A HISTORY OF BUDDHIST PHILOSOPHY

A HISTORY OF BUDDHIST PHILOSOPHY

Continuities and Discontinuities

David J. Kalupahana

University of Hawaii Press ■ Honolulu

Printed in the United States of America
92 93 94 95 96 97 5 4 3 2 1

Library of Congress Cataloging-in-Publication Data

Kalupahana, David J., 1933–
A history of Buddhist philosophy : continuities and discontinuities / David J. Kalupahana.
p. cm.
Includes bibliographical references and index.
ISBN 0–8248–1384–7 (cloth : acid-free paper). — ISBN 0–8248–1402–9 (pbk. : acid-free paper)
1. Buddhism—Doctrines—History. 2. Philosophy, Buddhist––History. I. Title.
BQ4090.K36 1992
181'.043—dc20 91–37326
CIP

University of Hawaii Press books are printed on acid-free paper and meet the guidelines for permanence and durability of the Council on Library Resources

Designed by Paula Newcomb

This work, completed three days before an accident that left our youngest son, Milinda, paralyzed, is dedicated to our friends and well-wishers, at home and abroad, especially my colleagues Eliot Deutsch and Larry Laudan, whose gracious support lessened the trauma for both Milinda and the family.

CONTENTS

Part Two: Continuities and Discontinuities

INTRODUCTION

In 1976 the University of Hawaii Press published my introductory text on Buddhist thought entitled *Buddhist Philosophy: A Historical Analysis*. I was pleasantly surprised by the enthusiastic response to that work. Within a few years permission was sought for a Chinese translation of the book, and the translation was published in 1983. Introducing that work the publisher stated: "This book is largely an outgrowth of his [the author's] many lectures over the past fifteen years on the subject of Buddhist philosophy." To be specific, Part I contained the results of my own research on the early Buddhist tradition, while some chapters in Part II, especially those dealing with Mādhyamika and Yogācāra, contained the interpretations of these traditions by classical as well as modern scholars. My evaluation of these schools assumed the correctness of these interpretations and I was therefore arguing that these were incompatible with the doctrines of early Buddhism. However, during the next fifteen years, I undertook my own research into the later Buddhist traditions and realized the possibility of reading the more mature works of Nāgārjuna and Vasubandhu in a manner that would make them extremely compatible with the teachings of early Buddhism. This research was published in two volumes: *Nāgārjuna: The Philosophy of the Middle Way* (1986) and *The Principles of Buddhist Psychology* (1987).

The present work is therefore a consolidation of thirty years of research and reflection on early Buddhism as well as on some of the major schools and philosophers associated with the later Buddhist traditions. In a sense it is a complete rewriting of the earlier work, including the section on early Buddhism, which is simply an expansion rather than a reinterpretation.

In recasting the section on early Buddhism, I attempted to synthesize two modes of explanation. The first explains Buddhist doctrines in terms of the philosophical themes that are gaining currency in the modern world. This should enable a student of Western philosophy and religion to look at early Buddhism in terms of the problems and categories with which he/she is familiar. The second retains the classical Buddhist categories, such as the four noble truths and the noble eightfold path, in an attempt to pour old wine into new bottles ("pouring new wine into old bottles" being incompatible with the anti-foundationalism and anti-structuralism of early Buddhism). This enterprise may be frowned on by those who are against comparing an ancient (sixth century B.C.) Asian tradition with one founded on extraordinary developments in mathematics, science, and technology. Yet it is undeniable that some of the leading philosophers of the twentieth century have often renounced the ideas with which they started. Thus we have early and later Wittgenstein, early and later Russell, early and later Ayer, early and later Quine, and so on. In a very broad sense, the term "early" in these characterizations represents some form of foundationalism, and the term "later" signifies an anti-foundationalism. To bring out the very sophisticated character of early Buddhist thought and its non-absolutist approach, I decided that the chapter on pre-Buddhist thought should be more comprehensive. Chapter I of the present work therefore explains the absolutist character of all the major philosophical trends during this early period, with one philosopher, Sañjaya, adopting an equally absolutist skepticism as a response. Only against this background is it possible to highlight the middle standpoint adopted by early Buddhism in its explanation of epistemology, ontology, ethics, and logic.

The examination of early Buddhist thought begins with Chapter II, a brief account of the life of Siddhārtha, the historical Buddha, outlining the background to his attainment of enlightenment and the impact it had on Indian religious, social, and political life.

Chapter III, "Knowledge and Understanding," is a vastly expanded version of the chapter on epistemology in the previous work. It includes a comprehensive examination of the various sources of knowledge—sense perception, yogic insight, inference and logic—and emphasizes the non-absolutist standpoint from which the Buddha explained these themes.

The central conception of Buddhism, namely, the "theory of dependent arising," previously explained under the rubric of causality, is now treated in Chapter IV under two themes, namely, "the dependently arisen," representing what is experienced, and "dependent arising," which is the theory formulated on the basis of such experience.

A new chapter on "Language and Communication" (Chapter V) has been added to explain the variety of uses of the term *dhamma* (Skt. *dharma*). It demonstrates how this term was used in five different senses, enabling the Buddha to relate the content of experience to both language and textual traditions. It was this method that prevented some of the Buddhist schools from getting involved in essentialist enterprises such as the study of etymology and grammar (these being the work of Buddhist monks of a later date, in both Sri Lanka and Burma). Instead, the early Buddhists engaged in hermeneutical studies that produced two treatises, the *Peṭakopadesa (Introduction to the Canon)* and *Netti (Guide),* both of which gained semi-canonical status.

The five chapters (VI–X) that follow recast and expand material included in Chapters 4 through 7 of the previous work. Chapter VI presents the various categories, such as the aggregates, elements, and the twelvefold formula, which the Buddha used to explain the conception of a human person, avoiding the Spiritualist and Materialist theories of "self." Chapter VII analyzes the conception of the world of experience—physical, psychological, and moral. Chapters VIII, IX, and X deal with the four noble truths. Chapter VIII shows how the principle of dependent arising is used to explain human suffering and its causation. Chapter IX is devoted to the nature of freedom and happiness. The chapter entitled "Nirvana" in the previous work was very polemical, directed at those who considered freedom *(nirvāṇa)* to be an absolute. Since it has served its purpose, I felt that a straightforward presentation of the Buddha's conception of freedom was now appropriate. Chapter IX therefore examines freedom in relation to epistemological, behavioral, and psychological dimensions, concluding with an analysis of the unanswered questions pertaining to the freed person. Chapter X appraises the nature of the moral life advocated in Buddhism. Herein the eightfold path receives a detailed treatment.

Chapter XI, "Popular Religious Thought," is new. It does not deal with the multifarious religious rituals practiced by the equally divergent Buddhist communities. Instead, it discusses one of the simplest Buddhist rituals, practiced in almost every tradition, and explains how even such a basic ritual reflects the teachings of the Buddha without doing violence to their important philosophical content.

The second part of the book, entitled "Continuities and Discontinuities," deals with the constant emergence of absolutist tendencies and an equally persistent attempt by some later Buddhist philosophers to criticize and reject such tendencies. Those who wanted to uphold the radical non-substantialist position of early Buddhism were faced with the dual task of responding to the enormously substantialist and absolutist thinking of the non-Buddhist traditions as well as to those within the Buddhist tradition who fell prey to such thinking. Chapter XII is therefore devoted to tracing such absolutist tendencies within Buddhism.

Interpretation of the Abhidharma canonical texts has continued to baffle the tradition, especially because of the exalted state assigned to them (taking the term *abhi-dharma* to mean "higher dharma"), and also because the reasons for compiling these treatises were soon forgotten. Thus at a rather early stage the commentarial tradition, both in Pali and in Sanskrit, tended to interpret the Abhidharma texts as dealing with ultimate realities. Modern interpreters who have relied on these commentaries have continued to present such substantialist explanations, whereas I have examined one of the canonical Abhidharma texts for clues to an understanding of the entire Abhidharma tradition. Moggalīputta-tissa's *Kathāvatthu* throws invaluable light on the innumerable problems that a student confronts when reading these extremely terse and non-discursive texts. Chapter XIII therefore discusses the *Kathāvatthu* and applies its basic philosophical themes to explaining the remaining books of the Abhidharma. A threefold method of treating subject matter is adopted in Abhidharma discourse: enumeration, classification, and synthesis. By this method the Abhidharma is able to clarify the meanings of concepts and their relationships. This constitutes the content of Chapter XIV.

Chapter XV outlines the methodology of the Prajñāpāramitā literature, especially the *Vajracchedikā*. Even though it is slightly different from that of the Abhidharma, the ultimate purpose is the same, namely, the clarification of concepts without allowing for substantialist or nihilist, realist or nominalist associations. This methodology can be designated as one of enumeration, deconstruction, and reconstruction.

The process of deconstruction was utilized by Nāgārjuna, whose ideas are examined in Chapter XVI. His profuse use of this method, especially at a time when substantialist and idealist metaphysics were becoming rampant, culminating in the *Saddharmapuṇḍarīka-sūtra* (Chapter XVII) and *Laṅkāvatāra-sūtra* (Chapter XVIII), left the impression that he was a nihilist, an accusation leveled against him in the latter work. As a result, classical as well as modern interpreters of Nāgārjuna have failed to appreciate the reconstructive aspects of his philosophy. Examining Nāgārjuna's philosophy in terms of both deconstructive and reconstructive aspects, I have now related him to the Buddha himself and his doctrines of non-substantiality *(anātma)* and dependent arising *(pratītyasamutpāda),* avoiding the transcendentalism I attributed to Nāgārjuna in *Buddhist Philosophy*.

The next major philosopher of the Buddhist tradition was Vasubandhu, whose views are examined in Chapter XIX. The unfortunate manner in which Nāgārjuna's contributions came to be evaluated during the two centuries after his death provided an important lesson for Vasubandhu, whose mature work, the *Vijñaptimātratāsiddhi,* contains both deconstructive and reconstructive aspects. The first part of that work, consisting of twenty-two verses (hence called *Viṃśatikā*), is devoted to a deconstruction of substantialist metaphysics, while the second part, consisting of thirty verses (therefore referred to as *Triṃśikā* or, more correctly, *Triṃśatikā*), can be seen as a reconstruction of meaningful concepts. Vasubandhu resorted to an extremely subtle deciphering of the psychological process of conceptualization, drawing inspiration from the Buddha's own analysis of human psychology. Yet the careful manner in which these philosophers presented their analyses was often undermined when enthusiastic commentators rushed to conclusions, placing inappropriate labels on them. Thus, because of Vasubandhu's psychological treatment of the conceptual process, it did not take long for him to be considered a proponent of absolute idealism.

Non-absolutism is not new to Western philosophy. However, in the field of logic, which was almost totally dominated by the two-valued system of Aristotle, absolutism seems to have reigned supreme longer than in any other discipline. Hence I thought that a chapter on Dignāga (Chapter XX), not included in the previous work, would help students understand how non-absolutism and non-substantialism can work even in the sphere of logic.

I have argued that one major text and three prominent philosophers generally identified with Mahāyāna are representative of the non-substantialist and non-absolutist teachings of the Buddha himself, rather than of the doctrines formulated in the more popular Mahāyāna treatises. Since I was born and bred in a Theravāda stronghold, I have naturally earned the wrath of some reviewers for relabeling these prominent texts and philosophers, for centuries identified with Mahāyāna. However, these reviewers are unaware of the equally strong condemnation of my writings by traditional scholars from Theravāda countries in South and Southeast Asia. With no apologies to either, what little was said in the previous work about the patriarch of Theravāda, Buddhaghosa, is here presented in greater detail. Chapter XXI is thus devoted to an examination of the *Visuddhimagga,* the major work of the philosopher who was named "Voice of the Buddha" *(buddhaghosa)* and who is said to have been born at Buddhagayā (Bodhgayā, where the Buddha attained enlightenment), although in fact he was a South Indian brahman. An analysis of its philosophical standpoint, even though it is difficult to identify one, reveals that his was no voice of the Buddha.

Chapters XXII and XXIII concern the traditions that emphasize chanting and meditation, respectively. Here I was compelled to be a bit more polemical, especially at the beginning of each chapter, because of the pervasive nature of the dogmatism with which these traditions have been interpreted. However, the primary purpose of both chapters is to examine the chanting and meditation traditions to discover what in them is and is not consistent with the teachings of early Buddhism.

My concluding remarks (Chapter XXIV) focus on the ideological conflict between Theravāda and Mahāyāna. Being non-absolutist, the Buddhist tradition had to recognize some form of relativism. The question is: How can there be harmony in the context of a plurality of views? The conclusion outlines the Buddha's own way of dealing with relativism without contributing to conflict, although a change in that paradigm during the second century A.D. led to the unfortunate ideological rift that has survived until the present day.

Although we are unaware of the specific language used by the Buddha, there seems to be no doubt about the way he used whatever language in vogue. His philosophy of non-substantialism and radical empiricism compelled him to make minimal use of the active voice and to employ the passive forms, the aorists, and the past participles, as is evident in the discourses preserved in the Prakrit languages, both Pali and the Northern Prakrits, like Gandhari, as well. Two written languages that emerged subsequently and were associated primarily with Buddhism, even though their spoken forms may have existed before the introduction of Buddhism to these countries, are the classical languages of Sri Lanka and Tibet. Classical Sinhala became a literary medium only after the introduction of Buddhism to Sri Lanka in the third century B.C., and classical Tibetan, including the alphabet, was developed in order to translate Buddhist texts after the introduction of Buddhism to that country in the sixth century A.D. Nurtured by Buddhist ideas, especially the recurrent initial statement in the discourses, *evam me sutaṃ* or *evam mayā śrutam* ("thus has been heard by me"), these two languages adopted passive forms to an extent rarely noticed in any other language. Nagarjuna's primary philosophical treatise, the *Mūlamadhyamakakārikā,* is a conscious attempt by a leading Buddhist philosopher to retain the spirit of the Buddha's teachings by using the passive forms only, even when composing his verses in Sanskrit, a language that is artificial and essentialist in the extreme. As someone educated in both Sinhala and English, I have been in the habit of writing what is sometimes referred to as "Singlish" (Sinhala idiom rendered into English). As a pragmatist I felt compelled to allow the copy editor the freedom to modify my style of writing so that the Western reader would not have to struggle with an unfamiliar mode of expression, even though it may not reflect the spirit of the Buddha's philosophy.

I am grateful to the staff of the University of Hawaii Press, especially to executive editor Iris Wiley, managing editor Cheri Dunn, and my editor, Sharon Yamamoto, for the patience and enthusiasm with which they attended to the publication of this work.

ABBREVIATIONS

A	*Aṅguttara-nikāya*
AA	*Manorathapūraṇī (Aṅguttara-nikāya-aṭṭhakathā)*
Adv	*Abhidharmadīpa-vṛtti (Vibhāṣāprabhāvṛtti)*
AK	*Abhidharmakośa*
Akb	*Abhidharmakośa-bhāṣya*
Cpd	*Compendium of Philosophy* (tr. of Abhidhammatthasaṅgaha), by S. Z. Aung and C. A. F. Rhys Davids (London: PTS, 1910).
D	*Dīgha-nikāya*
DA	*Sumaṅgalavilāsinī (Dīgha-nikāya-aṭṭhakathā)*
Dhp	*Dhammapada*
DhpA	*Dhammapadaṭṭhakathā*
DhsA	*Atthasālinī (Dhammasaṅganī-aṭṭhakathā)*
GS	*The Book of Gradual Sayings* (tr. of Aṅguttara-nikāya), by F. L. Woodward and E. M. Hare, 5 vols. (London: PTS, 1932–1936).
It	*Itivuttaka*
J	*Jātaka*
Kārikā	*Mūlamadhyamakakārikā*
KS	*The Book of Kindred Sayings* (tr. of Saṃyutta-nikāya), by C. A. F. Rhys Davids and F. L. Woodward, 5 vols. (London: PTS, 1917–1930).
Kvu	*Kathāvatthu*
KvuA	*Kathāvatthu-aṭṭhakathā*
Laṅkā	*Laṅkāvatāra-sūtra*
M	*Majjhima-nikāya*
Miln	*Milinda-pañha*
MLS	*The Collection of the Middle Length Sayings* (tr. of Majjhima-nikāya), by I. B. Horner, 3 vols. (London: PTS, 1967).
PS	*Pramāṇasamuccaya*
PTS	Pali Text Society, London
PTSD	*Pali Text Society's Pali-English Dictionary,* ed. T. W. Rhys Davids and W. Stede (London: PTS, 1959).
Pug	*Puggalapaññatti*

S	*Saṃyutta-nikāya*
SBB	*Sacred Books of the Buddhists* (London: PTS, 1899–1921).
Sdmp	*Saddharmapuṇḍarīka-sūtra*
Sn	*Sutta-nipāta*
TD	*Taisho Shinshu Daizōkyō,* ed. J. Takakusu and K. Watanabe (Tokyo: Daishō Shuppan Company, 1924–1934).
Thag	*Theragāthā*
Thig	*Therīgāthā*
Triṃś	*Triṃśikā (Vijñaptimātratāsiddhi)*
Ud	*Udāna*
Vajra	*Vajracchedikā-prajñāpāramitā*
Vims	*Viṃśatikā (Vijñaptimātratāsiddhi)*
Vin	*Vinaya Piṭaka*
Vism	*Visuddhimagga*

PART ONE
EARLY BUDDHISM

CHAPTER I

Indian Philosophy and the Search for Ultimate Objectivity

Brahmanism

Early Indian philosophy, before its gradual systematization in what came to be known as "Brahmanism," is represented by the observations and reflections of a large number of philosophers, like Aghamarṣaṇa, Prajāpati Parameṣṭhin, Brāhmaṇaspati, Dīrghatamas, Nārāyana, Hiraṇyagarbha, and Viśvakarman, encapsulated in their belief statements included in the *Vedas.*[1] In the reflections of these thinkers one can witness a variety of philosophical trends, some embodying genuine forms of skepticism, others admitting the role of human perspective in any explanation of the ultimate questions in philosophy, and still others constantly struggling to reach ultimate objectivity in philosophical discourse. These provided a foundation for the vast range of metaphysical and theological concepts that were eventually woven into one elaborate system called Brahmanism.

In the absence of detailed philosophical discussions, it is not possible to say whether skepticism appeared in the *Vedas* as a systematically worked out theory in epistemology and/or psychology. Yet one can perceive sudden outbursts on the part of reflective thinkers strangled in a web of metaphysical views, especially those pertaining to the origin or the first cause of the universe. Questions such as "What is the tree or wood out of which the universe was fashioned?"[2] were often raised. Apart from certain purely theistic conclusions, the most general tendency was to assume the existence of some primordial substance representing a form of real existence *(sat)* out of which everything came to be fashioned. However, the philosopher could not easily repose in the conception of such existence. The conception of non-existence *(asat)* constantly frowned on him, and he could not remain completely oblivious to such an idea.

The *Nāsadīya-sūkta* refers to several strands of thinking prevalent during this period. Even though various ideas available at the time are taken up for examination, no attempt is made to reach a definite conclusion. The text of the hymn reads as follows:

1. Not non-existent was it nor existent was it at that time: there was not atmosphere nor the heavens which are beyond. What existed? Where? In whose care? Water was it? An abyss unfathomable?
2. Neither mortal was there nor immortal then; not of night, of day was there distinction: That alone breathed windless through inherent power. Other than That indeed there was naught else.
3. Darkness it was, by darkness hidden in the beginning: an undistinguished sea was all this. The germ of all things which was enveloped in void, That alone through the power of brooding thought was born.
4. Upon That in the beginning arose desire, which was the first offshoot of that thought. This desire sages found out (to be) the link between the existent and the non-existent, after searching with the wisdom in their heart.
5. Straight across was extended their line of vision: was That below, was That above? Seedplacers there were, powers there were: potential energy below, impulse above.
6. Who, after all, knows? Who here will declare—arose whence this world? Subsequent are the gods to the creation of this world. Who, then, knows whence it came into being?
7. This world—whence it came into being, whether it was made or whether not—He who is its overseer in the highest heavens surely knows—or perhaps He knows not![3]

As K. N. Jayatilleke has pointed out,[4] this hymn is interesting because, after taking into account almost all the available theories regarding the origin of the world, it ends on a skeptical note. However, there seem to be a few more theories mentioned in the hymn than Jayatilleke perceived. First, there is the basic epistemological issue of whether or not there can be knowledge of the beginning of the world. Those who hold that such knowledge is possible could maintain either that the world was created or that it was not. The former alternative would generate at least four views, namely, that the world was created from Being *(sat),* from non-Being *(asat),* from both Being and non-Being *(sad-asat),* or from neither Being nor non-Being *(na-sat-na-asat).* The latter alternative would involve the idea that the world had no beginning, which is different from the more radical view that there is no knowledge. These alternatives can be presented diagrammatically in a way that is slightly different from Jayatilleke's presentation (see chart on p. 5). The hymn begins with the assertion of the last proposition, namely, that there was an origin, but what existed at that time *(tadānīm)* cannot be described, and hence it was neither non-Being nor Being *(nāsadāsīt no sadāsīt tadānīm).* Yet for the early Indian thinkers this was not satisfactory because it involved a negative description. A positive description was needed, represented by the combination of Being and non-Being *(sad-asat),* as exemplified by the statement "That alone breathed windless." Yet the more vexing problems were "What is Being?" and "What is its relationship to non-Being?" The

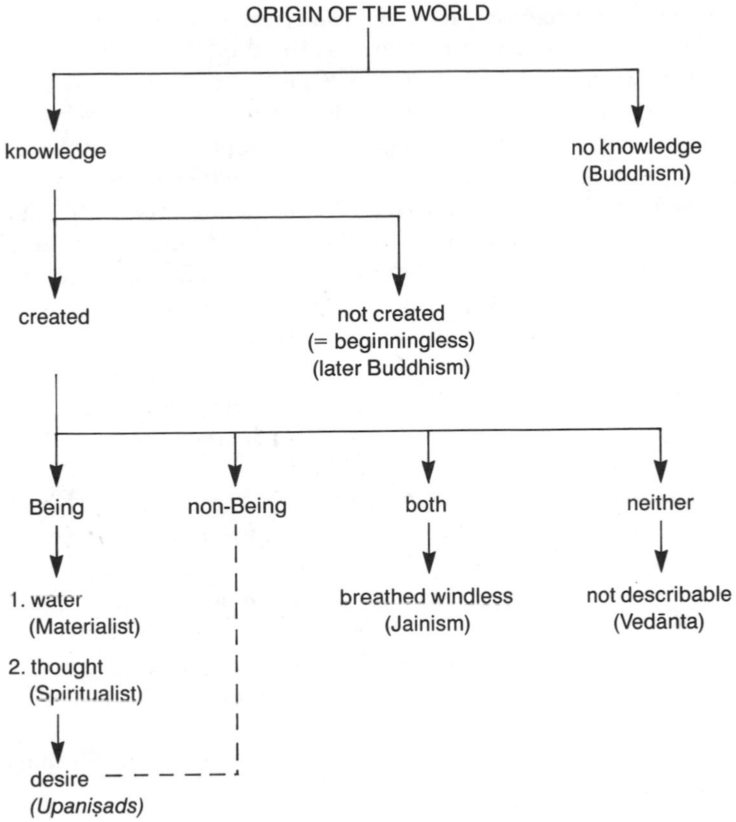

conception of water *(ambhas)* is suggested as a possible entity, but it was not appealing except to the Materialist. Hence we have the spiritual entity represented by *thought.* "That alone through the power of brooding thought was born. Upon That in the beginning arose desire, which was the first *offshoot of that thought*" (emphasis mine). It is this desire that the sages, searching their hearts with wisdom, found to be the link between non-Being and Being.

There are two important ways of looking at this hymn, which represent two philosophical standpoints that emerged subsequently. If we start at the top of the diagram and come down the ladder, first recognizing an origin of the universe, attributing that origin to Being, identifying that Being with "thought," explaining the relationship between Being and non-Being as "desire," and, finally, insisting that it was this "desire," as the seed of existence, that was revealed to the sages at the highest level of *tapas* (practice of austerity), then we have cosmology revealed to the sages in their meditation. Desire becomes a cosmic desire that the sage discovers at the highest level of meditation, where he becomes one with the absolute "thought" ("I," the *ātman*). The early *Upaniṣads,* as will be shown later, seem to have taken this route, even though the more developed Vedānta seems to have moved toward adopting the transcendentalist perspective (neither Being nor non-Being), while the Jainas opted for the third alternative (Being and non-Being). In contrast, if we begin from the bottom of the diagram, it is possible to adopt a totally different perspective, insisting that the germinal "thought" in which the sages discovered the seed of existence, namely, desire, is no more than a human conception, for it is human conception that generates desire for producing things (being) that did not exist before (non-being). But the question as to whether that "thought" was originally existent, non-existent, both, or neither will have to be left unanswered *(avyākata),* and the question of origin itself renounced. This would also mean the acceptance of the more radical alternative mentioned at the outset, namely, that absolute origin is unknowable and, therefore, inconceivable *(anamatagga).* This, as will be seen, is the position adopted in Buddhism.

It is the first philosophical standpoint embedded in the hymn that became rather popular until the emergence of Buddhism. In the hymn, we see a philosopher confronted with the problems of both existence *(sat)* and non-existence *(asat),* initially forcing him into a skeptical mood. The rationalist tradition in which he grew up weighed heavily in favor of a substantialist solution to the problem of existence. "Water" *(salila)* is suggested as a primordial substance, probably because it was seen as an element which, in its various forms, could reflect the character of other physical elements as well. However, it was enveloped in darkness (= ignorance?).

At this stage, the rationalist's perspective is replaced by that of the empirically minded sage whose "searching with the wisdom in [his] heart" was believed to be a way of eliminating ignorance. Yet the philosopher's meditations are to lead him in a different direction. He is willing to recognize a link between non-existence and existence and identify that link with "desire" *(kāma).*

This was a significant step, although it contributed to certain unpalatable philosophical consequences. The conception of "desire," whether human or divine, injects an element of subjectivity into the explanation of a phenomenon that the philosopher would rather understand as a natural process. The recognition of desire as a productive cause of existence would mean the denial of objective determinism. Philosophical explanation of natural existence will be compelled to accommodate varying human motives and desires, thereby depriving that explanation of any objectivity. Pure objectivity has no place in the context of a particular view or perspective.

Thus, the limitations imposed on philosophical discourse by any recognition of a perspective would render all theories gray, indistinct, and therefore unsatisfactory. The search for the "clear and distinct" will be lost in a welter of possibilities, all of which are shadowy and vague. Furthermore, certainty in the sphere of knowledge and understanding will never reach the level that most philosophers generally crave. For these reasons the Vedic philosopher could not help relapsing into yet another skeptical mood. These are some of the reflections of Prajāpati Parameṣṭhin, to whom the *Nāsadīya-sūkta* is attributed.

Another philosopher takes a bolder stand. He solves the riddle of existence *(sat)* by simply asserting it to be "one" *(ekam)* that is designated by the wise in a variety of ways as Agni (god of fire), Yama (lord of death), or Mātarīśvan (god of wind).[5] A distinction is immediately drawn between a designation, a name or a concept, and the real. This again implies ultimate objectivity independent of any activity of naming, designating, or conceptualizing, which inevitably involves human perspective. An understanding of reality is achieved only when the human perspective is completely left out.

It is interesting to note that in most of the speculations of the early Vedic thinkers, attention is focused on the objective world, as in the case of the physical sciences in the modern world, where one discovers a persistent attempt to reach the limit of objectivity.[6] Yet, unlike in modern science, the trend of thought in the *Vedas* is toward the idea of a single absolute and self-subsistent principle *(sat)* that is infinite in the sense of being an inexhaustible power. All finite things are products of self-evolution, representing one universal system and plan. The search was for one single, ordaining, sustaining, coordinating principle of which all known forces, laws, and movements are manifestations. The earliest conception that satisfied all these conditions was *ṛta,* and for a while it proved sufficient because it embodied not only physical but also spiritual (= sacrificial or ritualistic) and moral laws. It was not created, but found a guardian in Varuṇa.[7]

Unfortunately, the conception of *ṛta* gradually faded into oblivion and was soon replaced by the conception of *ātman.* The reason is obvious. While *ṛta* satisfied an almost universal human yearning for ultimate objectivity in explaining the physical as well as the moral world, it did not account for the reality of the human being. *Ṛta* was almost always external to the human person, who appeared more as an automaton than as part of it. Even the caste system, which was an inalienable part of Brahmanical teachings—and which was viewed as the product of a cosmic sacrifice[8] and, for that reason, as part of *ṛta*—turned out to be an objective phenomenon involving no human contribution. With the social structure being a purely objective phenomenon, the moral laws that were based on it became equally objective. The ground was thus prepared for introducing the conception of self *(ātman),* which dominated speculations during the period of the *Upaniṣads.*

The *Upaniṣads* are generally considered to be statements of the contemplatives or yogins. As such, they should reflect ideas similar to those attributed to the sages in the *Nāsadīya-sūkta* referred to earlier. The purely objective phenomenon of *ṛta* should have been replaced by a conception of a world order in which the human person plays a significant role. But even though, by emphasizing the conception of self *(ātman)*, Upaniṣadic thinkers may have intended to highlight the significant role of the subject of experience in explaining the world process, the way they did so left a completely different philosophical legacy, which subsequent thinkers in the Brahmanical tradition continued to justify. The following statement from the *Bṛhadāraṇyaka Upaniṣad* is a classic example:

1. In the beginning this world was Soul *(Ātman)* alone in the form of a Person. Looking around, he saw nothing else than himself. He said first: "I am." Thence arose the name "I." Therefore, even today, when one is addressed, he says first just "It is I" and then speaks whatever name he has. Since before *(pūrva)* all this world he burned up *(uṣ)* all evils, therefore he is a person *(pur-uṣ-a)*. He who knows this, verily, burns up him who desires to be ahead of him.
2. He was afraid. Therefore one who is alone is afraid. This one then thought to himself: "Since there is nothing else than myself, of what am I afraid?" Thereupon, verily, his fear departed, for of what should he have been afraid? Assuredly it is from a second that fear arises.
3. Verily, he had no delight. Therefore one who is alone has no delight. He desired a second. He was, indeed, as large as a woman and a man closely embraced. He caused that self to fall *(pat)* into two pieces. Therefrom arose a husband *(pati)* and a wife *(patni)*. Therefore this [is true]: "Oneself *(sva)* is like a half-fragment," as Yajñavalkya used to say. Therefore this space is filled by a wife. He copulated with her. Therefrom human beings were produced.
4. And she then bethought herself: "How now does he copulate with me after he has produced me just from himself? Come, let me hide myself." She became a cow. He became a bull. With her he did indeed copulate. Then cattle were born. She became a mare, he a stallion. She became a female ass, he a male ass; with her he copulated, of a truth. Thence were born solid-hoofed animals. She became a she-goat, he a he-goat; she a ewe, he a ram. With her he did verily copulate. Therefrom were born goats and sheep. Thus, indeed, he created all, whatever pairs there are, even down to the ants.
5. He knew: "I, indeed, am this creation, for I emitted it all from myself." Thence arose creation. Verily, he who has this knowledge comes to be in that creation of his.
6. Then he rubbed thus. From his mouth as the fire-hole *(yoni)* and from his hands he created fire *(agni)*. Both these [i.e., the hand and the mouth] are hairless on the inside, for the fire-hole *(yoni)* is hairless on the inside.

   This that people say, "Worship this god! Worship that god!"—one god after another—this is his creation indeed! And he himself is all the gods.

Now, whatever is moist, that he created from semen, and that is Soma. This whole world, verily, is just food and the eater of food.
That was Brahma's super-creation: namely, that he created the gods, his superiors; likewise that, being mortal, he created the immortals. Therefore was it a super-creation. Verily, he who knows this comes to be in that super-creation of his.

7. Verily, at that time the world was undifferentiated. It became differentiated just by name and form, as the saying is: "He has such a name, such a form." Even today this world is differentiated just by name and form, as the saying is: "He has such a name, such a form." He entered in here, even to the fingernail-tips, as a razor would be hidden in a razor-case, or fire in a fire-holder. Him they see not, for [as seen] he is incomplete. When breathing, he becomes breath *(prāṇa)* by name; when speaking, voice; when seeing, the eye; when hearing, the ear; when thinking, the mind: these are merely the names of his acts. Whoever worships one or another of these—he knows not; for he is incomplete with one or another of these. One should worship with the thought that he is just one's self *(ātman),* for therein all these become one. That same thing, namely, this self, is the trace *(padanīya)* of this All, for by it one knows this All. Just as, verily, one might find by a footprint *(pada),* thus—. He finds fame and praise who knows this.
8. That self is dearer than a son, is dearer than wealth, is dearer than all else, since this self is nearer. If, of one who speaks of anything else than the self as dear, one should say, "He will lose what he holds dear," he would indeed be likely to do so. One should reverence the self alone as dear. He who reverences the self alone as dear—what he holds dear, verily, is not perishable.
9. Here people say: "Since men think that by the knowledge of Brahma they become the All, what, pray, was it that Brahma knew whereby he became the All?"
10. Verily, in the beginning this world was Brahma. It knew only itself *(ātmānam):* "I am Brahma!" Therefore it became the All. Whoever of the gods became awakened to this, he indeed became it; likewise in the case of seers *(ṛṣi),* likewise in the case of men. Seeing this, indeed, the seer Vāmadeva began:—

   I was Manu and the sun *(sūrya)!*

   This is so now also. Whoever thus knows "I am Brahma!" becomes this All; even the gods have not power to prevent his becoming thus, for he becomes their self *(ātman).*
   So whoever worships another divinity [than his Self], thinking "He is one and I another," he knows not. He is like a sacrificial animal for the gods. Verily, indeed, as many animals would be of service to a man, even so each single person is of service to the gods. If even one animal is taken away, it is not pleasant. What, then, if many? Therefore it is not pleasing to those [gods] that men should know this.
11. Verily, in the beginning this world was Brahma, one only. Being one, he was not developed. He created still further a superior form, the *kṣatra-*

hood, even those who are *kṣatras* (rulers) among the gods: Indra, Varuṇa, Soma, Rudra, Parjanya, Yama, Mṛtyu, Īśāna. Therefore there is nothing higher than *kṣatra.* Therefore at the *rājasūya* ceremony the *brahman* sits below the *kṣatriya.* Upon *kṣatra*hood alone does he confer this honor. This same thing, namely *brahman*hood *(brahma),* is the source of *kṣatra*hood. Therefore, even if the king attains supremacy, he rests finally upon *brahman*hood as his own source. So whoever injures him [i.e., a brahman] attacks his own source. He fares worse in proportion as he injures one who is better.

12. He was not yet developed. He created the *viś* (the commonalty), those kinds of gods that are mentioned in numbers: the Vasus, the Rudras, the Ādityas, the Viśvedevas, the Maruts.
13. He was not yet developed. He created the *śūdra* caste *(varṇa),* Pūṣan. Verily, this [earth] is Pūṣan, for she nourishes *(√puṣ)* everything that is.
14. He was not yet developed. He created still further a better form, Law *(dharma).* This is the power *(kṣatra)* of the *kṣatriya* class *(kṣatra),* viz., Law. Therefore there is nothing higher than Law. So a weak man controls a strong man by Law, just as if by a king. Verily, that which is Law is truth. Therefore they say of a man who speaks the truth, "He speaks the Law," or of a man who speaks the Law, "He speaks the truth." Verily, both these are the same thing.
15. So that *brahma* [appeared as] *kṣatra, viś,* and *śūdra.* So among the gods Brahma appeared by means of Agni, among men as a *brahman,* as a *kṣatriya* by means of the [divine] *kṣatriya,* as a *vaiśya* by means of the [divine] *vaiśya,* as a *śūdra* by means of the [divine] *śūdra.* Therefore people desire a place among the gods in Agni, among men in a *brahman,* for by these two forms [preeminently] *brahma* appeared.

    Now whoever departs from this world [i.e., the world of the *ātman*] without having recognized it as his own, to him it is of no service, because it is unknown, as the unrecited *Vedas* or any other undone deed [do not help a man].

    Verily, even if one performs a great and holy work, but without knowing this, that work of his merely perishes in the end. One should worship the Self alone as his [true] world. The work of him who worships the Self alone as his world does not perish, for out of that very Self he creates whatsoever he desires.
16. Now this Self, verily, is a world of all created things. Insofar as a man makes offerings and sacrifices, he becomes the world of the gods. Insofar as he learns [the *Vedas*], he becomes the world of the seers *(ṛṣi).* Insofar as he offers libations to the fathers and desires offspring, he becomes the world of the fathers. Insofar as he gives lodging and food to men, he becomes the world of men. Insofar as he finds grass and water for animals, he becomes the world of animals. Insofar as beasts and birds, even to the ants, find a living in his houses, he becomes their world. Verily, as one would desire security for his own world, so all creatures wish security for him who has this knowledge. This fact, verily, is known when it is thought out.[9]

This passage embodies the central themes of the Brahmanical philosophical system, which were subsequently elaborated in the *Bhagavadgītā*. Three stand out clearly: (1) the metaphysics of the self and the world, combined in the one concept of *ātman;* (2) the social philosophy, with the fourfold caste system as its basis; and (3) the moral ideal based on the caste system, which is designated *brahma*.

The conception of *ātman* is the most prominent. Unlike the notion of *ṛta,* which was confined to an explanation of the external world, *ātman* was here intended to highlight the subject. Yet the attempt to reach ultimate objectivity in explaining the subject of experience compelled the Upaniṣadic thinkers to present a conception of "I" *(aham)* as the primordial "self" *(ātman),* thereby combining the philosophical perspectives suggested by the Cartesian *cogito* as well as the Kantian "transcendental unity of apperception." The Cartesian doubt is eliminated by the assertion that certainty is associated with the knowledge of itself. The *ātman,* looking around, sees nothing but himself. It is this "self" that comes to be embodied in the notion of "I." It is not only a condition of experience but, like the Kantian postulate, a necessary prerequisite for all rational thinking. "Therefore, even today, when one is addressed, he says first just 'It is I' and then speaks whatever name he has." However, the Upaniṣadic thinker is interested in utilizing this conception of "self" not only to account for certainty regarding human knowledge or for a rational justification of knowledge, but also to explain the origin and continuity of the world. Hence the "self" becomes a self-transforming or self-reproducing ultimate reality joining together the individual and the external world. The "self" *(ātman)* at once becomes both metaphysical subject and metaphysical object.

In the context of such an ultimate reality, all differences are dissolved. Plurality or multiplicity exists only in relation to "name and form." Concepts, words, even propositions do not designate anything real. The real transcends language and convention.

This view had far-reaching consequences in the area of moral discourse. The Upaniṣadic thinkers could not recognize the view that moral principles are relative or that the social structure on which such principles are based is a mere convention. If they viewed the caste system as a mere convention, it certainly would be different from the reality of the self as well as that of the world, for the latter is no convention. In brief, there would be no connection whatsoever between fact and value. Thus the search for ultimate objectivity in moral phenomena was initiated.

In the Brahmanical system, the term *dharma* generally stands for moral law or principle. The Upaniṣadic thinkers could have linked *ātman* (the factual world) directly with *dharma* (values). However, such a linkage would have excluded the social structure so sacred to the

Brahmanical thinkers, for whom it was more important to relate ethical principles to the caste system itself, since the former are derived from the latter, not vice versa.

Thus, after explaining the ultimate objectivity of the self and the world, the Upaniṣadic passage quoted above proceeds to elaborate on *brahma,* the source and ultimate reality of the social structure. While value-laden concepts are conspicuously absent in the portion explaining the conception of *ātman,* they are introduced for the first time in the analysis of *brahma.* What is significant is that the passage places *brahma* on a par with *ātman.* The two descriptions are almost identical. Both are sources for whatever follows.

Brahma is the source of *kṣatra* (the sword or the warrior class), which, interestingly, is referred to as a "superior" *(sreyas)* form. This represents a slight change from the first formulation of the caste system in the *Ṛgveda,*[10] where the Brahman class (= *brahma*) is identified with the mouth of the cosmic person *(puruṣa),* while the warrior class *(kṣatriya)* represents his arms, the superiority of the Brahman class being implied in its symbolization. However, in the Upaniṣadic passage, the *kṣatra* is specifically referred to as a superior form. This change could reflect the gradual emergence of the warrior class as a powerful force in the social life of the Indians, and the attempt on the part of the Brahman class to deal with it. Yet even though the warrior class is described as a superior form, the passage goes on to assert the importance of *brahma* as the source of the *kṣatra,* thus laying the foundation for the later legal system that considered harming a *brāhmaṇa* a heinous crime. The two other classes, the *viś* (ordinary citizens) and *śūdra* (the menials), arise in due order from *brahma.*

It is only after the creation of the three classes from *brahma* that one hears of the emergence of *dharma,* a form that is even more superior to the *kṣatra.* In fact, the warrior class wields no power unless it is endowed with *dharma* or law, which is a creation of *brahma.* This is another way of taking away the power passed on to the warrior class with the earlier pronouncement about its social standing.

The moral law *(dharma)* is thus directly linked to the original principle *(brahma)* out of which emerged the three other classes in society. For this reason, the moral law becomes the truth *(satya)* in an absolute sense. At least in principle, any violation of that law could not be permitted, for it was not a conditional but an absolute law.

The ultimate truth *(ātman)* and ultimate value *(brahma)* are thus combined in a salvific realization that is considered to be the highest blissful attainment a human being can achieve. Even though the realization of *brahma* was considered to be blissful, the development of aesthetics to be on a par with ontology and ethics took a few more centuries. The science of aesthetics recognized the experience of *brahma (brahmāsvāda)* as the ultimately objective standard of aesthetic judgment. With it, the Platonic trinity of good, beauty, and truth was complete.

Materialism

The first reaction to the Brahmanical speculations outlined above came from the Materialist thinkers of India. They represented one branch of the naturalistic tradition, the other being the school popularly known as the Ājīvikas. The Materialists were known by different names—the Cārvākas, the Lokāyatikas, or the Bārhaspatyas. Ajita Kesakambali, Pūraṇa Kassapa, and Pakudha Kaccāyana were prominent teachers among the early Materialists. Even though they are often referred to as ascetics *(samaṇa)* and brahmans *(brāhmaṇa),* their teachings are generally considered part of the heterodoxy, primarily because they were opposed to the orthodox Brahmanical system.

All Materialists agreed in considering matter to be the ultimate fact of the universe, reducing all phenomena, including the phenomenon of consciousness, to transformations of material elements. Yet it is possible to discern two slightly different trends in Materialist thinking. The first represents an extreme form, in that it reduced all phenomena, including material bodies, to their ultimate constituents—namely, earth, water, fire, and air. These four basic material elements never change, even though the things that are derived from them are in a process of constant flux. The assumption that the elements are eternal and permanent and that all their derivatives are in a state of impermanence and change compelled these Materialists to view the former as real and the latter as unreal. For them, the search for ultimate objectivity can be satisfied only by the recognition of material elements that are permanent and eternal. Furthermore, only such material elements follow a fixed pattern or law of self-nature *(svabhāva).* Everything else tends to be irregular and therefore unreal in its behavior. This was the nihilistic school of Materialism.[11]

The second school of Materialists avoided such reductionism and accepted the reality not only of material elements but also of the physical bodies constituted by them.[12] Unlike the nihilistic group, which resorted to a more rationalistic explanation of material phenomena, this group seems to have emphasized sense experience as a valid source of knowledge. In giving equal validity to the material elements and the physical bodies constituted by such elements, this second group of Materialists seems to have paid more attention to the human personality. For them, the identity of a person was based on the physical body, which enjoyed the status of ultimate reality.

This perspective may have made a difference to their conception of human behavior. Those who considered the human personality to be a mere lump of material particles maintained that killing a human person is not a matter of serious consequence, for all that is done is that a sword is inserted through that lump of matter. In contrast, the Materialists who believed in the reality of the physical body maintained that its evolution in the form of a body is a natural phenomenon *(svabhāva)* and that the destruction of that body is an act against nature. This is a more enlightened form of Materialism.

However, both schools denied any continuity of the human personality after death. For the nihilistic school, every form of moral judgment is meaningless talk, whereas according to the more enlightened form of Materialism, only those moral judgments based on belief in the survival of the personality are meaningless. Unfortunately, although a distinction regarding the metaphysics of the two schools has been found, no such distinction is mentioned regarding their moral discourse. This is probably because Materialist teachings were preserved by their critics rather than by the Materialists themselves. It seems that the critics lumped together the different schools of Materialism and condemned them all for being opposed to moral discourse. And whatever the contribution of the Materialists in denying the ultimate reality of a self—for they were the first *anātmavādins* (no-soul theorists) of India—their recognition of matter and/or physical bodies as ultimately real was no more than another journey toward the limit of objectivity in human knowledge and understanding.

The Ājīvikas

The second school of Naturalists was called the Ājīvikas, and their leader is believed to have been Makkhali Gosāla. The Ājīvikas shared a conception of matter with the Materialist thinkers. However, they differed from the Materialists in assuming that the physical personality of a human being can survive death. Indeed, they were proponents of evolutionary biological systems with no *known* beginnings and ultimate destinies, hence beyond the power of human control. Their naturalism is expounded in terms of three major concepts: fate *(niyati)*, species *(saṅgati)*, and inherent nature *(bhāva, svabhāva)*.[13]

Fate explains—or, rather, leaves unexplained—how a being *(satta)* comes into existence either as a human or as an animal. Such occurrence is predetermined or fixed *(niyata)*. No attempt is made to explain this predetermination. Yet once it has come into existence, it belongs to one or the other species *(saṅgati)*, which is determined by the coming together *(saṃ + gati)* of various characteristics. Once a being has come to possess certain characteristics, its nature *(bhāva, svabhāva)* as well as its behavior are determined solely by the species to which it belongs. This process of evolution may continue for several lives until it is able, without any effort on its part, to end that process.

The most prominent doctrine of the Ājīvikas is the rejection of any human effort or will. Nature is so fixed and determined that no human effort can change its course. The Ājīvikas appear to have been the first Indian philosophers to face squarely the philosophical problem of determinism and free will. Like some modern philosophers, they seem to have possessed the courage to openly accept determinism and reject free will.

The rejection of free will did not compel the Ājīvikas to deny freedom as well. They admitted the possibility of coursing through the cycle of existences and ultimately achieving freedom and purity *(saṃsāra-suddhi)*, but without any effort on the part of the individual.[14] The process is compared to a ball of thread thrown from the summit of a mountain, which will unwind to its full length. No other condition will make any difference to its length.

Here again, one can notice the attempt to reach the limit of objectivity in the explanation of human life and experience. Even human effort, let alone human perspective, cannot make any difference to the real world. The ultimately real world, determined by forces beyond human understanding, will remain what it is regardless of all the different views of it expressed by human beings.

Jainism

Jainism is another heterodox school of thought with two prominent teachers, Pārśvanātha and Mahāvīra, the latter being the real systematizer of Jaina doctrines, although he was a follower of the former. Mahāvīra is credited with blending the asceticism of Pārśvanātha with the naturalistic teachings of the Ājīvikas, especially Makkhali Gosāla, thus producing a philosophy described as dynamism (or, more appropriately, vitalism).[15] He was a senior contemporary of the Buddha; interesting dialogues between the Buddha's disciples and Mahāvīra are recorded in the Jaina discourses, while dialogues between Mahāvīra's disciples and the Buddha are included in the Buddhist discourses. However, there is no evidence that the two teachers met face to face.

As mentioned earlier, the Ājīvikas, though following the ascetic *(śramaṇa)* tradition, denied the efficacy of human effort and free will and advocated a theory of biological determinism. Mahāvīra, who at one time was a friend of the Ājīvika teacher Gosāla, was interested in accounting for free will without having to abandon biological determinism. This compromise compelled him to give equal consideration to the objective and the subjective.

We have already seen how the Brahmanical thinkers attempted to reach ultimate objectivity in the explanation of the subject as well as the object, thereby admitting a metaphysical self *(ātman)* to account for both. Since Mahāvīra retained biological determinism, which is itself a movement toward ultimate objectivity, he could not get involved in an empirical analysis of human psychology simply to justify the validity of free will, because his theory of biological determinism would have sublated any psychological theory that was not equally objective. Hence he needed a theory of psychology and morality that was as objective as biological determinism. His ingenuity lies in formulating a doctrine of action *(kiriya)* without simply returning to the Upaniṣadic notions of *ātman* and *brahma,* and thereby renouncing the Brahmanical conceptions of society and morals. Thus the conception of action *(kiriya)* emerges as the central conception in Jainism.

Action *(kiriya),* according to Mahāvīra, is threefold: bodily, verbal, and mental. The most important feature of this theory is that all three forms are accorded equal status. To do this, Mahāvīra had to ignore the psychological springs of action that came to be emphasized by the Buddha. Empirical psychology has often spoiled the purity of philosophical discourse.[16] The clarity and precision one can attain in the study of physical phenomena cannot be achieved in the analysis and explanation of human psychology. Therefore, Mahāvīra opted for a more physicalistic explanation of action, rather than a psychological analysis. Instead of a theory of intentionality, we meet with what may be called, in modern philosophy, an action theory of mind. Action dictates what the so-called mind is, rather than the mind determining what action is.

It is for this reason that Mahāvīra believed that any bodily action, whether intentional or unintentional, will produce consequences for which the agent of action is responsible. By ignoring the intentionality of human action, Mahāvīra was able to give a more systematic and precisely formulated account of the relationship between action and consequence or action and responsibility. Arguing against the Buddhists, a disciple of Mahāvīra says:

> If a savage puts a man on a spit and roasts him, mistaking him for a fragment of the granary; or a baby, mistaking him for a gourd, he will not be guilty of murder! . . . If anybody thrusts a spit through a man or a baby, mistaking him for a fragment of the granary, puts him on the fire and roasts him, that will be a meal fit for the Buddhas to breakfast upon. . . . Well-controlled men cannot accept your denial of guilt incurred by [unintentional] doing harm to living beings. . . . It is impossible to mistake a fragment of the granary for a man; only an unworthy man can say it.[17]

According to this assertion, action results in responsibility, regardless of whether the action is performed with or without intention, with or without knowledge. Thus Mahāvīra is able to link an action with its consequence without having to face the dilemma of one and the same action appearing to have two different consequences. A good action is invariably associated with good consequences, never evil ones. Similarly, an evil action is always associated with evil results, never good ones. The relationship between action and consequence is never conditional but always absolute.

By explaining action *(kiriya)* in this manner, Mahāvīra was prepared to contrast it with biological determinism. Because it is human action, it is internal to the person, whereas biological determinism is external. Action explains free will, for every action is willed. It is free because it is not part of biological determinism. This is the sense in which Mahāvīra's statement that "there are things that are determined and things that are not determined" *(niyayāniyayaṃ saṃtaṃ)*[18] can be understood.

The above explanation of human action and biological determinism may have compelled Mahāvīra to adopt a non-absolutistic standpoint regarding ordinary human knowledge and understanding. Thus we have the famous Jaina theory of "possibilities" *(syādvāda)* as well as of "standpoints" *(naya)*.

Before Mahāvīra, the skeptic Sañjaya had proposed four negative propositions in order to avoid errors in philosophical discourse. These negative propositions were stated in the following form:

1. A is not B.
2. A is not $\sim B$.
3. A is not $(B \cdot \sim B)$.
4. A is not $\sim(B \cdot \sim B)$.

Mahāvīra, a younger contemporary of Sañjaya, found these alternatives too skeptical. His explanation of existence had to accommodate both positive and negative propositions, together with the assumption that both are possibilities *(syād)*. The later Jaina writers have listed these possibilities as follows:

1. It is possible that A is B.
2. It is possible that A is $\sim B$.
3. It is possible that A is $(B \cdot \sim B)$.
4. It is possible that A is $\sim(B \cdot \sim B)$, that is, unspeakable *(avaktavya)*.
5. It is possible that A is B and $\sim(B \cdot \sim B)$.
6. It is possible that A is $\sim B$ and $\sim(B \cdot \sim B)$.
7. It is possible that A is $(B \cdot \sim B)$ and is $\sim(B \cdot \sim B)$.[19]

The recognition of varying epistemological possibilities would also mean the existence of a variety of ways in which the meanings of propositions could be analyzed. The later Jaina thinkers have proposed seven standpoints as guides *(naya)* for the determination of meanings. The seven standpoints are divided into two groups, the substantial *(dravya)* and the linguistic (*paryāya;* lit., "synonyms"). Under the former category are included three—the teleological *(naigama),* the universal *(saṃgraha),* and the conventional *(vyavahāra)*—and under the latter category, four—the particular *(ṛjusūtra),* the semantic *(śabda),* the etymological *(samābhirūḍha),* and the contextual *(evaṃbhūta).*[20]

The teleological standpoint *(naigama-naya)* is intended to pinpoint the goal in terms of which the meaning of a statement can be understood. For example, when I am scribbling this statement on a sheet of paper, if someone were to ask me, "What are you doing?" and I were to respond, "I am writing my book on Buddhist philosophy," my statement would make sense only in terms of what I propose to achieve, not what I am actually doing now. In other words, the book on Buddhist philosophy is yet not a reality apart from pencil marks on a sheet of paper. The Jaina commentators assumed that this is the standpoint developed by the Vaiśeṣika school.

The universal standpoint *(saṃgraha-naya)* focuses on the whole instead of the parts, the latter deriving their meaning only in relation to the former. Thus one cannot speak of spokes or hub or rim except in the context of a wheel. This is looked upon as the perspective of Vedānta. Finally, the conventional standpoint *(vyavahāra-naya)* attempts to accommodate both the part and the whole, as in the Sāṅkhya school.

It is interesting that the linguistic standpoints include what is called the particular or the *ṛjusūtra.* Literally, the term *ṛjusūtra* means "straight line," that is to say, a *series* of disconnected phenomena that gives the false appearance of a connected whole, which is a mere name *(nāma).* The Jaina commentators identified this with the standpoint of the Buddhists. The semantic standpoint *(śabda-naya)* deals with synonyms. Thus the terms Śakra, Indra, and Purandhara all refer to one and the same individual, the powerful god of the Vedic tradition, although the etymological standpoint *(samābhirūḍha-naya)* distinguishes them. The current-etymological or contextual standpoint *(evaṃbhūta-naya)* produces further distinctions, in that a term like "Purandhara," even though generally applied to the god Indra, makes no sense if it is applied to him when he is not involved in the act of "destroying fortresses" (the literal meaning of *purandhara*). Thus, while a synonym can have a universal application, it also has to be contextual.

These standpoints were undoubtedly elaborations by later philosophers of the Jaina tradition, for they refer to theories that emerged subsequently in the Indian tradition, such as those of the Vaiśeṣika, the Sāṅkhya, Vedānta, and even the theory of momentariness developed by the later Buddhists. Yet one cannot deny that they also represent the spirit of the epistemological standpoint of Mahāvīra himself.

Examining Mahāvīra's doctrine of action *(kiriya)*, one cannot avoid the conclusion that it is the ordinary unenlightened person who assumes that the same action can lead to two different consequences. An enlightened one cannot make any mistake about the one-to-one relation. Yet the epistemological theories of "possibilities" and "standpoints" leave Mahāvīra in a position where such mistakes are unavoidable if a person adopts any one of the possibilities or standpoints. Thus, if an enlightened one is to make no mistake whatsoever, he must adopt all the possibilities or standpoints each time he makes a predication. This would account for Mahāvīra's recognition of "omniscience" *(sarvajñatva)* as the highest form of knowledge. Indeed, Mahāvīra was the first religious teacher in India to claim such omniscience,[21] which can be described as the most comprehensive way of reaching ultimate objectivity.

Although the Jaina theory of action *(kiriya)* seems to have led to a relativistic or non-absolutistic theory of knowledge that culminated in the recognition of "omniscience," the Buddha perceived this view of action as not much different from the Ājīvika conception of biological determinism, and hence as another way of reaching out for objectivity. While recognizing the Jainas for highlighting the doctrine of human action at a time when most heterodox schools were rejecting it, the Buddha criticized them for equating bodily action with motivation or the psychological springs of action.[22] He found that with such an equation, the Jainas were not only presenting an extremely deterministic theory, which he referred to as *pubbekatahetuvāda* (the theory that every human experience is due to past action), but also were creating difficulties with regard to the explanation of freedom *(nirvāṇa)*. It is at this point that the Jainas were compelled to accept certain aspects of the Brahmanical notion of self *(ātman)*.

If human action were as determined as the Jainas believed it to be, it would be difficult to explain how an evil person could change the course of his life and become a good person. The Jainas responded to this by maintaining that the soul is originally pure and that it is soiled by adventitious karmic particles. This notion of an originally pure soul is not very different from the Brahmanical conception of *ātman*. This again is a view wrongly attributed to the Buddha.[23] Furthermore, the Jainas conceived of these adventitious karmic particles in the form of material elements. Such a materialistic view of action may have helped them explain the correlation between action and consequence in a more objective way, but it did not help solve the problem of freedom from karma. Indeed, the Buddha ridiculed the Jaina view that one can free oneself from present karma by non-action and expiate one's past karma by extreme penances.[24] He maintained that Jainas who practiced penances and experienced extreme pain would, by their own reckoning, be full of past evil karma, and that buddhas who enjoyed extreme happiness were inheritors of past good karma.

The Jainas' theory of action, which made no distinction between motivated and unmotivated or volitional and non-volitional action, had a far-reaching impact on their moral philosophy as well as their religious observances. In moral philosophy they advocated an extreme form of non-violence *(ahiṃsā)*, which may be an extremely praiseworthy ideal. Strict vegetarianism seems to have originated with the Jainas. However, *ahiṃsā* also led to other extreme practices, such as wearing a piece of cloth over the nose and the mouth to prevent inhaling any form of invisible life and sweeping the ground on which one would be walking to avoid stepping on tiny creatures even by accident.

Conclusion

The four major philosophical traditions before the rise of Buddhism—Brahmanism, Materialism, Ājīvikism, and Jainism—seem to have been generally reluctant to admit any element of uncertainty or skepticism regarding human knowledge. Even the Jainas, who were forced into adopting a relativistic standpoint in their attempt to reconcile the problems of determinism and free will, finally abandoned that relativism in favor of a doctrine of omniscience. The only philosopher who seriously addressed the problem of skepticism was Sañjaya. Unfortunately, Sañjaya could provide no solution to it and therefore refrained from making any positive statement. Sañjaya differed from the Absolutists in that he resorted to negative pronouncements without asserting an ultimate reality that transcends empirical description, as the Brahmanical thinkers did.

The historical fact that two of Sañjaya's leading disciples, Upatissa and Kolita, left him after learning about the Buddha's teachings and were converted almost immediately, becoming the Buddha's two chief disciples after assuming the names Sāriputta and Mogallāna, respectively, is of extreme ideological significance. They probably became disciples of Sañjaya because they were genuine skeptics. If they had been totally dissatisfied with the skeptical traditions they could easily have embraced one that emphasized absolute certainty regarding an ultimate reality, such as the Brahmanical teachings or even the doctrines of the Ājīvikas or the Jainas, if not those of the Materialists. Yet they remained disciples of Sañjaya until they found a tradition that combined skepticism with some more positive teachings. This explains why they were attracted to the Buddha's doctrine even after getting to know of it through reports. Here they seem to have discovered a new solution to the problem of skepticism, not comparable to those offered by the preceding schools. In fact, Sāriputta's report to Moggallāna about the nature of the Buddha's teachings clearly indicates what was unique in the Buddha's solution to the problem of skepticism:

> Whatever be the phenomena that arise from causes, the Tathāgata has expounded their causation as well as their cessation. The great recluse is such a theorist.
> *(Ye dhammā hetuppabhavā tesaṃ hetu tathāgato āha, tesañ ca yo nirodho evaṃvādī mahāsamaṇo.)*[25]

Whereas Sañjaya was reluctant to make any positive pronouncements through fear of falling into error, the Buddha was willing to recognize the limitations of human knowledge and provide a reasonable description of truth and reality without reaching out for ultimate objectivity. This approach allowed him to avoid any ontological or metaphysical commitments and deal with language in a more meaningful way. For these reasons, he refrained from either raising or answering questions relating to ultimate origins or destinies, questions that had haunted Indian philosophers for centuries. Indeed, it was a discussion of such metaphysical issues between the Buddha and a wanderer Dīghanakha that served as the occasion for Sāriputta to attain enlightenment, convinced of the futility of attempting solutions to such problems.[26]

If Absolutism is the result of reaching out for ultimate objectivity in philosophical discourse, and if extreme skepticism is the reason for the failure of such an enterprise, the Buddha, in his explanation of human experience, seems to have renounced the search for such objectivity and confined himself to a middle way, thereby renouncing both Absolutism and extreme skepticism.

CHAPTER II

Life of the Buddha

The story of the life of the Buddha has become enshrined in all forms of myths and legends, as in the case of many religious teachers of the past. Distinguishing historical facts from myths and legends is not only a difficult task but one that is generally resisted by the overenthusiastic devotee. Such resistance can seem justified if the interpreter of the myths tends to assume that they are mere imaginations of the faithful disciple. Yet a more sober and careful analysis reveals that these myths symbolize important emotional or psychological events connected with the personalities involved or with actual historical incidents that called for dramatic explanations.

In recent times the reconstruction of the life of the historical Buddha, the sage of the Śākya clan *(Śākyamuni)*, has been attempted by many scholars. One classic is E. J. Thomas' *The Life of Buddha as Legend and History* (1927). A second work of rare scholarship is by Bhikkhu Ñyāṇamoli. His *The Life of the Buddha* (1972) consists of translations of selections from the Pali canon and commentaries carefully sorted out and identified by their authors, such as reports by Ānanda or Upāli, who were the Buddha's immediate disciples, or explanations by traditional commentators. Working with scanty references to historical events, another way of reconstructing the life of the Buddha is to pay serious attention to the philosophical ideas he expounded and see how far these are reflected in his life and conduct. Such an attempt was made in *The Way of Siddhartha: A Life of the Buddha* (1982). The present work being an outline of the philosophical teachings of the Buddha, it seems appropriate to preface it with a chapter summarizing the contents of that work.

Buddha, meaning "the enlightened one," is a term by which Siddhārtha Gautama came to be known after his attainment of enlightenment. Siddhārtha's father, Suddhodana, was the ruler of a small kingdom, called the country of the Śākyans, at the foothills of the Himalayas. It was a city-kingdom with Kapilavastu as its center. Siddhārtha's mother, Māyā, is said to have died immediately after his birth. Pajāpatī Gotamī, Māyā's younger sister, nursed Siddhārtha in his childhood. Brought up in comfortable surroundings, enjoying privileges not available to the vast majority of children in a caste-ridden social structure, Siddhārtha was well educated in the traditional academic disciplines, martial arts, and other fields of study appropriate for a prospective ruler. However, early in life he seems to have come into conflict with his father, who wanted him to be the heir to the throne rather than a philosopher or religious leader who would challenge traditional ideas and values. These conflicts are symbolized in some of the myths about his early life, especially those of the prognostications of the sage Asita Kāladevala and of his father preventing him from witnessing birth, illness, old age, and death. Traditional learning included study of the *Vedas* as well as the six ancillary sciences: phonetics *(śikṣā)*, ritual *(kalpa)*, grammar *(vyākaraṇa)*, etymology *(nirukti)*, metrics *(chandas)*, and astronomy *(jyotiṣ)*.[1] The Buddha's insightful criticisms of the *Vedas,* knowledge of the meaning and gradual evolution of the rites and rituals, critical evaluation of current social and political structures, detailed analysis of moral conventions, and illuminating thoughts about the nature and function of language, all of which can be clearly seen in the discourses attributed to him, could not have been the result merely of a sudden enlightenment, much less of omniscience, which he openly disclaimed. Instead, his enlightenment can be considered the combination of a mature response to the traditional learning that he received as a student and a penetrating understanding of human life and the nature of existence.

Doubts have been raised about whether the Buddha was married and had a family because there are no specific references to these matters in the early discourses. Yet his own statements regarding the luxuries his father provided in order to keep him tied to a household life do not rule out the possibility of his having married (a woman named Yasodharā) and fathered a son (Rāhula).

An extremely critical mind like Siddhārtha's, exposed to learning that considered the *Vedas* to be revealed texts and the *Upaniṣads* to be the culmination of human knowledge and understanding, could naturally revolt. Ascetics and brahmans like Ajita Kesakambali, Makkhali Gosāla, Pakudha Kaccāyana, Pūraṇa Kassapa, Sañjaya Bellaṭṭhiputta, and Mahāvīra had already reacted against such traditional dogmas. Siddhārtha was to be the last of these major thinkers of the heterodoxy.

Most of the six so-called heretical teachers were ascetics who had experimented with both reason and experience in order to understand the nature of human life and the world. With his critical attitude, Siddhārtha could not simply depend on the authority either of the traditionalists or of the heretics. Thus he was compelled to adopt the life of an ascetic against the will of his parents,[2] who wanted him to remain a householder and be the next ruler of the Śākyans. No mention of his wife's objections to his renunciation is made in the early sources. Being a faithful wife in a traditional family, Yasodharā no doubt realized the need to support her husband's ideology, and thus remained a docile partner in Siddhārtha's quest for answers to the riddle of existence. The legend about Siddhārtha's leaving home while his wife and new born baby were asleep, while highlighting the emotional stress in his renunciation, also symbolizes Yasodharā's acceptance of her husband's decision. Any other interpretation of his renunciation would do violence to the character of a person who propounded an extremely enlightened form of love and compassion for oneself as well as others.

Wandering ascetics had criticized the Brahmanical tradition for several centuries before Siddhārtha began to realize its weaknesses and its unfortunate impact on morality and social harmony. However, Siddhārtha was not as negative as the Materialists and Ājīvikas were toward morals as well as spirituality. Hence, immediately after leaving home and country, he moved south into Magadha, in Central India, where he joined two leading contemplatives, Āḷāra Kālāma and Uddaka Rāmaputta, both representatives of the Upaniṣadic tradition. Under their guidance Siddhārtha learned meditation techniques specifically directed at the appeasement of mind rather than the development of insight. Dissatisfied with their spiritual attainments, he is said to have left them and joined a band of ascetics who were practicing self-mortification. In the company of Kondañña, Bhaddiya, Vappa, Mahānāma, and Assaji, Siddhārtha practiced severe forms of self-mortification in the hope of gaining knowledge and freedom. Even his friends were surprised at the extreme levels to which he carried such practices. His fasting reduced his body to a mere skeleton, and at one stage he is said to have been on the verge of death.

Six long years of mortification of the flesh made him realize the futility and meaninglessness of such deprivation, and he abandoned this way of life. At this point his five friends, who had been helping and watching him with great anticipation left him in disgust. After regaining his strength, Siddhārtha moved to a quiet place on the banks of the Nerañjarā River near Gayā. The opposite bank was a hub of ritual activities where ascetics and brahmans performed fire sacrifices and the like. Seated under a *ficus* tree, which subsequently became famous as the *bodhi* tree or "tree of enlightenment," Siddhārtha decided to revert to the meditational practices he had cultivated under the tutelage of Āḷāra Kālāma and Uddaka Rāmaputta. These yogic exercises, as mentioned earlier, were intended to appease the mind. Continuing with these exercises rather vigorously, he was able to move onto a stage beyond what he had experienced earlier. This was a state in which all perceptions and what had been experienced *(saññāvedayita)* came to an end or cessation *(nirodha)*.

Where his predecessors had assumed that the higher states of meditation provided a glimpse into the nature of ultimate reality, Siddhārtha, through his ability to stop all perceptions and experience, realized the non-cognitive nature of that state. Therefore, he emerged from that state and devoted most of his time to a cognitive understanding of existence. The process of meditation that led to the cessation of perception also involved excessive concentration and flexibility of mind. Equipped with these, he spent much time reflecting on his own past (= retrocognition or *pubbenivāsānussati*). Looking at the information provided by such reflection, without adopting too many presuppositions, such as the existence of a permanent and eternal substance, Siddhārtha understood how his life had been conditioned by various factors. Developing the cognitive capacity called clairvoyance *(dibbacakkhu)*, he perceived how the lives of other human beings are conditioned in the same way. He realized that, in addition to factors such as one's parents and environment, one's own behavior *(kamma)* contributes to the manner in which human life evolves. He was probably aware of the physicalistic explanation of behavior presented by Mahāvīra. Siddhārtha was looking for an explanation, not the neatness or clearness associated with it. He was not ready to push things under the rug because they stood in the way of formulating absolute laws. This involved him in a massive psychological enterprise. Even though he understood that human life is often conditioned by factors for which one is not fully responsible, examining the psychological springs of human behavior, he came to realize that there is a ray of hope for freedom. It was this realization that prompted him to analyze the psychological springs of action, or motivation, and distinguish behavior on the basis of its intentionality or non-intentionality. The rest of his investigations thus focused on discovering the motives that dominate human action and lead to unfortunate and evil consequences. Greed *(lobha)* and hatred *(dosa)* headed the list.

While this realization may not appear to be startling, the difficulty lay in eliminating such negative motives without adopting a totally negative attitude toward human emotions. In other words, Siddhārtha wanted to discard passion and be dispassionate without simultaneously losing the capacity for compassion. The method he finally adopted was to appease his dispositional tendencies without either allowing them to grow into states of greed, lust, or attachment or actually annihilating them, which was tantamount to suicide. This psychological struggle continued until he emerged from it claiming that he had appeased or calmed his dispositions *(sabbasaṅkhārasamatha)* and attained the cessation of lust *(rāga)* and hatred *(dosa)*.

The elimination of lust and hatred and appeasement of the dispositions enabled him to adopt a restrained attitude about the view he had adopted of the world. Without running after ultimate objectivity or abandoning all perspectives—that is, without looking for any form of absolute or permanent existence, or of nihilistic non-existence—he examined the nature of human conception. Appeasement of the dispositions enabled him to look at conception itself as possessing pragmatic value rather than absolutistic implications. This eliminated the last of the hurdles or obstacles, namely, confusion *(moha).*

The elimination of lust, hatred, and confusion *(rāgakkhaya, dosakkhaya,* and *mohakkhaya)* constituted his enlightenment and freedom, and this final knowledge and insight is referred to as "knowledge of the waning of influxes" *(āsavakkhaya-ñāṇa).* It represents a transformation of his whole personality, cognitive, conative, and emotive. With that transformation, Siddhārtha was able to perceive the world paying attention to the human predicament and the way out of it, which he summarized in the four noble truths *(ariya-sacca).*

In the context in which he lived, where the search for ultimate objectivity reigned supreme, his non-absolutist and non-substantialist view of the world and human life would have been received with little enthusiasm. Therefore, he was hesitant to preach what he had discovered. Yet his moral concern, symbolized by an invitation from Brahma, prompted him to go out into the world and propound his ideas for the sake of the few who were prepared to listen to him. Thus was initiated a missionary career that was to last for the next forty-five years.

By this time, his two instructors in the methods of yogic contemplation, Āḷāra and Uddaka, had passed away. Therefore, he went in search of the five friends in whose company he had practiced severe self-mortification, who were living in Bārānasi. At first they received him with suspicion and uncertainty, but they soon began to notice the transformation of his personality. Respect and admiration followed. They were willing to listen to him, and thus an audience was instantly created. Since these ascetics were enamored with self-mortification, the Buddha may have felt the need to explain the futility of such a life. Therefore, his first discourse to the world pertained to the *practical* middle path that avoids the two extremes of self-indulgence and self-mortification.[3] It was an exposition of the noble eightfold path and the fruits of life to be reaped, by oneself as well as others, by following it. It did not involve a discussion of the philosophical middle standpoint, which was the *raison d'être* of the moral life. The *philosophical* middle path was the topic on which he later discoursed to Kaccāyana, whose concerns were more epistemological and theoretical than practical.[4]

The first of the five ascetics who realized the significance of the Buddha's doctrine was Kondañña. Abandoning the self-mortification they had practiced for years, the five ascetics applied themselves to the teachings of the Buddha and soon attained enlightenment and freedom. The rapid progress they made should not be surprising, for they were men of great earnestness and spiritual maturity. The same can be said of many others, like Sāriputta and Moggallāna. In pre-Buddhist India, religious or spiritual pursuits were confined mostly to men, female participation being extremely rare. For this reason those who joined the Order during the early stages were mostly men. However, the Buddha's teachings injected a spirit of tolerance and critical reflection into Indian life, resulting in an erosion of the social, political, and religious conventions of the Brahmanical tradition.

The first of the Brahmanical conventions that fell into disrepute was social discrimination based on the age-old caste system. In the early discourses, the caste system remains the second most criticized theory, next to the doctrine of *ātman*. Not only did the Buddha provide innumerable arguments against this conception of caste, he also practiced what he preached by opening the doors of Order to any person who came to him looking for moral and spiritual guidance.

For a variety of pragmatic reasons, the Buddha seems to have adopted a more restrained attitude toward the Brahmanical system that discriminated against females. The rather cautious steps he took before admitting females into the congregation can be appreciated only against the background of the significant social, political, and religious revolution that was gradually taking place in India. Already thousands of males had renounced the household life and were living in congregations at various monasteries donated by lay disciples. This, as mentioned earlier, was a historical accident or situation created by the Brahmanical tradition. The sudden influx of females into such congregations could have created innumerable difficulties for monastic life and discipline. Furthermore, the Buddha was being criticized for eroding the family life of the Indians. He was denounced not only for destroying the so-called family *dharma* (caste system) but also for his unrestricted acceptance of renunciation by men who carried heavy family responsibilities.[5] The Buddha seems to have taken this latter criticism more seriously than the former. For this reason, he had to be more cautious in the most important venture of admitting women to the Order, and when he realized that the time was ripe, he did take that step. Even a superficial reading of the *Therīgāthā*[6] provides a clear view of the Buddha's attitude toward women and of the exalted status they enjoyed in the Buddhist Order. Indeed, Buddhism was the first religious tradition to recognize women's ability to attain the highest spiritual status attainable by any man, including the Buddha himself, and thus one in which they actually did so.

The second Brahmanical convention that the Buddha disrupted was the political one. Many formidable rulers of Magadha and the surrounding kingdoms were attracted to the teachings of the Buddha. Bimbisāra and Pasenadi became ardent followers and often sought the Buddha's advice on matters pertaining to political thought. The conception of a "universal monarch" *(cakkavatti)* whose authority depended on popular consensus and moral integrity rather than divine ordination was often emphasized by the Buddha. Punitive measures were replaced by moral rehabilitation. The story of Angulimāla's[7] attainment of moral perfection and spiritual freedom after spending most of his adult life as a murderer clearly exhibits the Buddha's way of dealing with problems of crime and punishment. His political philosophy was to leave a lasting impression not only on the Indian conception of monarchy, faithfully followed by Emperor Aśoka, but also on those of the South and Southeast Asian countries.

In the area of religious practices, the Buddha rejected only those ritualistic elements that contained no perceivable psychological and moral significance. As a result the brahman class lost the opportunity to practice its meaningless sacrifices and was deprived of its privileged position of intermediary between humanity and divinity. Although not every Brahmanical religious teacher or philosopher was willing to renounce his practices and ideas, some leaders, such as the Kassapa brothers,[8] were converted along with their large retinues.

Recognizing the futility of attempting to bring about a total revolution in human society and institutions, and assuming that "small is beautiful," the Buddha proceeded to organize the Order of monks and nuns in a manner that reflected his own philosophy. The ultimate goal of the *religious* life, as will be explained later, is the absence of constraints (*vimutti, nibbāna,* etc.). Thus a life of ultimate purity is also a life where possessive individualism should be renounced. This idea had to be reflected in the monastic life. Monks and nuns were to have no private property except the bowl and three robes. A monastery was a place of residence for all members of the Order, whether they came from north or south, east or west.

Virtues *(sīla)* recommended by the Buddha and conforming to the moral principles *(dhamma)* he formulated were adhered to as rules of discipline *(vinaya)* until more elaborate ones were adopted as occasions demanded. As the monastic institutions expanded and multiplied, the need for more and more specific rules gradually gave rise to an extensive corpus of literature called the *Books of Discipline (Vinaya Piṭaka).* Yet this vast collection of rules and regulations embodies the fundamental spirit of the Buddha's philosophy, in that they are not inviolable laws valid for eternity. Their validity was recognized only as long as they were functional, and the pragmatic spirit of the teachings often called for revisions and sometimes even for revocations.

The first Western writers who studied the principles governing the Buddha's monastic organization were impressed by its democratic temper. The Saṅgha has been designated "a system of government formed by the Bhikkhus (monks), for the Bhikkhus and of the Bhikkhus."[9] This means that it is a democratic institution set up by the Buddha for the good of its members as well as mankind. It is significant that when the question of a successor in whom the disciples could take refuge was raised during the Buddha's last days, he responded by saying that the doctrine *(dhamma)* he had preached and the discipline *(vinaya)* he had instituted would be their guides.[10] This was a novel idea, unknown to the political and religious organizations contemporary with or prior to Buddhism.[11] It is important to note that the Buddha's conception of democracy was not based strictly on a majority-minority distinction. The underlying moral principle was the welfare of oneself and others; the concept of "other" could vary, depending on context (see Chapter x).

As the Buddha's word swept across the northern part of the Indian continent and his fame as the founder of the religion spread, it was inevitable that his daily routine would change. Instead of his traveling about to meet people, more and more people from all walks of life visited him and sought his counsel. As a result there came to be a group of disciples, headed by Ānanda, who seem to have assumed responsibility not only for taking care of the Buddha but also for maintaining order in the constant flow of people who came to see him. Often the Buddha was not willing to isolate himself from the people, and when one of his attendants tried to prevent someone from seeing him, he would prevail upon them to allow that person an audience.[12]

The Buddha's strenuous life as a constant guide to thousands of people on matters moral and spiritual gradually began to take a toll on his health. The aftereffects of his six years of self-mortification also seem to have played a part. References are not wanting in connection with the latter part of his life, when he would interrupt a sermon or a discourse to retire to his living quarters, allowing one of his disciples to complete the discourse.[13] He had great confidence in most of his disciples, including nuns, who had attained enlightenment and freedom, and often recognized their expertise in the doctrine. While the unenlightened disciples tended to worship him as their sole savior, which appears to be the traditional Indian way of respecting someone who initiates a new tradition, the Buddha was struggling to avoid any "cult worship" by insisting that what was more important was the doctrine *(dhamma)* he had preached. The doctrine was to be their guide, not anything else.

As he reached the age of eighty and realized that his life would not last long, the Buddha traveled north, probably with the intention of returning to his homeland. However, his health deteriorated to such an extent that he passed away at Kusinārā, almost on the border between the country of Brahmanical domination, which he had attempted to change, and his own land of the Śākyans, which had given birth to the new movement.

CHAPTER III

Knowledge and Understanding

The wide variety of philosophical speculation in India before the advent of Buddhism indicates a vast range of experimentation with different sources of knowledge. The Buddhist discourse that refers to sixty-two metaphysical views regarding the nature of self and the world maintains that these were the products of two primary sources: experience and reason.[1] However, the two were not exclusive. The empiricists seem to have utilized reason just as much as the rationalists recognized experience. The major difference between them seems to have been the almost complete rejection of yogic insight by the rationalists and the total dependence on such insights by the empiricists. Thus the empiricists are described as those who follow the methods of exertion *(ātappa)*, application *(padhāna)*, concentration *(anuyoga)*, and reflection *(manasikāra)*,[2] while the rationalists adopted two primary techniques, deduction *(takka)* and investigation *(vīmaṃsā)*.[3]

The sources just mentioned, with the exception of yogic insight, are generally utilized by philosophers the world over. Yet the Buddha claimed that these very sources of information were the basis for what he considered to be metaphysical speculations in the Indian context. He referred to them as *adhivuttipada*,[4] a term that literally means "overstatement." The characterization of metaphysics as "overstatements" raises many important philosophical issues. What is the relationship between an experience and a statement about that experience? Are all experiences veridical and the statements about them false? How are we to decide which statement is true and which is false, that is, which is a statement of fact and which is an overstatement? Can what makes a statement false also render the experience itself false? These were some of the questions that invited the Buddha's attention, especially because he was not willing to subscribe totally to any of the theories presented by the pre-Buddhist philosophers.

In Chapter I it was pointed out that most of the theories of the four major schools of thought before the Buddha—Brahmanism, Materialism, Ājīvikism, and Jainism—were dominated by a search for ultimate objectivity in philosophical explanation. Although they were attempts to leave behind the human perspective and provide a completely objective description of phenomena, the Buddha found that they were indeed dominated by one or the other, or a combination, of the following attitudes or perspectives: (1) faith or confidence *(saddhā),* (2) likes or preferences *(ruci),* (3) tradition *(anussava),* (4) reflection on form *(ākāra-parivitakka),* and (5) delighting in the contemplation of views *(diṭṭhi-nijjhānakkhanti).*[5]

Faith or confidence can pertain to the source of knowledge, to the relationship between knowledge and description, or even to predictability on the basis of that knowledge. Faith in the source of knowledge can often blind us to such an extent that, even if there were undeniable evidence against what is revealed by such a source, we would insist on its veracity. Confidence regarding the relationship between knowledge and description can lead us in two different directions: we can either insist that the description is an exact copy of knowledge or the content of knowledge (= a picture theory of language), or we can assume that knowledge transcends all forms of description. Finally, confidence regarding predictability has provided greater and greater confidence regarding that particular kind of knowledge, and unpredictability has often been the reason for rejecting even what may be called veridical knowledge.

The same can be said of other attitudes or perspectives. This inclined the Buddha to maintain that,

> There are five things that have a twofold result in this life. What five? [Knowledge based on] faith, likes, tradition, reflection on form, and delight in views. . . . Even if I know something on the basis of best faith, that may be empty, hollow, and confused, while what I do not know on the best faith may be factual, true, and not otherwise. It is not proper for an intelligent person, safeguarding the truth, to come categorically to the conclusion in this matter that such alone is true and whatever else is false.[6]

Here the Buddha is emphasizing the idea that a theory accepted on the basis of faith or confidence, likes or preferences, tradition or report, reflection on form or logical consistency, or delighting in the contemplation of views or obsession with views is not necessarily true. This means that the criterion for deciding what is true or false lies elsewhere. The question is, where?

Considering the difficulties confronted by his predecessors, the Buddha was not willing to abandon all human perspectives when formulating a view, perhaps realizing from the outset the impossibility of doing so. Therefore, he was compelled to analyze in detail the nature of sense experience, the means by which we come to have yogic intuition, and the process of rational reflection. This involved an enterprise that no Indian philosopher before him had attempted. Neither do any of his contemporaries elsewhere in the world, either in China or in Greece, seem to have engaged in anything comparable. In short, this involved him in a detailed analysis of human psychology.

Sense Experience

It is interesting that the Buddha undertook his most comprehensive analysis of the psychology of sense perception in a context in which questions were raised as to why there are so many conflicting views in the world.[7] Even though his statement explaining the process of sense experience is rather brief, its implications are wide-ranging:

> Depending upon the visual organ and the visible object, O monks, arises visual consciousness; the meeting together of these three is contact; conditioned by contact arises feeling. What one feels, one perceives; what one perceives, one reflects about; what one reflects about, one is obsessed with. What one is obsessed with, due to that, concepts characterized by such obsessed perceptions assail him in regard to visible objects cognizable by the visual organ, belonging to the past, the future, and the present.[8]

In the first place, the principle according to which sense experience begins to take place is "dependence" *(paṭiccasamuppāda)*. The conception of a "self" *(ātman)* that functions as the agent is thereby eliminated. Second, the first reference is to the visual organ, which is part of the physically identifiable personality. The physical personality itself being part of the psychophysical personality *(nāmarūpa)*, i.e., a conscious human being, the notion of a tabula rasa on which experience is said to leave its impressions is also abandoned.

Third, even though the object of experience is mentioned after the sense organ, the description gives equal importance to both. It is in dependence on the sense organ and the object that the process of perception begins. While the object is mentioned as one of the primary conditions, there is no attempt to determine what that object is. Neither is the object referred to as a vague sense datum that eventually gets unfolded as the process of perception proceeds. What is implied is that the sense object itself has to attune to the sense organ, for an object that is not compatible with the sense cannot be perceived. The Buddha's emphasis is on what a reflective human being does with the so-called object or what happens to the object when the process of experience takes place, rather than on determining what the ultimate nature of the object is or on providing an ultimately objective description of the object itself.

Fourth, his realization that ultimate objectivity regarding the object itself cannot be achieved and that the human perspective is unavoidable is underscored by his statement regarding the initial stage of sense experience, that is to say, "depending upon the visual organ and the visible object arises visual consciousness." Where can a philosopher go to determine the nature of the object while avoiding the consciousness of the object? If consciousness is not a tabula rasa but part of the psychophysical personality and hence conditioned by previous experiences, there are many other elements that will enter the scene when a decision is made regarding the object. It is to explain the complex nature of consciousness, while at the same time allowing for the retention of some measure of objectivity of the object, that the Buddha underscores the dependence of consciousness on the sense organ and the object. Furthermore, there is no suggestion of epi-phenomenalism, that is, that consciousness is a by-product of matter, and therefore generated at each moment as a result of the contact between the sense and the object.

The suggestion that consciousness at this stage is rather noetic and gradually progresses as it goes through the other stages does not seem appropriate, either. The reason is that the intermediary stage between contact *(phassa)* and perception *(saññā),* namely, sensation or feeling *(vedanā),* does not add to the *content* of the perception in terms of precision or clarity, but rather to its *character.*

The coming together of the sense organ, the object of sense, and the consciousness conditioned by them is called contact *(phassa).* The term "contact" is to be understood in its broader sense, as in statements such as "I am in contact with John," not in the more restricted sense of "bare touch." Because the term is used in a more extended or comprehensive sense, the Buddha is able to say that all philosophical theories about the world are dependent on contact *(phassa-paccayā).*[9] Contact thus expresses the idea of familiarity.

The inevitable result of contact is feeling *(vedanā),* which introduces the emotive element, and this can be pleasant, unpleasant, or neutral. Familiarity breeds not only contempt but also admiration and indifference. For the Buddha, the emotive aspect of sense experience is most important, because it enables him to ground moral decisions in the world of experience instead of leaving them as arbitrary decisions unrelated to the factual world. However, the Buddha was not unaware that feelings can grow into monstrous forms, overwhelming human beings to such an extent that they lose all rationality. In other words, emotions, which are inevitable elements in our experiences, can also cause most of our confusion and suffering.

To express this idea, the Buddha changes the language he employed to explain the process of perception. Instead of using the language of "dependence," as in "depending upon feeling arises perception" *(vedanā-paccayā saññā),* he utilizes the language of agency: "What one feels, one perceives" *(yaṃ vedeti, taṃ sañjānāti).* This is an extremely sophisticated way of indicating how a causally conditioned human personality with its own identity can give rise to the conception of an independent and self-subsistent self *(ātman)* through hyperactive emotions. It also demonstrates how that overextended emotion is generally accommodated in ordinary language, and how a more impersonal language can bring about a change in the emotions themselves without eliminating them altogether. This fascinating view that conceptions themselves can change human emotions is discussed further below.

The statement that "what one feels, one perceives" is an intriguing way of stating that our perceptions are *normally* determined by our emotional life. It is a clear admission that our interests, whether simple interests or more extended emotions, such as likes and dislikes, play an important role in our perceptions. Indeed, no perception can be totally free from perspectives—perspectives determined minimally by interest and maximally by likes and dislikes, that is, by prejudices.

The next step in the process of experience is reflection *(vitakka),* which can lead the perception in two different ways. Reflection provides an opportunity to evaluate the consequences of perception, whether it leads to bondage and suffering or freedom and happiness. If reflection continues to justify the existence of an ego, an independent and self-subsistent entity *(ātman),* it leads to obsession *(papañca).*

It should be remembered that the cause of this obsession is the emergence, as a result of overstretched emotion, of the conception of an ego or self-subsistent entity. However, once that obsession is generated, its influence is felt in relation not so much to the perception *(saññā)* itself as to the conception *(saṅkhā)* of that perceived object. In fact, in another passage obsession is specifically connected with conception, e.g., *papañca-saṅkhā.*[10] To some extent one can be obsessed with a perception only so long as one clings to the notion of an ego, although an obsession can also pass away with the waning of that immediate experience. In contrast, an obsession can be lasting if it is associated with the conception of the object of experience, and it is this conception that can relate itself to the objects of the past, present, and future. In other words, it is easier to be enslaved by a concept that gives the impression of being permanent and incorruptible than by a perception that is obviously temporal and corruptible. In modern Western thought, the idea that concepts, being substitutes for percepts, should not be looked upon as incorruptible found a strong advocate in William James.[11]

The above analysis of sense experience alone would suffice as a refutation of the Brahmanical notions of the self and the world as eternal and incorruptible entities *(ātman).* Yet because the Brahmanical tradition claimed that its conceptions were the product not of sense experience but of yogic intuition, the Buddha was compelled to conduct a detailed analysis of the psychology of yogic intuition.

Yogic Experience

The Buddha received instruction in meditation under two traditional teachers of the Brahmanical school, Āḷāra Kālāma and Uddaka Rāmaputta.[12] When reporting about the training he received from them, the Buddha simply mentions the ultimate stage of mental development each one had attained. The probable reason is that these teachers were more interested in the ultimate state of experience than in the means of reaching it. As a trainee, even the Buddha himself may have focused on that experience. As mentioned earlier, the Buddha was not impressed by their attainments and left them. After six long years of self-mortification, when he returned to meditative practices, he seems to have paid attention to the means as well as the goal, thus noticing the usefulness as well as the limitations of the yogic method. As in the case of sensory experience, we here encounter the first ever detailed statement regarding the psychology of yoga.

After being a critic of yoga as well as its beneficiary, the Buddha paid attention to all the minute details at every step of the way. He realized that a strong moral life is a prerequisite for mental concentration. Excessive desire *(kāma)* and unwholesome mental tendencies *(akusala dhamma)* naturally obstruct concentration. Therefore, during the initial stage a person is expected to cultivate aloofness from such tendencies.

Aloofness from unwholesome states of mind is said to produce an emotional experience or stage in which reflection and investigation are active and which is permeated by a sense of joy and happiness born of that aloofness. Reflection and investigation are here taken to be the most important sources of information, the former providing an account of the historical background, and hence being comparable to radical empiricism, while the latter concentrates on the present or on immediately given information. Together they serve as a comprehensive method for understanding any experience. The moral integrity of the person involved in such reflection and investigation has been assured by the first stage of meditation.[13]

The search for ultimate explanations has often compelled those who reflect and investigate to be dissatisfied with the information available from these two sources. Consequently, they continue to reflect and investigate until they reach a stage where they either assert *something* that is totally different from what is empirically given or fall into complete skepticism. In either case there cannot be much progress at this second stage of meditation.

At this point the only way out is to suspend reflection and investigation and concentrate on the information already available through such means. This is the third stage of meditation. While reflection and investigation are temporarily suspended, appreciation of the given information continues. Therefore the emotional state generated as a result of the first stage, namely, joy and happiness, also continues.

Yet joy can grow into a state of jubilation, which can hinder the unbiased evaluation of the data of experience and render the mind rigid and inflexible. Thus, in the final stage of this particular process of meditation, an attempt is made to eliminate joy. The resulting state is one in which the mind becomes extremely flexible, pliable, and considerate *(upekkhā),* without any prejudices. This fourth stage of meditation is considered to be a state of equanimity rather than a blank mind emptied of all conceptions.

These are the four preparatory stages of contemplation *(jhāna)* and are said to belong to the world of material form *(rūpa).* Unfortunately, a wrong translation of the terms *vitakka/vicāra* as discursive thought/initial thought instead of reflection/investigation has led to the belief that at the end of these four stages, all mental processes, such as discrimination and analysis, are eliminated. The final state is therefore understood as indifference (= *upekkhā?*) toward normal sensory experiences and the beginning of a non-sensuous yogic intuition. In the interpretation of yoga, it thus becomes the watershed between transcendentalism and empiricism. Even though the contemplatives of the Brahmanical tradition may have opted for the former, the Buddha clearly sided with an empiricist interpretation of the four stages.

This becomes evident from the Buddha's way of analyzing and evaluating the higher, formless *(arūpa)* stages of contemplation. First is the contemplation of "space" *(ākāsa).* One cannot contemplate space if all sensory experiences and thoughts are abandoned in the previous stage. However, it is an interesting way of initiating the gradual abandoning of the world of material form *(rūpa).*

Why would anyone want to abandon the world of material form when trying to understand the nature of the self and the world? The answer is obvious: sense experience has not provided satisfactory information. The Brahmanical thinkers had lost confidence in sense experience as a valid source of knowledge. At this stage the Buddha was simply following their methodology in order to evaluate its signficance and relevance.

It is natural to remain satisfied with any experience or conception until one reaches a problematic situation. One could remain satisfied with the reflection on "space" and be unruffled by notions of multiplicity, for space is vast and usually empty. Yet reflection on empty space can always engender questions regarding its limits *(anta).* How far can it stretch? Is there a limit? The idea that space is unlimited does not satisfy the gnostic mind; the alternative, namely, agnosticism, is also not satisfactory. The contemplative therefore takes no delight in the idea of space, for he has already abandoned any joyous involvement in what he perceives. In that process he realizes that the attempt to reach the limit of space is being made in his own "consciousness" *(viññāṇa).*

This second stage of higher contemplation can be a fruitful epistemological source for "idealism" *(viññāṇavāda?)*. However, the contemplatives who instructed the Buddha before his enlightenment were not interested in terminating the process at this level, for consciousness often implies a relationship between subject and object, a duality that did not conform to what they were looking for during their speculations.

Therefore, the third stage represents an attempt to get rid of the substantiality or reality of consciousness. This can be achieved by contemplating "no-thing" *(akiñci)*. At this point the contemplative can realize the non-substantiality of all phenomena, physical or psychological and, as a result, abandon the belief in a permanent and eternal self *(ātman)*. Some of the contemplatives of the heterodox schools that propounded materialistic and biological theories did precisely this. The traditional brahman contemplatives were not satisfied with such a conclusion. In their search for evidence in favor of a unitary self accounting for the reality of both "oneself and others," they appear to have pressed on and reached a state they characterized as "neither perception nor non-perception" *(neva saññā nāsaññā)*. It seems obvious from this negative description that the contemplative is here faced with a dilemma. He feels that he has a positive experience, yet he is unable to relate it to any ordinary sense experience. Linguistic description fails him.

The Buddha's response to this was twofold. First, while he was a trainee under Uddaka Rāmaputta, he claimed to have reached such a state. However, he was not quite enamored with it; hence his parting company with Rāmaputta. Second, when he reverted to this meditative practice, he claimed that he proceeded beyond it and reached the state of cessation of perception and of what has been experienced *(saññāvedayitanirodha)*.

The important question is, Why did the Buddha claim that he was able to go beyond Rāmaputta's attainments and achieve a state of cessation? Did Rāmaputta not proceed further because he was preoccupied with seeking a "certain," unique experience not couched in sensory terms? Considering how subsequent yogins of the Brahmanical tradition, such as Patañjali, advocated the elimination of discriminative thought (i.e., sensory and conceptual thinking) during the initial stages of meditation, and how the Buddha did not do so, it is possible to maintain that the Buddha had already abandoned the intellectual obstacle (i.e., the search for a mysterious experience) during the preliminary stages, and that he had no reason to remain satisfied with a state described as "neither perception nor non-perception." In fact, cessation, which is the stopping of all experience, is a non-cognitive state.

Hence the twofold response of the Buddha represents his solution to the Brahmanical contemplative's dilemma. The Buddha's renunciation of Rāmaputta's tutorship constitutes his rejection of the Brahmanical claim that contemplation leads to the knowledge of an extra-sensuous and extra-linguistic ultimate reality such as *ātman,* while his second response indicates that he recognized the possibility as well as the value of cessation without assuming its cognitive capacity. The Buddha's constant practice of this state of cessation when he was advanced in years, especially before his passing away,[14] strongly suggests that it is a state in which one is able to relax and enjoy a moment of peace and serenity of mind. For this reason, he maintained that this state is to be experienced with the body *(kāyena sacchikaraṇīya).*[15]

The fact that the state of cessation has no cognitive value, other than bodily relaxation and serenity of mind, is further confirmed by the Buddha's statement that when he emerged from that state he realized the non-substantiality *(anatta)* of all phenomena.[16] The ability to terminate the normal processes of experience *(saññā, vedanā)* without destroying the sensory faculties (as in the case of death) or gaining any cognitive awareness in the process compelled the Buddha to rely heavily on sensory experience in formulating his worldview. Indeed, the state of cessation is sometimes compared with death, the only difference being that, while in both states all dispositional tendencies *(saṅkhāra),* bodily, verbal, and mental, cease, in the former life continues and the faculties *(indriya)* remain extremely bright and clear *(vippasanna).*[17] All this leads to the conclusion that, according to the Buddha, cognitive awareness requires not only the availability of the sensory faculties but also the presence of bodily, verbal, and mental dispositions, and that any attempt to abandon these dispositions (= human perspectives) is epistemological suicide.

As a result of this realization, the Buddha's evaluation of the so-called higher forms of knowledge *(abhiññā)* also takes a different turn. The usual list of higher knowledge consists of psychokinesis, clairaudience, telepathy, retrocognition, and clairvoyance. The Brahmanical tradition seems to have utilized some of these knowledge-claims to justify the doctrine of karma as well as rebirth. However, their conception of rebirth was based on the belief in an immutable "self" *(ātman).* Some of the higher forms of knowledge, such as retrocognition and clairvoyance, could be used to suggest the existence of such an immutable self. But the Brahmanical thinkers were not completely satisfied with them, for such knowledge involved duality as well as multiplicity. They were looking for a non-dual ultimate reality that would unite the individual self with the reality of the world. Therefore, while considering the higher forms of knowledge as well as sensory experience to be practical knowledge *(vijñāna),* they opted for what they considered to be the highest form of knowledge, i.e., the non-dual *(advaya),* which is said to sublate all other forms of knowledge. The state of cessation of perception and experience thus proved to be a more valuable source of knowledge for the later Brahmanical yogin, as well as for some Buddhists who were enamored with transcendence (see Chapters XVIII and XXI).

The Buddha was reluctant to admit any ineffability in the state of cessation *(nirodha),* primarily because it is a non-cognitive state. Once he abandoned any notion of ineffability, he was inclined to give more validity not only to sense experience but also to the higher forms of knowledge, especially retrocognition and clairvoyance. To highlight the relationship between sensory experience and the extraordinary perceptions, the Buddha introduced two other forms of knowledge that he gained subsequent to the four preliminary stages of concentration. It is rather unfortunate that these two forms of perception, mentioned in one of his earliest discourses, the *Sāmaññaphala-suttanta,* have gone unnoticed by both classical and modern scholars. The discourse is viewed as one of the earliest and most authentic sources for the study of the heterodox traditions. Here the Buddhist yogin, following his attainment of the fourth stage of contemplation, directs his attention to his own psychophysical personality, unlike his Brahmanical counterpart:

> With his thought thus serene, made pure, translucent, cultured, devoid of evil, supple, ready to act, firm and imperturbable, he applies and bends down his thought to knowledge and vision. He comes to know: "This body of mine has material form, it is made up of the four great elements, it springs from mother and father, it is continually renewed by so much rice and juicy foods, its very nature is impermanence, it is subject to erasion, abrasion, dissolution, and disintegration, and there is in this consciousness of mine, too, bound up, on that it depends."[18]

This is an extremely important reflection, following immediately after the fourth preliminary stage of contemplation *(jhāna),* which, as mentioned earlier, has been wrongly interpreted as a state where all discursive and initial thought are abandoned. It is an unequivocal statement that some of the so-called higher forms of knowledge pertain to the nature of the physical body, the inalienable part of the human personality. It refers not only to the source and nature of the physical personality but also to the fact that there is consciousness associated with it, which makes it a complete person.

Against the background of the theories of the six heterodox teachers referred to in Chapter 1, this description of the human person is significant. While the heterodox teachers attempted to provide an objective explanation of the human personality by focusing on either the physical body or physical action, which they felt to be easily and objectively identifiable, the Buddha here introduced consciousness as an inalienable part of the human personality, even though it is not so objectively identified and analyzed. Thus he rejected the purely physicalistic explanation of the human personality as well as human behavior.

After understanding the nature of the psychophysical personality, the

Buddha directed his knowledge and understanding toward a more complex and vexing problem, namely, the function of the mind *(mano):*

> With his thought thus serene . . . and imperturbable, he applies and bends his thought to the creation of a mind-made body *(manomayaṃ kāyam).* From this body he creates another body, having material form, made of mind, possessed of all limbs and parts, nor deprived of any organ.[19]

The reference to the excessive creativity of the mind *(mano),* contrasted with the functioning of consciousness or awareness *(viññāṇa)* in the previous passage, is noteworthy. While consciousness, which is invariably associated with dispositions *(saṅkhāra),* accounts for knowledge and understanding, the mind is here represented as leaping over those boundaries to create figures that are perfect and incorruptible. By implication, this is a criticism of the Brahmanical notion of self *(ātman).*

These two forms of knowledge made the Buddha cautious in dealing with the contents of the extraordinary perceptions *(abhiññā)* mentioned above. Psychokinesis was admitted as a possibility. It consisted of certain powers such as levitation. The Buddha, however, was reluctant to utilize such powers to convert people to his way of thinking,[20] perhaps realizing that they produce a feeling of awe rather than conviction. Clairaudience, the ability to hear sounds that escape the auditory faculty not associated with a concentrated mind, was also recognized but rarely utilized.[21] Telepathy, the ability read the thought processes of other people, served as a useful means of understanding the intentions of his listeners and communicating with them in a more effective way.[22] It is this effectiveness in communication that his opponents may have viewed as a "magical power of conversion" *(āvaṭṭanī māyā).*[23]

For the Buddha, the most important among the higher forms of knowing were retrocognition and clairvoyance. Retrocognition was of particular significance. Avoiding the search for ultimate objectivity or ultimate realities, the Buddha was compelled to look at human experience from a contextual or historical standpoint. Knowledge of one's own past, as far as one can reach, was therefore essential. Under normal circumstances, memory is generally not regarded as a trustworthy source of knowledge, since it is often vague and indistinct and frequently fails us. Such inadequacies are sometimes attributed to our own prejudices, our reluctance even to think of such memories, our tendency to suppress memories that are unpleasant and recall those that are pleasant. Such a process is not at work in the case of the yogin, for he has already cleansed his mind by going through the first four preliminary stages. He is prepared to look at his memories whether they be pleasant or unpleasant. His moral standing, at least for the moment, prevents him from being hypocritical in dealing with the information.

Therefore, if memory were to be backed up by a strong sense of morality as well as excessive concentration, there is no reason that the information provided by it should be as suspect as in ordinary cases. Indeed, the Buddha often encouraged his disciples to use mindfulness *(satipaṭṭhāna)* as one of the foremost methods of attaining knowledge and freedom.[24] Mindfulness *(sati)* is not merely an awareness of what is immediately given in experience, but understanding the present in relation to the past. Thus in retrocognition, consciousness is said to function in the wake of memory *(satānusārī viññāṇaṃ)*.[25] The evolution of one's own personality, conditioned by various factors, good or bad, is most comprehensively understood through retrocognition. The question of how retrocognition can be extended to previous lives despite the interruption of the physical personality is discussed in Chapter VI.

The fifth higher knowledge is clairvoyance *(dibbacakkhu)*. As defined by the Buddha, it does not involve knowledge of the future. While clairvoyance is sometimes used in the sense of perceiving events taking place at a distance, and is comparable to clairaudience, more often it refers to knowledge of the evolution of other human beings as they are conditioned by their karma. The recognition of such a form of knowledge appears to be extremely arbitrary on the part of anyone claiming to be an empiricist. The question is often raised as to how an empiricist can explain knowledge of other-minds, let alone their evolution through several existences. It seems that doubts about the existence of other-minds are generated more by philosophers who attempt to reach ultimate objectivity in their explanations. In the Indian context, the Materialists, the Ājīvikas, and even the Jainas seem to have been confronted with such problems. In the case of the Buddha, the issue was to a great extent dissolved by his adoption of a philosophical standpoint that simply avoids generating such problems. When subsequent Buddhist philosophers adopted such objective standpoints, they were compelled to compile treatises justifying the existence of other-minds, as exemplified by Vinītadeva's *Santānantarasiddhi (Establishment of Other-Minds)*.[26]

It is possible to adopt two extreme attitudes about the five forms of knowledge referred to above. The skeptic who looks for an objective explanation can insist on the meaninglessness of such knowledge-claims, for they are not compatible with his notion of verifiability, which is confined mostly to the physical. The spiritualist, in contrast, believes that such knowledge is mystical and has nothing to do with ordinary experiences. The middle path adopted by the Buddha avoids both these extremes. Without being unduly skeptical or excessively enamored with them, he was willing to accept whatever information was available through such means as long as it possessed any pragmatic value. Karma and rebirth, two doctrines that the Buddha came to accept on the basis of some of these experiences, were justified not only on empirical grounds but also on pragmatic ones,[27] the latter being highlighted for the benefit of the skeptic.

This brings us to the highest form of knowledge recognized by the Buddha, namely, knowledge of the waning of influxes *(āsavakkhaya)*, often referred to as wisdom or insight *(paññā,* Skt. *prajñā)*. The fact that it comes at the end of a list of higher forms of knowledge, all of which are viewed as extraordinary and even mystical in some sense, leaves the impression that this form of knowledge must be equally mystical, if not more so. Thus wisdom is often considered to be totally unrelated to sensory experiences, despite the Buddha's own admission that there is no significant difference between consciousness *(viññāṇa)* and insight *(paññā)*.[28] Indeed, those who perceived a sharp dichotomy between the life process and freedom are the ones who insisted on a dichotomy between consciousness and insight.

The term *āsavakkhaya-ñāṇa* literally means "knowledge of the waning of influxes." Influxes are defilements produced in the individual's mind as a result of responses to the objects of experience. Even though this cognition pertains to the absence of such influxes, there is a positive content to such knowledge, namely, the human mind that is free from influxes and hence pure. Thus it cannot be looked upon as non-dual *(advaya)* in a metaphysical sense, although it may be non-dual in a moral sense, because a person who has developed this form of knowledge is not egoistic and therefore does not make a sharp distinction between himself and others.

The moral content of the knowledge of the cessation of influxes is most important, because it is the culmination of the moral rectitude with which the process of meditation began (i.e., the first stage of contemplation). If a person does not reach this final stage but only the higher forms of contemplation *(jhāna)* and knowledge *(abhiññā)*, he can immediately revert to the state in which he first set out on the practice of meditation, thus rendering temporary what is achieved in the first stage of contemplation. The waning of influxes *(āsavakkhaya)*, which is a synonym for freedom *(nibbāna)*, therefore represents the elimination of the defiling tendencies once and for all.

The waning of influxes is a moral transformation that takes place in the individual. Whether one allows oneself to be overwhelmed by such influxes after they have been overcome depends on various factors, such as the conviction that they are harmful and the determination not to be lured by them. Because this refers to self-knowledge, or knowledge of the moral transformation taking place in oneself, the enlightened ones have claimed certainty about this form of knowledge more often than any other. The paeans of joy they give voice to after realizing this state reveal such a jubilant, exultant emotional triumph over suffering and frustration that it seems almost impossible for them to revert back to a state of bondage. This is often expressed in their claim: "[Future] births have waned, the higher life has been lived, done is what has to be done, there is no more of this in the future."[29]

Omniscience

The terms *sabbaññū, sabbavidū* ("all-knowing") and *sabbadassāvī* ("all-perceiving") occur in the early discourses.[30] The general tendency among modern interpreters of Buddhism is to assume that this is a knowledge-claim comparable to the "omniscience" claimed by Mahāvīra or in the theistic tradition, where it is attributed to divinity. Although the Buddha disclaimed such knowledge in the *Tevijja-Vacchagotta-sutta,*[31] insisting that he possessed only the threefold higher knowledge (the last three forms discussed above), scholars are more inclined to interpret the last, namely, wisdom *(paññā),* as "omniscience." It is true that some of the later Buddhist metaphysicians like the Sarvāstivādins propounded ideas that can serve as a basis for such knowledge-claims. Modern interpreters therefore attempt to attribute these ideas to the Buddha himself despite a mass of evidence against doing so.

To understand what the Buddha meant by "all-knowing" or "all-perceiving," it is first necessary to analyze the use of the term "all" *(sabbaṃ)* in the early discourses. Interestingly, an important discourse relating specifically to this problem is attributed to the Buddha:[32]

> Thus have I heard. Once the Fortunate One was living at Sāvatthi, in the monastery of Anāthapiṇḍika, [situated] in the Jeta's Grove. Then the Fortunate One addressed the monks: "O, monks!" They responded: "Yes, O Venerable One!" and the Fortunate One spoke thus: "Monks, I will preach to you 'everything.' Listen to it. What, monks, is 'everything'? Eye and material form, ear and sound, nose and odor, tongue and taste, body and touch, mind and concepts. These are called 'everything.' Monks, he who would say, 'I will reject this *everything* and proclaim another *everything,*' he may certainly have a theory [of his own]. But when questioned, he would not be able to answer and would, moreover, be subject to vexation. Why? Because it would not be within the range of experience."

This discourse makes the Buddha's position abundantly clear. For the Buddha, "all" or "everything" represented the subject defined in terms of the six senses and the object explained in terms of the six sense objects. However, to be "omniscient" it is necessary that one knows everything, not only of the past and present but also of the future. It is possible to claim that the obvious past and the future can be known directly if one can perceive the *essence* of everything. That essence being permanent and eternal, one glimpse of it at any point would mean knowledge of everything. This is certainly how the Buddhist school of Sarvāstivādins attempted to justify omniscience, but such a view cannot be attributed to the Buddha. Not only did he refuse to recognize knowledge of such an essence or substance as existing in the future, he also claimed that he failed to perceive any such entity surviving in the immediate past or in the present.

This is the implication of a disciple's statement: *Na tuyhaṃ adiṭṭhaṃ asutaṃ amutaṃ vā ato aviññātaṃ kiñcanaṃ atthi loke.*[33] This statement is sometimes interpreted as "You are omniscient," that is, "There is nothing that you have not seen, heard or conceived."[34] This is an extremely superficial and reckless rendering of an important statement. The statement is to be understood in the light of the definition of an "enlightened one" in the early Buddhist context. In fact, the term *akiñcana,* "one who does not look for something" (*kiñci;* other than what is given in sensory experience, *à la* discourse on "everything" quoted above), is used to refer to the enlightened one.[35] Hence, the above statement in Pali is more appropriately rendered as: "You do not have (or recognize) something *(na kiñcana)* that is not seen, heard, conceived, or cognized in this world," which would be a negation rather than an assertion of the very metaphysics that serves as the basis for "omniscience." This idea was highlighted centuries later by the famous Buddhist philosopher Nāgārjuna (see Chapter XVI).

Limitations of Experience

One of the important features of cognitive experience admitted by the Buddha, whether of sensory experience or of extraordinary perception, is its limitation. Neither sense experience nor extraordinary perception gives us knowledge of "everything," including the so-called obvious past and the future. The flux of experience is often confined to the immediate past and the present. Thus, in the passage describing the process of perception, when he referred to the objects of the past, present, and future, the Buddha was confining himself to concepts *(saṅkhā)* relating to objects, not to experience or perception *(saññā)* itself. For this reason, whenever he had to speak of experience or objects of experience, he was careful to use participles such as "has been" *(bhūta)* or "has remained" *(ṭhita),* "made" *(kata),* "dispositionally conditioned" *(saṅkhata),* or "dependently arisen" *(paṭiccasamuppanna).*

Undoubtedly the Buddha realized that this is not sufficient. There was a need to speak of the future, if not of the obvious past. Man has a strong inclination to know the future. In the modern world, predictability has become the hallmark of science. Other disciplines, such as economics, politics, and even psychology, are trying to emulate this scientific spirit. For the Buddha, predictability is only a *guide,* not an insurance. Ultimately objective laws are means by which human beings have often tried to guarantee predictability. The Buddha was not fascinated by them:

> Beings, dominated by prediction *(akkheyya)*, established upon prediction, not understanding prediction, come under the yoke of death. However, having understood prediction, one does not assume oneself to be a foreteller. When such a thought does not occur to him, that by which he can be spoken of, that does not exist for him.[36]

When predictability is not asserted as having absolute validity, absolute identities vanish, leaving room for possibilities, change, and creativity. When the Buddha said, "that by which he can be spoken of, that does not exist for him," he was simply emphasizing the idea that when a person truly understands the nature and function of predictability, he does not cling to beliefs in permanent and eternal identities. This also enables him to avoid the problems of determinism and free will, problems that seem to have plagued philosophers who were engrossed with absolute predictability. Yet the renunciation of such predictability does not mean that one has to commit oneself to the other extreme, namely, the belief in absolute unpredictability. The middle path between these two extremes is inductive knowledge *(anvaye ñāṇa)*.[37]

Inductive inference is generally considered to be circular. It is assumed to be an inference from several experienced events to a future possibility. Yet even after the experience of a thousand instances, it is not possible to assume that the next instance will be similar. Such a criticism is valid in the context of essentialist philosophies that recognize discrete entities as objects of experience. In such cases, the relations among these discrete entities are mere mental fabrications. However, in a system that repudiates such rational distinctions and recognizes that relations between events are often revealed in experience, these experienced relations themselves serve as guides for possible future experiences. Uniformities are thus abstractions, and imagination functions more in the formulation of such uniformities than in the experience of relations themselves. Inductive inference thereby turns out to be an explanatory extension of sensible continuity into the obvious past and the future. If the search for ultimate objectivity is to be abandoned in the analysis of the data of sensible experience, there seems to be no reason why it should be retained in the evaluation of other sources of knowledge, such as inference. Thus the Buddha's theory of non-substantiality applies equally to all data of human thought and experience—objects of experience and relations among events, as well as uniformities.

Logic and Truth

The spirit of the Buddha's doctrine of non-substantiality and of his renunciation of the search for ultimate objectivity is reflected most prominently in his conception of truth and his system of logic. Absolute truths had no place in the Buddha's view of experience or reason, as should be evident from the preceding discussion. That explanation of experience and reason left no room for a sharp dichotomy between the true and the false. The essentialist logic of the later Indian philosophers, based on the Brahmanical notions of truth as existence *(sat)* and falsity as non-existence *(asat),* could not be accommodated in the Buddhist system of thought. For this reason, in dealing with the language of propositions, especially the search for truth-values in statements, the Buddhist analysis of experience does not facilitate any logical enterprise requiring that "each *statement* be true once and for all or false once and for all, independently of time."[38] Neither is there any attempt to formulate such "timeless" truths in "tenseless" statements.[39] As emphasized earlier and in the discussions that follow, the Buddha's philosophical terminology is confined primarily to past participles, that is, to language that expresses the immediate past and the present together.

The avoidance of any absolutistic notions of truth does not mean the wholehearted sponsorship of skepticism, either in its absolute form, as reflected in a philosopher like Sañjaya, or in its less severe form, portrayed in the Jaina logic of *syādvāda,* where everything is a possibility or a "maybe." The difficulty lay in discovering a middle path between these extremes. In the first place, the Buddha had to admit that every rational human being needs to recognize certain things as true and others as false. Otherwise human life would be chaotic. Therefore, to the question of whether there is a variety of truths (regarding the same matter), the Buddha declared that "truth is one and there is no second" *(ekaṃ hi saccaṃ na dutīyam atthi).*[40] Second, it was necessary to prevent this truth from deteriorating into an absolute truth, as reflected in the statement "This alone is true, everything else is false" *(idam eva saccaṃ mohgaṃ aññaṃ).*[41] This latter statement, which the Buddha refused to recognize, has a significant bearing on his conception of truth. By rejecting it the Buddha was, in fact, renouncing several theories or conceptions of truth or reality.

The statement "This alone is true" *(idam eva saccaṃ)* is different from the statement "This is true" *(idam saccaṃ).* The demonstrative "this" *(idaṃ)* emphasizes the particular or the individual, and may be taken as an instance of an empirical truth. However, the addition of the emphatic particle "alone" *(eva)* may not make it an absolute truth if the reference is to an empirical truth as substantiated by the demonstrative. Therefore, "this alone is true" can more appropriately refer to an essential truth, the phrase "this alone" isolating that experience from anything else or eliminating any relationship it bears to any other thing or event. In a sense, it refers to an immediate impression, comparable to that recognized by Hume, with no fringes or relationships. Furthermore, it implies a pure perception.

This purity of perception naturally causes problems relating to its future identification: inference from one event to another becomes impossible, so that prediction can never be accomplished. This again was the Humean dilemma. The second part of the statement, "all else is confusion or falsehood" *(mogham aññaṃ)*, represents a process of exclusion, subsequently developed into a theory called *apoha* by the Buddhist logician Dignāga (see Chapter xx). The process of exclusion is intended to achieve several things. First, in an indirect way, it is looked upon as a means of further purifying the perception involved in the first part of the statement. Second, it is meant to provide a guarantee for the prediction, which was weakened by the way experience is defined in the first part of the statement. Third, even though such exclusion can be made at a purely conceptual level, involving universals, the statement enabled the pre-Buddhist metaphysician to tie up the pure individual with the pure universal, or the pure perception with the pure conception, an enterprise carried out with great precision by the later Indian philosopher of language Bhartṛhari.

For the Buddha, neither perception nor conception is as pure as it was assumed to be by the pre-Buddhist Indian philosophers. His conception of truth *(sacca)* had to be presented in an altogether different manner. This seems to be why the Buddha wanted to dissolve the absolutistic true/false dichotomy and replace it with a trichotomy—the true, the confused, and the false—the first accounting for what is available in the present context, the second allowing for the possible, and the third explaining the impossible. The Buddha refers to truth as *sacca,* confusion or the confused as *musā,* and the false as *kali.*

This repudiation of the absolute true/false distinction, comparable to one unsuccessfully attempted by William James in Western philosophy,[42] seems to leave the Buddha with a method of providing truth-value to propositions very different from the methods adopted in the essentialist or absolutistic systems. An extremely interesting passage in the *Aṅguttara-nikāya* (misinterpreted by K. N. Jayatilleke[43] because of his careless handling of the terminology used by the Buddha) clarifies the Buddha's position:

> *I know* what has been seen, heard, thought, cognized, attained, sought, and reflected upon by the people, including the ascetics and brahmans. If *I know* what has been seen . . . by the people . . . and if I were to say, "I do not know it," that would be confusion *(musā)* on my part. And if I were to say, "[It is both that] I know it and I do not know it," that too would be confusion on my part. [However,] if I were to say, "[It is both that] I neither know it nor do not know it," I would be committing a sin *(kali)* on my part.[44]

The truth-values Jayatilleke assigned to the last three statements seem to be inconsistent with the terminology the Buddha used to characterize them. The four statements may be summarized as follows:

i. I know *p* (truth, *sacca*).
ii. I do not know *p* (confusion, *musā*).
iii. [It is both that] I know and do not know *p* (confusion, *musā*).
iv. [It is both that] I neither know nor do not know *p* (sin, *kali*).

According to the Buddha, if i is true, both ii and iii are confusions *(musā)* and iv is false *(kali)*. Compared with the term *musā,* the term *kali* expresses the heightened sense of epistemological sin.

The logician brought up in the essentialist tradition is bound to be startled by the following result:

i. p (true)
ii. $\sim p$ (contrary)
iii. $(p \cdot \sim p)$ (contrary)
iv. $\sim(p \cdot \sim p)$ (contradictory)

It seems that for the Buddha, if something is empirically true, then its denial is not to be characterized as absolutely false, but as something that is simply contrary to the situation. For this contrary to appear as a contradiction, it must be pitted against either an absolute truth or a constructed universal statement that does not allow for exceptions. Thus the statements "All swans are white" and "Some swans are not white" are contradictories because the former is taken to be an absolute truth. Realizing the nature of experience as well as conception, the Buddha was not willing to grant such absolute truths. To eliminate such absolutism, he adopted two strategies. The first was to redefine the conception of "all" *(sarvam),* confining it to what has been experienced. This is clear in his discourse on "everything" or "all" *(sabbaṃ)*. The second strategy was to concretize every universal statement with the use of the demonstrative. Thus we have statements such as "All *this* is suffering" *(sabbam idaṃ dukkhaṃ),* never "All is suffering" *(sabbaṃ dukkhaṃ).*

In the context of such an epistemic evaluation of truth and falsity, a statement that can be counted as false is one that denies not only the empirical truth but also any possibilities. Therefore, for the Buddha, the simultaneous rejection of both assertion and denial [$\sim(p \cdot \sim p)$] does not represent an excluded middle—either to be known by some means other than sensory experience or described in a language other than ordinary language, or even not describable at all—but a clear denial of knowledge as well as description. Thus an empirical statement would be contradicted only by a statement that represents a *total rejection* of both knowledge and description, and for the Buddha this would also involve a denial of all possibilities of knowing or describing, which is the effect of the fourth proposition. By describing the fourth proposition as "(epistemological) sin" *(kali),* the Buddha is here condemning the transcendentalists of the Upaniṣadic tradition, as well as the Jainas, for giving truth-value to it. For the Buddha, a truly contradictory statement implies not only indescribability as this or that but also the absence of any possibility of knowing.[45] Proposition iii, $(p \cdot \sim p)$, does not rule out the possibility of knowledge altogether and is, therefore, a contrary rather than a contradiction. It is this non-absolutism that appears in the system of logic presented by Dignāga during the fifth century A.D. (see Chapter XX).

The Fourfold Negation

It was remarked that the Buddha's system of logic deals more with contraries than with contradictions. We have already reached the conclusion that contradictions deny the possibility of both knowledge and description. If our conclusion is valid, then there is no mystery regarding the Buddha's statement of the fourfold negation.

The fourfold negation has generally been interpreted as a way of ascertaining a truth that transcends language and description. However, we have consistently held the view that these four negations are applied primarily to metaphysical questions.[46] These are questions that cannot be answered on the basis of any knowledge. In that sense, they are meaningless. Furthermore, unlike the four alternatives discussed earlier, where propositions ii and iii are contraries rather than contradictions, prompting the Buddha to use the term "confusion" *(musā)* to refer to them, no such characterization is made of any of the components of the fourfold negation. Each one is simply negated, without making any knowledge-claim. In fact, according to the Buddha, no knowledge-claim is possible with regard to the content of any of these propositions:

i. The world is eternal.
ii. The world is not eternal.
iii. The world is both eternal and not eternal.
iv. The world is both neither eternal nor not eternal.

When these propositions are symbolized utilizing S = world and P = eternal, we have the following four propositions:

i. S is P
ii. S is $\sim P$
iii. S is $(P \cdot \sim P)$
iv. S is $\sim(P \cdot \sim P)$

Symbolized as such, these do not appear to differ from the symbolization of the four propositions discussed earlier. Hence the temptation to give truth-values to them utilizing the true/false dichotomy in Eastern as well as Western philosophy. Nowhere in the early discourses did the Buddha provide truth-values to any one of these propositions; all four assertions were negated. The distinction between this fourfold negation and the four earlier propositions, for which the Buddha was willing to give truth-values, needs to be recognized. That distinction must be clarified if we are to distinguish between negation and denial, a distinction of great epistemological significance for Buddhism.

An assertion or denial of something is generally made after verification through the available means of knowledge. Hence it is possible to say that such and such is the case or is not the case. This form of denial is expressed by the Buddha with the phrase "it is indeed not the case" *(no h' etaṃ).*[47] In these cases the Buddha was trying to decide what is true, confused, and false. However, in the case of the fourfold negation, there is no way of presenting such a denial, for there is no means of knowledge *(na pamāṇam atthi).*[48] The negation therefore takes place at an earlier level, that is, at the level at which the question is raised, the negation being formulated with a prohibitive particle: "Indeed, do not [say or question] thus" *(mā h' evaṃ).*[49] Such questions are meaningless or unfruitful *(anatthasaṃhitaṃ)* in an extreme sense, for there is no possibility of verifying their meaning, unlike in the case of contraries.[50] The conclusion is irresistible that the fourfold negation has nothing to do with logic, if by logic we mean the science that helps distinguish true statements from confused or false ones.

It was mentioned that the four propositions for which the Buddha was willing to provide truth-values and the four propositions which he negated are almost identical when symbolized, though epistemologically they do not belong to the same discourse. An artificial symbolic language may facilitate the process of reasoning by developing "techniques that enable us to get along without thinking"—a paradoxical situation indeed.[51] However, the Buddha perceived danger in such enterprises, for a system of logic that focuses primarily on forms *(ākāra-parivitakka)* to the neglect of their content, whether these forms be empirical or conceptual, may not always lead to the discovery of truth or falsity relating to a statement or statements.[52]

The most important question arises at this stage: What is the criterion by which a true statement can be distinguished from either a contrary or a contradictory one? The characterization of proposition iii as a "contrary" rules out coherence as the primary criterion, even though such a criterion is operative in the decision regarding proposition iv. Proposition iii, which asserts $(p \cdot \sim p)$ as a contrary and not as a contradiction, goes against not only the coherence theory but also the correspondence theory of truth, because of the essentialism embedded in the latter, with its true/false dichotomy reflecting the existence/non-existence dichotomy. The Buddha is thus left with only a pragmatic criterion of truth, and this is what we come across in the *Discourse to Prince Abhaya (Abhayarāja-kumāra-sutta).*[53]

This discourse speaks of the propositions asserted by the Buddha and those that are not asserted. These are classified in terms of their truth-value, utility (or disutility), and emotive content. If propositions can be true *(bhūta, taccha)* or untrue *(abhūta, ataccha),* useful *(atthasaṃhita)* or useless *(anatthasaṃhita),* pleasant *(piya, manāpa)* or unpleasant *(appiya, amanāpa)* to the hearer, we get eight possibilities:

1.	True	useful	pleasant
2.	True	useful	unpleasant
3.	True	useless	pleasant
4.	True	useless	unpleasant
5.	Untrue	useful	pleasant
6.	Untrue	useful	unpleasant
7.	Untrue	useless	pleasant
8.	Untrue	useless	unpleasant

It is significant that the text does not even refer to propositions 5 and 6, the implication being that they are not possible.

The epistemological significance of the criterion used for deciding what is true and untrue, as outlined in the *Discourse to Prince Abhaya,* cannot be appreciated if one indiscriminately adopts an essentialist conception of truth and falsity in understanding the terminology used. On the contrary, it requires a careful analytical study. The term for truth with which we are already familiar, namely, *sacca,* has the implication of "existence." Its opposite is *musā* or "confusion," not non-existence *(a-sacca).* Therefore it was necessary for the Buddhist to retain the conception of existence without contrasting it with non-existence. This existentialist implication of the term *sacca* is retained when, in its place, the term *taccha,* meaning "such," is used. To strengthen the specific Buddhist sense of "truth," the *Discourse to Prince Abhaya* introduces a totally different term, *bhūta* ("become"). When these two terms are used together, they convey what the Buddhist meant by the term "true."

Indeed, the past participle *bhūta,* meaning "become," when used as a synonym for "true," brings out clearly the anti-essentialist implication of the Buddha's conception of truth. The analysis of experience in the earlier part of this chapter should confirm the view that Buddhism leaves no room for an essentialist conception. Experience, whether sensory or extraordinary, does not provide us with "ready-made" truths. *Bhūta* or "become" highlights that very idea. What is true is what has "come to be," and what is false is what "has not come to be" *(abhūta).*

Now, the best epistemological criterion for distinguishing what has come to be and what has not come to be is simply usefulness or utility.

What has not yet come to be is not useful to anyone. This is precisely why the discourse does not even mention any alternatives that are untrue and useful at the same time, that is, statements 5 and 6.

It is extremely important to reflect on the relationship between the "not become" *(abhūta)* and "confusion" *(musā)*. If "become" *(bhūta)* is understood in the sense of "true" *(sacca)*, the temptation is to equate the "not become" *(abhūta)* with "false" *(kali)* rather than with "confusion." This would throw the Buddha into the muddle into which a philosopher like Bertrand Russell fell as a result of his essentialism.[54] For example, the theory of the indestructible atom remained true and functional until the advancement of physics gave rise to theories that made the earlier atomic theory appear false. This embarrassment would have been avoided if truth and falsity had been explained in terms of "become" and "not become." Equating the "not become" with "confusion" would then explain a significant epistemological fact, namely, the function of human interest or perspective as a determinant of the worldview that continues to change in different directions. In this sense, the system of logic utilized by the Buddha allows for change and creativity without falling into the abyss of Absolutism.

The past participle *bhūta*, "become," turned out to be the most appropriate term to express the radical empiricism of the Buddha, which avoided the essentialist enterprise of searching for ultimate objectivity. This is to be contrasted with the terminology of the essentialists in India, such as *astitva*, "being, existence" (in pre-Buddhist thought), and *bhāva*, "being" (in the post-Buddhist systems). As seen earlier, the *Discourse to Prince Abhaya* provided a pragmatic foundation for that radical empiricism. The best form of knowledge, according to the Buddha, thus turns out to be knowledge of things "as they have become" *(yathābhūta)*,[55] not knowledge of things "as they really are." Here we have a pragmatic criterion of truth that steers clear of the two extremes of correspondence and coherence. It is the Buddha's response to the "views from nowhere" that dominated the pre-Buddhist background.

CHAPTER IV

Experience and Theory *(Paṭiccasamuppanna* and *Paṭiccasamuppāda)*

Abandoning the search for ultimate objectivity, the Buddha had to renounce most explanations of reality presented by his predecessors. The Brahmanical notion of self *(ātman),* the Materialist and Ājīvika conceptions of nature *(svabhāva),* and even the Jaina theory of action *(kiriya)* appeared to him too metaphysical. Absolute skepticism, such as that of Sañjaya, was one form of response to such metaphysics. The Buddha was compelled to avoid these extremes if he were to say anything new and original. His doctrine had to steer clear of notions of permanent existence and nihilistic non-existence, strict determinism and chaotic indeterminism. Epistemological justification for whatever view he proposed had to avoid the extremes of absolute certainty and unrestricted skepticism. A middle standpoint was needed not only in epistemology, but also in ontology and ethics. Even if he were to allow for the so-called wondrous and the marvelous *(acchariya-abbhuta-dhamma),* which is no more than the "unusual," the principle he adopted in explaining such events had to avoid mystery altogether. The Buddha realized that it is inconsistent to advocate an absolute, inviolable law or uniformity and then take refuge in its violations in order to account for the "unusual." Similarly, he was not willing to consider the mental life and freedom as anomalies to be sacrificed at the altar of the nomological or the natural.

The Buddha's explanation of the nature of existence is summarized in one word, *paṭiccasamuppāda* (Skt. *pratītyasamutpāda*),[1] meaning "dependent arising," a theory that he formulated on the basis of the experience of dependently arisen phenomena *(paṭicca-samuppanna dhamma).*[2] The meaning of the former is best elucidated by clarifying the implications of the latter.

The term "dependently arisen," being a past participle, refers to some thing, event, or idea that "*has* occurred." Its usage in Buddhist texts distinguishes it from expressions such as "*had* occurred," which carry strictly past connotations with no reference to the present in any form. The strictly defined temporal category of the obvious past as distinguished from the present is expressed more often by verbal forms such as the aorist.[3] The epistemological importance of the use of the past participle was the subject matter of Chapter III. In the area of metaphysics, especially relating to the problem of causation, the use of the past participle highlights the effect rather than the cause. While the term "arisen" *(samutpanna),* taken in itself, can refer specifically to the effect, the prefix, which is a gerund meaning "having moved or gone toward," connects that obvious effect with its possible cause or causes, which may or may not be given *immediately.* In this sense, the phrase "dependently arisen" provides a description of phenomena in conformity with the radical empiricism of the Buddha outlined in Chapter III.

The description of phenomena as "dependently arisen" constitutes a middle way in that it steers clear of two extremes. First, it avoids the assumption of a mysterious underlying substance relating the cause and the effect, an assumption involved in most theories that uphold absolute identity or identities. The Buddha rejected such a conception of identity *(ekatta)* as metaphysical.[4] Second, it eschews the equally metaphysical absolute distinction *(puthutta),*[5] thereby ruling out atomistic theories of existence, which are normally based on rationalistic rather than empiricist analysis of time into past, present, and future. Therefore the terms expressive of the concepts of atoms *(paramāṇu)* or moments *(khaṇa)*[6] are conspicuously absent in the early discourses.

After explaining all experienced phenomena *(dhamma)*—and these include conditioned events as well as related ideas or concepts (the latter being designated by the term *dhamma* in its restricted sense),[7]—as "dependently arisen" *(paṭiccasamuppanna),* the Buddha formulated a general principle that became the central conception in Buddhism, namely, "dependent arising" *(paṭiccasamuppāda).*[8] In his own words, the principle of dependent arising is an extension of the experience of dependence into the obvious past and the future.[9] It is an abstraction from the concrete experiences of dependence—hence the use of the abstract noun *dhammatā* (Skt. *dharmatā*), a term that can mean the "nature of phenomena."[10] It is interesting that the later Buddhist tradition preserved this abstract sense when it constructed an abstract noun in Sanskrit, *pratītyasamutpannatva,*[11] out of the Pali past participle *paṭiccasamuppanna,* even though such a term is not found in the early discourses of the Buddha.

The Buddha's most significant statement regarding the existential status of this principle of dependent arising occurs in the discourses several times, and thus is quoted here in full, along with the original Pali text, retaining the punctuation given in the Pali Text Society edition:

> What, monks, is dependent arising? Dependent upon birth, monks, is decay and death, whether the Tathāgatas were to arise or whether the Tathāgatas

> were not to arise. This element, this status of phenomena, this orderliness of phenomena, this interdependence *has remained.* That the Tathāgata comes to know and realize, and having known and realized, he describes it, sets it forth, makes it known, establishes it, discloses it, analyzes it, clarifies it, saying: "Look."
> *(Katamo ca bhikkhave paṭiccasamuppādo. Jātipaccayā bhikkhave jarāmaraṇaṃ, uppādā vā tathāgatānaṃ anuppādā vā. Thiṭā va sā dhātu dhammaṭṭhitatā dhammaniyāmatā idappaccayatā. Taṃ tathāgato abhisaṃbujjhati abhisameti, abhisambujjhitvā abhisametvā ācikkhati deseti paññapeti paṭṭhapeti vivarati vibhajati uttānīkaroti passathā ti cāha.)*[12]

This is repeated with regard to the other relations of the twelvefold formula (see Chapter V) as well.

Remaining faithful to the epistemological standpoint discussed earlier, the Buddha was prepared to make a limited claim for the validity of the causal principle. The noteworthy feature in this statement is his return to the use of the past participle *(ṭhita,* Skt. *sthita)* to explain the existential status of dependent arising. Thus all he is asserting is that this principle *has remained* valid so far. To claim anything more than this would be tantamount to rejecting the very criticism he made of absolute predictability. The idea is repeated in his choice of the term *dhammaṭṭhitatā* to describe the "status of phenomena," for its literal meaning is the "has-remained-ness of phenomena." After clarifying the sense in which he is claiming existential status for the causal principle, the Buddha proceeds to speak of the uniformity of phenomena *(dhammaniyāma)* as well as their interdependence *(idappaccayatā).*

This status attributed to the principle of dependence needs to be kept in mind when analyzing the meaning of the terms used to describe four main characteristics of that principle:[13] objectivity *(tathatā),* necessity *(avitathatā),* invariability *(anaññathatā),* and conditionality or interdependence *(idappaccayatā).*

The objectivity of the principle of dependence needed to be highlighted, especially in a context in which the Brahmanical thinkers apparently abandoned notions of space, time, and causality in favor of the eternal self *(ātman),* and in which some of the heterodox schools, like the Materialists and Ājīvikas, looking for *ultimate* objectivity, raised it to the level of an absolute reality or an inexorable, inviolable law *(svabhāva).* The Buddha's use of the abstract noun *tathatā* (from *tathā,* "such") connects his notion of objectivity directly to his conception of truth as "become" *(bhūta),* for the synonym of "become" is a semantic and grammatical equivalent of *tathatā,* namely, *taccha* (see Chapter III). Thus the Buddha avoided the rather inconsistent method of attributing one type of existential status to the experienced event *(dhamma)* and a diametrically opposed existential status to the principle *(dhammatā)* that explains such events. Otherwise, he would have failed to ground the principle of explanation on the experienced event, which would have led him to a hierarchy of truths, one ultimate and the other provisional. With that he would have been advocating a double standard of truth—"the way of truth" and "the way of opinion"—which is not much different from the Platonic method. The Buddha would thus have donned two different garments at the same time, that of the empiricist when explaining experience, and that of the absolutist when explicating the principle or theory of that experience. A discussion of the theory of two truths is more appropriately taken up in connection with Nāgārjuna's philosophy (see Chapter XVI).

If we are able to associate the notion of necessity with the principle of dependence, it is in a negative way only, involving a denial of arbitrariness, which is implied in the term *avitathatā.* Again, the literal meaning of the term, "no-separate-true-ness" *(a-vi-tatha-tā),* can throw much light on its philosophical implication. Philosophers who raised questions about the possibility of necessary connections were often those who resorted to the extreme analytical methods, maintaining that "what is distinguishable is also separable." Emphasis on absolute distinctions can be a reaction against using the conception of necessity in the sense of absolute inevitability. Therefore, if the meaning of separateness is not overextended to imply absolute distinctness, the use of the concept of necessary connection can be toned down. This seems to have been the Buddha's intention in presenting a negative term to express a positive meaning. It is also the effect of the term *anaññathatā* (*an-aññatha-tā,* lit., "non-otherwise-ness"), which expresses a more restrained sense of "invariability."

After presenting these first three characteristics of the principle of dependent arising and ensuring that they were not overstretched or overstated (thereby avoiding metaphysics, which he characterized as the process of overstating, *adhivuttipada;* see Chapter III), the Buddha focused on the most important of the four, namely, interdependence (*idappaccayatā,* lit., "this-condition-ness"). Sometimes the term is used not merely as one of the characteristics or features of the principle of dependence, but also as a synonym for it.[14] This interdependence is further elaborated in the abstract formula that often precedes a concrete statement explaining the conception of an empirical self or human person in terms of the twelve factors (*dvādasaṅga;* see Chapter VI):

> When that is present, this comes to be; on the arising of that, this arises. When that is absent, this does not come to be; on the cessation of that, this ceases.
> *(Imasmiṃ sati, idaṃ hoti; imassa uppādā idaṃ uppajjati. Imasmiṃ asati, idaṃ na hoti; imassa nirodhā idaṃ nirujjhati.)*[15]

This description seems to preserve most of the salient features of the Buddha's conception of the principle of dependent arising discussed above. First, the so-called *locative absolute* construction in Pali and Sanskrit grammar ("when that, then this") enabled the Buddha to express his radical empiricism more satisfactorily. It has the advantage of expressing the temporal relation, which remains unexpressed in the hypothetical or the conditional syllogism implied by the "if-then" formula recognized in the more substantialist systems of logic. Second, the "that" (Skt. *asau*) as related to "this" *(idaṃ)* highlights the experiential component of the relation rather than the rational. "This" refers to the effect that is experienced rather than inferred, and "that" refers to the cause that has already been experienced. In other words, it is the statement of the "dependently arisen." Third, the that/this distinction does not necessarily wipe out the relationship between the two events signified, for it is not a relation constructed purely on conception (like Hume's "relations of ideas"), where the process of exclusion *(apoha)* is applied (see Chapter xx).

This means that the two statements of the formula—the positive (when that, then this) and the negative (when not that, then not this)—do not constitute the fallacy of denying the antecedent because they are not intended as components of a hypothetical syllogism where the relationship is viewed as necessary and sufficient. On the contrary, the positive and the negative statements strengthen the relationship between the two events, providing a more precise premise for the Buddha without making it an absolute truth. In addition, the general or abstract formula is intended to account for two different types of relations. Relativity is indicated by the statement, "when that is present, this comes to be," while genetic relations are accommodated in the statement, "on the arising of that, this arises."

Formulating the principle of dependent arising in this manner, the Buddha was attempting to avoid the search for any mysterious entity or substance in the explanation of phenomena. For example, if we are to stay with the premise "Humans are mortal," there is a possibility that we will continue to look for a hidden something that could account for human mortality. Appealing to the available evidence, without extending reflection and investigation beyond their limits—and, in the above instance, depending on the fact that no human has been immortal—the Buddha was renouncing that search for a mysterious something *(kiñci)*. The renunciation of mystery does not mean abandoning all inquiry and adopting an attitude of absolute skepticism; rather, it represents the acceptance of a middle standpoint with regard to knowledge and understanding. This moderation is reflected in the explanation of phenomena in terms of dependent arising when it is called a middle path *(majjhimā paṭipadā)*.

The Buddha's discourse to Kaccāyana (the *Kaccāyanagotta-sutta*)[16] presents in a nutshell the principle of dependence as a philosophical middle standpoint. Considering the importance most major philosophers of the Buddhist tradition attach to this brief discourse, as reported by Ānanda, it is quoted here in full:

> Thus have I heard: The Fortunate One was once living at Sāvatthi, in the monastery of Anāthapiṇḍika, in Jeta's Grove. At that time the venerable Kaccāyana of that clan came to visit him, and saluting him, sat down at one side. So seated, he questioned the Fortunate One: Sir [people] speak of "right view, right view." To what extent is there a right view?
>
> This world, Kaccāyana, is generally inclined toward two [views]: existence and non-existence.
>
> To him who perceives with right wisdom the uprising of the world as it has come to be, the notion of non-existence in the world does not occur. Kaccāyana, to him who perceives with right wisdom the ceasing of the world as it has come to be, the notion of existence in the world does not occur.
>
> The world, for the most part, Kaccāyana, is bound by approach, grasping, and inclination. And he who does not follow that approach and grasping, that determination of mind, that inclination and disposition, who does not cling to or adhere to a view, "this is my self," who thinks, "suffering that is subject to arising arises; suffering that is subject to ceasing, ceases"—such a person does not doubt, is not perplexed. Herein, his knowledge is not other-dependent. Thus far, Kaccāyana, there is "right view."
>
> "Everything exists"—this, Kaccāyana, is one extreme.
>
> "Everything does not exist"—this, Kaccāyana, is the second extreme.
>
> Kaccāyana, without approaching either extreme, the Tathāgata teaches you a doctrine by the middle. Dependent upon ignorance arise dispositions; dependent upon dispositions arises consciousness; dependent upon consciousness arises the psychophysical personality; dependent upon the psychophysical personality arise the six senses; dependent upon the six senses arises contact; dependent upon contact arises feeling; dependent upon feeling arises craving; dependent upon craving arises grasping; dependent upon grasping arises becoming; dependent upon becoming arises birth; dependent upon birth arise old age and death, grief, lamentation, suffering, dejection and despair. Thus arises this entire mass of suffering.
>
> However, from the utter fading away and ceasing of ignorance, there is ceasing of dispositions; from the ceasing of dispositions, there is ceasing of consciousness; from the ceasing of consciousness, there is ceasing of the psychophysical personality; from the ceasing of the psychophysical personality, there is ceasing of the six senses; from the ceasing of the six senses, there is ceasing of contact; from the ceasing of contact, there is ceasing of feeling; from the ceasing of feeling, there is ceasing of craving; from the ceasing of craving, there is ceasing of grasping; from the ceasing of grasping, there is ceasing of becoming; from the ceasing of becoming, there is ceasing of birth; from the ceasing of birth, there is ceasing of old age and death, grief, lamen-

tation, suffering, dejection and despair. And thus there is the ceasing of this entire mass of suffering.

Conclusion

The principle of dependent arising is intended as an alternative to the Brahmanical notion of an eternal self *(ātman)* as well as to the conception of nature *(svabhāva)* presented by some of the heterodox schools. As an alternative, it not only avoids mystery but also explains phenomena as being in a state of constant arising and ceasing. The Buddha realized that even though such a principle is verifiable *(ehipassika)*, it is not easily perceived *(duddasa)* by ordinary human beings,[17] who are engrossed and delight in attachment *(ālaya)* to things as well as views.[18] Such leanings can blind them to such an extent that they ignore even the most evident facts. Thus the difficulty in perceiving and understanding dependence is due not to any mystery regarding the principle itself but to people's love of mystery. The search for mystery, the hidden *something (kiñci)*, is looked upon as a major cause of anxiety and frustration *(dukkha)*. Therefore the one who does not look for any mystery *(akiñcana)*,[19] and who perceives things "as they have come to be" *(yathābhūta)*, is said to enjoy peace of mind that elevates him intellectually as well as morally. This explains the characterization of dependent arising as peaceful *(santa)* and lofty *(panīta)*.[20]

CHAPTER V

Language and Communication

The Buddha's term for "discourse" is *dhamma* (Skt. *dharma*). A discourse represents an attempt on the part of the Buddha, a human person, to formulate in linguistic terms or symbols an event, series of events, or state of affairs available to him in a continuum of experience. The Buddha's followers perceived a rich variety of senses in which he used the term *dhamma,* distinguishing five applications of the term:[1] (1) *guṇa* (quality, nature); (2) *hetu* (cause, condition); (3) *nissatta* (= *nijjīva,* truth, non-substantiality); (4) *desanā* (discourse); and (5) *pariyatti* (text, canonical text).

In an extremely comprehensive research project, Wilhelm and Magdelene Geiger tried to identify the fivefold use of the term *dhamma* in the vast collection of early discourses included in the Pali Nikāyas.[2] The present chapter is devoted to a philosophical evaluation of these five applications and to an examination of how the flux of experience relating to the material as well as the moral life is best communicated through the linguistic medium. The five applications of the term *dhamma* begin with the more specific and end with the most general. Let us begin our analysis with the most general and work toward the more specific uses. *Dhamma* as text *(pariyatti)* involves us in two philosophical issues. A text is intended to communicate some idea, and language, whatever its form, is the primary means of such communication. Thus our first philosophical problem is to determine the nature of linguistic convention. The second relates to the authenticity of the text.

The Nature of Language

The Buddha, who perceived the world of human experience as being in flux, was not willing to recognize language as a permanent and eternal entity. Like everything else, language (*loka-sāmaññā* = generality of the world, *loka-vohāra* = usage of the world, *loka-sammuti* = convention of the world) is in flux. The basic constituent of language, namely, the word *(akkhara),* does not represent an incorrigible entity (as the Indian term *akṣara* implies), but rather a conventional symbol *(saṅkhā)* that people adopt depending on circumstances.[3] In a sense, the word substitutes for a human conception, the hard words being those that have remained stable and constant, and the soft ones, the more variable and fluctuating. If human conceptions are affected by changes in the natural environment and material culture, there is no reason to assume that the symbols expressing such conceptions should remain unchanged and eternal. It is only recently that psychobiologists of language have come to realize that natural environment and material culture affect the relative frequency of the occasions for using various words.[4] This means that "the more frequent a word, the more readily it is expected; the more readily it is expected, the more erosion it is apt to tolerate and still be recognized for what it is intended."[5] The Buddha's way of describing how words and conceptions come to be is couched in a language that avoids the implications of arbitrariness as well as absoluteness: "a word occurs" *(akkharaṃ anupatati)* or "a conception takes place" *(saṅkhaṃ gacchati).*[6] The fact that words and conceptions are neither absolute nor completely arbitrary is clearly recognized in the following passage:

> When it is said: "One should not strictly adhere to the dialect of a country nor should one transgress ordinary parlance," in reference to what is it said? What, monks, is strict adherence to the dialect of a country and what is transgression of ordinary parlance? Herein, monks, the same thing *(tad eva)* is recognized in different countries as *pāti,* as *patta,* as *vittha,* as *sarāva,* as *dhāropa,* as *poṇa,* as *pisila* [these being dialectical variants for the word "bowl"]. When they recognize it as such and such in different countries, a person utilizes this convention, obstinately clinging to it and adhering to it, [saying]: "This alone is true; all else is falsehood." Thus, monks, is strict adherence to the dialect of a country and transgression of ordinary parlance. And what, monks, is the strict non-adherence to the dialect of a country and the non-transgression of ordinary parlance? In this case, monks, the same thing is recognized in different countries as *pāti,* as *patta,* as *vittha,* as *sarāva,* as *dhāropa,* as *poṇa,* as *pisila.* Thus they recognize it as such and such in different countries. "These venerable ones utilize it for this purpose," and thus saying he utilizes it without grasping. And thus, monks, is strict non-adherence to the dialect of a country and the non-transgression of recognized parlance.[7]

Here there are two significant assertions about language. First is the recognition of the kinship of words, based on usage rather than on simple etymology adopted by the grammarians, a feature noted more recently by philosophers of language.[8] Second is what is now referred to as "language drift,"[9] which is a repudiation of the absolute structures of language that are supposed to be revealed by linguistic analysis. Here again, drift is caused by usage. This language drift represents a midway position between strict adherence *(abhinivesa),* more appropriately described as linguistic or conceptual constipation, on the one hand, and transgression *(atisāra)* or, literally, "linguistic or conceptual diarrhea," on the other.

In the Brahmanical system, the *Vedas* were considered to be revealed texts, which prompted the preservation of every word and every syllable unchanged, thus generating the so-called science of etymology *(nirukti)* and grammar *(vyākaraṇa)* as part of the studies ancillary to the *Vedas* themselves.[10] In contrast, the Buddha's attitude toward language seems to have compelled his disciples to concentrate on hermeneutical problems. The situation was rendered more complicated when the Buddha permitted his disciples to use their own languages in disseminating the teachings.[11] Thus the textual tradition *(pariyatti),* whatever the language in which it is preserved, was an important means of preserving and communicating the Buddha's doctrine *(dhamma).*

Authenticity of the Texts

Ever since the Buddha's first discourse, which is referred to in the collection of discourses as the *Tathāgatena-vutta (Said by the Thus-Gone-One)* and which came to be popularly known as the *Dhammacakkappavattana-sutta (Discourse on the Establishment of the Principle of Righteousness),* the Buddhist tradition has debated the relative value of the textual *(pariyatti)* and the practical *(paṭipatti).*[12] It is interesting to note that during the earlier period of Buddhist history, especially the time following the Buddha's death, Buddhist monks argued for the importance of practice *(vinaya)* as the lifeline of the teachings.[13] However, as time passed they seem to have realized the need to preserve the Buddha-word.[14] According to the Buddha himself, verbal testimony *(sadda),* whether preserved as an oral tradition or as a recorded one, is neither an absolute source of knowledge nor an utterly useless means of communication. Seeing and hearing, as indicated earlier, are two important sources of knowledge. For the Buddha, the voice of another *(parato ghosa)* constitutes an important means of knowledge, not in itself, but supplemented by investigative reflection *(yoniso manasikāra).*[15]

The "voice of another" can be very ambiguous. It can be the voice of anyone, an enlightened person or an unenlightened one. Even if it is the voice of the Enlightened One, it needs to be checked and rechecked.[16] However, while not claiming divine authority and absolute sacredness for his statements of doctrine *(dhamma)* and discipline *(vinaya),* the Buddha probably felt the need to perpetuate them without too much distortion. Hence toward the end of his life he recommended certain hermeneutical principles that his disciples could employ whenever there was controversy regarding the teachings. These four hermeneutical principles are significant because they are intended not to determine whether or not the teachings embodied in the literature are correct but to ensure that they are the statements of the Buddha. Disciples are given some latitude to interpret the Buddha-word without sticking to the absolute etymological and literal meanings of the language or adopting a laissez-faire attitude. Thus this represents another instance in which the Buddha adopted a "middle of the road" standpoint. The four hermeneutical principles are referred to as *mahāpadesa* ("primary indicators"). The first of them is stated as follows (1):

> Herein, monks, if a monk were to say: "I have heard such in the presence of the Fortunate One; I have received such in his presence: 'This is the doctrine *(dhamma),* this is the discipline *(vinaya),* this is the message of the teacher *(satthusāsana).*' " Monks, the statement of that monk should neither be enthusiastically approved nor completely condemned. Without either enthusiastically approving or completely condemning, and having carefully studied those words and signs, they should be integrated with the discourses *(sutta)* and instantiated by the discipline *(vinaya).* However, when they are being integrated with the discourses and instantiated by the discipline, if they do not integrate with the discourses and are not instantiated by the discipline, on that occasion one should come to the conclusion: "This indeed is not the word of the Fortunate One, the Worthy One, the Perfectly Enlightened One, instead, it is wrongly obtained by this monk." And so should you, monks, reject it. . . . However, when they are being integrated with the discourses and instantiated by the discipline, if they integrate with the discourses and are instantiated by the discipline, on that occasion one should come to the conclusion: "This indeed is the word of the Fortunate One, the Worthy One, the Perfectly Enlightened One, it is well-obtained by this monk." This, monks, is the first great indicator.[17]

The remaining indicators are explained in identical terms, except that they refer to the interpretation of the Buddha-word received (2) directly from a certain senior monk residing in some place; (3) from a community of senior monks who are educated, conversant with the tradition, and custodians of the doctrine and discipline as well as the formulae; and (4) from a single monk who is not merely a senior monk as described in (2) but, like those described in (3), educated, conversant with the tradition, and a custodian of the doctrine and discipline as well as the formulae.

Thus, throughout the centuries, the more enlightened disciples of the Buddha have not only continued to study the literary tradition but have also compiled extensive treatises dealing with the interpretation of that tradition, namely, with problems of hermeneutics. Two of these treatises are particularly prominent: the *Nettippakaraṇa (The Guide)* and the *Peṭakopadesa (Discourse on the Collections).*

The Content of the Text

What comes to be embodied in the literature *(dhamma = pariyatti)* is the doctrine *(dhamma = desanā)*. In the Buddhist context, just as there is no absolutely perfect language, so there is no absolute truth to be expressed in linguistic terms. It is not easy to find a passage where the Buddha claims that *he has realized a truth that transcends linguistic expression.* What is actually stated is that the doctrine is not within the sphere of *a priori* reasoning *(a-takkāvacara)*,[18] for the *a priori* is dependent more on one's perspective as to what ought to be than on what has been the case, a perspective that is generally avoided in the Buddha's doctrine. The Buddha steered clear of any apriorism that produces insoluble metaphysical problems by recognizing four types of questions requiring four different answers: (1) questions to be explained unequivocally *(ekaṃsa-vyākaraṇīya)*; (2) questions to be explained after counterquestions *(paṭipucchā-vyākaraṇīya)*; (3) questions to be set aside *(ṭhapanīya)*; and (4) questions to be explained after analysis *(vibhajjavyākaraṇīya)*.[19]

The character of the Buddha's discourse is illustrated by these four types of questions. The questions calling for unequivocal answers do not imply the existence of ultimate or essential truths to be stated in conceptual terms that correspond to them in any absolute manner. Instead, they are questions that require positive answers on the basis of the most convincing empirical evidence at hand. The second type allows for the possibility of the question being unclear or ambiguous, so that clarification is sought through counterquestions. The questions to be set aside are those that do not permit any reasonable answers on the basis of empirical evidence. Such questions are meaningless (as stated in Chapter III). The recognition of questions to be answered analytically exemplifies a fundamental characteristic of the Buddha's conception of truth. One of the important characteristics of the non-absolutist or pragmatic conception of truth is that it is contextual. As noted in Chapter IX, even the experience and conception of freedom *(nibbāna)* is contextual. The Buddha looked upon fruitfulness as a means of verifying contextual truths. If fruitfulness is contextual and not predetermined, constant analysis and verification of such fruitfulness become the inevitable means of determining what is true.

Discourse *(dhamma)* as non-substantiality *(nissatta + nijjīva)* is a narrowing down of the scope of the discourse by focusing on an all-pervasive yet negative doctrine. The non-foundationalism of the Buddha's doctrine—its non-recognition of a permanent and eternal structure in the explanation of human knowledge, of the nature of the individual and the world, of morals and society, and of linguistic convention (= discourse) —is expressed by *dhamma* as non-substantiality *(nissatta)*.

The more positive doctrine of dependent arising *(paṭiccasamuppāda)* is denoted by the discourse *(dhamma)* as cause or condition *(hetu)*. The centrality of the conception of dependence was unequivocally expressed when the Buddha maintained: "He who sees dependent arising perceives the doctrine" *(Yo paṭiccasamuppādaṃ passati so dhammaṃ passati)*.[20] As explained in Chapter IV, the Buddha utilized the conception of dependence to explain almost every event, thing, or phenomenon wherein he refused to perceive any underlying substance, structure, or foundation. Discourse as non-substantiality *(nissatta)* and discourse as dependence *(hetu)* are thus complementaries.

The denial of permanent and eternal substances did not leave the Buddha with a conception of the universe consisting of discrete entities. The theory of dependent arising would be inexplicable in the absence of relations among events. However, without analyzing experience into two distinct categories as events *and* relations, the Buddha often spoke of related events *(paṭiccasamuppanna dhamma)*. Conceiving in this manner or speaking such a language, the Buddha had to accommodate both the concrete and the abstract. The concrete conception of the "dependently arisen" *(paṭiccasamuppanna)* is meaningless without an element of abstraction represented by the conception of "dependent arising" *(paṭiccasamuppāda)*, and vice versa. It is similar with the impermanent *(anicca)* and impermanence *(aniccatā)*, the non-substantial *(anatta)* and non-substantiality *(anattatā)*, the empty *(suñña)* and emptiness *(suññatā)*, and so on. It is this inevitable element of abstraction in the Buddha's discourse that came to be designated by quality *(guṇa)*. Examples quoted by the commentators to illustrate this aspect of discourse *(dhamma)* include *jarā-dhamma* ("decaying nature"), *maraṇa-dhamma* ("dying nature"), and *vipariṇāma-dhamma* ("evolving nature").[21] This quality or nature of experienced phenomena is referred to by the abstract noun *dhammatā*, derived from the word *dhamma* itself.[22] The commentators also included the moral principle *(dhamma)* under this category,[23] even though it could come under *dhamma* in the sense of *paṭiccasamuppāda*.

Being neither absolute nor ultimate in itself, embodying neither absolute nor ultimate truth or truths, the Buddha's discourse turned out to be rather flexible. The discourse as well as its contents were pragmatic in nature. Thus, like the moral principle (*dhamma;* see Chapter X), the discourse *(dhamma)* itself came to be compared to a raft *(kulla)* fulfilling a pragmatic function.

The Method of Discourse

We often find references to four stages in which the Buddha would initiate and conclude a discourse.[24] The first stage is represented as "pointing out" *(sandasseti)*, that is, indicating the problem. If it was in reference to an individual, the Buddha would explain that person's present situation. If it concerned an event, thing, or phenomenon, the Buddha would explain the problem as it existed. During the second stage, the Buddha would attempt to create some "agitation" *(samuttejeti)* by emphasizing the non-substantiality of the individual, event, thing, or phenomenon. This is the process of deconstruction, intended to avoid any ontological commitment. If the discourse is concluded at this point, the person to whom it is addressed will be left in a state of anxiety. During the third stage, the agitation is immediately appeased *(sampahaṃseti)* by pointing to a way out of the problem. This is the process of reconstruction or redefinition, which is achieved through the positive doctrine of dependent arising explaining the subject, the object, and morality and freedom. In doing so, the Buddha recognized the capacity of language to communicate the content of human experience, whether that relates to facts or values. In the final stage, the Buddha makes no effort to convert the hearer to his way of thinking, for the hearer tends to accept his explanation without much ado *(samādapesi)*.

The discourse *(dhamma)* formulated in terms of language thus becomes the means of communication. Communication, not only among those who speak different languages but also among those who speak the same language, becomes impossible if one adopts either of the approaches toward language criticized by the Buddha, namely, strict adherence or transgression. The first would imply that each conception utilized in language has its incorruptible object (ontological commitment) unavailable to human experience, while the second would imply that human experience is incommunicable through language (that is, linguistic transcendence). The Buddha seems to have realized that the former is more perverse than the latter. His method of communication therefore deals first with the problem of ontological commitment and then with linguistic transcendence.

This is an extremely significant method of communication and conversion, based on the Buddha's understanding of human psychology. His contemporaries, who failed to understand the psychological significance of this method of discourse, saw him as a person possessed of the magical power of conversion *(āvaṭṭanī māyā)*.[25] Yet there was no magic or mystery involved. All that the Buddha did was carefully observe the intellectual maturity and psychological state of each person and provide a discourse that would produce beneficial consequences for him. The Chinese version of the Āgama passage that refers to the four stages rightly characterizes them as the Buddha's "skill in means."[26]

"Skill in means" does not imply converting someone by discoursing on something that is obviously false. In fact, the two stages of causing agitation *(samuttejana)* and appeasement *(sampahaṃsana)* correspond, respectively, to deconstruction of solidified conceptions through analysis *(vibhāga),* which is the function of the doctrine of non-substantiality *(anatta),* and reconstruction of the same conception by the method of explanation *(vyākaraṇa),* which is achieved through the principle of dependence *(paṭiccasamuppāda).* Both these processes allow for a great degree of flexibility and are intended to eliminate both absolutism and nihilism.

CHAPTER VI

The Human Personality

One of the most controversial views expressed by the Buddha concerns the nature of the subject—the self or the human person who experiences the objective world. It is generally assumed that, as a strong advocate of what is popularly known as the doctrine of "no-self" *(anatta, anātman),* the Buddha was unable to give a satisfactory account of human action and responsibility, not to speak of problems such as knowledge and freedom. Such criticisms were directed at him by his contemporaries as well as by some classical and modern writers on Buddhism.

For some of his contemporaries, the continuity in the human personality could be accounted for only by recognizing a spiritual substance different from the physical body *(aññaṃ jīvaṃ aññaṃ sarīraṃ).*[1] For others, only a sensibly identifiable physical body *(taṃ jīvaṃ taṃ sarīraṃ)* was required.[2] Those who opted for a spiritual substance could not depend on ordinary events, such as continuity in perceptual experience and memory, in order to speak of a self, because such events are temporal and changeable. Their search culminated in the conception of a permanent and immutable spiritual substance. Those who assumed the self to be identical with the physical body were not merely claiming that the self survives recognizably from birth to death and not beyond; they were also denying any conscious activity on the part of that self. When the Buddha rejected the self as a spiritual substance, he was perceived as someone who, like the latter group, advocated the annihilation of a really existing conscious person.[3]

The Buddha had a difficult task before him, especially when he realized that the negation of a subjective spiritual entity would produce great anxiety in ordinary human beings.[4] However, he also felt that such anxieties had to be appeased without doing violence to critical thinking or sacrificing significant philosophical discourse. The method he adopted in dealing with the Spiritualist as well as the Materialist views is evidently *analytical.* His teachings therefore came to be popularly known as a "philosophy of analysis" *(vibhajjavāda).* A truly analytical philosophy is generally believed to advocate no theories. Analysis is intended as a method of clarifying the meaning of terms and concepts without attempting to formulate alternative theories, even if such theories were meaningful. However, the Buddha seems to have perceived analysis as a means, not a goal. We will need to keep this in mind when we examine the Buddha's response to the Spiritualists as well as to the Materialists. His response to the former is more popular in the early discourses, for theirs was the more widespread view in pre-Buddhist India.

The Doctrine of Aggregates *(Khandha)*

To the question of what constitutes a human person, the Spiritualist's answer was almost always "There exists a spiritual self, permanent and eternal, which is distinct from the psychophysical personality." The Buddha therefore concentrated on the analysis of the so-called psychic personality in order to discover such a self. Every time he did so, he stumbled on one or the other of the different aspects of experience, such as feeling *(vedanā)*, perception *(saññā)*, disposition *(saṅkhāra)*, or consciousness *(viññāṇa)*. If anything other than these psychic elements constituted the human personality, it was the body *(rūpa)*.[5] Yet none of these factors could be considered permanent and eternal; all are liable to change, transformation, and destruction—in brief, they are impermanent *(anicca)*. As such, whatever satisfaction one can gain from them or through them will also be limited. Often such satisfaction can turn into *dis*satisfaction. Hence the Buddha looked upon them as being *un*satisfactory *(dukkha)* (see Chapter VIII).

Arguing from the impermanence and unsatisfactoriness of the five aggregates, the Buddha involved himself in a discussion of the problem of "no-self" *(anatta)*. Although his treatment seems to be very analytical, its interpretation by some of the classical and modern scholars appears to take an absolutist turn. The Buddha's assertion regarding "no-self" is presented in three separate sentences. Referring to each one of the aggregates, he says,

> It is not mine. He is not me. He is not my self. *(N' etaṃ mama. N' eso aham asmi. Na m' eso attā.)*[6]

Only the first statement refers to the aggregates; hence the subject is in the neuter form:

> It is not mine
> *(N' etaṃ mama)*.

What is denied in this first statement is the existence of a mysterious entity to which each of the aggregates is supposed to belong. Thus the

Buddha's argument begins with the question of *possession* or *ownership*. Examining the process of sense perception we pointed out that, as a result of overstretched emotions *(vedanā)*, a natural process of experience gets solidified into a metaphysical subject that henceforward is taken to be the agent behind all experiences. A feeling of possession arises not simply on the basis of one's interest but as a result of one's desire. The Buddha is here arguing that, in order to explain the functioning of the body, feeling, perception, disposition, and consciousness, it is not necessary to posit a mysterious entity that is perceived as the *owner* of such experiences. Hence the statement that follows,

> He is not me
> *(N' eso aham asmi)*,

refers directly to that mysterious entity negated in the first statement. This explains the use of the masculine pronoun *(eso)* instead of the neuter *(etaṃ)* of the previous sentence. It also makes a big difference in his argument. The Buddha is not denying each and every conception of "I" *(ahaṃ)* that is associated with the aggregates but only the metaphysical presupposition behind the statement "Such and such an aggregate belongs to such and such a self." The assumption that a certain term has one meaning only and no other was contrary to the Buddha's conception of language. This is why, after rejecting the conception of "I" adopted in the Brahmanical system, he continued to use the very same term throughout his discourses.

Equally important to the Buddha was safeguarding the use of the term "self" without rejecting it altogether as absolute fiction. Hence the necessity for repeating the previous sentence, replacing "I" *(ahaṃ)* with "self" *(atta)*:

> He is not my self.
> *(Na m' eso attā)*.

This accounts for the constant use of the term "self" *(atta)* in a positive sense in the discourses, along with its negation, "no-self" *(anatta)*. It seems appropriate to say that there are two different meanings or uses of the terms "I" and "self," one metaphysical and the other empirical. The metaphysical meaning cannot be accounted for by any of the aggregates, and this is the thrust of his argument in the above context.

If a metaphysical self cannot be explained in terms of the aggregates, can a non-metaphysical or empirical self be accounted for by them? The general tendency among Buddhist scholars is to assume that the aggregates serve only the negative function of denying a metaphysical self. However, a careful reading of the early discourses reveals that these five aggregates also perform the positive function of clarifying what an empirical self is.

Body or material form *(rūpa)* is the first of the five, which is not surprising since the theory of aggregates was intended to replace the Spiritualist conception of "self." By allowing the physical personality such a prominent role, the Buddha was simply insisting on the importance of *sensible* identity as one of the requirements for maintaining the identity of a human person, the "I" or "self." Of course, this physical identity is not permanent even during the time the body survives, but it is a convenient way of individuating and identifying a person, albeit not the only way. In this connection it is interesting that the early discourses do not speak of a human person without a body or material form *(arūpa)*. *Arūpa,* the formless or the immaterial, is more often a state of contemplation, such as the four higher *jhānas* discussed in Chapter III, or a symbolization of such a mental state in the form of a divine life *(deva)*.

Feeling or sensation *(vedanā)* refers to the emotive content of human experience, which is another important aspect or constituent of the personality. It accounts for emotions, which are an inalienable part of a living person, whether he be in bondage or has attained freedom *(nibbāna)*. Feelings are of three types: the pleasant or the pleasurable *(manāpa, sukha),* the unpleasant or the painful *(amanāpa, dukkha),* and the neutral *(adukkhamasukha)*. Except in the higher state of contemplation *(jhāna)* characterized by cessation *(nirodha)* of all perception and of the experienced or the felt (which, as stated earlier, is a non-cognitive state), feelings are almost inevitable in experience. Such feelings can be twofold, depending on how far they are stretched: in the most rudimentary form, they can account for self-interest; if overstretched, they can produce continuous yearning or thirsting, even for feelings themselves.

Perception *(saññā)* stands for the function of perceiving *(sañjānātīti saññā)*. As in the case of feelings, the perceptions are related to all other constituents of the human personality, so they are not atomic impressions that are compounded into complex entities as a result of activities of mind such as imagination. Each of our perceptions is a mixed bag of memories, concepts, dispositions, and material elements. A pure percept, undiluted by such conditions, is *not* recognized by the Buddha or any subsequent Buddhist psychologist who has remained faithful to the Buddha. A pure percept is as metaphysical as a pure *a priori* category.

Dispositions *(saṅkhāra)* explain why there cannot be pure percepts. In the Buddha's perspective, this is *the* factor that contributes to the individuation of a person, and therefore of his perceptions. Almost everything, including physical phenomena is strongly influenced by this most potent cause of evolution of the human personality and its surroundings.

Indeed, the dispositions are responsible not only for the way we groom the physical personality with which we are identified, but also for partly[7] determining the nature of a new personality with which we may be identified in the future. It is not merely the human personality that is molded or processed by dispositions. Our physical surroundings, even our amenities of life, housing, clothing, utensils, and, in a major way, our towns and cities, art and architecture, culture and civilization—and, in the modern world, even outer space—come to be dominated by our dispositions. Karl Popper calls this the World Three.[8] For this very reason, the Buddha, when describing the grandeur of a universal monarch, his palaces, elaborate pleasure gardens, and other physical comforts, referred to them all as dispositions *(saṅkhāra)*.[9]

Epistemologically, the dispositions are an extremely valuable means by which human beings can deal with the world of experience. In the absence of any capacity to know everything presented to the senses, that is, omniscience, dispositional tendencies function in the form of interest, in selecting material from the "big blooming buzzing confusion"[10] in order to articulate one's understanding of the world. In other words, recognition of the importance of dispositions prevented the Buddha from attempting to formulate an ultimately objective *view* of the world.

Consciousness *(viññāṇa)* is intended to explain the continuity in the person who is individuated by dispositions *(saṅkhāra)*. Like the other constituents, consciousness depends on the other four aggregates for existence as well as nourishment. Consciousness is not a permanent, eternal substance or a series of discrete, momentary acts of conscious life united by a mysterious self. Thus consciousness cannot function if separated from the other aggregates, especially material form *(rūpa)*, but must act with other aggregates if thoughts are to occur. When consciousness is so explained, it is natural to conclude that it is a substantial entity, which was how the substantialists responded to the Buddha, who replied that consciousness is nothing more than the act of being conscious *(vijānātīti viññāṇaṃ)*.[11]

Thus the analysis of the human personality into five aggregates is intended to show the absence of a metaphysical self (an *ātman*) as well as the presence of an empirical self.

The Theory of Elements *(Dhātu)*

While the theory of aggregates remains more popular in the discourses, there is occasional reference to the conception of a human person consisting of six elements *(cha-dhātu)*.[12] The six elements are earth *(paṭhavi)*, water *(āpo)*, fire *(tejo)*, air *(vāyu)*, space *(ākāsa)*, and consciousness *(viññāṇa)*. Unlike in the theory of aggregates, here we find a more detailed analysis of the physical personality, and this may have served as a refutation of the Materialist view of a human person.

While it is true that the first four *dhātu* represent the basic material elements *(mahābhūta)*, to which is added space, there is here no attempt to deal with them as purely objective phenomena; they are almost always defined in relation to human experience. Thus earth represents the experience of solidity, roughness, and so on; water stands for fluidity; fire refers to the caloric; and air implies viscosity.[13] The Buddha recognized space as an element that is relative to these four material elements. The fact that space is not generally included in the list of material elements led to much misunderstanding and controversy regarding its character. The scholastics, like some modern-day scientists, believed that space is absolute, hence unconditioned *(asaṃskṛta)*.[14] In contrast, the early discourses recognized the conditionality of space, for the experience of space is dependent on the experience of material bodies.[15] Just as the Buddha refused to recognize a psychic personality independent of the physical, so he refrained from considering the physical personality independent of conscious life *(viññāṇa)* as a complete human person.

Explaining the physical personality in terms of material elements, all of which are understood from the perspective of human experience, the Buddha was able to avoid certain philosophical controversies generated by a more objective physicalistic approach. Prominent among them is the mind-body problem. It is true that the Buddha spoke of the human person as a psychophysical personality *(nāmarūpa)*. Yet the psychic and the physical were never discussed in isolation, nor were they viewed as self-subsistent entities. For him, there was neither a "material-stuff" nor a "mental-stuff," because both are results of reductive analyses that go beyond experience. On rare occasions, when pressed to define the physical and psychic components by an inquirer who had assumed their independence, the Buddha responded by saying that the so-called physical or material *(rūpa)* is contact with resistance *(paṭigha-samphassa)* and the psychic or mental *(nāma)* is contact with concepts *(adhivacana-samphassa)*, both being forms of contact[16] (see Chapter III for a discussion of contact). Such an explanation of the psychophysical personality brings into focus the relationship between language and consciousness, for *adhivacana* literally means "definition."

The description of the human personality in terms of the five aggregates as well as the six elements is an elaboration of the knowledge and insight referred to in the *Sāmaññaphala-suttanta* discussed in Chapter III. A human being so constituted is referred to as a *bhūta* (lit., "become").[17] The Buddha refers to four nutriments that are essential for such a being to remain human *(bhūtānaṃ vā sattānaṃ ṭhitiyā)* and for human beings who are yet to come *(sambhavesīnaṃ vā anuggahāya)*:[18] (1) material food, gross or subtle *(kabaliṅkāro āhāro oḷāriko vā sukhumo vā)*; (2) sensory contact *(phasso)*; (3) mental dispositions or volitions *(manosañcetanā)*; and (4) consciousness *(viññāṇa)*.

These four nutriments, in fact, define what a human person is. The

Buddha's non-recognition of a human person independent of a physical personality is reinforced by his insistence that material food is the first and foremost nutriment. The second nutriment suggests that people are sensory-bound. Stopping sensory contact for the sake of temporary rest may be useful, as in the state of cessation *(nirodha-samāpatti),* but suppressing it altogether would mean the destruction of the human person. The inclusion of mental dispositions or volitions—or what may be called "intentionality"—as a nutriment indicates the importance attached to the individual's decision-making or goal-setting capacity. This aspect of the human person has led to much controversy among philosophers, and is generally known as the problem of the will. Tradition records that the Buddha abandoned the disposition to live *(āyu-saṅkhāra)* at a place called Cāpāla almost three months before he passed away.[19] In other words, the continuity of human life is not a mere automatic process: the human disposition is an extremely relevant condition for its survival. Finally, consciousness, which is generally associated with memory *(sati),*[20] is needed to complete the human personality, for its absence eliminates a person's capacity to coordinate his life. Without it, the human being is a mere "vegetable." These four nutriments are founded on craving *(taṇhā)* and hence contribute to suffering, a process that is explained in the popular theory of the twelve factors *(dvādasāṅga).*[21]

The Theory of Twelve Factors *(Dvādasāṅga)*

Having rejected the *substantial* existence of an individual self, the Buddha did not remain silent so as to give the impression that the real person is beyond description. His discourse to Kaccāyana (see Chapter IV) states in no uncertain terms that the middle way adopted by the Buddha in explaining the human personality is "dependent arising" *(paṭiccasamuppāda),* as explicated in terms of the twelve factors. In its positive statement, this twelvefold formula represents an explanation of a person in bondage, while the negative statement that immediately follows explains the process of freedom.

Enlightenment is a necessary precondition for freedom. Therefore, it is natural to begin explaining the life of a person in bondage as that of someone who is engulfed in ignorance *(avijjā).* And as mentioned earlier, no concept becomes more important in a discussion of the human personality than that of the dispositions *(saṅkhāra),* which are defined as follows in the discourses:

> Disposition is so-called because it processes material form *(rūpa),* which has already been dispositionally conditioned, into its present state.

This statement is repeated with regard to feeling *(vedanā),* perception *(saññā),* dispositions *(saṅkhāra),* and consciousness *(viññāṇa).*[22]

According to this description, while dispositions are themselves causally conditioned, they process each of the five factors of the human personality, thereby providing them with the stamp of individuality or identity. Hence the most important function of individuating a personality belongs to the dispositions, which are an inalienable part of the personality. They can function in the most extreme way, for example, in creating an excessively egoistic tendency culminating in the belief in a permanent and eternal self *(ātman)*. This may be one reason the Buddha considered the self *(ātman)* as a mere "lump of dispositions" *(saṅkhāra-puñja)*.[23] Thus ignorance can determine the way human dispositions function *(avijjāpaccayā saṅkhārā)*, either creating the belief in permanent existence *(atthitā)* or denying the value of the human personality altogether *(n'atthitā)*.

The elimination of ignorance and the development of insight would therefore lead to the adoption of a middle standpoint in relation to dispositions. It has already been mentioned that the elimination of dispositions is epistemological suicide. Dispositions determine our perspectives. Without such perspectives we are unable to deal with the sensible world in any meaningful or fruitful manner. The Buddha realized that subdued dispositions are enlightened perspectives—hence his characterization of freedom *(nibbāna)* as the appeasement of dispositions *(saṅkhāra-samatha)*.

Thus the dispositions, while carving an individuality out of the "original sensible muchness,"[24] also play a valuable role in the continuity of experiences. The development of one's personality in the direction of imperfection or perfection rests with one's dispositions. These, therefore, are the determinants of one's consciousness *(saṅkhārapaccayā viññāṇaṃ)*. Consciousness *(viññāṇa)*, wherein dispositions function by way of providing an individuality, determines the continuity (or lack of continuity) in a person's experiences. Therefore, it is sometimes referred to as the "stream of consciousness" *(viññāṇasota)*.[25]

The Indian philosophical tradition in general, and the Buddhist tradition in particular, uses the term *nāmarūpa* to refer to the complete personality, consisting of both the psychological and physical components. Although this psychophysical personality comes to be conditioned by a variety of factors, such as one's parents, immediate associates, and environment, the Buddha believed that, among these various factors, consciousness is preeminent *(viññāṇapaccayā nāmarūpaṃ)*.[26] It is this perspective that induced him to emphasize the individual's capacity to develop his own personality, morally as well as spiritually, in spite of certain external constraints. Dispositions and consciousness, in combination, are referred to as "becoming" *(bhava)*.[27] When a person—including one who has attained freedom, like the Buddha—is referred to as "become" *(bhūta)*,[28] this explains how dispositions and consciousness function together to form his personality within the context of the physical environment. In this sense, neither the psychic personality nor its achievements, like freedom, need be viewed as anomalous phenomena, as was the case in some of the pre-Buddhist traditions and with some of the more prominent philosophers of the Western world, such as Immanuel Kant[29] and Donald Davidson.[30] The Buddha's is another way of resolving the determinism / free-will problem.

The next five factors in the twelvefold formula explain the process of perception and the way an ordinary unenlightened person may react to the world of experience. As long as a psychophysical personality exists and as long as its sense faculties are functioning, there will be contact or familiarity *(phassa)* with the world and feeling or emotive response *(vedanā)* to that world. These are inevitable. However, because of the presence of ignorance and, therefore, of extreme dispositional tendencies, the unenlightened person can generate craving *(taṇhā)*—or its opposite—for the object so experienced. Craving leads to grasping *(upādāna),* for both pleasurable objects and ideas. Grasping conditions becoming *(bhava)* and, if this process were to be continued, one would be able, under the proper conditions, to attain whatever status one aspired to in this life or even in a future life.

This process of becoming *(bhava),* which allows for the possibility of achieving goals and satisfying desires, whatever they may be, is not denied in Buddhism. Satisfaction *(assāda),* even that derived from pleasures of sense *(kāma),* is admitted.[31] To begin with the lowest level of satisfaction, a person misguided concerning his goals may achieve the fruits *(attha)* of his action by, say, depriving another human being of life. In his own small world, he may derive satisfaction *(assāda)* by doing so, but soon the unfortunate consequences *(ādīnava)* of that action could lead him to the greatest suffering and unhappiness. Instead of being a fruit *(attha),* the action would turn out to be "unfruitful" *(anattha),* and hence bad *(akusala).*

At another level, a person may, without hurting himself or others, derive satisfaction from having a spouse, children, comfortable lodging, and sufficient food and clothing. These may be considered satisfaction *(assāda)* derived from pleasures of sense *(kāma).* Indeed, there is no unqualified condemnation of these satisfactions, as with those derived from the destruction of human life mentioned above, although it is recognized that these satisfactions are meager, neither permanent nor eternal, and that they can eventually lead to dissatisfaction.[32] These are the satisfactions that one enjoys under great constraint. The nature of such constraints will be analyzed in Chapter IX in connection with the problem of freedom *(nibbāna).* The *final* result of all this is impermanence, decay and death, grief, suffering, and lamentation. Constant yearning for this and that, thirst for sense pleasures, and dogmatic grasping of ideas—these are the causes and conditions of bondage and suffering. It is a life that will eventually lead to one's own suffering as well as to the suffering of others, the prevention of which represents the highest goal of Buddhism.[33]

Through understanding this process, a person is able to pacify his dispositions and develop his personality *(nāmarūpa)* in such a way that, freed from grasping *(upādāna),* he can lead a life that not only avoids suffering and unhappiness for himself but contributes to the welfare of others as well. Getting rid of *passion* and developing a *dispassionate* attitude in life, the freed one is able to cultivate *compassion* for himself as well as others. At the time of death, with ignorance gone and dispositions annihilated, his consciousness will cease without establishing itself in another psychophysical personality.[34]

Conclusion

Pre-Buddhist speculations on the nature of the subject or the human person had fossilized into two distinct theories: eternalism and annihilationism. The concepts employed in its explanation had also solidified. There was not much flexibility; it was an either/or situation. The categories discussed above—the five aggregates, the six elements, and the twelve factors—are repetitious. Such repetition seems unavoidable in a context calling for comprehensive articulation of the concept of a person, with all its relations and ramifications. To follow a middle path avoiding fossilized theories and solidified concepts was no easy task.

The categories just discussed were presented at different times to instruct individuals of various inclinations and dispositions on a variety of issues. Therefore they had to embody not only the concept of a person but also that of his relation to the material world, other human beings, social and political life, morality, and, above all, knowledge and understanding. Such ramifications of the concept of a person need further elaboration. However, there is an underlying theme in all the categories, and that is the Buddha's conception of a "selfless self."

CHAPTER VII

The Object

In the early discourses, objects are described from two different perspectives: objects known and objects of knowledge. The former are very specific, in the sense that they have already served as the objects of experience. The latter are a general category that includes even possible objects. Following the emphasis on the epistemological significance of the experienced, that is, the objectivity of the dependently arisen in formulating a theory of dependent arising (see Chapter IV), it seems appropriate to begin the present discussion with the objects known.

Objects Known

The objects known or experienced often appear in a list of three and four. Sometimes this list is extended to seven items. The first four are: (1) the seen *(diṭṭha),* (2) the heard *(suta),* (3) the conceived *(muta),* and (4) the cognized *(viññāta).*[1] The second list adds: (5) the attained *(patta),* (6) the sought *(pariyesita),* and (7) the reflected *(manasā anuvicarita).*[2]

It is significant that all these objects are described using the past participle form. These are the concrete objects of knowledge with which a perceiving individual has become familiar, within the context in which he is placed. The first two are the objects known through the first two sense faculties, the eye and the ear. Objects known through these faculties are more susceptible to variation, corruption, and misinterpretation than those cognized through the other three physical sense faculties, the nose, tongue, and body. Yet they are the most important among the five. When these two faculties do not function properly, a person is deprived of a major part of sensible experience, as in the case of one who is both blind and deaf. At the same time, these are faculties that can be refined so as to bring more clarity and precision to the objects known through them. Hence the inclusion of clairvoyance or divine eye *(dibba-cakkhu)* and clairaudience or divine ear *(dibba-sota)* among the higher forms of knowledge (see Chapter III). It is in this sense that the objects seen and heard become primary in the Buddhist schema.

The non-inclusion of the objects known through the nose, tongue, and body may baffle the reader of Buddhist texts, but they seem to have been omitted for very pragmatic reasons. While there is no denial of the objects of smell, taste, and touch, the Buddha was more concerned with those that are more problematic, especially in the explanation of the external world.

The next two objects in the list, the conceived *(muta)* and the cognized *(viññāta),* are as important as the first two. Indeed, they are even more susceptible to variation, corruption, and misunderstanding than objects that are seen and heard. The conceived here seems to refer to the object cognized by the mind *(mano);* hence the use of the past participle *muta* (from *maññati, manyate*). Mind, according to the Buddha's analysis, is the faculty that accounts for reflection or memory. In this sense it is said to be capable of sharing the objects of the other five physical faculties. Ordinarily, the object of mind is referred to as *dhamma,* meaning "idea" or "concept." However, in the present context—the reference being to concepts already formed, and thus requiring use of the past participle—the term *muta* has been preferred to the more general term *dhamma,* since the latter does not preclude any possible conceptions.

Even though conceiving is an indispensable means of knowing, the Buddha found it to be the most unrestrained activity and therefore responsible for the greatest amount of confusion regarding the nature of the object. Thus, while the conceived or the conceptualized object can be based on data provided by the sensory faculties, it can also be totally independent, as demonstrated by the Brahmanical conception of self *(ātman).* According to the Buddha, most of the so-called objects that are believed to transcend both sensory experience and conceptualization, and that serve as the objects of an extra-sensuous intuition, are, in fact, the conceived or the conceptualized objects.

The function by which we identify the numerically distinct objects of sense experience is conception, which operates on the basis of the sense of sameness. For this reason objects of conception *appear* to have a greater degree of incorruptibility and immutability than sense experience. However, for the Buddha, such conceiving operates on the basis of the data provided by the senses. The concreteness of a conception depends on the extent to which it is grounded in the data of experience. This allows abstract concepts like "dependent arising," "emptiness," "impermanence," "unsatisfactoriness," and "non-substantiality" to be viewed as objects, not pure fabrications on the part of human imagination, because they represent a conceptual extension of experienced temporal events such as "the dependently arisen," "the empty," "the impermanent," "the unsatisfactory," and "the non-substantial," respectively. Their apparent incorruptibility or immutability is no more than their atemporality, that is, their applicability to events of the obvious past and of the future. The term "atemporal" *(akālika)*[3]—used in Buddhist texts to refer to "the doctrine" *(dhamma),* one aspect of which is "dependent arising" *(paṭiccasamuppāda;* see Chapter v)—does not imply the "timeless" or the eternal *(akāla, kāla-vimutta),*[4] for that would mean recognition of time as a category separable from the events that are experienced. On the contrary, the atemporality of abstract concepts allows for the utilization of long-forgotten perceptual instances from which those concepts have flowered, and which merge again in the particulars of present and future perceptions with the help of those abstract concepts. Thus a human person can move back and forth in dealing with sensible experience without remaining docile as a "sessile sea anemone."

The Buddha accepted the validity of certain objects of conception. Thus, addressing a man named Citta, he says:

> Citta, just as from a cow comes milk, and from milk curds, and from curds butter, and from butter ghee, and from ghee junket, yet, when there is milk, there is no conceiving as "curd" or "butter" or "ghee" or "junket"; instead, on that occasion there is conceiving as "milk."[5]

However, the conception does not always end with objects so conceived. It can go far beyond its limits to conceive of objects that transcend concrete experiences. The following is a pre-Buddhist Upaniṣadic description of a class of objects not given in concrete experience:

> He who inhabits the earth, yet is within the earth, whom the earth *does not know,* whose body the earth is, and who controls the earth from within—he is your self, the inner controller, the immortal.[6]

This statement is repeated in relation to the concepts of water, fire, sky, air, heaven, sun, quarters, moon and stars, space, darkness, light, beings, breath, speech, eye, ear, mind, skin, intellect, and the organ of generation. The Buddha, as a radical empiricist, could not proceed that far with his conceptualization. Therefore, in the *Mūlapariyāya-sutta,* he takes up the object conceived by the Upaniṣadic thinkers relating to the various aspects referred to above, and insists that one should not conceive of an object such as the self "to be made by earth, to be made of earth, to be the possessor of earth" *(paṭhaviyā maññati, paṭhavito maññati, paṭhaviṃ me ti maññati).*[7] As in the *Upaniṣads,* this statement is repeated in connection with other objects of experience as well as conception. For the Buddha, this is an instance where the conceived object *(muta)* has transcended its limit. He therefore emphasized the need to restrain this faculty in order to arrive at a more sober view of the object conceived.

The object cognized *(viññāta)* is not as problematic as the objects conceived *(muta)* because the cognized is generally confined to the six senses, even though the sixth sense, the mind *(mano)*, is responsible for the conceptualization mentioned above. If the mind were to restrict itself to the ideas *(dhamma)* formed on the basis of the information provided by the five other senses, the objects cognized would pose no problems. For this reason, there is no reference to the cognized being restrained. To restrain cognitions would be to prevent any new cognitions from arising. This would eliminate the possibility of cognizing any novelty in regard to the objective world.

However, the Buddha was insistent that with regard to the seen, the heard, the conceived, and the cognized, there is no mysterious something *(kiñci)* that is "not seen, not heard, [and not conceived]" *(na . . . adiṭṭhaṃ asutaṃ amutaṃ kiñcana atthi),*[8] a statement which, as pointed out earlier, has been wrongly translated and interpreted as implying omniscience. Instead of looking for a mysterious something, the Buddha's advice is to take the object as a given, i.e., as the mere seen *(diṭṭhamatta)*, the mere heard *(suttamatta)*, the mere conceived *(mutamatta)*, and the mere cognized *(viññatamatta)*.[9] The adjective "mere" *(matta,* Skt. *mātra)*, used here as a suffix, has a negative as well as a positive connotation. While its negative connotation as "mere" is significant, in that it is intended to deny any mysterious entity, its positive meaning as "measure" is even more important, for it signifies a measure of objectivity without fixing that objectivity. For example, the suffix often occurs with numerals, such as *tiṃsamatta* or *saṭṭhimatta,* which can be translated as "thirty" and "sixty," respectively, even though literally they would mean "about thirty" and "about sixty." By affixing *-matta,* an attempt is made to avoid absolute fixity or determination of the number, thereby leaving room for slight variations. This attitude is even more important in determining the nature of an object than in defining numbers.

The second list of objects may appear rather intriguing. The attained *(patta)* represents an ideal or a goal already achieved; the sought *(pariyesita)* represents an ideal or goal aimed at or pursued; and the reflected *(manasā anuvicarita)* represents an ideal or a goal constantly being examined or considered. The notable feature in this description is that these three objects are not mentioned independently of the first four, indicating that the Buddha recognized the primacy of the latter, just as he admitted the importance of the seen and the heard among the list of four.

It is tempting to define the last three items on the list as objectives rather than objects. However, to do so would be to deprive them of any objectivity at all, creating a sharp dichotomy between objectives, goals, or ideals on the one hand, and objects on the other. The next step would be to characterize the former as mere hallucinations and the latter as ultimate reality. Such a perspective would then serve as a basis for the fact/value distinction as well as for the dichotomy between instrumentalism and realism that has haunted philosophers for centuries.

However, if the last three objects are considered to be objects even though they are dependent on the first four objects, then any absolute distinctions made between the real and the nominal or ideal will be dissolved to some extent; all that is asserted is that the element of subjectivity plays a bigger role in the case of the last three objects than in that of the first four objects. Thus, the issue is the degree of subjectivity involved rather than a sharp distinction between object and non-object. While what is taken as the *most objective*—that is, the seen *(diṭṭha)*—is not free from an element of subjectivity, what is generally explained as *merely subjective*—that is, the ideal—is not without an element of objectivity, unless it is described in contradictory terms, which is how it is presented in the absolutistic systems.

This appraisal of the object is certain to arouse objections, for the most important criterion that is applied in determining objectivity, namely, verifiability, cannot be applied with the same measure of success to the second category of objects, or even to the last two in the first category. However, for the Buddha, verifiability was based on consequences *(attha),* and he was probably prepared to be the devil's advocate and admit the enormous influence of concepts and ideals on human behavior, far more than the influence of sensible objects. This is not to say that the Buddha was therefore prepared to accept any and every ideal as an ultimate reality. On the contrary, he emphasized the need to modify the ideal whenever it came into conflict with the actual, whether in the world of physical reality, in the sphere of biology, or in human life—social, economic, political, or moral (for the Buddha's conception of the moral ideal, see Chapter x).

Objects of Knowledge

After outlining the variety of objects that are experienced, and discouraging any attempt to look for a mysterious entity in its explanation, the Buddha presented a general description of the object. This is part of the twelve "gateways" *(āyatana)* of experience. He lists six objects: (1) material form *(rūpa),* (2) sound *(sadda),* (3) smell *(gandha),* (4) taste *(rasa),* (5) touch *(phoṭṭhabba),* and (6) concept *(dhamma).*[10] Here the Buddha is aiming at comprehensiveness. The previous analysis was selective; its purpose was to highlight the most objective object and the most subjective object. Since this general description is not confined to what *has been experienced* but can be extended to objects of the obvious past as well as of the future (that is, to possible objects), the Buddha takes up all the available faculties—eye, ear, nose, tongue, body, mind—and examines their respective objects. This is evidence for his renunciation of a non-sensuous intuition, since he perceived the mind's functioning to be more epistemologically reliable when it is in association (rather than dissociation) with the data of sensory experience.

The object of the eye *(cakkhu)* is generally referred to as material form *(rūpa)*. This does not mean that the other four objects—sound, smell, taste, and touch—are not material. The capacity of the visual organ is more confined to form, which is also determined by color.[11] Thus the description of material form here is more comprehensive than the one discussed earlier, namely, material form *(rūpa)* as one of the five aggregates constituting the human personality, where the reference is more to the physical body than to the object of experience (see Chapter VI). In the early discourses one does not come across a detailed description of what constitutes the objects of the six senses. A microscopic analysis of objects is met with in the later commentaries and manuals, and such analyses have often generated metaphysical problems the Buddhists were never able to solve satisfactorily.

The precaution taken when dealing with the object known or experienced is avoidance of a search for something *(kiñci)* more than what is given. However, in dealing with the general objects of knowledge listed above, the Buddha warns against reducing them to substances and qualities: "Having seen a material form with the eye, one should not grasp either a substance *(nimitta)* or a secondary quality *(anuvyañjana)*."[12] This is not to advocate a preconceptual object, for the reference is to a complete perception. What is to be avoided is the reduction of that object to substance and secondary qualities. What the Buddha was most concerned about was reification of the object. He recognized the variegated objective world, leaving room for appreciation of the beautiful, yet often insisting that "desirability" is not an inevitable characteristic of that world. Desire *(kāma)* represents the emotional impact of an object on an individual, resulting from a wrong perspective about that object. Rectifying that perspective was seen as one of the ways to avoid unhappiness and suffering without having to eliminate the object itself. It is this emotional aspect of the objective experience that the Buddha highlighted when he characterized it as the desired *(iṭṭha)*, the enjoyable *(kanta)*, the pleasing to the mind *(manāpa)*, the pleasurable *(piyarūpa)*, tending toward desire *(kāmūpasaṃhita)*, and enticing *(rajanīya)*.[13]

The Buddha often advised his disciples to view the world *(loka)* as "empty" *(suñña)*, "non-substantial" *(animitta)*, and "ungrounded" *(appaṇihita)*. The notion of a substance is generally looked upon as a necessary condition for explaining changing or fleeting experiences. That necessity arises as a result of not considering these experiences as "dependently arisen" *(paṭiccasamuppanna)*, but rather as discrete and separate entities. Extreme analysis can thus fix the boundaries so sharply that the fringes can no longer remain to account for possible relations. Avoiding such an analysis of objects eliminates the need for grounding them *(pra-ni-√dhā)* in substances. Thus the objects of experience are without fixity *(appaṇihita),* without substance *(animitta),* and therefore empty of substantial existence *(suñña).*

Such a perspective is deemed necessary to reduce the emotional impact of the object on the individual and to prevent him from being enamored with it *(abhinandati),* extolling it *(abhivadati),* and becoming obsessed with it *(ajjhosaya tiṭṭhati).* The delight *(nandī)* so produced can be the cause of much disappointment and suffering *(dukkhasamudaya).*[14] Just as the Buddha emphasized the non-substantiality *(anatta)* of the subject not in order to deny individuality but to rectify the perspective from which that individuality is viewed, so the non-substantiality of the object is intended to refine the perspective from which the objective world is viewed, not to cause the abandonment of all views about the object.

CHAPTER VIII

The Problem of Suffering

The Buddha recognized four truths about human existence. These truths are articulations of his wisdom or insight *(paññā)*.[1] They are: (1) suffering *(dukkha)*, (2) the arising of suffering *(dukkhasamudaya)*, (3) the ceasing of suffering *(dukkhanirodha)*, and (4) the path leading to the ceasing of suffering *(dukkhanirodhagāminī-paṭipadā)*.

It is evident that these are not truths in the ordinary sense of the word, namely, truths that are distinguished from untruths or falsehood primarily on the basis of cognitive validity or of rational consistency, in terms of correspondence or of coherence. In the context of these definitions of truth, what the Buddha referred to as a truth about existence may be termed a psychological truth. However, the Buddha spoke of them as "noble truths" *(ariya-saccāni)*. This means that they are not merely epistemological or rational truths. The conception of "nobility" involves a value judgment. Value is not decided in terms of higher or lower, as the term "noble" sometimes signifies; instead, it implies relevance or worth. The noble is thus qualified by the "fruitful" *(atthasaṃhita)*, while the ignoble *(anariya)* is defined in terms of the "fruitless" *(anatthasaṃhita)*.[2]

The four truths are therefore more appropriately explained as factual truths with moral relevance. The *Discourse to Kaccāyana* (Chapter IV) brings out the distinction between the conception of truth in the Brahmanical tradition, on the one hand, and the Buddha's own definition, on the other. There, the conception of suffering is contrasted with the notion of self *(ātman)*. The Buddha's advice to Kaccāyana is not to cling to a view such as "This is myself," but to concentrate his attention on suffering instead. The nature of the Brahmanical notion of self was explained in Chapter I. It is a view from nowhere, for the conception of an eternal self is a product of the renunciation of all human perspectives. When such metaphysical speculation is avoided, one cannot help adopting a human perspective. The conception of truth comes to be determined on the basis of its relevance or irrelevance to human life. The pragmatic conception of truth presented by the Buddha is therefore not only epistemologically relevant but also ethically significant.

Yet the Buddha was reluctant to present suffering as a universal or all-inclusive truth. "All or everything is suffering" *(sabbaṃ dukkhaṃ)* is a statement that is conspicuously absent in the early discourses attributed to the Buddha. A general statement about suffering is always concretized by the use of the relative pronoun "this" *(idaṃ)*. Thus the most general statement one can find in the discourses reads, "All this is suffering" *(sabbam idaṃ dukkhaṃ)*. This allows the Buddha to specify and elaborate on the conception of suffering.

A concrete explanation of the truth of suffering occurs in his very first discourse, popularly known as the *Dhammacakkappavattana-sutta:*

> Birth is suffering; old age is suffering; sickness is suffering; death is suffering. Sorrow, lamentation, and dejection are suffering. Contact with what is unpleasant and separation from the pleasant are suffering. Not getting what one wishes is suffering. In brief, clinging to the five aggregates of the personality—body, feeling, perception, disposition, and consciousness—as possessions of "my self" is suffering.[3]

Taken at face value, this passage can easily contribute to the belief that Buddhism represents an extremely pessimistic view of human life. Yet a careful analysis reveals that what is defined as suffering belongs to three temporal periods, beginning with the past, moving on to the immediate present, and reaching out into the future for a possible solution. The immediate suffering is, of course, contact with what is unpleasant and separation from the pleasant, as well as not achieving the fulfillment of one's wishes. The problem faced by a philosopher with serious moral concerns is beautifully summarized by William James:

> A look at another peculiarity of the ethical universe, as we find it, will still further show us the philosopher's perplexities. As a purely theoretic problem, namely, the casuistic question would hardly ever come up at all. If the ethical philosopher were only asking after the best *imaginable* system of goods he would indeed have an easy task; for all demands as such are *prima facie* respectable, and the best simply imaginary world would be one in which *every* demand was gratified as soon as made. Such a world would, however, have to have a physical constitution entirely different from that of the one which we inhabit. It would need not only a space, but a time, of n-dimensions, to include all the acts and experiences incompatible with one another here below, which would then go on in conjunction—such as spending our money, yet growing rich; taking our holiday, yet getting ahead with our work; shooting and fishing, yet doing no hurt to the beasts; gaining no end of experience, yet keeping our youthful freshness of heart; and the like. There can be no question that such a system of things, however brought about, would be the absolutely ideal system; and that if a philosopher could create universes *a priori,* and provide all the mechanical conditions, that is the sort of universe which he should unhesitatingly create.[4]

The Buddha was no such idealist. Being a radical empiricist and a pragmatist, he was not willing to reconstruct such an *a priori* world even for the satisfaction of those who crave it. Taking the bull by the horns, he was prepared to deal with the riddle of existence without running away from it. His first priority, then, was to recognize the fact of suffering. Human beings are guided by dispositions that can transform themselves into wishes and desires of the extreme sort, bringing them into conflict with the very constitution of the universe, namely, arising and ceasing (= dependent arising); in the case of the human universe, this constitution represents birth, old age, sickness, and death. Birth has already occurred, and the question of suffering would not have arisen without it. The individual person may or may not have contributed in some measure to that event. To continue to worry about how birth came to be—to try to determine *precisely* what contributed to it, even if some veridical memories of the past are available and the contributions of one's parents are observable without a great deal of effort—is to involve oneself in a fruitless and endless reflective enterprise, which the Buddha designated as speculation about the past *(pubbanta-kappanā)*[5] or running after the past *(pubbanta-atidhāvana)*.[6]

The Buddha's analysis of the problem of suffering thus took him back to the point of birth. Birth of a human person has taken place. According to the principle in terms of which it has occurred, that person is liable to old age, sickness, and death. The Buddha was unwilling to dissociate birth from other occurrences, such as old age, sickness, and death. His perspective did not lead him to believe that birth is the greatest good and death the worst evil. For him, *if* death were to be viewed as suffering, then birth, without which death could not take place, should be perceived in a similar way.

This is not to give up hope altogether, for if birth has initiated a process that eventually ends in death, every effort should be made to minimize the suffering that a human person experiences between birth and death. Therefore, examining carefully the conditions that render immediate experiences painful and frustrating, the Buddha presents a way out of that suffering: "In brief, the clinging to the five aggregates of the personality—body, feeling, perception, disposition, and consciousness—as possessions of 'my self' is suffering." Here there is no judgment that the five aggregates *(pañcakkhandha)* are suffering. What is condemned is grasping *(upādāna)* the five aggregates as the possession of a mysterious entity or an ego. In doing so the Buddha traces the cause of the problem of suffering to the way in which the human personality or the subject is perceived.

This leads to the evaluation of the objective world, for the impact of the human perspective is as evident in the objective world of experience as it is in the case of the subject. The use of the term *dukkha* in describing the world of objectivity is more appropriately understood as "unsatisfactory" than as "suffering." This is a more abstract use of the term *dukkha,* for it is an extension of a subjective attitude (namely, "suffering") to explain what may be called an objective experience. With this the human perspective is retained once again, where other philosophers would permit a totally non-subjective or value-free description.

Very often, the reason for considering an object unsatisfactory *(dukkha)* is that it is impermanent *(anicca)* and subject to transformation or change *(vipariṇāma-dhamma).*[7] Unless this assertion is examined carefully in the light of other statements relating to the world of experience, it can once again lead to a misunderstanding of the Buddha's worldview. For example, according to our previous analyses of the subject and object (Chapters V and VI), the Buddha left no room for the recognition of any permanent and eternal substratum (*ātman, svabhāva,* etc.) in the world of experience. All phenomena are non-substantial *(sabbe dhammā anattā).* Whatever is non-substantial is dependently arisen *(paṭiccasamuppanna),* that is, subject to arising and ceasing depending on conditions, which means that all phenomena are impermanent and liable to change or transformation. Thus the conclusion is inevitable that all phenomena are unsatisfactory, and if the Buddha were to arrive at such a conclusion, there would be no reason a statement such as "all phenomena are unsatisfactory" *(sabbe dhammā dukkhā)* should not be found in any of the discourses. Yet the Buddha judiciously avoids making any such statement. Therefore, the statement that whatever is impermanent is unsatisfactory should not be universalized. It needs to be qualified, and it is this qualification that is spelled out in the statement "All dispositions are unsatisfactory" *(sabbe saṅkhārā dukkhā).*[8]

Dispositions are certainly subjective. Yet the Buddha is here referring to certain objects that have come into existence or are produced solely to satisfy the dispositional tendencies in human beings. Such objects are generally referred to as the "dispositionally conditioned" *(saṅkhata)* and are included in the more comprehensive category of objects referred to as "the dependently arisen" *(paṭiccasamuppanna).*[9]

At this point, it would be tempting to regard the dependently arisen as the natural and the dispositionally conditioned as the artificial. Any phenomenon that involves the activity or influence of the dispositions—and this would include views or perspectives about such phenomena—would then fall under the category of the artificial, while the natural would transcend all dispositions, and therefore all views or perspectives. This amounts to transcendence, to abandoning all views, a position contrary to the ideas expressed in Chapter IV regarding the nature of the principle of dependent arising.

The only way to avoid such a situation is to explain the principle of dependence as involving both the natural and the dispositional, the latter accounting for human perspective as well as for the limitations of experience that make it impossible to know everything "as it is." In other words, the principle of dependent arising takes into account the natural happenings in the subjective as well as objective spheres on a limited scale revealed by limited human experiences, without admitting absolutely determined psychological or physical laws that are totally independent of experience.

However, such dispositional functions need to be distinguished from those that take the upper hand in determining a person's subjective life, compelling him to admit metaphysical entities such as the self *(ātman)* or influencing his objective experience, which compels him to look for mysterious substances *(svabhāva)*. These dispositional tendencies that take the upper hand are the solidified dispositions, which find expression in the form of greed *(lobha)*, lust *(rāga)*, craving *(taṇhā)*, or hatred *(dosa)*, and which are referred to as the cause of suffering[10] (i.e., the second noble truth).

It is now possible to explain why the Buddha, after saying that what is impermanent is suffering *(yad aniccaṃ taṃ dukkhaṃ)*, proceeded to specify the "what" *(yad)*. He was referring to the dispositions as implied in the statement "All dispositions are impermanent" *(sabbe saṅkhārā aniccā)*,[11] because all dispositions, unless they are appeased or desolidified, lead to suffering *(sabbe saṅkhārā dukkhā)*.[12] This eliminates the necessity of considing all phenomena *(sabbe dhammā)*, even if there were an element of disposition involved in their determination, to be unsatisfactory *(dukkha)*.

Thus, speaking of the grandeur of a universal monarch *(cakkavatti rājā)* and the facilities he enjoys, such as palaces, pools, and pleasure gardens, the Buddha refers to them as "dispositions" that eventually come to decay and destruction.[13] Being impermanent and dispositionally conditioned, if one were to be obsessed by them, clinging to them as one's own, one would eventually experience suffering. The unsatisfactoriness of dispositionally conditioned phenomena *(saṅkhata)* thus lies in the fact that they leave the mistaken impression that they are permanent and eternal entities. Only a correct understanding of how such things are produced or have come to be *(yathābhūta)* will enable a person to avoid any suffering consequent upon their destruction or cessation.[14]

The Buddha's statement that phenomena are unsatisfactory is limited to those that are determined solely by dispositions, for they are the ones that affect the individual most and from which he is unable to free himself easily. The realization that such phenomena are impermanent and unsatisfactory, and that all experienced phenomena are non-substantial and dependently arisen, constitutes the cessation of suffering and the attainment of freedom and happiness.

CHAPTER IX

Freedom and Happiness

The analysis of freedom *(nibbāna)* and the happiness *(sukha)* associated with such freedom, independent of the problem of suffering discussed in the previous chapter, can lead to much misunderstanding. The first and second noble truths relate to the problem of suffering and its cause, respectively. Even though all dispositions are considered to be suffering or unsatisfactory *(dukkha),* they are not looked upon as the cause of suffering. The cause of suffering is almost always referred to as lust *(raga),* craving *(taṇhā),* greed *(lobha),* attachment *(ālaya),* grasping *(upādāna),* hatred *(dosa),* aversion *(paṭigha),* and other psychological tendencies.

Epistemological Freedom

The distinction between the first noble truth and the second is crucial. It has already been pointed out that the dispositions are necessary conditions for human knowledge and understanding. Abandoning all dispositional tendencies is tantamount to committing epistemological suicide; they are necessary not only for knowledge and understanding but also for the continuity of the life process that begins with birth. The reason is that dispositions are not purely mental *(mano),* they are physical *(kāya)* and verbal *(vaci)* as well, that is, habitual bodily behavior and similarly habitual verbal behavior. Annihilation of these dispositional tendencies would eliminate the functioning of the physical organs and make it almost impossible for a human being to continue to respond to the world. The Jaina practice of not performing any new actions, except those mortifications intended to expiate for past actions,[1] comes close to such an elimination of bodily and verbal responses. When such practices are carried to their conclusions, they can mean actual suicide.

Thus allowing the dispositions to have complete mastery over one's knowledge and understanding results in dogmatism, while their annihilation is equivalent to epistemological suicide. Similarly, allowing dispositions to overwhelm one's behavior can lead to bondage and suffering, whereas annihilating them means complete inaction or even suicide. The middle standpoint recommended by the Buddha is the appeasement of all dispositions *(sabbasaṅkhārasamatha)*, which is equivalent to freedom *(nibbāna)*.[2] Hence freedom pertains both to human knowledge and understanding and to human behavior. For the Buddha, the first form of freedom is a necessary condition for the second.

The term *nibbāna* (Skt. *nirvāṇa*) conveys the same negative sense associated with the conception of freedom whenever the latter is defined as "absence of constraint." Epistemologically, a view or a perspective becomes a constraint whenever it is elevated to the level of an absolute *(parama)* or viewed as embodying the ultimate truth.[3] It is such absolutizing of views that contributes to all the contention in the world, where one view is pitted against another, one perspective looked upon as superior and another as inferior.[4] The Buddha carefully avoided formulating any eternal truths *(saccāni . . . niccāni)*[5] and provided a definition of truth that is non-absolutistic, thereby leaving room for its modification in the light of future possibilities (see Chapter III). Yet the body of knowledge or variety of perspectives that has remained functional is respected as the "ancient tradition" *(sanātana dhamma)*[6] and is not discarded altogether. The Buddha was emphatic in stating that one cannot hope to attain purity either by clinging to one view *(diṭṭhi)* or by having no-view *(adiṭṭhi)*.[7] If he had assumed that there can be only one view that leads to freedom and purity, then only those who lived in India during the sixth century B.C. could have attained such freedom, for that one view could not be applied to any other context, where the content of human knowledge would be different. But since he did not believe that there is one absolutely true view, the Buddha could claim that his conception of truth is not confined to any particular time, i.e., that it is atemporal *(akālika)*.[8]

Freedom is sometimes referred to as a state of stability *(accutaṃ padaṃ)*[9] and as a state in which there is no fear from any quarter *(akutobhaya)*.[10] These definitions have more epistemological than behavioral significance. How often is one's stability disturbed by the shattering of a perspective cherished for a whole lifetime? What fear can be greater than that arising from thinking of the sun not rising tomorrow? Analytical knowledge intended to get rid of dogmatic views was symbolized in the form of a "diamond" *(vajira)*.[11] The fear driven into the hearts of the dogmatic philosophers as a result of such analysis was symbolized as Vajrapāṇi, "the demon with the diamond (or thunderbolt) in hand."[12] Disruption of cherished views can bring instability and fear worse than what one experiences as a result of losing property or those who are near and dear. It is for this reason that freedom is considered to be release from excessive involvement *(yogakkhema)*.[13] With no such excessive involvement in perspectives, and being able to modify them in the light of new information or different interests, a person can remain at peace *(khema)* and without fear *(appaṭibhaya)*.[14] With fear gone, one can enjoy unswerving happiness *(acalaṃ sukhaṃ).*[15] It is a stable happiness, not one that fluctuates.

Behavioral Freedom

In terms of behavior, freedom as "absence of constraints" means the ability to act without being constrained by unwholesome psychological tendencies such as greed and hatred. It is not the ability to function without regard for each and every principle of nature, physical, biological, or psychological. While those physical, biological, or psychological principles that are wholly determined by human dispositions *(saṅkhata;* see Chapter VIII) can be brought under control as a result of an enlightened person's appeasement of dispositions, he still has to function in a world where the principle of "dependent arising" *(paṭiccasamuppāda)* prevails. Thus he may be almost immune to disease because of his healthy way of living; indeed, the only ailments the historical Buddha suffered seem to have been aftereffects of the severe self-mortification he practiced before enlightenment. Yet even the Buddha was unable to prevent the onset of old age, decay, and, finally, death. The principle of dependent arising that brought about his death was initiated when he was born in this world, an occurrence over which he had no complete control. However, if a person's desire for survival *(bhava-taṇhā)* is one of the contributory factors to such survival, with the elimination of such desire he can anticipate the possibility of overcoming future rebirth. Thus the overcoming of rebirth is the result of his spewing out craving in the present life. It is primarily in this sense of not being reborn *(a-punabbhava)* that we can speak of immortality *(amata).*[16]

Seen in this light, we must reconsider the implications of the famous discourse in the *Udāna* used by almost every modern interpreter of Buddhism as evidence for an absolutistic conception of freedom *(nibbāna).* The discourse reads:

> Monks, there is a not-born, not-become, not-made, not-dispositionally-conditioned. Monks, if that not-born, not-become, not-made, not-dispositionally-conditioned were not, no escape from the born, become, made, dispositionally-conditioned would be known here. But, monks, since there is a not-born, not-become, not-made, not-dispositionally-conditioned, therefore an escape from the born, become, made, dispositionally-conditioned is known.[17]

Note that the negations pertain to concepts referred to by the past participles not-born *(a-jāta),* not-become *(a-bhūta),* not-made *(a-kata),* and not-dispositionally-conditioned *(a-saṅkhata),* indicating that they involve events that have already occurred. Their nominal forms—birth *(jāti),* becoming *(bhava),* making or doing *(kamma),* and dispositions *(saṅkhāra)*—explain the world of bondage and suffering (see Chapter VIII). Therefore, their negation is simply a negation of the bondage and suffering that a person experiences as a result of the process that has already taken place. Since part of that process involved human dispositions, the opportunity to restrain that process by the appeasement of dispositions is also recognized. In other words, it is an explanation of the possibility of freedom, not in an absolutistic sense, but in a limited sense of "absence of constraint." The fact that the passage refers only to those events which are predominantly conditioned by dispositions and not to those that are "dependently arisen" *(paṭiccasamuppanna)* seems to indicate that this is a reference to the freedom and happiness one can attain in the present life, in contrast to its bondage and suffering.

Behaviorally, freedom finds expression most clearly in the attitude one adopts toward life in the world. This is best illustrated by the simile of the lotus *(puṇḍarīka).*[18] Like a lotus that springs up in the muddy water, grows in it, and, rising above it, remains unsmeared by it, so one who has spewed out greed and hatred, though born in the world and remaining in it, yet manages to be unsmeared by the world *(lokena anupalitto).* This world of experience is sometimes described in couplets: gain and loss, good repute and disrepute, praise and blame, happiness and suffering.[19] A person who has attained freedom is not overwhelmed by such experiences; hence he remains unsmeared by them, freed from sorrow, taintless and secure.[20] This is not to say that he does not experience that world.

To remain unsmeared by the world of present experience (i.e., the third noble truth) by the elimination of the cause of suffering, which is greed or craving (the second noble truth), it is necessary to understand the problem of suffering (the first noble truth). Thus the behavior of the person who has attained freedom can be understood only in terms of the conception of suffering discussed earlier (see Chapter VIII).

The Buddha's discussion of suffering, as has been pointed out, focused on immediate experiences without ignoring the past and future. Therefore his explanation of happiness should do likewise. The general tendency is to view the birth of a human being as a joyous event and death as a mournful one. The Buddha perceived both birth and death as suffering, yet the solution is neither to rejoice in both nor to bemoan them both. The elimination of craving and appeasement of dispositions enabled the Buddha to adopt a more sober attitude toward death. This attitude is expressed in the words of one of his chief disciples:

> Neither do I take delight in death nor do I rejoice in life. I shall discard this body with awareness and mindfulness. Neither do I take delight in death nor do I rejoice in life. I shall discard this body, like a hireling his earnings.[21]

It is possible to interpret this attitude as one of reckless abandon bordering on pessimism, but the statement simply expresses the fruitlessness of any attempt to avoid death when birth has already occurred. If death is unavoidable by a human being who has come to be born, either as a result of a previous craving for survival or of circumstances beyond his control, he ought neither waste time worrying about death and trying to find a way out of it in the present life nor commit suicide, but rather deal with the problem of immediate suffering with compassion for himself as well as others.

This attitude is also reflected in the Buddha's advocacy of fearlessness in the service of humanity. Yet it is necessary to distinguish this from conscious, deliberate self-immolation. Self-sacrifice or unrestrained altruism is neither a means nor a goal. However, if, in the process of helping oneself and others attain happiness, one were to face unforeseen death due purely to circumstances (that is, to dependent arising), and if it is *not something sought after (apariyiṭṭha),* the Buddha's conception of life and death allows for that form of death to be hailed as noble.[22] This qualification necessarily rules out any decision to take a course of action knowing that it will certainly lead to death either for oneself or for others, in complete contrast to the ideal presented in the *Bhagavadgītā,* as well as in some of the later Buddhist texts like the *Jātakas*[23] and the *Saddharmapuṇḍarīka-sūtra.*[24]

Thus it is not only the abandoning of greed *(lobha)* and hatred *(dosa)* that constitutes freedom, but also overcoming confusion *(moha).* A clear understanding of the nature of life, even according to the limited sources of knowledge available to human beings, is a necessary condition for freedom and happiness. An enlightened person is one who has overcome the perversions of knowledge and understanding *(vipallāsa).*[25] The four types of perversions pertain to perception *(saññā),* thought *(citta),* and views *(diṭṭhi).* They constitute the identification of (1) the impermanent with the permanent *(anicce niccan ti),* (2) the not unsatisfactory with the unsatisfactory *(adukkhe dukkhan ti),* (3) the non-substantial with the substantial *(anattani attā ti),* and (4) the not pleasant with the pleasant *(asubhe subhan ti).*

Here the subject represents the impermanent, the not unsatisfactory, the non-substantial, and the not pleasant about which permanence, unsatisfactoriness, substantiality, and pleasantness are predicated as a result of confusion. If the subject stands for what is experienced—and this would include the cognitive as well as the emotive aspects of experience, the so-called world of fact and value, bondage *(saṃsāra),* and freedom *(nibbāna)*—then the predication that renders the identification a perversion *(vipallāsa)* would make it impossible for freedom *(nibbāna)* to be considered permanent, unsatisfactory, substantial, and pleasant.

Most interpreters of Buddhism would refrain from asserting *nibbāna* as a permanent and substantial entity, at least as far as its cognitive aspect is concerned. However, they often insist on the permanence and substantiality of its emotive character. Thus, even if *nibbāna* is not an ultimate reality *(paramattha)* in an ontological sense, there is a tendency to regard it as ultimate reality in the sense of permanent and eternal happiness, and hence as a sort of transcendental emotional experience that has nothing to do with the feelings and sensations of ordinary human beings.

The evidence that *nibbāna* does not consititute a permanent and eternal cognitive reality has been presented above. What remains to be discussed is the nature of the emotive experience—namely, the sort of happiness—associated with the attainment of freedom or *nibbāna*.

Psychological Freedom

The term for happiness is *sukha* (etymologically explained as *su-kha,* meaning "having a good axle-hole," that is, a vehicle moving smoothly without constraints). The early discourses refer to two forms of happiness. The first is worldly or material happiness *(āmisa-sukha),* the term *āmisa* (derived from *āma,* meaning "raw") expressing the sense of raw, sensual appetite.[26] The second is expressed by the negative term *nirāmisa,*[27] understood as mental or spiritual happiness, which is contrasted with the happiness derived from satisfaction of the five physical senses. For this reason there has been a general reluctance to associate this form of happiness with any feeling or sensation *(vedanā),* which is inevitable in sense experience.[28] The happiness of freedom is perceived as beyond the pale of sense experience, and therefore of any satisfaction relating to the senses. Thus so-called worldly or material happiness *(āmisa-sukha)* becomes identical with whatever happiness is derived from following one's desires *(kāma-sukha).*

Yet the Buddha does not seem to have advocated the view that feelings *(vedanā),* and even sense experience *(saññā),* are necessarily evil and conducive to unhappiness. As pointed out earlier (Chapter III), the suppression of all perceptions and whatever is felt *(saññāvedayitanirodha)* was intended as a deconstructive method, never as a goal in itself. Once the deconstruction process has taken effect, feelings and perceptions can serve their proper functions without running the risk of reifying either their cognitive content or their emotive component.

The fact that the person who has attained freedom continues to experience through the same sense faculties he possessed before, and that he continues to have agreeable *(manāpa)* and disagreeable *(amanāpa),* pleasurable *(sukha)* and painful *(dukkha)* experiences, is clearly admitted by the Buddha.[29] This means that there is no qualitative difference between the feelings of someone who is in bondage and someone who is freed. All that is asserted is that, in the case of a person who has attained freedom, there is an absence of the greed, hatred, and confusion that are *generally* consequent upon sense experience. For this reason the distinction normally made between material happiness *(āmisa-sukha)* and spiritual happiness *(nirāmisa-sukha)* needs to be reconsidered.

In fact, Buddha does not appear to be condemning so-called material happiness indiscriminately. The discussion of material inheritance *(āmisa-dāyāda)* and spiritual inheritance *(dhamma-dāyāda)* in the early discourses seems to support this view.[30] A disciple of the Buddha is represented as experiencing great physical discomfort as a result of fasting, and as refusing to eat some food left by the Buddha because he believes that a true disciple should not be heir to the Buddha's material possessions. The Buddha does not consider this to be appropriate behavior. Material or physical comfort in itself is to be neither abandoned nor condemned. Physical deprivation, according to the Buddha, is as disruptive of moral and spiritual development as is indulgence in physical comfort. Thus so-called spiritual happiness *(nirāmisa-sukha)* need not be qualitatively distinct from material comfort or happiness. It is the cognitive and emotional slavery to the objective world (see Chapter IV) that constitutes suffering, and it is this slavery that is referred to as bondage, whereas freedom from such slavery constitutes the highest happiness *(paramaṃ sukhaṃ* or *nirāmisaṃ sukhaṃ)* that a human being can enjoy while alive.

To assume that this happiness is permanent and eternal would mean that there is a permanent and eternal person who continues to have such experience. This is to admit a Supreme Being who, even if he is not the creator and preserver of the universe, is at least present during the past, present, and future, for without him one cannot account for the experience of permanent and eternal happiness. The Buddha and his disciples cannot deny George Berkeley's conception of God and continue to speak of permanent and eternal happiness. There cannot be the experience of such happiness unless one admits the existence of an experiencer who is permanent and eternal. All that can be asserted without contradiction is that if a person were to follow such and such a perspective and adopt such and such forms of behavior, he would be able to experience such and such a happiness, comparable to that experienced by the Buddha and his enlightened disciples. The concept of previous and future buddhas can be meaningful only in such a context. Thus non-substantiality *(anatta)* pertains not only to the world of bondage *(saṃsāra)* but also to freedom *(nibbāna)*. The Buddhists were therefore prepared to admit that freedom as well as conception *(paññatti)* are undeniably non-substantial *(anatta)*.[31] One of the discourses relating to freedom underscores this characteristic:

> Non-substantiality is indeed difficult to see. Truth certainly is not easily perceived. Craving is mastered by him who knows, and for him who sees there exists no something *(akiñcana).*[32]

Freedom is an experience. As such, it can find expression in language, as any other human experience does. Hence it is a truth *(sacca)* or, more specifically, a noble truth *(ariyasacca),* which also makes it a noble view *(ariyā diṭṭhi).*[33] However, those who adopt a substantialist perspective regarding truth (see Chapter III) are prone to distinguish freedom from the person who experiences it. Attributing ultimate objectivity to freedom, they create an elephant of enormous size for which they are unable to provide a reasonable description. Obsessed with their extremely restricted views and unable to touch the fringes, one person will explain the animal only as a huge pot and *nothing else,* for he has touched the animal's head. Another person insists that it is *none other* than a winnowing basket, because he has felt only the animal's ear. Still another defines it as a ploughshare and *nothing else,* since he confined his experience to the animal's tusk. The search for ultimate objectivity has blinded them completely.[34] After creating something *more,* they struggle with their descriptions, whereupon language fails them. The inevitable result is the assertion that freedom is beyond linguistic description. The Buddha was striking at the root of the problem when he insisted that freedom, like any other phenomenon, is non-substantial *(anatta).*

Unanswered Questions

There are two sets of unanswered questions relating to the person who has attained freedom. One concerns the living person and the other pertains to the dead person. In both cases the term used is *tathāgata,* meaning the "thus-gone-one." Unfortunately, it is this notion of the "thus-gone" that led to the emergence of many metaphysical issues relating to the conception of freedom, because it is when a freed person is so described that questions such as Where did he go? can arise. If he is living, then his life must be different from that of everyone else. If he is dead and is not reborn like everyone else, then he must be surviving in a totally different form of existence.

The two sets of questions are posed in the form of six propositions to which the Buddha does not provide an answer:

1. The soul is identical with the body. *(Taṃ jīvaṃ taṃ sarīraṃ.)*
2. The soul is different from the body. *(Aññaṃ jīvaṃ aññaṃ sarīraṃ.)*
3. The *tathāgata* exists after death. *(Hoti tathāgato parammaraṇā.)*
4. The *tathāgata* does not exist after death. *(Na hoti tathāgato parammaraṇā.)*

5. The *tathāgata* both exists and does not exist after death. *(Hoti ca na ca hoti tathāgato parammaraṇā.)*
6. The *tathagata* neither exists nor does not exist after death. *(N' eva hoti na na hoti tathāgato parammaraṇā.)*[35]

The first two propositions are generally considered to be references to the metaphysical notions of self *(ātman)* and not in any way related to the problem of the *tathāgata,* whereas the last four refer specifically to the *tathāgata* "after death" *(parammaraṇā).* However, in response to questions raised by a monk named Yamaka regarding the dead *tathāgata,* Sāriputta, one of the Buddha's leading disciples, raised further questions relating to the first two propositions:

1. Is the *tathāgata* identical with the body? (This question is repeated with regard to the other aggregates, feeling, perception, disposition, and consciousness).
2. Is the *tathāgata* different from the body? (Repeated with regard to the other aggregates.)
3. Is the *tathāgata* in the body? (Repeated with regard to the other aggregates.)[36]

These questions, of course, pertain to the living *tathāgata.* Yet the inquiry is not about the ordinary conception of *tathāgata* but about one who exists in truth *(saccato)* and reality *(thetato).* In this latter sense, the explanation of the *tathāgata* goes beyond normal objectivity. It is an ultimately real *tathāgata,* beyond change and impermanence, permanent and eternal, that is sought for. In that sense, the *tathāgata* is not different from the soul or self *(ātman, jīva)* of the Brahmanical thinkers, who believed that it is different from the ordinary human personality. The denial of such a *tathāgata* would be similar to the notion of self posited by the Materialists, for whom the self is identical with the body.

Thus the assumption of a metaphysical yet living *tathāgata* is not radically different from the supposition of a *tathāgata* after death. For the Buddha, these are theories based on the transcendence of all human perspective, and hence are views from nowhere. There is no way in which questions about them can be answered from the human perspective. Therefore the Buddha was not willing to make any statement, for any statement would have committed him to either an assertion or a negation about the content of the question. If the content of the question is such that it can neither be asserted nor negated, the Buddha finds the question itself to be metaphysical.

There is a belief that the Buddha observed "silence" on all these matters, indicating his reluctance to make any statement because these are matters that transcend lingustic expression. While it is true that "whereof one cannot speak, thereof one must be silent," such silence is justified only if these questions continue to be raised despite the reasons given for not answering or explaining them *(avyākata)*. However, it must be noted that the Buddha was not simply silent when such questions were raised. In fact, he protested vehemently against raising such questions, because the questions themselves were meaningless, let alone the answers (see Chapter III). Such questions are not only epistemologically meaningless and unanswerable[37] but pragmatically irrelevant, for answers to them do not in any way help solve the problem of immediate human suffering.[38]

What, then, is the Buddha's own conception of the living *tathāgata?* It is the conception of freedom with substrate *(sopādisesa-nibbāna):*

> Herein, monks, a monk is a worthy one who has destroyed the defiling impulses, lived the [higher] life, done what has to be done, laid aside the burden, achieved the noble goal, destroyed the fetters of existence, and is freed through wisdom. He retains his five senses, through which, as they are not yet destroyed, he experiences pleasant and unpleasant sensations and feels pleasure and pain. His cessation of craving, hatred, and confusion is called the freedom with substrate.[39]

The Buddha recognized the possibility of the survival of human life after death, the condition for such survival being the excessive craving and grasping for life. Therefore, when he spoke of freedom as the absence of constraints such as craving, hatred, and confusion, the Buddha was compelled to explain what happens to the *tathāgata at death,* even though he was reluctant to answer questions about the *tathāgata after death*. The description of freedom without substrate *(anupādisesa-nibbāna)* is intended for this purpose:

> Herein, monks, a monk is a worthy one who has destroyed the defiling impulses, . . . [as in the passage just quoted], is freed through wisdom. Monks, all his experiences [lit., "things he has felt"], none of which he relished, will be cooled here itself. This is called freedom without substrate.[40]

Speculation regarding the afterlife of a freed person is dominant among those who are still obsessed with survival in one form or another, but not among those who have attained freedom. Unsmeared by such speculations, the freed person leads a life conducive to the welfare of as many people as possible, including himself, with compassion for all the world.

A controversy between a monk named Udāyi and a carpenter named Pañcakaṅga, recorded in a discourse called *Multiple Experiences (Bahuvedanīya),*[41] throws light on the Buddha's conception of happiness. The carpenter believed that the Buddha spoke of two kinds of feelings or sensations: pleasant and unpleasant (happy and unhappy, *sukha* and *duk-*

kha). He included neutral feelings under the category of the pleasant or happy. However, the monk argued that the Buddha spoke of three varieties: pleasant or happy *(sukha),* unpleasant or unhappy *(dukkha),* and neutral *(adukkhamasukha).* When the matter was reported to the Buddha, he found fault with both for rejecting each other's views, because both were right. At different times the Buddha spoke of two categories, three, five, and so on, up to 108 categories. These are all contextual *(pariyāya).*

The Buddha begins his explanation by referring to the normal forms of pleasant feelings or sensations, namely, the five strands of sense pleasure *(pañca kāmaguṇa),* such as a material object cognizable by the eye, desirable, pleasant, liked, enticing, associated with the pleasures of sense, and alluring. Yet the Buddha was not willing to accept these as the highest form of pleasantness or happiness *(sukha).* Other forms are more excellent and exquisite, which he proceeds to enumerate. These include the happiness or pleasant sensations associated with the higher contemplations *(jhāna),* including the state of cessation of perception and what is felt *(saññāvedayitanirodha).* At this stage the Buddha anticipated that other teachers would recognize the state of cessation as "happiness in itself" and continue to speculate as to what it is and how it is. The Buddha was not prepared to identify happiness with one particular feeling or sensation. For him, happiness is contextual. Wherever *(yattha yattha)* it is obtained, through whatever source *(yahiṃ yahiṃ),* he was prepared to recognize happiness. In other words, he was not willing to speak of happiness in an abstract way. This was his anti-essentialist approach.

CHAPTER X

The Moral Life

The moral life is generally distinguished from the good life,[1] a distinction that pertains to their nature as well as their quality. As far as their nature is concerned, the good life is founded on human emotion and disposition, while the moral life has its roots in the ultimately objective moral law, often associated with the divine, either as its guardian or as its author. For this very reason, the moral life is assumed to override the good life. This distinction also determines their qualitative difference. The moral life constitutes permanent and eternal happiness bearing the stamp of spirituality and sacredness. In contrast, the good life is one of temporary enjoyment and happiness associated with the sensory experiences of human beings, and is therefore materialistic and profane.

In the preceding chapter on freedom and happiness, it was pointed out that the Buddha avoided a sharp dichotomy between the happiness in *nibbāna* and the happiness associated with ordinary human life. This enabled him to recognize a more intimate relationship between the freed person and the ordinary human being, *nibbāna* and *saṃsāra,* the common denominator being human life itself, which needs to be protected and nourished.

The Buddha seems to have realized that if the moral life meant conforming to an absolute moral law that can override the good life, it could bring harm to human life. The history of mankind is replete with such instances. He therefore advocated a position in which human life could override the moral life. This is the implication of his famous statement that even "what is good has to be abandoned, let alone evil" *(dhammā pi . . . pahātabbā pageva adhammā).*[2] In other words, human life is not made for morals; morals are made for human life. An ideal, if it is formulated by human beings, is based on an understanding of particular forms of good. Therefore that ideal must be modified when it comes into conflict with more concrete instances of good as human experiences continue to unfold. The Buddha used the simile of a raft to illustrate the pragmatic value of the moral ideal. William James expressed a similar sentiment when he argued for leaving part of the ideal behind when it came into conflict with the actual.[3]

The Buddha's renunciation of the conception of an absolute moral law and recognition of the validity of concrete or contextual moral conceptions may leave the impression that he justified a form of moral relativism. Relativism is generally frowned upon in ethics, primarily because, if it is true, then any and every act or principle adopted by a person or group of people, from barbarians to the most civilized, has to be recognized as right. Utilitarianism, in its two most popular forms, attempts to determine the *rightness* of an act or a rule. On a superficial level of understanding, one may be tempted to compare such relativism or utilitarianism with Buddhism. However, a warning from the Buddha may prevent such a comparison.

The Buddha was not prepared to decide the rightness or wrongness of an action or a rule in itself. There are acts or rules that may appear to be right in particular contexts or situations. For the Buddha, the rightness or wrongness of an action or a rule does not consist in its situational or contextual validity alone, but rather in what it does to the person or the group of people in the particular context or situation. Thus simply performing an act or adopting a rule because it is viewed as right does not constitute morality. It is the impact of the action or rule on the total personality or the group involved that gives it a moral character—hence the Buddha's statement, "Be moral or virtuous without being made of morals or virtues" *(sīlavā no ca sīlamayo).*[4] The former is genuine; the latter is artificial. A moral person does not go about collecting moral medals. Instead, he or the social group that includes him grows with every moral action performed.

The path of morality thus turns out to be a gradual path. The *Rathavinīta-sutta*[5] is a classic description of this path of moral progress, illustrated by the simile of a journey that requires a relay of seven chariots. Just as a traveler, by means of a relay of chariots, eventually arrives at the end of his journey, so a person eventually reaches freedom and happiness through the cultivation of moral principles. Freedom and happiness thus constitute the ultimate goal or fruit *(paramattha),* that is, a life of knowledge and compassion replacing the ordinary life of greed, hatred, and confusion.

The path to moral perfection constitutes the fourth noble truth and is generally described as the noble eightfold path, which consists of:

1. Right view *(sammā diṭṭhi)*
2. Right conception *(sammā saṅkappa)*
3. Right speech *(sammā vācā)*
4. Right action *(sammā kammanta)*
5. Right livelihood *(sammā ājīva)*

6. Right effort *(sammā vāyāma)*
7. Right mindfulness *(sammā sati)*
8. Right concentration *(sammā samādhi)*

These eight factors illustrate the comprehensive nature of the path of moral perfection recommended by the Buddha. Commenting on the eightfold path, Rhys Davids says, "If this Buddhist ideal of perfect life is remarkable when compared with the thought of India at that time, it is equally instructive when looked at from the comparative point of view."[6] What is instructive from a comparative perspective is that it incorporates the functions of several philosophical traditions which, in the modern world, have tended to remain distinguishable from one another. For example, modern ethical philosophers who belong to the Analytic tradition confine their philosophical enterprise to a mere analysis and clarification of ethical concepts and theories, viewing ethics as a purely descriptive enterprise. Others—for example, some of the Existentialists, like Kierkegaard—consider it a valuable part of the philosopher's vocation to recommend ways of life or modes of conduct that are conducive to the well-being of the individual as well as society (i.e., ethics is a prescriptive enterprise as well). The noble eightfold path is both descriptive and prescriptive. It involves an analytical study of knowledge as well as conception, and highlights factors that are relevant to any prescriptive theory in moral philosophy.

The term *sammā* (Skt. *samyak*) prefixed to the eight factors is generally translated as "right," not because it is based on an absolute truth but because it is comprehensive or complete (as in *sammāsambuddha,* the completely or perfectly enlightened). *Sammā* is the contrary of "wrong" *(micchā,* Skt. *mithyā),* which again is not based on the absolutely false but on the partial or the confused. The moral conceptions of right and wrong are therefore corollaries of the epistemological notions of the true and confused, not of the absolutist true/false dichotomy.

Right View

It is significant that the first factor on the list is right or comprehensive "view" *(diṭṭhi).* Most of the theories prevalent during the Buddha's day were based either on totally subjective perspectives or on ultimately objective perspectives. The *Upaniṣads* seem to have regarded morality as ultimately objective, while the Materialists considered it to be totally subjective. The Buddha considered these to be partial truths *(pacceka-sacca)* established on distinct perspectives *(puthu-niviṭṭha).*[7] For him, a comprehensive view had to account for subjectivity as well as objectivity; hence the importance of "right view" *(sammā diṭṭhi)* as the first step in the path of moral perfection.

The discourse to Kaccāyana, quoted in full in Chapter IV, was delivered in response to a question regarding the nature of right view. According to the Buddha, the world is generally inclined toward two views, one of existence and the other of non-existence. Although he looked upon both as unsatisfactory, the theory of existence *(atthitā)* was what attracted most of his attention. Even though it was meant to be a theory about an objective reality, *atthitā* was an extremely subjective view arising out of a misinterpretation of ordinary self-awareness and culminating in a metaphysical theory of a permanent and eternal self or soul *(ātman)*. The Buddha perceived such a view as generating excessive attachment, which beclouds our perception of the human predicament (i.e., the problem of suffering). The theory of non-existence *(n'atthitā)* is simply a strong reaction against the excessively subjective view, and another attempt to reach out for objectivity that turns out to be equally excessive. The right view, according to the Buddha, is a middle perspective that avoids the excesses of subjectivity and objectivity.

Right Conception

The adoption of wrong views may be considered a result of our inability to understand the nature and function of conception *(saṅkappa)*. Conceptions are formed in various ways by human beings. A conceiving mind is necessarily involved; however, not every conception so conceived earns the status of a meaningful conception. It must relate to an object, whether mental or material, that a community of intelligent beings can agree on. In this sense, the difference between a conception and a convention is reduced to a great extent. In another sense, a conception is a substitute for our experience, and its validity depends on its experiential reference. Very often this experiential reference is extended beyond its limit with a view to discovering the meaning of a conception, and the empirical content is thereby obliterated. The end product is the incorruptible Platonic "idea" (see Chapters III and XX). As in his analysis of views *(diṭṭhi)*, the Buddha realized that a person's excessive attachment to conceptions *(saṅkappa-rāga)* poses difficulties to understanding their functional value.[8]

In the descriptions of the noble eightfold path, two types of conceptions are referred to. These are moral conceptions of negative as well as positive value. The negative moral conceptions are: conception of pleasures associated with lust *(kāma-saṅkappa)*, conception of ill-will *(byāpāda-saṅkappa)*, and conception of harm *(vihiṃsā-saṅkappa)*.[9] The conceptions of positive moral quality are: conception of renunciation *(nekkhamma-saṅkappa)*, conception of good-will *(abyāpāda-saṅkappa)*, and conception of non-harming or compassion *(avihiṃsā-saṅkappa)*.[10] It is easy to see how the negative moral conceptions are related to the wrong conceptions about experiential objects or reference. They are the corollaries of the views pertaining to absolute existence and non-existence referred to earlier. Similarly, the positive moral conceptions are the counterparts of the conception of "dependent arising" *(paṭiccasamuppāda)*, which recognizes the value of both subject and object and prevents the generation of both attraction and revulsion *(anurodha-virodha)*,[11] the source of most human suffering *(dukkha)*. Right views and right conceptions thus serve as springboards on the path toward moral progress.

Right Speech

Refraining from speaking falsehood is one of the five basic moral precepts *(pañca-sīla)* recommended for the layperson. For the philosopher, this may appear to be simple "moralizing." However, for the Buddha, it goes far beyond that because it involves the conceptions of truth and relevance.

The Buddha's doctrine *(dhamma)* is often described as being well spoken *(svakkhāta)*, not because it conforms to or mirrors an ultimate truth but because it is based on experience *(sandiṭṭhika)*, which is not confined to a particular time *(akālika)* but is verifiable *(ehipassika)* and goal-directed *(opanayika)*, and whose meaning is realizable by intelligent human beings *(paccattaṃ veditabbo viññūhi)*.[12] Indeed, any speech that does not fulfill these requirements would be harmful or even meaningless. We have already discussed the contents of the *Discourse to Prince Abhaya (Abhayarājakumāra-sutta)* in Chapter III; there speech or statements *(vācā)* are classified according to their truth-value, pragmatic character, and emotive content. This means that the relevance or goal-directedness of speech provides a moral justification for avoiding wrong speech, such as falsehood, slander, harsh words, and frivolous talk or gossip.[13] Right speech is thus defined as "that which does not lead to one's own torment *(tapa)* nor to another's injury *(vihiṃsā)*." Positively, it is speech that is pleasant to others without simultaneously contributing to evil. The best speech leads to the cessation of suffering and the attainment of freedom, and such speech is attributed to the enlightened ones.[14]

Right Action

The Buddha avoided the behaviorism advocated by some of the Indian Materialists by almost always speaking of three forms of behavior *(kamma)*—mental *(mano)*, verbal *(vaci)*, and bodily *(kāya)*.[15] Furthermore, the importance attached to conception and speech, as mentioned earlier, eliminated any behavioristic model of explanation. More troublesome than the behavioristic model was the explanation and evaluation of action adopted by the orthodox school of Indian thought and by Jainism. While the orthodox school provided a rather deterministic view of action combined with an absolutistic criterion, namely, the conception of duty based on the caste system, the Jainas advocated an extremely deterministic view of past action *(pubbekatahetu)* that eliminated any choice or free will (see Chapter 1). The Buddha's explanation of human action as part of a more comprehensive process of dependent arising, and the evaluation of action in terms of consequences or fruits *(attha)*—i.e., a pragmatic criterion—compelled him to emphasize the need for constant mindfulness or reflection. This idea is clearly expressed in the Buddha's discourse to the novice Rāhula, his own son. A passage from the discourse reads as follows:

> What do you think about this, Rāhula? What is the purpose of a mirror?
> Its purpose is reflection, reverend sir.
> Even so, Rāhula, a deed is to be done with the body [only] after repeated reflection; a deed is to be done with speech . . . with the mind [only] after repeated reflection.
> If you, Rāhula, are desirous of doing a deed with the body, you should reflect on that deed of your body, thus: "That deed which I am desirous of doing with the body is a deed of my body that might conduce to the harm of myself and that might conduce to the harm of others and that might conduce to the harm of both; this deed of body is unskilled, its yield is anguish, its result is anguish." If you, Rāhula, reflecting thus, should find, "That deed which I am desirous of doing with the body is a deed of my body that would conduce to the harm of myself and to the harm of others and to the harm of both; this deed of body is unskilled, its yield is anguish, its result is anguish"—a deed of body like this, Rāhula, is certainly not to be done by you. But if you, Rāhula, while reflecting thus, should find, "That deed which I am desirous of doing with the body is a deed of my body that would conduce neither to the harm of myself nor to the harm of others nor to the harm of both; this deed of body is skilled, its yield is happy, its result is happy"—a deed of body like this, Rāhula, may be done by you.[16]

If there were any ultimate criterion for deciding what right action is, it would be the happiness of oneself as well as of others. In the context of a world of impermanence and change, an element of skepticism is involved, which, in turn, calls for a touch of heroism in human behavior. However, to prevent that heroism from deteriorating into some form of foolhardiness, the Buddha encouraged reflection or mindfulness *(satipaṭṭhāna)*, often described as the most significant and "royal" road to purity of human behavior.[17]

Right Livelihood

The Buddha's recognition that the highest form of life is one of freedom *(nibbāna)* from craving *(taṇhā)* has given rise to the impression that Buddhism inculcates an absolutely otherworldly life of asceticism and deprivation with no concern for satisfaction of the physical needs of the human being. Yet the number of his disciples who adopted such austere *(dhutaṅga)* lives is surprisingly small. Indeed, the Buddha allowed those who preferred such a life to adopt it, without making it a necessary condition of the higher life *(brahmacariya)*.[18] The higher life is the culmination of the moral life *(dhammacariya)*. As pointed out earlier, the moral life is not totally distinguished from the good life; rather, it turns out to be the common ground between the good life and the higher life.

The moral character of the good life of an ordinary layperson is fourfold. In his discourse to the banker Anāthapiṇḍika, the Buddha enumerated four characteristics of the good life: (1) well-being relating to resources *(atthi-sukha)*, that is, a life of sufficient means achieved through one's effort without resorting to fraud and trickery; (2) economic well-being *(bhoga-sukha)* or happiness resulting from the enjoyment of lawfully acquired wealth; (3) happiness consequent upon being free from debt *(anaṇa-sukha)*; and (4) the happiness of being free from blame *(anavajja-sukha)*.[19]

Right Effort

In the speculations of the thinkers of the pre-Buddhist *Upaniṣads*, the individual human will or effort received the "great extension," thereby paving the way for the recognition of a universal soul or self *(ātman)*, which, when combined with an absolute moral law *(brahman)*, ultimately led to denial of the efficacy of that individual or phenomenal will. The reaction of the Materialists to such a metaphysical conception led to similar consequences, for their view of nature *(svabhāva)* prevented any meaningful discussion of individual human initiative *(purisa-thāma, purisa-parakkama*; see Chapter 1). While denying a mysterious "ghost in the machine," the Buddha reduced the universal and objective laws to linguistic convention, thereby accommodating an element of skepticism. His explanation of causality as "dependent arising" eliminated the obsessive belief in error-free knowledge. This, in turn, requires human beings to process whatever information they obtain in order to construct their worldview. It is such processing, together with conforming to whatever discoveries are made through such processing, that is designated the will, and not any mysterious psychic principle. Thus the Buddha recognized four forms of effort *(padhāna)*:

1. Preventive effort *(saṃvara)*, that is, the non-grasping after conceptions of substance *(nimitta)* and qualities *(anuvyañjana)* on occasions of sense experience. This, as mentioned earlier, is the restraint of the senses that prevents the influx of unwholesome thoughts, etc.

2. Effort at relinquishing *(pahāna),* that is, the will or determination to abandon evil and unwholesome thoughts that have already arisen.
3. Effort to develop *(bhāvanā),* that is, to initiate and develop wholesome attitudes that are yet to arise. This is an extremely important part of culture, for it determines the direction in which life on this planet can move. The attitudes listed are seven in number (generally referred to as the seven factors of enlightenment, *satta-bojjhaṅga*), namely, mindfulness, discernment of the good, energy, rapturous joy, calm, concentration, and consideration. Although these have been explained in the tradition as the constituents of enlightenment *(bodhi),* there is no need to restrict that enlightenment to the individual; it also can mean the enlightenment and freedom of a society or even the whole of humanity. Taken in this larger context, it implies the effort to develop oneself as well as others. Indeed, the seven factors of enlightenment are more meaningful when their application is extended to society and morals.
4. Effort to maintain *(anurakkhaṇa),* that is, to maintain wholesome and favorable objects of concentration. Here again, the tradition is prone to interpret the object of concentration as referring to objects of individual meditative practices. In a more comprehensive sense, objects of concentration can include events, states, and processes *(dhammā)* that produce good consequences for the society as well. Programs and projects that are beneficial to a human being and to society are often initiated but rarely maintained. Again, the absence of absolutely deterministic laws is clearly asserted; hence the Buddha's advice to put forth effort to maintain what is good.[20]

Right Mindfulness

The essentialist search for truth and reality seems to have contributed to how mindfulness in Buddhism has been understood by some classical as well as modern interpreters. Mindfulness is often understood as a way of cleansing the mind of all discriminations and conceptions, leading to a preconceptual stage of perception. However, in the description of mindfulness available in the very popular discourse on *The Setting up of Mindfulness (Satipaṭṭhāna),* one is urged to reflect on or perceive retrospectively *(anupassanā)* the functioning of the physical personality *(kāya),* feelings or sensations *(vedanā),* thought *(citta),* and ideas *(dhamma).*[21] As with the previous factors of the moral path, reflective awareness is rendered necessary by the epistemological difficulties human beings face in trying to understand reality. Reflective awareness is an extremely important means of knowing when knowledge of things "as they really are" is not a possibility. It is radical empiricism—the recognition that experience is not atomic but a flux whose content is invariably associated with the past. This is the basis of the Buddha's conception of "dependent arising." While admitting the usefulness of knowledge of the past *(pubbante ñāṇa),*[22] the Buddha dissuaded his disciples from pursuing such knowledge much beyond the limits of experience, because this could lead to dogmatic views in relation to the past *(pubbantānudiṭṭhi).*[23]

Right Concentration

Right concentration is of extreme importance as *the* means of making a decision regarding behavior. The danger involved in following a radical empiricist approach, namely, that of generating dogmatic views about the origin of things by going beyond experience, is eliminated by following this step. That is to say, once past *experience* has provided some understanding of an event, state, or process, it becomes necessary to focus on that understanding (without undertaking a wild-goose chase) and use that understanding in order to act. What is focused upon is a healthy or wholesome event, state, or process, the criterion for healthiness or wholesomeness being the happiness of oneself and others.

The above analysis of concentration would mean that there is no absolutely true or real event, state, or process on which the wayfarer can focus. In the absence of absolute knowledge, constant revision of our understanding and behavior becomes inevitable. The Buddha was always prepared to adopt such revisions, as long as the reason for them was the welfare of all beings. It was due to his compassion for beings *(sattesu anukampā)* that he refused to assert statements about truth unconditionally.[24]

It is this form of revision that is embodied in the Buddha's statement that "even the good has to be abandoned, let alone the evil." He faithfully followed such revisionism by revoking the rules of monastic behavior *(vinaya)* for monks and nuns whenever he found that they were no longer useful.[25]

CHAPTER XI

Popular Religious Thought

The philosophical content of the Buddha's doctrine, as analyzed above, is often viewed as exotic or even incompatible with the popular beliefs and practices current among his ordinary lay disciples. After almost a century of modern Buddhist scholarship and Western academic struggle to decipher and understand the Buddhist conceptual framework, sociologists and anthropologists, following a paradigm developed by Robert Redfield and his associates at the Chicago School of Anthropology during the late 1950's, have come to distinguish between a "Great Tradition" and a "Little Tradition" in Buddhism.[1] The "Great Tradition" is supposed to be enshrined in the canonical Buddhist texts, espoused by Buddhist monks, scholars, and intellectuals, and propagated by the seats of higher learning in Buddhist countries. The "Little Tradition," in contrast, represents the popular religion practiced by the uneducated villager, who has no clues as to what the essential doctrines of Buddhism are and who has simply adopted pre-Buddhist animistic beliefs and religious rituals.

This interpretation of Buddhism as ordinarily practiced in the Asian countries ignores the significant fact that the basic teachings of the Buddha, whether these pertain to truth, morality, or any other topic, have permeated the ordinary religious consciousness through sermons delivered regularly by monks and nuns in village temples. Indeed, before the Western form of education was introduced, through a system of public and private schools, by the colonizers of Asian countries, the village temple was the sole educational institution for the dissemination both of moral and religious ideas and of knowledge of more mundane subjects, such as medicine and astrology. Local monks and nuns were the perpetuators of the Buddha's doctrine, and they depended heavily on Buddhist literature as their source material. Despite occasional quibbling over details of philosophical interpretation, it is possible to observe an unbroken continuity in philosophical standpoint, which is reflected in the popular and elaborate religious rituals of both the Theravāda and Mahāyāna traditions (see Chapter XXII). The same is true of the most basic ritual performed by every Buddhist layman *(upāsaka)* and laywoman *(upāsi-*

kā), whatever their sectarian differences. This basic ritual is generally referred to as "taking refuge" *(saraṇāgamana)* in the Three Gems *(ratana):* the Buddha, the doctrine *(dhamma),* and the community *(saṅgha).*

The idea of "taking refuge" derives primarily from how the so-called Three Gems are conceived, so it is extremely important to clarify their meaning before examining the nature and function of the ritual itself. The three statements uttered at the time of "taking refuge" provide an almost complete definition of the Three Gems, a definition that clearly demarcates what each conception is and is not.

The Buddha

In the Pali language, the description of the Buddha or the Enlightened One reads as follows:

> *iti pi so bhagavā arahaṃ sammāsambuddho vijjacaraṇasampanno sugato lokavidū anuttaro purisadamma-sarathī satthā devamanussānaṃ.*[2]

The statement simply refers to nine characteristics of the Buddha *(nava-guṇa).* These characteristics are best understood in the context of the body of doctrines available to us in the earliest source material, namely, the discourses of the Buddha.

The first characteristic of this person is that he is a "fortunate one" *(bhagavā).* The usual translation of the term as "Lord" carries the implication of domination or overlordship, an idea rejected by the Buddha himself.[3] A second rendering of the terms as "Blessed One" can have the sense of being blessed by someone else, an idea that gained currency in the later Buddhist tradition, when it was believed that every prospective buddha (i.e., *bodhisattva*) has to be blessed by a previous buddha. However, if we consider the conception of *bhagavā* in the context of early Buddhism, it is more appropriate to translate it as "fortunate one," thereby avoiding the two extreme implications of overlordship and other-dependence. A fortunate person is one who, provided with proper surroundings *(paṭirūpadesa),* makes use of them through right application *(attasammāpaṇidhi)* and reaches the pinnacle of moral perfection.

Second, the Buddha is "worthy" *(arhat)* of esteem and respect. His life is esteemed and his personality respected because of his achievements. Born into this world *(loke jāto)* like any other human being, conditioned by a multitude of factors and subjected to various forms of suffering, he has been able to overcome most of that suffering by developing a perfect moral character. As such, the esteem and respect he elicits from other human beings is altogether different from that elicited by an omnipotent being with unlimited creative power. Admiration is the cause of the veneration accorded to the Buddha, whereas fear and trepidation generate respect for and obedience to a supreme being. For this very reason, the "refuge" afforded by the former is different from that expected from the latter.

The third characteristic consists of his being perfectly enlightened *(sammāsambuddha)*. Perfect enlightenment does not mean "omniscience" *(sabbaññū)* in an absolute sense. The use of the conception of "all" or "everything" *(sabbaṃ)* is extremely limited in the Buddhist context (see Chapter III): it is limited to what is empirically given as well as to what can be inferred from such empirical knowledge. Perfection implies the absence of the defiling influxes *(āsava)*, one of which is the search for a permanent and absolute essence in the subject as well as in the object. One "taking refuge" in the Buddha, therefore, cannot expect him to provide answers to most of the questions generated by one's unbounded curiosity and inclination.[4] The Buddha's knowledge is confined to what is empirically verifiable and morally significant.

Fourth, he is endowed with knowledge and conduct *(vijjācaraṇasampanna)*. This does not simply mean that he has knowledge as well as conduct, but implies the more significant fact that his conduct is in conformity with his knowledge. Rejecting any claim to absolute knowledge, he does not assert any form of absolute moral principle. Without asserting any absolute moral principle, how can he lead a morally significant life? The fact is that, in order to lead a morally significant life, it is not necessary to claim any knowledge of an absolute moral law. Indeed, for the Buddha, it is the very adherence to an absolute moral law that prevents a person from recognizing the moral content of certain forms of behavior that may be incompatible with such a moral law. This is not very different from the context where claims to absolute knowledge prevent the admission of different possibilities. Conflict and strife are the end result. Not claiming any such absolute knowledge, the Buddha could recognize contextual and pragmatically relevant moral principles, and, as such, not take on a burden he could not carry. In fact, he is one who has laid aside the burden *(ohitabhāra)*, unlike his Chinese contemporary, Confucius, who regarded the practice of morality *(jen)* as a burden.[5] The Buddha's maximum claim in the sphere of the moral life was not to harm himself or others, a claim he was able to uphold until the last moment of his life.

The fifth characteristic implies that he is "well-gone" *(sugata)*, in the sense that he has achieved the highest happiness a human being can aspire to, namely, physical and psychological "well-being." Not only is he free of the suffering resulting from greed, hatred, and confusion, he also enjoys a life devoted to the service of others as a result of his knowledge, understanding, and compassion. His life is an achievement both for himself and for others.

The sixth characteristic is the Buddha's knowledge of the world *(lokavidū).* For him, knowing the world does not imply unraveling all the assumed mysteries. Metaphysicians view the world, for the most part, as either permanent and eternal or discontinuous and haphazard. Knowledge of these assumptions about the world is as good as knowledge of the world, for by understanding the inclinations and proclivities of the human beings who propound such theories, one can avoid the pitfalls into which one can fall when investigating the nature of the world. Thus the Buddha's explanation of the world as "dependently arisen" *(paṭicca-samuppanna)* is the result of the appeasement of such dispositions and the consequent renunciation of the search for mystery.

The seventh characteristic consists of his being "unexcelled" *(anuttara).* As someone who has reached the ultimate goal of human life, the Buddha may have his equals, especially those disciples who reached a similar state of moral perfection, but there is no one and nothing superior to him. Placing himself in such a situation, he avoids two absolutist assumptions: that there is a supreme being to whom all human beings are subordinate, and that there is an ultimate moral law to which all humans must conform. The only claim he made that distinguishes him from his disciples is the fact that he was the teacher *(satthā),* which is highlighted by the next two characteristics.

The eighth characteristic is the Buddha's ability to restrain or tame human beings like an expert charioteer *(purisa-damma-sārathī).* Although he could perform miracles, such powers were not what made him an incomparable tamer; rather, it was his knowledge of the psychological constitution of human beings, coupled with a deep sense of compassion, that made him the "best communicator." Murderers like Angulimāla and courtesans like Ambapāli were restrained and led to follow morally acceptable lives primarily through psychological treatment, not by magic or coercion. In modern terms, the Buddha would be regarded as a supreme psychiatrist.

Finally, the Buddha is a "teacher of gods and humans" *(satthā deva-manussānaṃ).* He is not a messiah bringing a message from someone else. Here again, the burden he assumes is not extraordinary; he simply claims to teach others what he himself has discovered through a strenuous process of mental and moral discipline. The effectiveness of his teaching speaks for the quality of that mental and moral perfection. While it is true that a successful teaching career compelled the Buddha's disciples to regard him as *the* incomparable leader, he refused to acknowledge such a status for himself.[6] Furthermore, he certainly denied that he was a savior, representing himself merely as a guide.[7]

This statement about the character of the Buddha is uttered by every Buddhist when he "takes refuge" in the first of the Three Gems. Indeed, it makes it impossible to anticipate any form of protection *(patiṭṭhā)* from him, for the Buddha is no more than the ideal person. However, to be constantly aware of such moral perfection can be of enormous benefit as one continues one's struggles in this world. In fact, the ordinary layperson who is raised in a Buddhist context normally "takes refuge" *(saraṇa)* in the Buddha while seeking protection or support *(patiṭṭhā)* from the gods, for gods are beings who have attained enormous powers as a result of leading virtuous lives,[8] even though they can never attain enlightenment and freedom *(nibbāna)* while in that state.

Thus "taking refuge" and seeking protection or support are two entirely different activities. To receive protection one has to placate the gods, be indebted or obliged to them. Hence the popular Buddhist practice of donating the merits of one's own good actions to the gods as a symbolic gift. No such offering is made to a buddha. In other words, one need not *surrender* anything when worshiping a buddha. Worshipping a buddha means respecting the ideal moral perfection and a person who has attained that ideal. Any religious person, whatever his religious creed, can appreciate such an ideal and respect such a person, even if he is from a different religious persuasion.

The Dhamma

"Taking refuge" in the doctrine or Dhamma is less problematic. The statement in Pali defining the Dhamma reads as follows:

> *svākhāto bhagavatā dhammo sandiṭṭhiko akāliko ehipassiko opanayiko paccattaṃ veditabbo viññūhi.*[9]

The first characteristic of the Dhamma is that it is well-taught by the Fortunate One *(svākhāto bhagavatā dhammo)*. It is well-taught not because it represents the ultimate and absolute truth but because whatever truth it embodies is presented with clarity, preciseness, and no ambiguity. Statements of truth couched in double negations, though extremely popular in traditional Indian philosophy, were condemned by the Buddha as epistemologically destructive or sinful *(kali;* see Chapter III). In so doing the Buddha was adopting a middle path in his assessment of both language and truth. While denying an absolute truth or truths, the Buddha also avoided extreme skepticism by asserting truths demarcated by epistemological and contextual boundaries. Similarly, without rejecting language as incapable of expressing truth or truths, he recognized the meaningfulness of linguistic convention, once again limited by epistemological as well as contextual boundaries. Without straining either the conception of truth or linguistic convention, the Buddha was able to formulate pragmatically relevant empirical truths in clear, unequivocal language.

This clarity of expression *(svākhāta)* leads to the second characteristic of the Dhamma, namely, experiential content *(sandiṭṭhika)*. The Buddha was emphatic that he did not speak of anything he had not experienced *(adiṭṭha)*,[10] this experience being confined to the six senses and their objective spheres.[11] The highest form of knowledge (as explained in the preceding section, under *sammāsambuddha*), is not totally divorced from sensory experience. *Paññā* (wisdom) is synonymous with cessation of defiling tendencies *(āsavakkhaya)*. This means that the difference between the experiences of an ordinary person and those of an enlightened one has nothing to do with the source or the object of experience; rather, it pertains to the approach one adopts on occasions of experience. This provides for a common denominator between ordinary experience and so-called enlightened experience, thus permitting the formulation of that experience in a language intelligible to the ordinary person. As such, it is a view *(diṭṭhi)* that can be shared. It is a right view *(sammā diṭṭhi)* involving right conception *(sammā saṅkappa)*, in contrast to the wrong views *(micchā diṭṭhi)* based on metaphysical conceptions *(micchā saṅkappa)*. The fact that the Dhamma represents a view that can be shared goes against the popular interpretation of it as "no-view."

The third characteristic is easily misunderstood. The term *kāla* means time; *kālika* would then mean temporal, and *akālika* could then be taken in the sense of atemporal, and therefore permanent and eternal. But such an interpretation would contradict most of the fundamental doctrines of Buddhism, such as those of impermanence and dependent arising. And if the truths recognized in Buddhism are not absolute and eternal, there is no need to speak of the statement of these truths (= Dhamma) as atemporal in the sense of being beyond time. In the context of non-absolutism, the term *akālika* is better understood as "not confined to a particular time," that is, applicable to different times. Relativism becomes an unpalatable conception only against the background of absolutism, but can gain more respectability in the context of non-absolutism.

The fourth characteristic of the Dhamma is verifiability *(ehipassika)*. Here there is no secret teaching revealed or passed down to a few. A person—regardless of caste or creed, without having to abandon a religious or philosophical point of view, and without prior commitment to follow it—can come and take a look. Indeed, what is examined is not an ultimate truth but the truth of the consequences of adopting a moral life—that is, the physical and mental health consequent upon abandoning greed and hatred, the calmness that descends as a result of renouncing the metaphysical search for mysterious substances (i.e., overcoming the cause of epistemological confusion).

The fifth characteristic is related to the fourth, in that the goal of the religious life is not something totally distinct from the empirical conditions of life but the consequence of eliminating the empirical causes of suffering, namely, greed, hatred, and confusion. A large number of discourses are devoted to explaining the evil consequences of these three elements. As it was for the Kālāmas,[12] it would be very difficult for a person to deny that greed, hatred, and confusion result in suffering for oneself as well as for others. The most significant feature of the Buddha's teaching is that this empirically verifiable condition of life (i.e., freedom from greed, hatred, and confusion) becomes the ultimate goal or fruit *(paramattha)* of the religious life. As a result of the ultimate goal being reduced to such experience, without being elevated to a transcendent reality, the Buddha had no difficulty claiming that the doctrine leads to the desired goal *(opanayika)*.

Finally, the Dhamma is to be experienced by oneself *(paccattaṃ veditabbo)*. Realizing the temperaments of human beings who would be rather reluctant to restrain their craving, greed, and the like even if they were willing to renounce hatred, the Buddha made the qualification that the Dhamma is to be experienced by the intelligent or the wise ones *(viññūhi)*. These are not simply people with the highest "intelligence quotient"; rather, they are prudent people who can realize the unfortunate consequences of the immoral life and who are willing to adopt a moral life conducive to one's own happiness as well as to the well-being of others.

The Dhamma so defined, like the conception of the Buddha, need not be an obstacle to anyone attempting to share it. There is no special sorting of human beings to find out whether or not they are capable of receiving instruction on it. One is not expected to have blind faith *(amulikā saddhā)* before one is initiated into it.[13] It is an open doctrine.

It is true that Buddhism recognizes a gradual path to ultimate enlightenment and freedom. Those who are enamored with mysterious substances within the subject as well as the object will need instruction from a teacher regarding the process of deconstruction, which will eventually make them realize the non-substantiality of all phenomena *(sabbe dhammā anattā)*.[14] According to the Buddha, this is the most difficult aspect of the doctrine to grasp,[15] because anxiety *(paritassanā)* prevents people from giving up the belief in a permanent and eternal self and in permanent, immutable substances.[16] However, in the process of receiving instruction, there is nothing mystical and indefinable that is passed on from teacher to student. It is rather unfortunate that the relationship between teacher and student, and the nature of the instruction imparted by teacher to student, have come to be so much mystified in the more recent explanation of Buddhism, making it seem that it is almost impossible to practice the Dhamma without shaving one's head, donning a yellow (or grey) robe, and sitting by a teacher for a special non-verbal transmission.

The Saṅgha

The last of the Three Gems is the Saṅgha or the Order of Disciples, described in the following manner:

supaṭipanno bhagavato sāvakasaṅgho ujupaṭipanno bhagavato sāvakasaṅgho ñāyapaṭipanno bhagavato sāvakasaṅgho sāmīcipaṭipanno bhagavato sāvakasaṅgho yadidaṃ cattāri purisayugāni aṭṭhapurisapuggalā esa bhagavato sāvakasaṅgho āhuneyyo pahūṇeyyo dakkhiṇeyyo añjalikaraṇeyyo anuttaraṃ puññakkhettaṃ lokassa.[17]

This lengthy description refers to only four characteristics of the disciples: that they are well-behaved *(supaṭipanno),* straightforward *(ujupaṭipanno),* methodical *(ñāyapaṭipanno),* and correct *(sāmīcipaṭipanno).*

The relationship between the means and the goal is highlighted by the terms "well-behaved" *(supaṭipanna)* and "well-gone" *(sugata).* Being "well-behaved," they are intent upon the ultimate goal achieved by a person who is "well-gone," which, as mentioned earlier, is one of the characteristics of the Buddha.

[To be well-behaved means to be straightforward in one's behavior, not deceptive. The recognition of an ultimate reality transcending the ordinary world of experience has sometimes contributed to the view that deceptive "means" can be justified by the "goal." The Buddhist conception of "skill in means" *(upāya-kosalla,* Skt. *upāya-kauśalya)* does not include such deceptive means, for the goal is not so far removed or distinguished from the means. Thus deception in any form, whether intended to achieve good or bad ends, is not condoned in Buddhism.]

It is possible to interpret this straightforwardness as pointing to a single definite path of behavior as the only right path, but this would contradict the conception of truth presented in our discussion of the Dhamma. Straightforwardness equated with rightness would generate the conception of "one way" *(eka-yāna).* Buddhism does not recognize one single way. Instead, it speaks of one goal *(ekāyana),* which is human freedom and happiness.[18] As such, one can speak of a gradual path *(anupada),*[19] and this involves the idea of an appropriate method *(ñāya).* The denial of an absolute truth does not mean that the world is chaotic or haphazard. The principle of dependent arising *(paṭiccasamuppāda)* avoids both strict determinism and chaotic indeterminism.[20] Reflective awareness *(anupassanā)* in the form of constant mindfulness *(sati)* is the means of discovering an appropriate method of behavior in a world of bewildering variety, richness, and creativity.[21] One who adopts such mindfulness is able gradually to develop a method of behavior that need not necessarily conform to a preordained conception of "duty."

Conforming to the nature of the world (i.e., impermanence, non-substantiality, and dependent arising), a mindful and alert disciple adopts a means that leads to his own happiness and the happiness of others. Such is the correct behavior *(sāmīci-paṭipanna)* with which a disciple is endowed.

If the disciples of the Buddha are endowed with these four characteristics, they are worthy of veneration, hospitality, magnanimity, and respect. They represent an incomparable source of merit *(puññakkhetta)* for the world, since they are the living aspirants to the moral ideal represented by the Buddha. If this moral ideal caused no problems for people of other faiths, there would seem to be no reason why the aspirants to that moral ideal should be looked upon as alien by people of different religious persuasions. The Saṅgha or community of disciples would then be a veritable source of merit not in its own right, but because it represents a community that cultivates a noble moral ideal *(dhamma-cārī).*

For these reasons, the translation of the term *saraṇa* as "refuge" needs to be reconsidered. We have already indicated that *saraṇa* is different from *patiṭṭhā.* In the case of the latter, there is at least an outside agency (i.e., powerful beings like gods) to provide protection. Yet such protection is not forthcoming regardless of whether a person is good or bad. Gods protect those who follow a virtuous life, not an evil one, for they themselves have become gods as a result of being virtuous. In the case of the former, there is no such outside agency: it is the moral life itself that becomes a source of protection *(dhammo have rakkhati dhammacāriṃ).*[22] In this sense, in "taking refuge" in the Three Gems, a person is taking refuge in himself *(attā hi attano nātho),*[23] in utilizing his own moral life as a shield against the hazards of existence. Thus "taking refuge" in the Three Gems means no more than depending on one's own moral behavior to ward off calamities. What is significant is that even though the refuge formulas are recited in Pali and ordinary followers are not normally conversant with the Pali language, they are not completely unaware of what is being recited. The reason for this is that the concepts involved are often discussed by Buddhist monks when they deliver a sermon. Books in the various indigenous languages of Buddhist countries elaborating on the nature and function of the Three Gems are available in abundance. For example, texts in Sinhalese like the *Butsaraṇa (Taking Refuge in the Buddha), Dahamsaraṇa (Taking Refuge in the Dhamma"), and Sangasaraṇa (Taking Refuge in the Sangha)* have been extremely popular for centuries. Thus it is not correct to maintain that ordinary laypeople follow the "Little Tradition," consisting of animistic beliefs and religious rituals. If the ordinary followers of Buddhism in the modern world have lost touch with the more academic understanding of their religion, this is primarily due to the introduction of the Western system of education since the colonization of these countries, and to the almost total elimination of the regular dissemination of Buddhist philosophical and moral ideas.

PART TWO
CONTINUITIES AND DISCONTINUITIES

CHAPTER XII

The Emergence of Absolutism

The Buddha's tough-minded approach toward theories of knowledge, conceptions of reality, morals, and language made him adopt a middle standpoint avoiding the extremes of absolutism, both eternalistic and nihilistic. Yet this was not a very comfortable *modus operandi* for some of his disciples, who had been born and reared in absolutistic Brahmanical surroundings. The emergence of absolutistic tendencies can be perceived both during the Buddha's lifetime and after his death.

Absolutistic Tendencies during the Buddha's Lifetime

The accuracy with which the canonical texts portray the Brahmanical response to the Buddha's teachings could not be more appropriately reflected than in the incident relating to the Buddha's first encounter with a human being after his attainment of enlightenment and freedom. On his way to Bārānasi, in search of the five friends with whom he had practiced severe self-mortification and who were to become his first disciples, the Buddha was resting under the cool shade of a tree in the hot afternoon, when an ascetic named Upaka approached him and inquired, "Whom do you follow, friend, upon leaving the world? Who is your teacher and whose doctrine do you profess?" Responding to Upaka, the Buddha claimed that he had eliminated all epistemological constraints in order to be free and happy without looking for authority and credentials derived from a tradition. Surprisingly, Upaka did not ask for clarification or elaboration but left the Buddha, saying, "So be it."[1]

Interestingly, the Buddhists who were responsible for collecting the Buddha's discourses and preserving them for posterity were not reluctant to report this rather inauspicious beginning. In fact, they seem to underscore its importance, probably to indicate that the Buddha's ideas constituted a revolution that did not appeal to the traditionalists.

The novel, the new, the creative, in whatever context it appears—epistemology, metaphysics, ethics, or any other discipline—is initially confronted by a traditional opponent, namely, absolutism, whose tentacles gradually embrace and squeeze the life out of it. The process of the absorption of the new by the old was beautifully summarized by William James when he spoke of the classic stages of a theory's career:

> First, you know, a new theory is attacked as absurd; then it is admitted to be true, but obvious and insignificant; finally it is seen to be so important that its adversaries claim that they themselves discovered it.[2]

The same was true of the ideas expressed by the Buddha. The reluctance of his five former friends even to receive him with some respect when he first visited them after his enlightenment is indicative of how the unusual is often received.

However, more pronounced is the way in which absolutism keeps raising its head. As pointed out earlier, the Buddha continued to oppose the idea that there can be absolute knowledge, except regarding the determination with which an enlightened one resists his own temptations. It is this latter knowledge that is reflected in the conception of freedom attained by the enlightened ones (see Chapter III). Yet some of his contemporaries soon began to speculate about the nature and scope of the Buddha's knowledge, sometimes attributing to him absolute "omniscience" *(sabbaññutā)* comparable to that claimed by his senior contemporary, Vardhamāna Mahāvīra.[3] These attributions reveal the tendency to single out and exaggerate the *intellectual* content of enlightenment, assuming that the Buddha could not have succeeded in converting people as he did unless he possessed absolute knowledge of everything in the past, present, and future. Some disciples began to look for infinite intellectual capacities, far beyond what the Buddha had claimed, and even to ignore the more important moral content of his life. He was being elevated to the level of a supreme being. But even though the overwhelming veneration with which he was treated by some of his unenlightened disciples, like Ānanda, may have provided an impetus for the transcendentalist and absolutist view of buddhahood,[4] more often it was the followers of the Brahmanical tradition who raised questions that eventually lent themselves to an absolutistic interpretation of the conception of a buddha. The most striking example is the discussion between the Buddha and a brahman named Doṇa.[5] Observing the serene and peaceful personality of the Buddha, Doṇa approached the Buddha and questioned him:

Doṇa:	Sir, are you a god *(deva)?*
Buddha:	Brahman, I am not a god.
Doṇa:	Sir, are you a *gandhabba* [water spirit]?
Buddha:	Brahman, I am not a *gandhabba.*
Doṇa:	Sir, are you a *yakkha* [powerful demon]?
Buddha:	Brahman, I am not a *yakkha.*

Doṇa: Sir, are you a human *(manussa)?*
Buddha: Brahman, I am not a human.

Doṇa was confused. He had tried to understand the Buddha in relation to every personality, human or non-human, known to him. The Buddha denied every identification Doṇa attempted. Hence the brahman asked, "Who, then, are you?" The Buddha's response was that he had eliminated and destroyed those influxes that would make him a god, a *gandhabba,* a *yakkha,* or a human. Like a lotus or water lily *(puṇḍarīka)* that grows in the water, is nourished by the water, but rises above and remains unsmeared by it, the Buddha has been born in this world, nourished by this world, but has risen above and remains unsmeared by it. Hence, said the Buddha, "Brahman, take me to be a *buddha* [enlightened one]."

The Buddha's response to brahman Doṇa is easily interpreted as an admission that buddhahood indeed goes beyond all other forms of existence known to human beings. This, in fact, is the statement utilized by the Transcendentalists in the *Kathāvatthu* to justify their conception of buddhahood (see Chapter XIII). This interpretation—or, rather, misinterpretation—is the result of a non-analytical treatment of the conceptions negated by the Buddha. We have already examined the Buddha's conception of a human person (see Chapter VI). Ordinarily, a human person is one who is born into this world and continues to live in it conditioned by various factors, one of which is consciousness *(viññāṇa)* functioning in terms of interest *(saṅkhāra),* the latter being easily transformed into craving *(taṇhā),* greed *(lobha),* and so forth. Craving and greed represent some of the so-called influxes *(āsava)* that the Buddha has spewed out *(khīṇa)* through appeasement of the dispositions. The difference between the conceptions of a god, *gandhabba, yakkha,* and human on the one hand, and of a *buddha* on the other, is the presence or absence, respectively, of the influxes. The non-analytical treatment ignores precisely this distinction that the Buddha was making. The appeasement of dispositions and the waning of influxes made a significant difference to his own personality. In fact, there was no comparable conception of an enlightened one *(buddha)* in the Brahmanical language, for the Brahmanical conception necessarily implied the permanence and eternality of the self that attains freedom. Hence the Buddha used a most appropriate simile to express his conception of a buddha, namely, the lotus that sprouts in the muddy water, grows in the muddy water, but rises above the water to remain unsmeared by it. There is no implication that the lotus becomes permanent and eternal after it has risen above the water.

It is this psychological and behavioral transformation of an enlightened one that is defined as "a state which is not born, not become, not made, and not dispositionally conditioned" *(ajātaṃ abhūtaṃ akataṃ asaṅkhataṃ;* see Chapter IX). This means that an enlightened one's life is "dependently arisen" *(paṭiccasamuppanna),* and when he, like the lotus, has passed away, one cannot speak about *his* eternal existence, because the very condition that would provide him with even *one more* life after death, that is, grasping after existence *(bhava-taṇhā),* is not found in him. Indeed, this latter discourse, which is one of four that occur together and pertain to freedom *(nibbāna-paṭisaññutta),* is preceded by one that emphasizes the difficulty of perceiving non-substantiality in relation to freedom (see Chapter IX).

Furthermore, when the absolutist failed to absolutize the life of a living buddha, he was quick to raise questions regarding the state of a buddha *after death (param-maraṇā).* The Buddha realized that absolutism can emerge in speculations relating to both states, especially if these speculations focus on ultimate concerns about truth and reality *(sacca, theta).* This is clearly reflected in a dialogue between Sāriputta, one of his leading disciples, and another monk named Yamaka (see Chapter IX).

Yamaka is reported to have misrepresented the Buddha when he maintained that "a brother who has attained the state of the waning of influxes *(āsavakkhaya)* is destroyed and perishes when the body breaks up: he becomes not after death." Sāriputta is represented as arguing that, just as the search for ultimate truth and reality in relation to the person who has attained enlightenment and freedom (= *tathāgata*) is a vain enterprise, so the pursuit of ultimate reality is futile in connection with the freed person after death. There is no question that the person who attains enlightenment and freedom is the human person. If there is no possibility of discovering an ultimate reality in that person (see Chapter VI), there exists no means by which an ultimate reality can be discovered in him when he attains enlightenment and freedom, either when he is living or when he has passed away. The non-substantiality of the means (= human person in bondage) applies equally to the goal (= a human person who has attained freedom, *tathāgata*). Enlightenment and freedom are achieved through non-grasping at either the means or the goal. Hence the Buddha's statement "Done is what has to be done. There exists no further [achievement] for me" *(kataṃ karaṇīyaṃ, nāparaṃ itthattāya).*[6] So much for the tendency to absolutize the conception of a buddha, a tendency that reflects the almost universal human propensity to reach a conception of absolute knowledge in the form of enlightenment *(bodhi).*

In the sphere of ontology, a similar tendency was responsible for the reintroduction of metaphysical entities to account for the uninterrupted continuity of persons and events. In the history of Buddhism, "Sāti's heresy" is a classic example.[7] Sāti held the wrong view that, according to the Buddha's doctrine, "it is this selfsame consciousness which transmigrates, not another." In fact, Sāti was led to believe in such a view because the

Buddha often spoke of consciousness *(viññāṇa)* as a factor that accounts for the survival of human life after death. Veridical memories of past lives being the most compelling evidence for a theory of survival, the Buddha was willing to recognize consciousness as a causal factor because consciousness *functions in terms of interest and, therefore, memory.* It is this aspect of conditionality that was missing in Sāti's explanation. Thus, before criticizing Sāti, the Buddha was cautious to obtain a further definition of consciousness from him. Without ado, Sāti admitted that consciousness as he understood it represents "*he* who speaks, feels, and *he* who experiences the effects of good and bad deeds in different contexts." What Sāti had in mind was the "owner" (see Chapter VI), the agent behind the acts of speaking, feeling, experiencing—that is, the "inner controller" *(antaryāmin)* of the Upaniṣadic thinkers. The Buddha found fault with Sāti not for explaining survival on the basis of consciousness, but because his description of consciousness was suggestive of a metaphysical agent rather than a function that is "dependently arisen" *(paṭiccasamuppanna)*.

Even though the disciples of the Buddha did not involve themselves in enthusiastic discussions about the ultimate reality of the objective material world, some were concerned with the nature of the aggregates *(khandha)* into which the Buddha analyzed the human personality. Their question probably was, Even if there is no metaphysical agent behind the aggregates, are the aggregates themselves ultimately real? However, the Buddha's continued emphasis on the idea that all five aggregates are impermanent *(anicca)*, unsatisfactory *(dukkha)*, and non-substantial *(anatta)*, as evidenced by the excessively large number of discourses on the subject (see the *Khandha-saṃyutta*),[8] kept his substantialist-minded disciples from raising such a question openly. His statement that "all experienced phenomena are non-substantial" *(sabbe dhammā anattā)*[9] was unambiguous and unequivocal.

Absolutistic Tendencies after the Buddha's Demise

As long as the Buddha was alive, he was able to keep a lid on the tendencies just discussed, thereby preventing the absolutist monster from raising its head. Yet his reluctance to appoint a successor and insistence that the doctrine he taught and the discipline he instituted serve as guides for his future disciples left them with a sense of freedom about interpreting the doctrine as they wished. Indeed, this was what prompted the Buddha to formulate the hermeneutical principles discussed in Chapter V; it was also what led to the holding of the First Council three months after his death. It took almost two and half centuries for the controversies to surface again. When they did, they pertained to three issues discussed earlier, namely, (1) the nature of the continuity of the individual, (2) the reality of the elements that constitute the individual, and (3) the status of the liberated person. These were the primary topics of philosophical controversy during the time of Emperor Aśoka.

Realizing that the Order was divided on doctrinal issues as well as practical affairs, Aśoka is said to have invited one of the most respected monks, Moggalīputta-tissa (see Chapter XIII), to convene a council for purging heretical views and restoring the purity of the Buddha's teachings. The proceedings of this Third Council are recorded in the *Kathāvatthu,* a text that gained canonical status in no time, despite being written by a disciple who lived almost 250 years after the Buddha. It was the doctrinal significance of this work that compelled later commentators to make a special effort to justify its authority and sanctity. This they did by claiming that (1) the Buddha predicted the authorship and contents of this work, and (2) when Moggalīputta-tissa compiled the treatise, he was faithfully following the principles *(naya)* and topics *(mātikā)* established by the Buddha.[10] Even if we suspect the first of these claims, there seems to be no reason to question the second, as long as we are willing to place the *Kathāvatthu* against the background of the discourses of the Buddha and analyze its contents.

Moggalīputta-tissa's analysis and refutation of the heretical views are discussed in Chapter XIII. In the present context, we are interested only in identifying these so-called heresies. It is interesting to note that among the 218 points debated, most of which pertain to minor rules of discipline and the like, there are three major philosophical issues.

Personalists

The *Kathāvatthn* begins with a question about the conception of a "person" *(puggala).*[11] The language in which the question is formulated is important. The question is not Is there a person? but rather Is there a person as an absolute truth, as an ultimate reality? or Is there a person in truth and reality? (*Upalabbhati puggalo saccikaṭṭha-paramaṭṭhenāti,* where the two terms *saccikaṭṭha* and *paramaṭṭha* are reminiscent of the terms *saccato* and *thetato* in the discussion between Sāriputta and Yamaka mentioned earlier and in Chapter IX).

It is the essentialist search for ultimate reality or meaning that left the absolutist dissatisfied with the empirical explanation of the human personality in terms of the five aggregates (see Chapter VI). The problem was confounded when a similar essentialist enterprise gradually gave rise to a theory of moments *(kṣaṇa),* according to which the five aggregates were viewed as having momentary existence. This theory of momentary existence made it most difficult, even for those who were not inclined toward the search for ultimate reality, to explain the identity as well as the continuity in the empirical human person.

The radical empiricism of the Buddha was being confused with atomistic empiricism, like that of David Hume in Western philosophy. Among the Buddhist schools that advocated the most extreme form of this atomism was the Sautrāntika school, whose followers argued that there is not even one moment when a phenomenon *(dharma)* remains in order to be cognized. Thus they were advocates of what came to be popularly known as "a theory of representative perception" *(bāhyārthanumeyavāda)*.[12] The recognition of a static moment *(sthiti-kṣaṇa)*, they argued, would violate the Buddha's conception of impermanence *(anitya)*.

The Sautrāntikas' conception of existence as consisting of momentary and atomic events also led them to insurmountable difficulties in the explanation of causation or dependent arising. At the time of the arising of a momentary event, there could be no other event on which the successor could depend for its arising, for that has already passed away. Hence the Sautrāntikas favored the view that all that is asserted by a theory of dependence is simply "succession" *(samanantara)*, one event following another with no perceivable asymmetric, or even symmetric, relations. They feared that the conceptions of duration and identity would necessarily rule out any notion of change or impermanence. Therefore they were compelled to accept a theory of "creation ex nihilo" *(a-sat-kārya)* of every momentary existence.

The Sautrāntikas' inability to account for the principle of dependence *(pratītyasamutpāda)* led them to a major doctrinal conflict pertaining to the concepts of impermanence and continuity, especially in relation to the human person. This eventually contributed to the specific thesis of the Vatsiputriyas, who propounded the view that there is a "real person" *(santaṃ pudgalaṃ)* who is neither a substance *(dravya)*, like material form *(rūpa)*, nor a mere designation *(prajñapti)*, like milk *(kṣīra)*, this latter being no more than an aggregate of substances.[13] The real person transcended both realistic and nominalistic explanations. The deliberate search for a true and ultimately real person, as recorded in the *Kathāvatthu*, now turns out to be the inescapable solution to a sophisticated philosophical dilemma. The doctrine of the non-substantiality of the human person *(pudgala-nairātmya)*, so faithfully followed by some luminaries of the Buddhist tradition, represents a concerted attempt to resolve or dissolve this dilemma and return to the non-substantialist teachings of the Buddha.

Realists

The second important topic of controversy in the *Kathāvatthu* is the real existence of "everything" *(sabbaṃ)* at all times *(sabbadā)*.[14] The rationalization for this view seems to be that, if there is no mysterious agent possessing the aggregates, at least the aggregates must be real and ultimate. This real and ultimate existence cannot be restricted to the past and present only, but must be extended to future events as well. The absolutist vein in this speculation is that uncertainty relating to future events ought to be overcome, and this can be achieved primarily by admitting that "nothing comes out of nothing." Hence the theory that the essence or reality of everything exists at all times.

The *Kathāvatthu,* of course, makes no attempt to define that essence or reality. That definition appears with the philosophical school known as Sarvāstivāda, a name derived from the very doctrine of "everything exists" *(sabbaṃ atthi,* Skt. *sarvam asti)* discussed in the *Kathāvatthu.* Faced with the difficulties of explaining continuity in the context of a doctrine of moments, as in the case of the Sautrāntikas, the Sarvāstivādins distinguished between a thing, event, or phenomenon and its intrinsic nature *(svabhāva).* This is one of the most explicit and unqualified essentialist views ever to appear in the Buddhist philosophical tradition. It is best illustrated by the ideas of one of its most prominent teachers, Dharmatrāta.[15]

According to Dharmatrāta, a thing, event, or phenomenon *(dharma)* passes through the three periods of time: past, present, and future. In that process, what changes is the manner or mode *(bhāva)* of its appearance, not its substance *(dravya).* It is this substance that came to be referred to as intrinsic nature *(svabhāva).* In the sphere of physical phenomena, the intrinsic nature is manifest, for example, in a piece of gold. A piece of gold may appear in different shapes or be given dissimilar shapes at different times, and these shapes or forms are relative to various conditions. Nevertheless, gold remains the same. In conceptual terms, gold remains a hard word.

Interestingly, Dharmatrāta avoids a positive assertion that there is a permanent *(nitya)* element over and above the changing forms, probably realizing that this form of assertion would openly contradict the Buddhist doctrine of impermanence. Yet such an evasion does not help Dharmatrāta, for the distinction he is making will remain meaningless unless he is committed to the view that the so-called substance is permanent and eternal.

The example taken from physical nature (in this case, gold) to justify the conception of substance is very appealing. However, when the explanation pertains to mental events, a similar substantialist conception can lead to unpalatable conclusions. Thus the recognition of a substantialist conception of pain or suffering *(duḥkha)* is seen to lead to a pessimistic view of life.[16] This fact is recorded in Vasubandhu's *Abhidharmakośabhāṣya,* where it is said, "According to some, there indeed is no feeling of happiness. Everything is suffering."[17] Such pessimism, it is hoped, can be counterbalanced by an equally strong optimism. But the latter requires another essentialist conception, which, in fact, was what the Buddhist metaphysician was proposing. Hence his assertion that "Happy feelings do indeed exist in terms of unique character" *(asty eva svalakṣaṇataḥ sukhā vedanā).*[18] This is no more than the recognition of non-reducible conceptions or conceptual schemes, which is the result of an essentialist perspective.

How this conception of self-nature or substance *(svabhāva)* led to a paradoxical situation regarding causation is evident from another conception introduced by the Sarvāstivādins, that of *kāraṇa-hetu,* generally translated as "material cause." However, its definition as "a material cause is [everything] other than itself" *(svato 'nye karāṇahetuḥ)*[19] would mean that *kāraṇa* as a relation *(hetu)* bears it to all and only the things that "do not bear it to themselves" *(svato 'nye).* To take a more popular example from Western philosophy,[20] a barber is a unique person so long as he shaves others, not himself. If a person were to shave himself, the conception of barber becomes superfluous, for the *service* rendered by a barber is needed only by those who do not shave themselves. This raises the question of whether the barber shaves himself. The answer to this question undercuts the definition of a barber. The search for uniqueness *(svabhāva)* thus leads to a paradox.

The above is the more sophisticated way of arguing that essentially everything exists *(sarvam asti).* When the *Kathāvatthu* controverted the view that "everything exists," it was not refuting an imaginary or harmless conception but one that was to grow cancerous, hence requiring the services of some of the best analytical minds—those of a linguistic philosopher (Nāgārjuna), a psychologist (Vasubandhu), and a logician (Dignāga).

Transcendentalists

The third major problem analyzed in the *Kathāvatthu* is the nature of transcendence attributed to the Enlightened One. This is a continuation of the same kind of absolutist thinking that was prominent during the Buddha's day. At first sight, the tendency to view the Buddha as someone who has *totally* transcended the world, and nirvana as a state of eternal life after death, may seem to be the product of an ordinary untrained, uncritical mind. It is a tendency that is generally said to go hand in hand with confidence or faith that leans toward devotion. It is assumed that this tendency is not found in an intellectual, a trained or a critical human person. This, however, is not always the case. Such tendencies are often uncovered in the intellectual and the non-intellectual, the trained and the untrained, the critical and the non-critical, for they are a product of uncertainty regarding life, which can cause anxiety in almost anyone.

The available evidence seems to suggest that the conception of the Buddha's transcendence was promoted by the scholastic Sarvāstivādins rather than by the Mahāsāṅghikas, who are said to have broken away from the more conservative Sthaviravādins (Pali, Theravādins) during the fourth century B.C. In fact, one of two texts that openly espoused the total transcendence of the Buddha, namely, the *Lalitavistara,* is considered to be a Sarvāstivāda work.[21] It was not impossible for a conception of transcendence to emerge in the Sarvāstivāda school, for even when the Buddha was living, questions about transcendence emerged in connection with speculation about the nature of his knowledge and understanding. Absolute omniscience *(sabbaññutā,* Skt. *sarvajñatva),* involving an unlimited range of perception, both spatial and temporal, was attributed to the Buddha despite his refusal to claim it. One of the major difficulties in claiming such omniscience is the inability to perceive past and future events in the same way present events can be perceived. However, if we accept a substantial entity *(svabhāva)* or an essential quality *(svalakṣaṇa),* it is not impossible to maintain that it exists in an atemporal sense. In spite of the Buddha's warning against such assertions, the Sarvāstivādins insisted on precisely this form of existence, that is, existence during all three periods of time *(sabbadā atthi).* The corollary of this view can be that, if events, things, or phenomena exist in this form, perceiving such form would mean knowledge of all events, things, or phenomena at all times. This is the absolute form of omniscience that the Sarvāstivādins attributed to the Buddha, an attribution based not on the uncritical understanding of an ordinary person but on the extremely sophisticated rationalization of an intellectual. Of course, once the idea is put forward by an intellectual, the uninitiated person is apt to follow it without much hesitation.

The Sarvāstivāda conception of existence, providing a foundation for a theory of omniscience, represents only the positive dimension of a conception of transcendence. However, the dimension of transcendence that became more popular and pervasive, especially after the Buddha's demise, was the negative one, which was in some ways incompatible with the realistic outlook of the Sarvāstivādins. Hence we have to look elsewhere for this more popular conception of transcendence.

The negative dimension of transcendence involves the negation of three conceptions: (1) the historical personality of the Buddha, (2) the authenticity of the doctrine expounded by the historical Buddha and recorded in the early discourses, and (3) the relevance of the Saṅgha as the living embodiment of the doctrine. In other words, what is required is the total replacement of the popular religion based on the *historical trinity* (see Chapter XI) by one that is founded on what may be called an *ahistorical trinity.* Once again, this can be the work of a sophisticated intellect rather than an ordinary, uneducated disciple.

It is of immense interest to note that the three points debated in the *Kathāvatthu* pertain precisely to the historical personality of the Buddha (xviii.1), the authenticity of the discourses (xviii.2), and the significance of the Saṅgha (xvii.6–11). It is also significant that the controversial views are attributed by the later commentators to the Vaitulyavādins, not the Sarvāstivādins. The commentary on the *Kathāvatthu* xvii.6 equates Vaitulyavāda with *mahāsuññatavāda* or "the theory of great emptiness."[22] If this later identification is valid, it would mean that Moggalīputta-tissa was confronted by a theory of transcendence advocated not by the Sarvāstivādins but by a school that was propounding an extreme form of emptiness *(śūnyatā)*.

Even a most superficial reading of some of the later Buddhist texts, *sūtras* as well as *śāstras,* would seem to indicate the existence of two theories of "emptiness," a moderate view and an extreme view. The moderate view can be associated with the middle path advocated by philosophers like Nāgārjuna and Vasubandhu (see Chapters xvi and xix), who emphasized "emptiness" *(śūnyatā)* without denying the empirical or historical content of Buddhist discourse. In contrast, the "great emptiness" *(mahā-śūnyatā)* seems to wipe out empirical and historical content completely. This idea comes into prominence in the *Saddharmapuṇḍarīka-sūtra,* which openly denies the historical Buddha, rejects the doctrinal significance of the early discourses, and condemns the community *(saṅgha),* including the early disciples of the Buddha like Sāriputta and Moggalāna (see Chapter xvii); it reaches its culmination in the *Laṅkāvatāra-sūtra* (see Chapter xviii).

CHAPTER XIII

Moggalīputta-tissa and the *Kathāvatthu*

Moggalīputta-tissa is one of the earliest among the celebrated personalities to appear in the Buddhist tradition after the death of the Buddha. As a result of the deep veneration and respect he elicited from his followers, his life came to be associated with miraculous events and happenings. Thus the *Mahāvaṃsa,* the chronicle of the Theravādins, speaks of the miraculous birth of Moggalīputta-tissa. He was born into a brahman family and during his early days mastered the three *Vedas*. It was a monk named Siggava, a close friend of his family, who was responsible for converting him to the Buddha's doctrine.

It is recorded that with the conversion of the Emperor Aśoka to Buddhism by the monk Nigrodha, the material prosperity of the Buddhist monasteries increased, thereby attracting many undesirables to join the Order. This is perceived as the reason for the emergence of heretical views and unhealthy practices among the Buddhists. Such views and practices are said to have necessitated the Third Council. The hundreds of minor points of discipline debated in the *Kathāvatthu* may vouch for the prevalence of much corruption during this particular period. However, the major doctrinal themes with which it deals—these being three out of 218 topics debated—cannot be issues that sprang up in such a short time. As pointed out in Chapter XII, these were problems that persisted even during the Buddha's day and that continued until Moggalīputta-tissa, urged by the Emperor Aśoka, devised ways and means of refuting them.

Even if we ignore the rest of the *Kathāvatthu,* the refutation of the three major doctrinal heresies alone—those of the Personalist *(puggalavādin),* the Realist *(sabbatthivādin),* and the Transcendentalist *(lokuttaravādin)*—could make Moggalīputta-tissa one of the greatest exponents of Buddhist philosophy since its first enunciation by the Buddha. The present chapter is therefore devoted to an analysis of these three doctrinal issues, and to an evaluation of Moggalīputta-tissa's refutation of the heresies relating to them.

Refutation of the Personalist

In Chapter XII, we saw how the conception of a person, whether ordinary or enlightened, was most susceptible to generating an absolutistic form of thinking. The *Kathāvatthu* is one of the earliest texts to deal with such emergent absolutistic tendencies in the Buddhist tradition. In fact, the conception of person *(puggala)* is the first issue it takes up for lengthy debate. Unfortunately, its subtle philosophical distinctions and abstruse dialogical arguments are couched in such dry, archaic prose that this important philosophical treatise has remained neglected for a considerable period. The first English translation, entitled *The Points of Controversy,* by Shwe Zan Aung and C. A. F. Rhys Davids, was published in 1915 by the Pali Text Society. Yet no detailed study of its contents appeared until 1980, when S. N. Dube published his *Cross Currents in Early Buddhism,* a work focusing more on historical analysis of the issues than on a philosophical interpretation.

The few available discussions of the philosophical method of the *Kathāvatthu* are completely influenced by ideas introduced by the commentator Buddhaghosa; these are accessible to Western scholars through the summaries of the *Abhidhamma Piṭaka* prepared by Nyanatiloka Mahāthera, as well as the translation of Buddhaghosa's commentary, entitled *The Debates Commentary,* appearing under the name of B. C. Law (1940).

Nyanatiloka Mahāthera was one of the earliest scholars from the West to present a detailed study of the Pali Abhidhamma. His *Guide Through the Abhidhamma Piṭaka* (1938) has helped many who did not have the patience to traverse the arid desert of Abhidhamma terminology, analysis, and categories. Unfortunately, his translations of the text and interpretation of the contents remain faithful to the absolutist or substantialist distinctions introduced into the Theravāda tradition, advertently or inadvertently, by Buddhaghosa. One of the most pervasive distinctions pertains to whole and parts. Buddhaghosa espoused the view that the Buddha rejected the whole as being a mere convention *(sammuti)* and the parts as being real, even though the Buddha never used the term "ultimate" *(paramaṃ)* to refer to the parts. Applying this to the problem of the human personality, the medieval Buddhist metaphysicians and most modern scholars reached the hasty conclusion that the personality is unreal, a mere convention, a name, and that the aggregates are ultimately real. In fact, in commenting on the terms *saccikaṭṭha* (absolutely true) and *paramaṭṭha* (ultimately real), Buddhaghosa introduces an essentialist explanation in terms of intrinsic nature *(sabhāva).*[1] Here, no doubt, is the distinction between the nominal and the real, a distinction that is inconsistent with the explanation of the subject or personality in the early Buddhist tradition (see Chapter VI).

Before analyzing the arguments in the *Kathāvatthu* against the conception of an ultimately real person, it is necessary to examine some of the terminology utilized in the text. As mentioned in Chapter XII, the terms *sacca* (truth) and *theta* (reality) were used in Sāriputta's rejection of the conception of a person upheld by Yamaka. In the *Aṭṭhaka-vagga* of the *Sutta-nipāta,* where the Buddha refused to recognize any view, conception, or idea as "ultimate" *(paramaṃ),* we find the cerebral form *aṭṭha,* instead of the dental *attha,* the latter being often used specifically to refer to the fruit or consequence. Even when the term *paramattha* occurs in the early discourses to refer to *nibbāna,* it is used in the sense of ultimate fruit. Thus there is clear evidence that *aṭṭha* and *attha* signified the distinction between reality and fruit, the former representing an absolutist or an essentialist perspective of truth, the latter a pragmatic one. If this is any clue, then Moggalīputta-tissa's selection of the cerebral forms of the two terms *saccikaṭṭha (satyaka-artha)* and *paramaṭṭha* (*parama-artha,* contrary to the available editions)[2] is significant, for what is being debated is the question of an ultimately real person, and not any and every conception of person.

Keeping in mind this important philosophical use of the terms, we can examine the controversy between the Theravādins and the Personalists. Presenting the debate between the two groups as he does, Moggalīputta-tissa does not use any special logical formula to refute the Personalist view, but simply allows each party to speak its own language and then proceeds to indicate which language is consistent with that of the Buddha. The Theravādin argues against the Personalist thus:

Theravādin:	Is a person *obtained* as an absolute truth, as an ultimate reality?
Personalist:	Yes.
Theravādin:	Is a person, as an absolute truth, as an ultimate reality, *obtained* in the way that an absolute truth, an ultimate reality, is *obtained?*
Personalist:	One should not say so.
Theravādin:	Admit your refutation.
	If you say that a person *is obtained* as an absolute truth, as an ultimate reality, then you should also say that a person *is obtained* as an absolute truth, as an absolute reality, in the way that an absolute truth, an ultimate reality, *is obtained.*
	What you state—namely, you should *say* that a person *is obtained* as an absolute truth, as an ultimate reality, and at the same time *not say* that a person *is obtained* as an absolute truth, an ultimate reality, in the way an absolute truth, an ultimate reality, *is obtained*—is wrong.
	If you should *not say* that a person *is obtained* as an absolute truth, an ultimate reality, in the way an absolute truth, an

> ultimate reality, *is obtained,* then you should *not say* that a person *is obtained* as an absolute truth, as an ultimate reality. What you state—namely, you should *say* that a person *is obtained* as an absolute truth, as an ultimate reality, and *not say* that a person *is obtained* as an absolute truth, as an ultimate reality, in the way an absolute truth, an ultimate reality, *is obtained*—is wrong.[3]

The two rather complicated propositions involved in the above argument are distinguished as follows:

1. A person is obtained as an absolute truth, as an ultimate reality. *(Upalabbhati puggalo saccikaṭṭha-paramaṭṭhena.)*
2. An absolute truth, an ultimate reality, is obtained. *(Upalabbhati saccikaṭṭho paramaṭṭho.)*

Most modern interpreters, like Schrayer, Bochenski, Nyanatiloka, Jayatilleke,[4] and, more recently, Jayawickrema,[5] have been misled by Buddhaghosa into believing that, while the first statement describes the *person (puggala),* the second refers to the *aggregates* (*khandha;* the real parts to which the person can be ultimately reduced). This led Jayatilleke to symbolize the first proposition as *p* and the second as *q*. He then worked out a logical calculus on the basis of the refutation provided at the end.

However, what Moggalīputta-tissa appears to have had in mind is something very different. If we are to understand his language properly, we have to symbolize the two propositions not as *p* and *q* but as

*p*TR (person in truth and reality) and
TR (truth and reality),

because Moggalīputta-tissa's intention is to draw out the implications of the terms *saccikaṭṭha* and *paramaṭṭha,* not the term *puggala.* Hence, when the Personalist admits a person as an absolute truth, an ultimate reality, Moggalīputta-tissa immediately brings up the question regarding an absolute truth, an ultimate reality. The Personalist neither asserts it nor denies it. Instead, he says that one should not say so *(na vattabbe).* This means that it is an inexpressible *(avyākata).* At this point Moggalīputta-tissa insists that without a *conception* of an absolute truth, an ultimate reality, one cannot have a *conception* of a person (or a thing) as an absolute truth, an ultimate reality. (This is not much different from the essentialist trap into which the Sautrāntikas of a later date fell; see Chapter XII.)

The rebuttal of the Personalist is equally significant. Not only does it throw light on the implications of Moggalīputta-tissa's argument; it also explains the Personalist's own view of the inexpressible:

Personalist:	Is a person *not obtained* as an absolute truth, as an ultimate reality?
Theravādin:	Yes.
Personalist:	Is a person *not obtained* as an absolute truth, as an ultimate reality, in the way an absolute truth, an ultimate reality [,*is obtained*]?
Theravādin:	One should not say so.
Personalist:	Admit your rebuttal. If a person is *not obtained* as an absolute truth, as an ultimate reality, then you should *say* a person is *not obtained* as an absolute truth, as an ultimate reality, in the way an absolute truth, an ultimate reality [,*is obtained*]. What you state—namely, one should *say* that a person is *not obtained* as an absolute truth, as an ultimate reality, and *not say* that a person is *not obtained* as an absolute truth, as an ultimate reality, in the way and absolute truth, an ultimate reality [,*is obtained*]—is wrong. If one should *not say* that a person is *not obtained* as an absolute truth, an ultimate reality, in the way an absolute truth, an ultimate reality [,is obtained], then one should *not say* that a person is *not obtained* as an absolute truth, as an ultimate reality. What you state—namely, you should *say* that a person is *not obtained* as an absolute truth, as an ultimate reality, yet *not say* that a person is *not obtained* as an absolute truth, as an ultimate reality, in the way an absolute truth, an ultimate reality [,is obtained]—is wrong.[6]

It is significant that both the Theravādin and the Personalist *disagree* with regard to the first proposition but *agree* with regard to the second. Both seem to assert that one should not speak *(na vattabbe)* of an absolute truth or ultimate reality (TR). Yet the Personalist proceeds to assert a person as an absolute truth, as an ultimate reality (*p*TR), while the Theravādin does not. The two standpoints may be represented thus:

	Personalist	Theravādin
*p*TR	obtained	not obtained
TR	inexpressible	inexpressible

This means that the Personalist believes that "what cannot be spoken of" *(na vattabbe)* can still be obtained or experienced, whereas the Theravādin insists that what is unspeakable is also not obtained or not experienced. In other words, the Personalist is attempting to provide empirical content for statements left unexplained *(a-vyākata = na vattabbe)* by the Buddha.

It is only after clarifying the meaning and use of the primary terms—absolute truth and ultimate reality—that Moggalīputta-tissa continues to debate with the Personalist in the format of the above refutation and rebuttal. What follows is an endless series of propositions relating to the concept of a person—whether it is identical with or different from the aggregates, actions, and so on—all couched in the language of absolute truth and ultimate reality.

The actual refutation comes only after the Personalist has quoted a few passages from the Buddha in support of his concept of a person. These include statements like "There is a person who follows his own welfare" *(Atthi puggalo attahitāya paṭipanno)* or "There is one person who arises in the world and who is intent on the welfare of the many, the happiness of the many, with compassion for the world, for the welfare, benefit, and happiness of the many."[7] Moggalīputta-tissa recognizes all of them, but counters with a series of quotations from the early discourses that emphasizes the non-substantiality *(anatta)* and emptiness *(suñña)* of all phenomena. Interestingly, the series begins with the famous statement of the Buddha, "All [experienced] phenomena are non-substantial" *(sabbe dhammā anattā).*[8] Moggalīputta-tissa administers the coup d'état by focusing on one conception: "pot of ghee" *(sappi-kumbha).* When the Personalist admits that the Buddha spoke of a "pot of ghee," Moggalīputta-tissa poses a question that probes in two directions, namely, the author and the constitution of the pot of ghee: "Is there someone who makes a pot of ghee?"[9]

Explicitly, the question pertains to the author of the "pot of ghee." This is what the Personalist wants to prove. Implicitly, however, Moggalīputta-tissa is raising the question of the constitution of the "pot of ghee" itself. Therefore he quotes a passage from the Buddha that refers to a whole series of *conceptions* relating to containers (such as "pot," "pan," "bag," and "pool") as well as to the contained (such as "ghee," "oil," "honey," "molasses," "milk," and "water"). These are:

1. Pot of oil *(thela-kumbha)*
2. Pot of honey *(madhu-kumbha)*
3. Pot of molasses *(phāṇita-kumbha)*
4. Pot of milk *(khīra-kumbha)*
5. Pot of water *(udaka-kumbha)*

6. Pan of water *(pāniya-thālaka)*
7. Bag of water *(pāniya-kosaka)*
8. Pool of water *(pāniya-sarāvaka)*

to which are added,

9. Regular meal *(nicca-bhatta)*
10. Thick broth *(dhuva-yāgu)*[10]

The attempt here is to show how concepts are interchangeable. For example, the term "pot" *(kumbha)* is common to all the phrases in the first category, and that term is replaced by three other terms in the second category. In the first category there are several different liquids, including water, while in the second category there is one liquid, namely, water *(pāniya)*. In the first list, the common term is for the *container,* and in the second, it is for the *contained.* Even though common terms occur in the eight phrases listed, no one of these concepts is identical with another.

The last two phrases are quoted to show that the belief in permanence generated by the apparent "sameness" of concepts, expressed by terms like "permanence" *(nicca)* and "substantial" *(dhuva),* can actually imply something else. Thus one can speak of a regular meal instead of a permanent meal *(nicca-bhatta),* still utilizing the same terms. Similarly, a "substantial broth" *(dhuva-yāgu)* can mean a thick broth and need not necessarily imply permanence. Moggalīputta-tissa concludes his argument by raising the question, "Is there any broth that is permanent, substantial, eternal, and not subject to change?" The Personalist responds in the same old fashion: "One should not say so." Moggalīputta-tissa retorts, "In that case, do not speak of a person as an absolute truth, as an ultimate reality."

Refutation of the Realist

Moggalīputta-tissa begins by asking whether "everything exists" *(sabbaṃ atthi).*[11] The Realist answers in the positive. Yet Moggalīputta-tissa's attempt to get a definition of what "everything" means—whether it implies all things "at all times" *(sabbadā),* "in every way" *(sabbena),* "in everything" *(sabbesu),* "in a unique way" *(ayogaṃ katvā),* "even in regard to the non-existent" *(yam pi n' atthi),* and, finally, "in the way of views" *(diṭṭhi)*—is frustrated by the Realist, who continues to insist that "one should not say so" *(na h' evaṃ vattabbe).*

Moving away from the general notion of "everything," Moggalīputta-tissa asks, "Does the past exist?" to which the Realist has a positive answer. Moggalīputta-tissa reminds him that, according to the Buddha, the past is generally referred to as "what has ceased, gone away, changed, gone to its end, and disappeared." When he admits this, Moggalīputta-tissa insists that he should not say that the past exists, and so on with regard to the other periods of time.

Taking the conception of "exists" as it relates to the present *(paccup-*

panna), Moggalīputta-tissa argues that if we are to follow this specific definition we have to say that the present *exists* because it has not ceased, not gone away, not changed, not gone to its end, not disappeared. However, if one applies the same definition of *exists* to the past and the future, the Realist is in difficulty—hence his response that "one should not say so."

Still more specific issues are taken up next. The question now revolves around the existence of past aggregates like material form *(rūpa),* and once again the Realist takes refuge in its inexpressibility. Moggalīputta-tissa then makes a distinction between "present[-ness]" *(paccuppanna)* and "form" *(rūpa),* and wants to know which of these the Realist would designate as existing and which he would perceive as passing away. Thus, when a present material form ceases, it is presentness *(paccuppannabhāva)* that it abandons, not its intrinsic material form *(rūpabhāva).* The Realist cannot disagree. However, when the question is whether this means abandoning its intrinsic material form *(rūpabhāva),* the Realist falls back on inexpressibility. Yet when the same question is put to him in negative form ("Does the material form not abandon its material formness [*rūpabhāva*]?"), the Realist answers in the positive. Moggalīputta-tissa immediately asks whether this does not imply the permanence of material form. The Realist is once again silent.

The debate proceeds in this manner, involving almost every phenomenon *(dhamma)* recognized in the Buddha's discourses, every possible combination, and temporal periods as well. The only passage the Realist quotes from the discourses of the Buddha to justify his contention that what belongs to the past, present, and future exists is one that defines the five aggregates. The Realist argues:

> Did not the Buddha state: "Monks, whatever material form belonging to the past, present, and future, subjective or objective, gross or subtle, inferior or superior, remote or immediate, this is called the aggregate of form"?[12]

This is only a reference to what may be designated or conceived as material form, without any implication that all of them exist in the present. Moggalīputta-tissa's rebuttal consists in quoting the most significant statement of the Buddha explaining the three linguistic conventions relating to time:

> There are these three linguistic conventions or usages of words or terms which are distinct, have been distinct in the past, are distinct in the present, and will be distinct in the future, and which are not ignored by the wise brahmans and recluses. Whatever material form *(rūpa)* has been, has ceased to be, is past and has changed is called, reckoned, and termed "has been" *(ahosi),* and not reckoned as "exists" *(atthi)* or as "will be" *(bhavissati)*. . . .

> [This is repeated for the other aggregates: feeling, perception, disposition, and consciousness.] Whatever material form has not arisen nor come to be is called, reckoned, or termed "will be" *(bhavissati),* and it is not reckoned as "exists" *(atthi)* or "has been" *(ahosi)*. . . . Whatever material form has arisen and has manifested itself is called, reckoned, or termed "exists" *(atthi),* and is not reckoned as "has been" *(ahosi)* nor as "will be" *(bhavissati).*[13]

In addition, Moggalīputta-tissa cites a passage from the discourses wherein the Buddha refused to admit a visual faculty *(cakkhu)* through which one could perceive a buddha of the past.[14] This is followed by a reference to another passage in which a monk named Nandaka declares that in the past he was overwhelmed by greed, which was unwholesome, and that now he is not, which is wholesome.[15]

Finally, the Realist and Moggalīputta-tissa battle it out with two passages, one which the former believes establishes his contention that the future exists *(anāgataṃ atthi),* because here the Buddha speaks about the possibility of rebirth, but which the latter contends negates the future. The argument proceeds thus:

Realist:	Should it not be said that the future exists?
Theravādin:	Yes.
Realist:	Did not the Buddha state: "Monks, there is greed, there is delight, there is craving in relation to gross food [*kabaliṅkāra āhāra,* one of the four nutritions that contributes to rebirth, the others being contact *(phassa),* volition *(manosañcetanā),* and consciousness *(viññāṇa)*]. Consciousness is established therein, and grows. Wherein consciousness is established and grows, therein is the entry of the psychophysical personality. Wherever the psychophysical personality exists, therein is the amplification of dispositions. Wherever there is amplification of dispositions, therein is future birth. Wherever there is future birth, there exists continued rebirth, decay, and death. Wherever there is rebirth, decay, and death, that is sorrow, that is worry, and that is anxiety"?
Theravādin:	Yes [he did].
Realist:	In that case, future exists.[16]

Moggalīputta-tissa quotes the passage that immediately follows, wherein the Buddha outlines the negative consequences of not having greed, delight, and craving in relation to gross food.[17] The Realist admits that in terms of this passage one cannot assert the existence of the future. It seems that the Realist failed to understand that the two passages represent an instance where the Buddha applied the general formula of the principle of dependence (see Chapter IV) in its positive and negative forms to explain how rebirth can take place and how it can be stopped.

Refutation of the Transcendentalist

Although references to the life of the Buddha are scanty and brief, there are extremely valuable and genuine discourses, such as the *Padhāna-sutta,* the *Ariyapariyesana-sutta,* and the *Mahāparinibbāna-suttanta,* to name a few, that contain important historical information. For this reason, when some of the Buddhists who lived before and during the time of Emperor Aśoka were influenced by absolutistic thinking and wanted to explain the Buddhist doctrine as a form of "transcendentalism" *(lokuttaravāda),* they were compelled to deny the historicity of the Buddha's personality.

The debate between Moggalīputta-tissa and the Transcendentalist, as recorded in the *Kathāvatthu,* reads as follows:

Theravādin:	Should it not be said that the Buddha, the Fortunate One, inhabited this world of human beings?
Transcendentalist:	Yes [it should not be said].
Theravādin:	But aren't there shrines, parks, monasteries, villages, towns, kingdoms, and countries where the Buddha lived?
Transcendentalist:	Yes [there are].
Theravādin:	If there are shrines, parks, monasteries, villages, towns, kingdoms, and countries where the Buddha lived, then you should say that the Buddha inhabited this world.[18]

Moggalīputta-tissa raises two more questions:

1. Is it not the case that the Buddha was born in Lumbini, attained enlightenment under the Bodhi-tree, established the principle of righteousness *(dhammacakka)* at Bārānasi, abandoned the disposition to live at the shrine called Cāpāla, and passed away at Kusinārā?[19]
2. Did not the Buddha make the following statements: "Once, monks, I was living at Ukkaṭṭha, at the foot of the giant *sāla*-tree, in the forest called Subhaga"; "Once, monks, before my enlightenment, I was living at Uruvelā by the Goatherd's Banyan," [and similar references to Rājagaha, Sāvatthi, and Vesāli, all of which are reports in the first person (i.e., *viharāmi*), not in the third person *(viharati),* as is often reported by Ānanda]?[20]

The Transcendentalist answers in the positive. However, he then raises a counterquestion:

Transcendentalist:	Did the Fortunate One inhabit the world of human beings?

Theravādin:	Yes.
Transcendentalist:	Is it not the case that the Fortunate One, born in the world, raised in the world, and, having overcome the world, lived unsmeared by the world?
Theravādin:	Yes [it is the case].
Transcendentalist:	If it is the case that the Fortunate One, born in the world, raised in the world, and, having overcome the world, lived unsmeared by the world, then you should not say: "The Buddha, the Fortunate One, inhabited the world of human beings."[21]

The debate ends here, leaving the impression that the Transcendentalist has carried the day. Going back to the passage that the Transcendentalist was quoting, namely, the Buddha's conversation with the brahman Doṇa (see Chapter XII), where the Buddha refused to identify himself with a human *(manussa)*, Moggalīputta-tissa seems to have been reluctant to assert that the Buddha remained in the "human world" *(manussa loka)*. What is surprising is that Moggalīputta-tissa makes no attempt to indicate this distinction to the Transcendentalist.

However, when the Transcendentalist wants to deny the authority of the Buddha's discourses, Moggalīputta-tissa seems to be more forceful. The first part of the argument reads thus:

Theravādin:	Should it not be said: "The doctrine was preached by the Buddha, the Fortunate One"?
Transcendentalist:	Yes [it should not be said].
Theravādin:	By whom was it preached?
Transcendentalist:	Preached by the created form *(abhinimmitena)*.
Theravādin:	The created form of the Victor is the Teacher, the Perfectly Enlightened One, the All-knowing, the All-seeing, the Master of the Doctrine, the Source of the Doctrine?
Transcendentalist:	One should not say so.
Theravādin:	Should it not be said: "The doctrine was preached by the Buddha, the Fortunate One"?
Transcendentalist:	Yes [it should not be said].
Theravādin:	By whom was it preached?
Transcendentalist:	It was preached by the Venerable Ānanda.
Theravādin:	Venerable Ānanda [then] is the Victor, the Teacher, the Perfectly Enlightened One, the All-knowing, the All-seeing, the Master of the Doctrine, the Source of the Doctrine.
Transcendentalist:	One should not say so.[22]

At the end of this debate, Moggalīputta-tissa quotes statements from the discourses, once again expressed in the first person by the Buddha, to justify the view that the doctrine, as embodied in the discourses, was actually preached by the historical Buddha.

The Transcendentalist, having questioned the historical personality of the Buddha as well as the authenticity of the doctrine embodied in the early discourses, continues to argue against the Theravādins regarding the status of the Community *(saṅgha)*.[23] The specific topics debated are:

1. Does the Community accept gifts *(dakkhiṇā)*?
2. Does the Community purify gifts (i.e., does a gift become pure by being offered to the Community, which is pure)?
3. Does the Community actually enjoy the gifts (i.e., are the gifts real)?
4. Do gifts to the Community bear fruit?
5. Do gifts to the Buddha bear fruit?
6. Does the purity of gifts depend on the giver or the receiver?

The questions seem to indicate the Transcendentalist's reluctance to recognize the usefulness of the Community of disciples, that is, those who follow the path and, in doing so, benefit the ordinary people. Interestingly, most of the questions focus on "gifts" *(dakkhiṇā)*. The gifts of food, clothing, and shelter provided by laypeople to those who are devoting themselves to spiritual development have generally been regarded as meritorious. The view that the purity of gifts depends on the purity of the recipient, who is himself struggling for perfection, was not acceptable to the Transcendentalist, who was not even willing to recognize the historical personality of the Buddha. Denying the historical Buddha and downplaying the reality of the human person seeking enlightenment and perfection, the Transcendentalist was prepared to evaluate a gift only in relation to a giver *(dāyaka)*.[24]

What emerges from this debate is philosophically significant. The Transcendentalist, who rejects the historical Buddha, the content of his discourses, and the Community that seeks perfection, cannot faithfully admit the reality of the giver of a gift. All he can do is accept the simple act of giving. This would mean that an action is to be evaluated on its own, not in relation to anything else. The absolutist conception of "duty" is clearly on the horizon.

CHAPTER XIV

Abhidhamma

It may seem like putting the cart before the horse to analyze the contents of the Abhidhamma following a discussion of Moggalīputta-tissa and the *Kathāvatthu,* especially when tradition considers the *Kathāvatthu,* the only text of the Pali *Abhidhamma Piṭaka* attributed to someone other than the Buddha, to be the last piece added to this collection. In any case, it is futile to try to decide which text is early and which is late.

Our reasons for examining the *Kathāvatthu* first are as follows. The Abhidhamma texts, except the *Kathāvatthu,* are not interpretative. Interpretations are available only from the fifth century A.D. onward, almost eight centuries after the compilation of the *Kathāvatthu.* These are the commentaries of Buddhaghosa. The commentaries on the Sanskrit version of the *Abhidharma Piṭaka* preserved by the Sarvāstivādins may be earlier than those of the Theravādins. Yet those commentaries (called the *Vibhāṣā*) are no more trustworthy than Buddhaghosa's in interpreting the contents of that collection. Indeed, the *Vibhāṣās* were much more controversial in the Indian context, giving rise to a variety of conflicting opinions, than were the commentaries of Buddhaghosa on the Theravāda version.

Because of the catechistical and non-discursive style of the Abhidhamma treatises, most modern interpreters have fallen back on the commentaries for an understanding of these texts.[1] Since Moggalīputta-tissa's *Kathāvatthu* was considered sufficiently authoritative to be accorded canonical status, the philosophical themes defended in it should be consistent with the philosophical temper of the other canonical works, in which no such themes are explicitly stated or defended. In any case, the *Kathāvatthu* represents a closer companion of the canonical texts than do the commentaries, and can thus serve as a guide to understanding other canonical Abhidhamma texts. Hence the appropriateness of treating the ideas in the *Kathāvatthu* before examining the philosophy of the Abhidhamma. At least absolutism and transcendentalism, essentialism or reductionism, all of which are explicitly abandoned in the *Kathāvatthu,* should not be utilized in explaining the Abhidhamma.[2]

The *Kathāvatthu*'s contribution to the study of the Abhidhamma lies precisely in its elimination of absolutist and essentialist or reductionist perspectives. No one reading the excessively long debate in the *Kathāvatthu* on the conception of a person can assert that the Abhidhamma deals with ultimate realities *(paramattha)*. Abandoning the search for such ultimate realities, it becomes possible to explain the contents of the Abhidhamma in terms of the two principal teachings of the Buddha, namely, non-substantiality *(anatta)* and dependent arising *(paṭiccasamuppāda)*.

If the intention of the discourses in analyzing the human personality into five aggregates was merely to indicate the absence of a metaphysical agent *(anatta)* and not to discover a set of irreducible elements called "ultimate realities," there seems to be no justification for the various psychological and physical items listed in the canonical Abhidhamma texts (both in Pali and in Sanskrit) to be considered ultimate realities. The *Kathāvatthu,* as mentioned earlier, serves as a warning against such an enterprise. Instead, the various lists represent simple enumerations *(saṅgani)* of psychological and physical items of experience. For the sake of comprehensiveness, the Ābhidhammikas traced out every element *(dhamma)* that they could find mentioned in the discourses. The different lists in the two major Abhidhamma traditions, both derived from the discourses of the Buddha, would indicate that they do not contain ultimate realities. The compilers of the Abhidhamma texts simply picked what *they* thought were the significant elements; hence the difference between the two traditions.

What appears to be new in the Abhidhamma enumeration of physical and psychological elements emerges from the need to account for an aspect of discourse that could not be accommodated in the Abhidhamma methodology. For example, in the discourses the human personality is analyzed into five aggregates. In this discursive system of exposition, there was no need to bring in ethical or moral problems, i.e., whether or not any of these aggregates is associated with a moral quality. That question is discussed in relation to the behavior of the human person. But the Abhidhamma method does not allow for such discursive treatment: it simply lists the physical and psychological constituents in a non-discursive way. Hence the need to account for moral quality and so forth in the very enumeration of these elements. It is this difference in the treatment of subject matter that Nyanatiloka tried to highlight when he said:

> Now, in the *Dhamma-Saṅganī,* the first three realities are treated from the ethical, or more exactly, the karmical standpoint, and divide accordingly into A. karmically wholesome phenomena *(kusala-dhamma),* B. karmically unwholesome phenomena *(akusala-dhamma),* C. karmically neutral phe-

> nomena *(avyākata-dhamma),* which make up the first Triad of the Abhidhamma Matrix.[3]

This is what prompted C. A. F. Rhys Davids to characterize the contents of the *Dhammasaṅganī* as "Buddhist Psychological Ethics."[4] It would be more appropriate to describe them as ethical psychology.

Simple enumeration of physical and psychological constituents of human experience could leave us with a sand-heap of discrete entities. To avoid such reductionism, the Abhidhamma adopted a system of classification *(vibhaṅga)* whereby each element is related to another in the different classifications. Often this classification is done in terms of the major categories recognized in the discourses, such as the aggregates, the faculties, the elements and the four noble truths. The classification is done in such a way that it brings out the innumerable implications and applications of each conception examined. For example, the conception of feeling *(vedanā)* one of the five aggregates is further classified as follows:

What is here the aggregate of feeling?

The aggregate of feeling is of:

1. A single nature: in being associated with sense impression *(phassa-sampayutta);*
2. Twofold: accompanied by root *(sahetuko),* unaccompanied by root *(ahetuka);*
3. Threefold: wholesome, unwholesome, neutral;
4. Fourfold: *kāmāvacara* (belonging to the world of sense pleasures), *rūpāvacara* (belonging to materiality), *arūpāvacara* (belonging to the immaterial), *lokuttara* (belonging to the supernormal world);
5. Fivefold: bodily ease, bodily pain, gladness, sadness, indifference;
6. Sixfold: born of eye-impression, ear-, nose-, tongue-, body-, and mind-impression;
7. Sevenfold: born of eye-impression, ear-, nose-, tongue, body-, of the impression of the mind-element *(mano-dhātu),* of the impression of the mind-consciousness-element *(mano-viññāṇa-dhātu);*
8. Eightfold: born of eye-, ear-, nose-, tongue-impression, born of body-impression, either pleasant or painful, born of the impression of the mind-element, of the mind-consciousness-element;
9. Ninefold: born of eye-, ear-, nose-, tongue-, body-impression, of the impression of the mind-element, of the mind-consciousness-element, which is wholesome, unwholesome, or neutral;
10. Tenfold: born of eye-, ear-, nose-, tongue-, body-impression, either pleasant or painful, born of the impression of the mind-element, of the mind-consciousness-element, which is wholesome, unwholesome, or neutral.[5]

Clearly, the attempt here is to account for every possible shade of meaning that the conception of feeling represents. According to the Ābhidhammikas, this is best achieved by placing that conception in every possible category, even if this involves some repetition. The attempt is to provide a method or framework whereby the meaning of the conception can be understood within each *context*. This may be contrasted with the definition of the conception of feeling *(vedanā)* by the later commentators.

The process of classification *(vibhaṅga)* is therefore no more than an analytical process that tries to determine the contextual meaning of a conception. However, the Ābhidhammikas were not content with this process alone. While relating a conception to the different categories, it was deemed necessary to demarcate the boundaries within which each conception falls. This process of determining what a conception is and is not constitutes the subject matter of the Abhidhamma text called the *Dhātu-kathā*. It is supplemented by the *Yamaka*, in which questions relating to "identity, subordination, and coordination of concepts"[6] are taken up. Even though this extensive work, consisting of ten chapters, has been referred to as "ten valleys of dry bones,"[7] its significance as a philosophical treatise attempting to clarify the meaning and application of concepts is immense. The work is sure to tax the patience of the reader, but it nevertheless demonstrates the determination and commitment of the Ābhidhammikas to close any avenues through which *absolute* meanings could be smuggled in. Let us examine one of hundreds of examples considered:

> Are wholesome phenomena *(kusala-dhamma)* wholesome roots *(kusala-mūla)?* [No,] there are only three wholesome roots, the remaining wholesome phenomena are not wholesome roots. But are wholesome roots wholesome phenomena? Yes.

Nyanatiloka[8] represents this diagrammatically as follows:

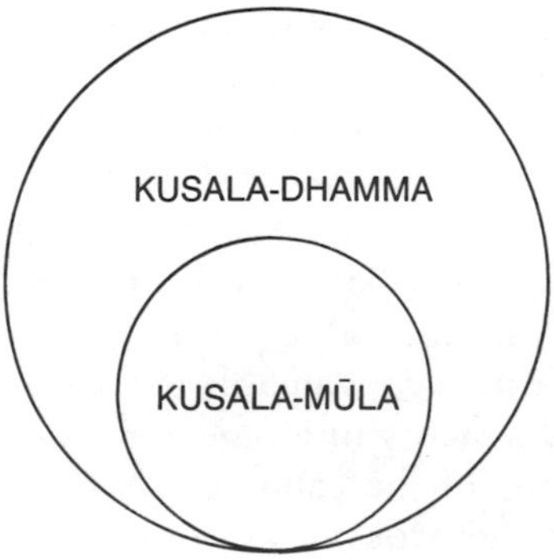

The enumeration and classification of concepts in order to determine their relative meanings and applications without accommodating any form of absolutism, thereby establishing their non-substantiality *(anatta)*, is followed by an exhaustive description of possible relations. This constitutes the Ābhidhammika explanation of the Buddha's positive teaching, namely, dependent arising *(paṭiccasamuppāda)*.

The theory of relations *(paccaya,* Skt. *pratyaya)*, like the other categories discussed earlier, constituted the common stock of the canonical Abhidhamma, even though the two traditions differed in terms of the numbers they recognized, as in the case of the physical and psychological categories. The two Abhidhamma traditions seem to have begun with a theory of four basic relations. The Theravāda expanded this into twenty-four. During Nāgārjuna's time there were still four types of relations recognized by the Indian Buddhist schools.[9] However, the Yogācāra interpreters of Abhidharma, while retaining these four, made further subdivisions to accommodate other relations they felt should be recognized.[10]

The four basic relations are as follows:

1. *Hetu-paccaya (pratyaya)* or the primary condition, which is primary in the sense of being a root-condition. According to the discourses, psychological springs of action such as greed, hatred, and confusion can be looked upon as root-conditions of human suffering.
2. *Ārammaṇa-paccaya (ālambana-pratyaya)* or the objective condition, which stands for the objective support for the manifestation of mental phenomena. The later commentators were keen on distinguishing the objective condition from other conditions, calling it non-productive *(ajanaka)*. This may have been due to the continuing debate among the phenomenalists, realists, and idealists regarding the status of the object.
3. *Adhipati-paccaya (pratyaya)* or the dominant condition, which accounts for the continued influence of a condition after the effect has come into existence as a result of conditions like the primary condition. The Sanskrit Abhidharma tradition provides a more comprehensive definition, calling it a universal condition. This enabled the Yogācāra interpreters to include under this category most of the new types of relations they envisaged.
4. *Samanantara-paccaya (-pratyaya)*, the proximate or immediately contiguous cause. Immediate contiguity can be obtained between two events, especially mental or psychological events. However, this relation became extremely valuable for the Buddhist metaphysician when he adopted a theory of momentary existence, which, interestingly, was not part of the canonical Abhidhamma. A momentary existence did not allow for one event to exert its influence on a sub-

> sequent event, especially when the momentary existence was defined as having no duration.

The remaining twenty relations accounted for every type of causal correlation that the Ābhidhammikas envisaged as a result of dealing with the wide variety of physical and psychological events mentioned in the discourses of the Buddha.

It may appear that there is no such theory of relations *(paccaya)* in the early discourses and that this is an innovation of the Abhidhamma. This is partly true. One certainly cannot find an elaborate theory of relations during the early period. Yet even in their discursive treatment, the discourses refer to relations such as roots *(mūlaṃ),* dominances *(ādhipateyya),* immediacy *(anantara),* and so on. The Ābhidhammikas, in contrast, were compelled to focus on relations because of their extensive but non-discursive enumeration and classification of events. Without a process of synthesis, enumeration and classification would have left them with a mass of disconnected events. The theory of relations thus serves the same function that "dependent arising" *(paṭiccasamuppāda)* fulfilled in the early discourses.

It may be noted that we have not yet commented on the *Puggalapaññatti,* whose counterpart in the Sanskrit Abhidharma canon is the *Prajñapti-śāstra.* The reason is twofold. First, its contents, like those of the *Kathāvatthu,* have been viewed from the perspectives of the absolutist and essentialist commentators of a subsequent date rather than from the standpoint of the earlier teachings. Nyanatiloka expressed his difficulties thus:

> This smallest of the seven Abhidhamma books appears to be somewhat out of place in the Abhidhamma Piṭaka as shown even by its title "Description of Individuals." For it is one of the main characteristics of the Abhidhamma that it does not employ conventional concepts like "individual" *(puggala),* etc. but deals only with ultimates, or realities in the highest sense *(paramattha-dhamma),* i.e., the mental and material phenomena, and their classifications into groups *(khandha),* bases, elements, etc.[11]

The contents of the *Puggalapaññatti* would not have seemed out of place in the Abhidhamma if Nyanatiloka had followed the explanations of Moggalīputta-tissa instead of Buddhaghosa. Moggalīputta-tissa, as mentioned in the previous chapter, rejected the conception of a person as an absolute truth, as an ultimate reality *(saccikaṭṭha-paramaṭṭha).* What the *Puggalapaññatti* deals with is only a "conception of a person," not a metaphysical conception of a person.

For the Abhidhamma, the non-metaphysical conception of a person is not different from the non-metaphysical explanations of the psychic and physical elements. Indeed, the commentarial explanation of "person" *(puggala)* as a mere convention *(sammuti),* and of the psychic *(citta, cetasika)* and physical *(rūpa)* elements as "ultimate realities" *(paramattha),* is completely rejected by the *Puggalapaññatti*'s enumeration of six concepts *(paññatti):*

1. The concept of aggregates *(khandha-paññatti)*
2. The concept of gateways *(āyatana-paññatti)*
3. The concept of elements *(dhātu-paññatti)*
4. The concept of truth *(sacca-paññatti)*
5. The concept of faculties *(indriya-paññatti)*
6. The concept of persons *(puggala-paññatti)*[12]

The first five groups of concepts are then explained in brief, because they had already been treated in great detail in other Abhidhamma treatises. The *Puggalapaññatti* is therefore devoted to an exhaustive analysis of the last of the six, the concept of a person. This fact should eliminate Nyanatiloka's second difficulty in understanding this text, namely, the absence of a detailed treatment of the aggregates, and so on. What is clear is that the text does not make any distinction between the first five categories of concepts and the last. It is interesting to note that, centuries later, the famous Buddhist psychologist Vasubandhu, who immersed himself in the study of the Sanskrit Abhidharma literature as well as the commentarial traditions *(vibhāṣā)* that introduced the substantialist (= Sarvāstivāda) and essentialist (= Sautrāntika) interpretations, abandoned the latter to write a treatise entitled *The Establishment of Conception Only* (*Vijñaptimātratāsiddhi;* see Chapter XIX).

Furthermore, the *contextual* analysis of the conceptions of aggregates and so forth in the previous books of the Abhidhamma is here adopted in the exposition of the different conceptions relating to a "person" *(puggala).* To accommodate such a contextual analysis, the work is divided into ten chapters, of which the first deals with single individuals, the second with pairs, the third with groups of three, and so on, up to a tenfold classification of persons. As Nyanatiloka himself observes, "It contains not merely brief definitions of the various human types, but also some fairly long descriptions, and a number of beautiful and elaborate similes."[13]

The first chapter lists fifty different types of persons.[14] These include every type mentioned in the early discourses, such as the "individualist" *(puthujjana),* the "noble" *(ariya),* the "ignoble" *(anariya),* the "trainee" *(sekha),* the "trained" *(asekha),* a person possessed of threefold knowledge *(tevijja),* of sixfold knowledge *(chaḷabhiñño),* the "perfectly enlightened one" *(sammāsambuddha),* the person who is freed through wisdom *(paññāvimutta),* freed through faith *(saddhāvimutta),* who follows the doctrine *(dhammānusārī)*, who follows faith *(saddhānusārī)*, the worthy one *(arahā)*, and so on. The detailed explanation that follows this matrix outlines the qualities on the basis of which each of the fifty can be identified.

The list of fifty conceptions focuses on the psychological constitution and moral standing of human persons, not their physical composition. It includes the ordinary person or the one who, in terms of his moral standing, can be described as an "individualist" *(puthujjana)*, as well as the person who has attained perfect enlightenment *(sammāsambuddha)* and who has reached such moral heights on the basis of an understanding of phenomena *(dhammā)* not previously available. The latter refers to the founder of the teachings. Between these two is a variety of persons who can be distinguished from one another in terms of their psychological constitution, moral development, and ethical behavior. However, to avoid any assumption that these concepts can be distinguished in terms of their ontological reference as well, the definitions that follow relate these concepts to others in the list. Thus the second, fourth, and, sixth, for example, are said to be related to the twenty first, namely, the noble *(ariya)*.

The passage that is most helpful in understanding the nature of the concepts dealt with in the Abhidhamma occurs in connection with the definition of three types of teachers *(satthā)*.[15] It reads thus:

1. There is one teacher who *proclaims* a self *(atta)*, in truth *(saccato)* and reality *(thetato)*, in this life, and *proclaims* a self, in truth and reality, in the life after.
2. There is one teacher who *proclaims* a self, in truth and reality, in this life, and *does not proclaim* a self, in truth and reality, in the life after.
3. There is a teacher who *does not proclaim* a self, in truth and reality, in this life, and *does not proclaim* a self, in truth and reality, in the life after.

The text goes on to identify the first as an eternalist *(sassatavādī)*, the second as a nihilist *(ucchedavādī)*, and the third as the perfectly enlightened one *(sammāsambuddha)*.

The use of the terms *sacca* (truth) and *theta* (reality)—which occur in the discussion between Sāriputta and Yamaka (see Chapter XII)—to qualify the conceptions of the eternalist and the nihilist seems to indicate that the conceptions referred to in the *Puggalapaññatti* are empirical, not substantialist or essentialist. It is this understanding of the nature and function of conceptions that compelled Moggalīputta-tissa to reject the theories propounded by the Sarvāstivādins as well as the Vātsīputriyas. The *Puggalapaññatti* can thus be considered the summation of the Abhidhamma technique of enumeration, classification, and synthesis. As indicated in the last passage quoted, it represents a middle standpoint in the explanation of conceptual thinking, avoiding the two extremes of absolutism, both eternalistic and nihilistic. It is, in fact, a continuation of the pragmatic approach adopted by the Buddha in dealing with conceptual problems.

CHAPTER XV

The Perfection of Wisdom in the *Vajracchedikā*

The history of the extremely popular Mahāyāna discourse, the *Vajracchedikā-prajñāpāramitā-sūtra,* is available in Hajime Nakamura's *Indian Buddhism* (1980). One important piece of information he has brought to our notice is that the earlier versions of this text, available through translation into Chinese by Ch'ih-ch'ien, follow introductions, similar to those of the early discourses, where the location of the sermon is given as Jetavana and the audience described as consisting of 1,250 *bhikkhus* only. There is no mention of any *bodhisattvas.* Furthermore, the Pūrvaśailas, a sect of the so-called Hīnayāna, are said to have possessed the *sūtra* in Prakrit.[1]

The inclusion of *bodhisattvas* as part of the audience would not be a major revision were it not for the fact that it obliterates the philosophical significance of the work by introducing an ideological conflict that only emerged subsequently, with the compilation of the *Saddharmapuṇḍarīka-sūtra* (see Chapter XVII). The *Vajracchedikā* undoubtedly represents a criticism of the same metaphysical ideas that the Buddha and some of his later disciples, such as Moggalīputta-tissa, rejected. But it is not necessary to interpret its philosophical content in a way that lends credibility to the so-called Hīnayāna-Mahāyāna conflict. In fact, the term "Mahāyāna" does not even occur in the discourse.

A consideration of the conception of "perfection" *(pāramitā)* can throw some light on the philosophical nature and content of the *Prajñāpāramitā-sūtras.* In the Buddhist context, the term *parama* is generally taken to mean the "greatest," "highest," "ultimate," or "perfect," more in the sense of an ideal or goal than a reality. Thus we have expressions like "Gains have good health as the greatest. Wealth has contentment as the greatest. Kinsmen have trust as the greatest, and freedom is the greatest (or ultimate) happiness."[2] The term *pāramitā* (or *paramatā*) represents the abstract noun, hence rendered as "perfection." This use of the term in the sense of goal is further strengthened by the more fanciful etymological explanation of the term as "(that by which) one has crossed over to the other shore" (*pāraṃ* = other [shore], *ita* = gone or moved). The absolutistic understanding of the concept of "goal" contrasted with "means"—an understanding that can generate polar theories such as realism and instrumentalism—has given rise to the view that *prajñāpāramitā* represents the perfection of wisdom, where wisdom stands for absolute knowledge, if not for knowledge of the Absolute, as opposed to all other forms of empirical or conceptual knowledge. If that were the case, then the six *pāramitās* of the Mahāyānists and the ten *pāramitās* of the Theravādins would leave us with six or ten absolutes relating to human activities such as generosity, virtuousness, renunciation, striving, effort, concentration, understanding, and so on. In contrast, a goal that is not absolute would enable a person who leads a moral life to be "virtuous" without being "made of virtues" (see Chapter x). Similarly, a person could be "wise" without being constituted or made of wisdom, the latter being taken in its nominal form to refer to an entity. It is such ontological commitment that the discourses devoted to expounding the perfection of wisdom *(prajnāpāramitā)* are trying to avoid. The philosophy of the *Vajracchedikā* is intended to achieve precisely this.

Analysis of the philosophical content of the *Vajracchedikā,* whose main purpose is to expound the "perfection of wisdom" *(prajñāpāramitā),* can begin with its reference to the Buddha's reminiscence of his previous birth as the sage Kṣāntivādī. *Kṣānti* is patience or tolerance, which is itself one of the perfections. The Buddha refers to one of his previous lives, in which he was said to have refrained from entertaining any idea of self *(ātma),* being *(sattva),* soul *(jīva),* or person *(pudgala),* even when his limbs were being chopped off one after another by order of the King of Kālinga. The reason he did not entertain any such idea was that he did not want to generate any thoughts of ill-will.

It is possible to argue that compassion, for example, cannot be generated unless there are "true and real" persons. Buddhism, however, holds that a belief in a "true and real" person involves ontological commitment, a commitment that leads to grasping after the subject or oneself. This grasping can lead in turn not only to greed *(lobha)* but also to its opposite, namely, hatred *(dveṣa)* or ill-will *(vyāpāda).*

Patience *(kṣānti)* thus turns out to be an extremely effective way of overcoming hatred and ill-will. The story of Kṣāntivādī is an idealized version of such patience. Yet the cultivation of patience is not achieved through external compulsion through a sense of duty, as in the absolutistic traditions, but through understanding. This is how the perfection of patience or tolerance comes to be related to the perfection of wisdom *(prajñāpāramitā).*

An interesting passage in the *Vajracchedikā* provides a clue to the nature and goal of the perfection of wisdom:

> The Fortunate One questioned: "What do you think, Subhūti, does it occur to the Arhat, 'By me has Arhatship been attained?' " Subhūti responded:

"No indeed, O Fortunate One, it does not occur to the Arhat, 'I have attained Arhatship.' And why? Because there is no thing *(dharma)* named 'Arhat.' Therefore, it is called 'Arhat.' If, O Fortunate One, it occurs to an Arhat, 'I have attained Arhatship,' that itself would be for him a grasping after a self, a grasping after a being, a grasping after a soul, a grasping after a person. And why? O Fortunate One, I have been referred to by the Tathāgata, the Arhat, the Perfectly Enlightened One as the foremost among those who live in peace *(araṇa-vihārī)*. I am, O Fortunate One, an Arhat, one who has abandoned lust *(vītarāga)*. O Fortunate One, it does not occur to me, 'I am an Arhat, one who has abandoned lust. If, O Fortunate One, it occurred to me, 'I have attained Arhatship,' the Tathāgata would not declare of me, 'The foremost among those who dwell in peace, Subhūti, the son of good family, dwells not anywhere. Therefore he is called 'a dweller in peace, a dweller in peace.' "[3]

Three significant assertions are included in this passage. First, Subhūti calls himself an Arhat, one who has abandoned lust, an epithet applied to the Buddha himself in this context, but an ideal that was subsequently condemned in the *Saddharmapuṇḍarīka* as being "low" *(hīna)*. Second, Subhūti is referred to as the foremost among those who dwell in peace *(araṇa-vīhārī)*. And, finally, Subhūti would not be considered the foremost among those who dwell in peace if he were to entertain the idea that he has attained or reached some thing referred to as Arhatship. In other words, he is not one who has made an ontological commitment as far as the conception of Arhatship is concerned.

Placing these three assertions in a historical setting, without relying on ideological conflicts that emerged long after, we can understand their philosophical significance, and through that the entire contents of the *Vajracchedikā*. The term *arhat* is used in the early discourses to refer to one who is "worthy" of respect as a result of cultivating a noble way of life. That noble way of life is the result of abandoning lust *(rāga)*. The Buddha and his immediate disciples are described as those who have reached such moral perfection, the former being singled out as the "perfectly enlightened one" *(sammāsambuddha)* as a result of being the founder of the path or doctrine unheard of before *(pubbe ananussuta)*.[4]

However, the more important assertion is the second. It would be an extremely unhistorical approach to analyze Subhūti's claim that he was declared to be the foremost among those who dwell in peace *(araṇa-vihārin)* without first taking a look at the Buddha's discourse entitled *Analysis of Peace (Araṇa-vibhaṅga-sutta)*.[5] Here the Buddha speaks of a "warring path" *(saraṇa-paṭipadā)* and a "peaceful path" *(araṇa-paṭipadā)*. One would normally expect the Buddha to define the former as the presence of lust, hatred, and confusion, which is bondage, and the latter as the absence of these three tendencies, which is freedom *(nibbāna)*. The elimination of lust and hatred may provide peace for oneself.

However, this alone does not provide a way of non-conflict in the world, for when we think of the world, which includes oneself as well as others, peace or non-conflict *(araṇa)* must involve the means of communication as well. It is for this reason that simple renunciation of lust and hatred is not sufficient. It has to be accompanied by the elimination of confusion *(moha),* which, in the *Vajracchedikā,* means cultivation of the perfection of wisdom. The *Analysis of Peace* defines the warring path as a dogmatic, extremist attitude toward concepts, and therefore toward language, and the peaceful path as a non-dogmatic, pragmatic attitude toward concepts and linguistic usage.

We have already quoted the most significant passage from this discourse, where the Buddha recommends a middle path that avoids the two extremes—one that views conceptual knowledge as self-sufficing and a revelation all by itself, and the other that views true experience as beyond all conceptual thinking. The first is an absolutist notion of conception and language; the second is a transcendentalist perspective. The Buddha emphasizes the utilization of language without grasping, i.e., without ontological commitment. He realized that many disputes in philosophy hinge on ill-defined words and ideas, each side claiming its own word or idea to be true. This leads to the third assertion referred to above, namely, that Subhūti would not be a dweller in peace if he were to entertain the idea that he has reached *some thing* designated by the term *arhatship.*

It may not be an exaggeration to say that the entire *Vajracchedikā* is one colossal attempt to avoid the extremist use of language, that is, to eliminate any ontological commitment to concepts while at the same time retaining their pragmatic value, so as not to render them totally empty of meaning. In the previous chapter, we saw how the canonical Abhidhamma texts adopted enumeration, classification, and synthesis to bring out the pragmatic meaning of concepts *(paññatti).* In doing so, the Abhidhamma attempted to be as comprehensive as possible, leaving no conception unanalyzed; hence the vastness of the collection. However, the *Vajracchedikā* tries to achieve the same in thirty-six printed pages. This is done by applying a formula, developed in the Prajñāpāramitā tradition, to a select number of concepts. Let us consider one such application.

> What was taught by the Tathāgata as heap of merit, as no heap of merit, that has been taught by the Tathāgata. Therefore, the Tathāgata teaches, "heap of merit, heap of merit."[6]

This statement, generally understood as if it were the Buddhist thesis of ineffability,[7] can be explained in terms of the threefold methodology of the Abhidharma, which, as pointed out in Chapter XIV, was intended as a way of establishing the doctrines of non-substantiality *(anātman)* and dependent arising *(pratītyasamutpāda).*

The Buddha, utilizing a linguistic medium, spoke of a heap of merit. His statement is immediately understood by a substantialist, either Buddhist or non-Buddhist, as a reference to a self-existent substance or unique entity *(svabhāva),* or to an essential characteristic *(svalakṣaṇa).* In either case, the concept stands for something *(kiñcit)* that is true and real in an ultimate sense. For this reason, the concept of heap of merit is immediately negated as no heap of merit. This is intended as the method of non-substantiality or the deconstruction of substantialist implications. Yet it is not an absolute or universal negation, but the negation of a particular definition of the concept of heap of merit. If the negation is not absolute or universal, then there can be other versions of the concept of heap of merit. As far as the Buddha is concerned, this is a concept that is dependently arisen *(pratītyasamutpanna).* Thus the assertion that follows the negation is no more than the recognition that the concept of heap of merit depends on a variety of conditions, and hence is not unique. It is significant that this third statement is presented in quotes which are expressed in the classical Indian languages by the phrase *iti* placed at the end of a term or a sentence,[8] and is different from the first. We may summarize the formula as follows:

1. Heap of merit, heap of merit = ontological commitment, a substantialist or realist explanation.
2. No heap of merit = deconstruction, negation of substance or unique character, with possible nominalist implications.
3. "Heap of merit, heap of merit" (in quotes), representing the reconstruction of the concept in terms of the principle of dependent arising. This would mean that each concept, instead of either representing a unique entity or being an empty term, is a substitute for a human experience which is conditioned by a variety of factors. As such, it has pragmatic meaning and communicative power without being absolute in any way.

The *Vajracchedikā* repeatedly applies this formula to a wide variety of concepts, such as material objects, the world systems, stream of thought, human personality, the fruits of the moral life, the Tathāgata, the Buddha, and the *dharma.*[9] One is reminded of the series of concepts analyzed by the Buddha in the *Mūlapariyāya-sutta.*[10] The conceptual categories to which the formula is applied may not be as exhaustive as the categories examined in the Abhidhamma, but they include most of the important concepts that received metaphysical interpretations at the hands of the substantialists.

The desubstantializing or desolidification of concepts by applying the above formula would mean that the *Vajracchedikā* is propounding a theory of "emptiness" *(śūnyatā).* Yet the term, so popular elsewhere in the Mahāyāna literature, never occurs in this text. This may be due to the fact that "emptiness," with its rather negative connotation, could sweep out the pragmatic meaning and use of concepts, and this latter is highlighted in the *Vajracchedikā* with a quotation from the early discourses of the Buddha. The quotation involves the simile of the raft (Pali, *kulla;* Prakrit, *kola),*[11] and concepts are to be utilized as one would use a raft—only for the sake of crossing over the sea of suffering—but not to be grasped as absolute truths. This is, indeed, the solution to the problem of ideological conflict and a way to lead a peaceful life *(araṇa-vihāra).*

The skepticism that led the Buddhists toward rejecting an absolutist notion of truth, and therefore of incorruptible concepts, which are supposed to reveal such truths, is expressed in a quatrain (whose counterparts are found in the early discourses)[12] that serves as the conclusion to the text:

> As stars, an eye-disease, a lamp,
> A mock show, dew drops or a bubble,
> A dream, a flash of lightning, or a cloud,
> So should one perceive what is dispositionally conditioned.[13]

It may be noted that the scheme or formula developed in the *Vajracchedikā* to deconstruct absolutist metaphysics became extremely popular in the East Asian Buddhist tradition, especially in Ch'an (Zen) Buddhism, where the *Vajracchedikā* was regarded as a *locus classicus* (see Chapter XXIII).

After repeated use of the formula to negate metaphysical ideas, the *Vajracchedikā* presents the more positive doctrine of the Buddha in two quatrains. Once again, these quatrains express a thought that is not unfamiliar to the early discourses:[14]

> Those who by my form did see me,
> And those who followed me by voice,
> Wrong the efforts they engage in,
> Me those people will not see.
>
> The Buddhas are to be seen through the *dharma,*
> For the *dharma*-bodies are the Guides.
> The nature of *dharma* should not be discerned,
> Nor can it be discerned.

It is tempting to interpret this as implying a theory of absolutism transcending ordinary sense experiences *(saṃjñā)* as well as cognitions *(vijñāna).* But this would mean abandoning every effort in the *Vajracchedikā* to eliminate mysterious substances, ultimate realities, and absolute truths by using the formula or schema discussed earlier. Instead, it is possible to explain the above statement as implying that what is important is the moral principle *(dharma)* as embodied in the Buddha's teachings *(dharma)*, which can lead a person to freedom and peace. The search directed at discovering who the Buddha essentially is, what buddhahood essentially means, contributed to endless conflicts even during the time of the Buddha, so much so that he once advised his disciples, "He who perceives the *dhamma*, he perceives me" *(Yo dhammaṃ passati so maṃ passati)*.[15] The *Vajracchedikā* is not a far cry from this.

However, in the interpretation of the life of the *bodhisattva*, the *Vajracchedikā* highlights a theme which eventually contributed to a belief that may not be so consistent with the teachings of early Buddhism. In the early discourses, three terms are often used to describe the state of release *(vimokkha)*, the highest among them being the "cessation of perception and what is experienced or felt" *(saññāvedayitanirodha)*, or simply the "attainment of cessation" *(nirodha-samāpatti)*. The three terms are *suñña* (empty), *animitta* (without a mysterious cause), and *appaṇihita* (unestablished).[16] We have already indicated that the state of cessation is not identical with the kind of freedom implied by the term *nibbāna* (see Chapter IX). The foregoing explanation of the "perfection of wisdom" *(prajñāpāramitā)* would, in a sense, rule out any identification of it with the state of cessation. Furthermore, a semantic equivalent of the term "unestablished" *(appaṇihita)* is used in the early discourses to refer to the consciousness *(viññāṇa)* of a freed person at the moment of death. It is said that such a person passes away without his consciousness being established anywhere *(appatiṭṭhitena viññāṇena)*.[17]

It is significant to note that the *Vajracchedikā* does not confine this last term, *apratiṣṭhita*, to a description of the state of cessation *(nirodha)*, which is a non-cognitive state, or the death of the freed person *(parinibbuta)*, but extends its use to include the behavior of the *bodhisattva* as well. This may seem harmless at first sight, for the aspirant to enlightenment is expected to abandon all lust, hatred, and confusion as he makes his way toward the final goal. Yet, in emphasizing this idea of not being established in anything, the *bodhisattva* was compelled to abandon any and every form of interest, not merely lust and hatred. It is this emphasis that may have eventually contributed to the theory of self-sacrifice or suicide as a means of salvation, espoused in the *Saddharmapuṇḍarīka* as well as in some of the *Jātakas* and *Avadānas*. It is, no doubt, an ideal that conflicts with what is found in the earlier tradition, where one's own welfare *(atta-d-attha)* as well as the welfare of others *(parattha)* needs to be recognized. In a sense, the conception of the "unestablished" *(apratiṣṭhita)*, when utilized in the explanation of the behavior of the *bodhisattva*, ushers in or makes room for the notion of "duty" so popular in the absolutistic traditions.

CHAPTER XVI

Nāgārjuna and the *Mūlamadhyamakakārikā*

According to most available accounts, Nāgārjuna was a brahman from South India. Archaeological discoveries at Amarāvatī confirm the fact that he was a friend of the Sātavāhana king, Gautamīputra Śātakarṇi, to whom he addressed his *Friendly Epistle (Sahṛd-lekhā).*[1] On the basis of this evidence, Nāgārjuna is believed to have lived during the latter part of the second century and the early part of the third century (ca. 150–250 A.D.).[2]

Two slightly differing accounts of his early life are available. Tibetan sources state that his parents decided to ordain him as a Buddhist monk early in his childhood, after learning from an astrologer that he was destined to die prematurely. The boy is said to have escaped this fate as a result of practicing the *amitāyur-dhāraṇī* under the tutelage of his teacher, Rāhulabhadra, at Nālandā.[3] Even if one is skeptical about the historicity of this account, there is no reason to doubt the efficacy of the practice of *dhāraṇī* (see Chapter XXII) or the association of Nāgārjuna with the Tibetan Buddhist tradition, where he is honored as a second buddha. The second account is available in Kumārajīva's *Kao-seng-chuan,*[4] which tells us that Nāgārjuna, in the company of two other friends, practiced psychokinesis *(ṛddhi),* made himself invisible, and, entering the royal harem, seduced its ladies. His friends were caught red-handed by the palace guards when they failed to make themselves invisible again, and were executed. Nāgārjuna narrowly escaped. This incident made him realize that craving for sense pleasures is a potent cause of suffering, which is the second noble truth in Buddhism; hence his decision to join the Buddhist Order. The allusion in this second story is as compelling as that in the first. While traditional yoga emphasized the mystical aspect, Buddhist yoga underscored its moral dimensions. One cannot find a better anecdote to illustrate this difference.

Here, then, we have a Nāgārjuna who was looking for the original Buddhist tradition. He discovered it in the Prajñāpāramitā tradition, allegorically explained as something he obtained from the *nāgas,* the Buddha being the foremost among them (hence his title, *mahānāga,* the "great serpent" or "great elephant," both symbolizing great powers of memory and discrimination). The Prajñāpāramitā tradition was gradually becoming popular in India at this time. We have already suggested the close relationship between the early discourses and the early Prajñāpāramitā tradition. The biographical accounts of Nāgārjuna agree in maintaining that, after being deeply satisfied with the *Prajñāpāramitā-sūtras,* Nāgārjuna went in search of the "other teachings of the Buddha."[5] The important question is, Where did he go looking for the "other teachings of the Buddha"? It would not have been very sensible for a philosopher like Nāgārjuna to depend on texts like the *Saddharmapuṇḍarīka-sūtra* (*Lotus Sūtra,* which was, in fact, gradually evolving during his day reaching its final form around 220 A.D.)[6] for any information about the Buddha's "other teachings." This was the first Mahāyāna *sūtra* that downgraded the early discourses as mere fodder for the unintelligent disciples who surrounded the Buddha. Nāgārjuna was probably not swayed by such theories, especially after being influenced by the sophisticated philosophical thinking embodied in the Prajñāpāramitā tradition. Indeed, Nāgārjuna's attitude toward the Pratyekabuddhas and the Śrāvakas is very different from that of many other extreme Mahāyāna thinkers.[7] This should eliminate any assumption of prejudice on his part against the early discourses.

Even a cursory glance at the *Mūlamadhyamakakārikā, Verses on the Fundamentals of the Middle Way* (abbreviated hereafter as the *Kārikā*) will leave the reader of this most significant work of Nāgārjuna with the impression that it is not only a grand commentary on the Buddha's discourse to Kaccāyana, the only discourse cited by name,[8] but also a detailed and careful analysis of most of the important discourses included in the Nikāyas and the Āgamas, especially those of the *Aṭṭhakavagga* of the *Sutta-nipāta.* In my *Nāgārjuna: The Philosophy of the Middle Way* (1986), I have provided a detailed analysis of the *Kārikā* in relation to the early discourses of the Buddha.[9] Here I will deal only with Nāgārjuna's basic philosophical approach, as embodied in his *Kārikā,* in order to understand his position among the various luminaries that dotted the history of the Buddhist tradition.

Moggalīputta-tissa, as described in Chapter XIII, was compelled to adopt a polemical standpoint, since he was confronted by an array of metaphysical thinkers as well as those who misinterpreted the simple rules of discipline *(vinaya).* This was forced on him by circumstances, especially the invitation of Emperor Aśoka to purify the Buddha's dispensation. Yet he demonstrated a philosophical acumen that remained unparalleled until the time of Nāgārjuna. Not burdened by any such responsibilities, Nāgārjuna was able to confine himself primarily to the philosophical issues, and therefore was able to produce one of the most remarkable treatises ever compiled by a Buddhist. It is also possible that Moggalīputta-tissa had to deal with philosophical issues relating to the conceptions of person *(puggala)*, phenomena *(dhamma)*, and transcendence *(lokuttaravāda)* in their nascent stages. By the time of Nāgārjuna, almost five centuries later, these metaphysical theories had come to be presented with greater sophistication, so the task was not made easy for him. Yet he seems to have risen to the occasion equipped with an extremely analytical mind.

Even though the metaphysical concept that was repeatedly rejected in the Prajñāpāramitā literature is referred to by the terms *ātma, sattva, jīva,* and *pudgala,* Nāgārjuna identifies the doctrines of the metaphysical schools with the two terms *svabhāva* (own-nature, self-nature, substance) and *ātman* (self). Yet his major problem was the Sarvāstivāda doctrine of substance.

Nāgārjuna seems to have realized that the problem of substance is the problem of explaining causality and change. These were two basic themes in the Buddha's explanation of existence. Therefore, before proceeding to establish the non-substantiality of all elements *(dharma-nairātmya)*, Nāgārjuna devoted two chapters to the clarification of these two issues. The Buddha's conception of "dependent arising" was an attempt to avoid introducing mysterious substances to account for causal relations. Nāgārjuna had no objection to the Abhidhamma formulation of causal relations so long as the relata are not regarded as having a unique nature or substance *(svabhāva)* in terms of which they are to be related.[10] Similarly, if a causal relation can be established without positing a unique substance, and if this causal relation can account for the experienced identity (which is not absolute), then there is no need to postulate absolute difference or otherness *(parabhāva)* either.[11] In other words, this is a rejection of the rationalist solution to the problem of causation. How that rationalistic explanation leads to a paradox has already been pointed out (see Chapter XII). Yet a total renunciation of the rational content of knowledge would not leave the empirical sound and secure. Hence Nāgārjuna turns to the pragmatic definition of an event as fruit *(artha)*, arguing against the rationalist that the fruit is dependently arisen, neither pre-existing as a substance nor something absolutely different, without at the same time arguing for an essentialist explanation that the fruit itself is a unique event.

A similar set of metaphysical theories relating to change is taken up next. Movement or motion being one of the most perceptible processes of change, he chooses three metaphysical views for criticism:

1. A moving entity moves.
2. A non-moving entity moves.
3. A moving and non-moving entity moves.

The first of these represents absolute identity between two events determined on the basis of motion, the second assumes absolute difference, and the third is a combination of the first two. Nāgārjuna's rejection of the three views is stated as follows:

> An existing mover does not carry out the movement in any of the three ways. Neither does a non-existing mover carry out the movement in any of the three ways. Nor does a person carry out a movement, both existing and non-existing, in any of the three ways. Therefore, neither the motion, nor the mover, nor the space moved is evident.[12]

A philosopher who recognizes a theory of dependence cannot speak of motion, a mover, or even the space moved in an essentialist way. Here, only the substantialist and essentialist perspectives are criticized by Nagarjuna, not any and every conception of causation and change. The substantialist and essentialist perspectives, as mentioned earlier, were advocated by the Sarvāstivādins and the Sautrāntikas, respectively.

The Non-substantiality of Elements *(Dharma-nairātmya)*

Chapters III to XV of the *Kārikā* are intended to establish the non-substantiality of elements *(dharma)* but not, as is generally believed, to eliminate the conception of elements altogether. Here our analysis relates to elements treated from an objective standpoint; the subjective standpoint will be considered in the next section. Three of the prominent categories of the early discourses as well as the Abhidhamma are at the top of the list. Categories discussed are as follows:

1. Faculties *(indriya)*
2. Aggregates *(skandha)*
3. Elements *(dhātu)*
4. Lust *(rāga)*
5. Dispositionally conditioned *(saṃskṛta)*
6. Action and agent *(karma-kāraka)*
7. Antecedent state *(pūrva)*
8. Fire and fuel *(agnīndhana)*
9. Prior and posterior ends *(purvāparakoṭi)*
10. Suffering *(duḥkha)*
11. Dispositions *(saṃskāra)*
12. Association *(saṃsarga)*
13. Self-nature *(svabhāva)*

Some of these categories constitute the subject matter of the Abhidhamma. These even reflect some aspects of the Abhidharma methodology, namely, enumeration, classification, and synthesis. While the first eleven categories represent enumeration and classification, avoiding the wearisome repetition of the Abhidhamma, the twelfth category accounts for synthesis.

Without taking into consideration the fact that Nāgārjuna was specifically criticizing the substantialist and essentialist interpretations of these categories, and misled by Candrakīrti's view that Nāgārjuna is here adopting the *reductio ad absurdum (prāsaṅgika)* method of analysis, many a modern scholar has been led to believe that Nāgārjuna was placing these categories under the executioner's block. However, a more cautious examination reveals that he was using a surgeon's scalpel to peel off the cancerous elements infecting a healthy body of conceptions.

We have mentioned that the categories discussed here relate to elements examined from an objective standpoint. It is well known that an objective standpoint can deteriorate into a view regarding ultimately objective realities independent of any human perspective, i.e., a view from nowhere.[13] Nāgārjuna's concluding statement after analyzing "elements" *(dhātu)* should serve as a corrective not only to the rather transcendentalist interpretation offered by Candrakīrti but also to that of the substantialist, whose conception of objectivity calls for an annihilation of the human perspective:

> Those who are of little intelligence, who perceive the existence as well as non-existence of existents, do not perceive the appeasement of the object, the auspicious.[14]

What Nāgārjuna is recommending is the appeasement of the conception of the object, neither its elevation to an ultimate reality nor its annihilation. It is not the elimination of any and every conception of it. Here he was faithfully following the footsteps of the Buddha (see Chapter VII). Thus, after performing a careful and delicate surgery in relation to all thirteen categories, Nāgārjuna, in Chapter XV, utilizes the executioner's block to get rid of the conception of substance *(svabhāva)*.

The metaphysical conception associated with the category of faculties *(indriya)* is taken up first, although it is the second mentioned in the early discourses as well as in the Abhidhamma. In doing so, Nāgārjuna is giving priority to epistemology. Among the faculties, he focuses on the eye *(cakṣu)*. Even though the chapter is called "The Examination of the Faculty of Eye" *(Cakṣur-indriya-parīkṣā)*, Nāgārjuna is not interested in examining the visual faculty itself, for there was not much controversy about it. The subject of controversy was the function of the eye, namely, seeing *(darśana)*. The metaphysical view that was prevalent, even as far back as the *Upaniṣads*, was that there were two processes involved in seeing: seeing itself, and seeing the object. According to the *Upaniṣads*, the latter is the experiencing of the object (= the bird enjoying the fruit), and the former, the coordinator of the perceptions of the object (= the bird who simply keeps on watching). In the rationalist traditions of the West, the seeing itself can be compared to the Kantian "transcendental unity of apperception," which is a necessary condition for the empirical understanding of the object. Among the Buddhist metaphysicians, this was consciousness perceiving itself *(svasaṃvedana),* which results in the dichotomies necessary for rational thinking (see Chapter XX). Nāgārjuna's criticism relates to this metaphysical conception only. A similar analysis is made of the remaining categories.

Arguments against the Conception of Substance

The chapter on "The Examination of Self-nature" *(Svabhāva-parīkṣa),* though brief (only eleven verses), is one of the most important. Nāgārjuna's main argument is that a conception of self-nature or substance cannot be reconciled with the doctrine of "dependent arising" *(pratītyasamutpāda)* or the theory, as developed in the Abhidhamma, that things, events, or phenomena are dependent on causes *(hetu)* or conditions *(pratyaya).* If substance were to arise as a result of causes and conditions, it has to be made *(kṛtaka).* This would be inconsistent with the very definition of substance. If it is not made *(a-kṛtaka),* then it is unique and has no relationship to or is not dependent on another. Self-nature or substance thus involves the conception of the "unique," the "unshared," or the "independent" (referred to in the later Theravāda tradition as *a-sādhāraṇa;* see Chapter XXI).

Having argued that the conception of substance is incompatible with a theory of dependence, Nāgārjuna makes a further claim that if self-nature or substance does not exist, one cannot speak of other-nature or a different substance, "for self-nature of other-nature is called self-nature."[15] The conceptual trap into which the Rationalist falls is then highlighted. If existence were understood in terms of identity (substance) and difference (otherness), then without these two aspects existence itself would be meaningless. If existence *(bhāva),* in this sense, is meaningless, non-existence *(abhāva)* is also not available. Yet it is the change of existence that people normally call non-existence. In other words, the conceptions of identity and difference militate against the recognition not only of dependence but also of change.

At this point Nāgārjuna refers to the Buddha's discourse to Kaccāyana[16] and draws the connections between self-nature and eternalism, on the one hand, and other-nature and annihilationism, on the other. Thus, when Nāgārjuna abandoned the conceptions of self-nature and other-nature, he was simply following the Buddha, who rejected the notions of eternalism and annihilationism.

The Non-substantiality of the Subject *(Pudgala-nairātmya)*

Here we begin with a discussion of the problem of transmigration, explained either in terms of the aggregates or of personal beings. The themes under examination are:

1. Bondage and release *(bandhana-mokṣa)*
2. Fruit of action *(karma-phala)*
3. Self *(ātma)*
4. Time *(kāla)*
5. Harmony *(sāmagrī)*
6. Occurrence and dissolution *(sambhava-vibhava)*
7. Thus-Gone-One *(tathāgata)*
8. Perversions *(viparyāsa)*
9. Noble truths *(ārya-satya)*
10. Freedom *(nirvāṇa)*

All these relate to the person who is either in bondage *(bandhana)* or has attained freedom *(mokṣa)*. As in the previous section, Nāgārjuna's attempt here is to weed out the metaphysical conception of a subtle personality *(pudgala)*, which is supposed to transmigrate from one life to another until the attainment of freedom, as well as the equally metaphysical conception of a permanent and eternal being who has attained freedom.

In the previous section, the conception that was criticized most often was that of the substantialist Sarvāstivādins, while the essentialist perspective of the Sautrāntikas took a secondary place. In the present section, it is mostly the conception of the essentialist Sautrāntikas that comes under fire. It is well known that the essentialism of the Sautrāntikas paved the way for the Vatsīputriyas to openly espouse the conception of a subtle personality, neither identical with nor different from the aggregates—a theory discussed at length by Vasubandhu in an appendix to his *Abhidharmakośa-bhāṣya.*[17]

In dealing with the problem of transmigration of a subtle personality, Nāgārjuna could not help being dialectical or argumentative. If something is permanent, then it is meaningless to say that it transmigrates. Transmigration implies moving from one place to another, i.e., disappearing from one place and appearing in another. Disappearing and appearing mean change, not permanence. Permanence would mean eternal presence, whereas if things are impermanent, in the sense of disappearing *(uccheda)*, they will never transmigrate.

Immediately after presenting the above argument, Nāgārjuna appeals to the empirical analysis of the human person provided by the Buddha. He says that after examining the five constituents of the human person, a transmigrating personality was not discoverable. The problem of moral responsibility (i.e., action and its fruits) is then taken up, and he carefully distinguishes the sense in which the Buddha explained them (i.e., in terms of dependent arising) from that of the metaphysician who relies on the conception of substance. Explaining moral responsibility in terms of dependence required not only abandoning the notion of a permanent self *(ātma)* but also renunciation of the metaphysical views pertaining to time *(kāla)*, harmony of causes and conditions *(sāmagrī)*, and the processes of occurrence and dissolution *(sambhava-vibhava)*.

✓ After dealing with the metaphysical issues relating to the human person, bondage, and moral responsibility, Nāgārjuna proceeds to examine similar metaphysical interpretations of the person who has "walked the way" *(tathāgata)*, that is, attained freedom. If non-substantiality is a synonym for dependent arising, and both conceptions explain the open-ended nature of the universe, which is neither eternal and fixed *(śāśvata)* nor discontinuous and haphazard *(uccheda)*, then that openness should allow for possibilities or new situations to occur without generating conflicts. Conflicts are often creations of human conceptualizations that tend to fix the empirical world of flux and change into eternal objects, truths, and events, as well as of concepts that are supposed to correspond to such eternal objects, truths, and events, respectively. The desolidification of such concepts allows for flexibility and change. Similarly, a person who has attained freedom from such conceptual obsessions is able to pursue a peaceful way of life *(araṇa-vihāra)* without becoming involved in any conflicts. The Buddha's statement, "Monks, I do not conflict with the world; the world conflicts with me,"[18] explains the behavior of the person who has attained freedom. The universe, when it is not structured by the solidified dispositions *(saṃskāra)* of human beings, is likewise. The true nature of the universe *(jagat)*—in contrast to the "world" fabricated by metaphysical conceptions—as well as that of a person who has "walked the way" *(tathāgata)* of that universe is not artificially put together or structured *(saṃskṛta)* but dependently arisen *(pratītyasamutpanna)*. Nāgārjuna's positive conclusion here is that, just as the universe *(jagat)* is non-substantial *(niḥsvabhāva)*, so is the person who has attained freedom.

The next three chapters of the *Kārikā* reflect Nāgārjuna's understanding of the extremely important aspect of the Buddha's discourse to Kaccāyana. In that discourse, the Buddha admonished Kaccāyana as follows:

> The world, for the most part, Kaccāyana, is bound by approach, grasping, and inclination. And he who does not follow that approach and grasping, that determination of mind, that inclination and disposition, who does not cling to or adhere to the view "This is my self," who thinks, "Suffering that is

> subject to arising arises; suffering that is subject to ceasing ceases," such a person does not doubt, is not perplexed. Herein, his knowledge is not other-dependent. Thus far, Kaccāyana, there is right view.[19]

The essentialist perspectives have left us with a dichotomy between fact and value. Facts are facts, whether we like them or not. They are true in the sense of being true always. The Upaniṣadic conception of self *(ātma)* fulfilled those requirements. For this reason, when the Upaniṣadic thinkers wanted to speak of values, they postulated a conception of *brahman.* The Buddha's pragmatic approach to the problem of truth left him with the belief that "what is true is useful" and that "what is useful is true." Nāgārjuna realized that, by renouncing the conception of an eternal self and focusing on the problem of suffering, the Buddha was defining truth in terms of relevance to human life: hence the four noble truths *(ārya-satya).* Perversions of knowledge, as the Buddha perceived, stood in the way of appreciating the four noble truths as truths, that is, being subjected to suffering as ordinary human beings and enjoying freedom and happiness as enlightened persons. If suffering is true, as the first noble truth asserts, and if freedom is true, which is the third noble truth, the two cannot be viewed as lower and higher, respectively. Furthermore, even the path leading from suffering to happiness is a noble truth, which implies abandoning the conception of a hierarchy of truths. This important consideration needs to be kept in mind when we explain Nāgārjuna's conception of two truths.

The two truths are generally understood as the conventional *(saṃvṛti)* and ultimate *(paramārtha).* Such an understanding would mean the abdication of the philosophical enterprise of the Buddha, the compilers of the canonical Abhidhamma, and Moggalīputta-tissa. It also would mean the renunciation of the entire analytical project that Nāgārjuna so ably pursued in the earlier part of the *Kārikā.* Thus the conception of two truths needs to be examined in a totally different light.

In fact, the four noble truths can easily be reduced to two truths, by including the first, second, and fourth under the category of conventional truth *(saṃvṛti-satya).* Their truth depends on normal consequences or fruits *(artha).* The third represents a truth in an ultimate sense *(paramārthataḥ)* only in terms of being an ultimate fruit *(parama-artha).* It is an ultimate fruit that any human being can enjoy, and this involves the happiness of oneself as well as of others. It is, indeed, the standard in terms of which a human person's moral life comes to be evaluated. It is not simply a rational standard or criterion, but one that has been achieved by the enlightened person. Nāgārjuna's controversial chapter on "Freedom" *(nirvāṇa)* is therefore an attempt to desubstantialize both the person who has attained freedom and freedom itself. Just as the Buddha surprised his disciples who had been brought up in the Brahmanical tradition, which recognizes *brahman* as a unique experience, by not admitting any experience as the unique experience of the happiness of *nibbāna* (see Chapter IX), so did Nāgārjuna cause astonishment in the minds of his contemporaries as well as ours by saying:

> The Buddha did not teach the appeasement of all objects, the appeasement of all obsessions, and the auspicious [all synonyms for *nirvāṇa*] as some thing to some one at some place.[20]

For Nāgārjuna, conception *(prajñapti)* becomes the key to every mystery in the world: it is dependent arising, it is emptiness, and it is the middle path.[21] There is no ultimate or absolute reality that transcends conceptual thinking.

Once absolutism, substantialism, and essentialism had been banished from the sphere of philosophical discourse, Nāgārjuna was at liberty to go back to the Buddha's explanation of the human person both in bondage and in freedom. He immediately returned to the conclusion of the Buddha's discourse to Kaccāyana, which represents the popular theory of the twelvefold formula of causation *(dvādasāṅga-pratītyasamutpāda),* its positive *(anuloma)* description explaining a person in bondage and its negative *(pratiloma)* description defining one who has attained freedom from suffering in the present life as well as in future lives, by not being reborn.

The *Kārikā*'s final chapter is on views *(dṛṣṭi).* The Buddha had referred to sixty-two views with which he disagreed; his own was the sixty-third. To insist on rejecting the sixty-two views and uphold a sixty-third would be dogmatism. Nāgārjuna did not want the Buddha's to be a dogmatic view. His was a pragmatic view that called for modification of any view depending on the context and its pragmatic value. It was not an absolute view. If views have contextual reference and pragmatic value, there is no reason to cling to any one of them as being absolute. Abandoning the grasping of any view as the ultimate one seems to be the inevitable way. This, indeed, is the final advice of Nāgārjuna.

CHAPTER XVII

The *Saddharmapuṇḍarīka-sūtra* and Conceptual Absolutism

The *Saddharmapuṇḍarīka-sūtra* or *Discourse on the Lotus of the True Dharma,* popularly known as the *Lotus Sūtra,* is the most important text of popular Mahāyāna Buddhism. It antedates Nāgārjuna but was probably completed during his lifetime or sometime after.[1] Leon Hurvitz, whose recent translation of the Chinese version of Kumārajīva has added significantly to our understanding of this work, summarizes the concerns of the text as follows: "First, it boasted that its practitioners were aiming at the salvation not merely of themselves but of all animate beings as well. Second, it concerned itself with the Universal and the Absolute, although these meant different things to different schools within that movement."[2] Hurvitz's first point refers to the moral philosophy inculcated in Mahāyāna, and the *Lotus* has much to say about it; his second refers to its metaphysics. Unfortunately, the *Lotus* gives us very little information as to what this Universal or Absolute is. If, as some modern scholars believe, Absolutism in Mahāyāna were to be established on the basis of "emptiness" *(śūnyatā),* the *Lotus* leaves us empty-handed. Commenting on the doctrine of emptiness in the *Lotus,* Hurvitz observes, "All the same, the *Lotus*'s references to 'emptiness,' if laid end to end, would not amount to much. The *Lotus*'s concern, after all, is much less with theory, than with practice."[3] For this reason, the only way the nature of this Absolutism can be clarified is by examining its scattered epistemological reflections to see whether they have any relationship to the doctrines of other schools of Buddhism, especially the conception of "emptiness" discussed in the previous chapter.

The Absolutism of the *Lotus* pertains to both the path and the goal. According to it, there is only one true path, not a second or a third. The following simile is used to illustrate this claim:

> It is just as the potter, O Kāśyapa, makes pots with the same clay. Among them some become pots for sugar lumps, some pots for clarified butter, some pots for curds or milk, while some become pots for inferior and filthy

> things; and just as there is no difference in the clay, but rather a supposed difference in the pots based solely on the things put into them, in just this way, O Kāśyapa, is there this one and only one vehicle, to wit, the Buddha Vehicle. There exists neither a second nor a third.[4]

It may be noted that the simile of the pot *(bhājana)* is the same as the one used by the Buddha, and quoted by Moggalīputta-tissa to illustrate the relativity of the meanings of concepts in order to criticize the claims of the Personalists (see Chapter XIII). Yet, if the simile were used to illustrate the existence of metaphysical entities like the ultimately real elements (*dharma,* like clay) out of which all things (such as pots) are made, then it would be inappropriate for the Mahāyānists to use this example to justify the ultimate reality of the one vehicle, for one of the most significant claims they made against most other schools concerned their own conception of the non-substantiality of elements *(dharma-nairātmya).* The important question, then, is, What does the pot, or the clay out of which the pot is made, refer to? Does the concept refer to something or to itself?

The problem is further complicated when the *Lotus* proceeds to define the one true conception of the goal. It says:

> Nirvāṇa, you see, Kāśyapa, comes from an understanding of the sameness of all dharmas *(sarva-dharma-samatāvabodha).* And it is one, not two, not three.[5]

The sameness *(samatā)* of all dharmas cannot be accounted for in terms of a substance *(svabhāva),* like the one postulated by the Sarvāstivādins, or the self *(ātma)* recognized by the Upaniṣadic thinkers. The chapter on "Medicinal Herbs" *(Auṣadha)* provides some clues to an understanding of the epistemology as well as the metaphysics of the *Lotus.* Here, while presenting the path as well as the goal as one ultimate truth or reality, the *Lotus* for the first time recognizes a hierarchy of truths. The first of these is the ordinary world of human bondage created by lust, hatred, and confusion; the second is the world of impermanent, empty, and non-substantial dharmas characterized by arising and ceasing; and the third represents the world of dharmas, "non-arisen, non-ceased, unbound, unreleased, not dark, not bright."[6] To account for this hierarchy, the *Lotus* also provides three levels or degrees of knowledge. The first may be taken as the ordinary sense experiences dominated by lust, hatred, and confusion. Human beings born with these three tendencies are referred to as those born blind *(jātyandha).* The second consists of the knowledge of those who have eliminated lust, hatred, and confusion through development of the five kinds of higher knowledge *(pañcābhijñā)*—namely, clairvoyance, clairaudience, telepathy, retrocognition, and psychokinesis, all of which enable a person to attain freedom *(vimokṣa)* from the cycle of births and deaths. This constitutes the knowledge and understanding of the *arhat* and the *pratyekabuddha*. (This is a dubious attribution on the part of the *Lotus*. According to the early discourses, no person attained freedom from the cycle of births and deaths through development of the five forms of higher knowledge without at the same time developing knowledge of the waning of influxes [*āsavakkhaya-ñāṇa*], this latter being often defined as wisdom [*paññā*].) Third is the highest intuition *(prajñā)*, through which one is able to perceive all dharmas as "non-arisen, non-ceased, unbound, unreleased, not dark, not bright."

The levels of understanding are illustrated by similes. The first form of knowledge and understanding is that of one seated in his inner house *(antargṛhaṃ nisanna)*. One who remains in the dark inner house perceives no colors or shapes; he is blind by birth. However, the Buddha is able to cure his blindness (= ignorance) by making him move outside and enabling him to perceive colors and shapes revealed by the light of the sun. This refers to the immediate disciples of the Buddha, who attained freedom from continued births and deaths by realizing the variety as well as impermanence of phenomena. Yet they are unable to enlighten or save others; to do that is the function of the Buddha, who is like the sun. A comparison with Plato's famous "parable of the cave" is irresistible.

This description of the degrees of knowledge and of reality can easily justify not only the ultimate reality of the one goal (= *buddha*hood) but also the ultimate reality of the one path leading to it (= *bodhisattva*-hood). However, considering the various schools that the *Lotus* was criticizing, it is still not easy to determine what it is negating and what it is asserting as far as philosophical thinking is concerned.

Let us assume that the people who are blind by birth are the substantialists, both non-Buddhist and Buddhist. Since they believe in permanent and eternal entities *(ātma, svabhāva)*, they are compelled to deny plurality as well as change and evolution. The second group of people would be those who have adopted the philosophical standpoint of non-substantiality *(anātma, niḥsvabhāva)*, supplemented by a theory of "dependent arising" *(pratītyasamutpāda)*, and who therefore are able to free themselves from suffering and the continued cycle of births and deaths. They can recognize plurality as well as change and evolution, as explained by the Buddha in the early discourses and faithfully adopted by the mainline Buddhist tradition, represented by the Abhidhamma, Moggalīputta-tissa, the Prajñāpāramitā tradition and Nāgārjuna. The most significant question then becomes, Who is left out? or, Who are the ones who adopt the third standpoint, which represents the highest degree of knowledge as well as the ultimate truth revealed by that knowledge?

If it is assumed that this ultimate standpoint involves recognizing an ultimate reality beyond all conceptual thinking and description, that reality certainly will not be any different from the permanent and eternal entities of the substantialists. The non-Buddhist substantialist, such as the Upaniṣadic philosopher, would not say that the self *(ātma)* is the object of conceptual knowledge, nor would the Sarvāstivādin proceed to define a substance *(svabhāva),* except by saying that it exists during the three periods of time. The only way the *Lotus* can avoid these forms of substantialism is by asserting the incorruptibility (i.e., the non-arisen, non-ceased, etc. character) of concepts. Indeed, the example it quotes to illustrate the reality of the *one* path or vehicle (see above) may point in this direction. Like the Platonic theory of incorruptible forms, where each form is sublated by one of higher generality until one reaches the ultimately incorruptible and eternal concept of the Good, the *Lotus* seems to arrive at the ultimately incorruptible, eternal, and all-pervading concept of Buddha. Such an interpretation of the reality recognized in the *Lotus* is further confirmed by the use of the term *sarvākārajñatā* ("knowledge of all *modes*")[7] instead of the more popular *sarvajñatva* ("knowledge of everything"). In terms of functions, the Buddha is comparable to the sun and the moon, which spread their light without discrimination,[8] or to the rain cloud *(megha)* that provides nourishment for every living thing in the universe, once again without making any distinctions.[9] Thus the Buddha becomes the embodiment of universal knowledge *(prajñā)* and compassion *(karuṇā).*

Even though the philosophy of the *Lotus* can therefore be distinguished from the substantialist thought of the non-Buddhists as well as of the Sarvāstivāda Buddhists, it hardly compares with the philosophical standpoint of either the Buddha or of the mainline Buddhist tradition. The reason is that non-substantiality *(anatta)* applies to the highest reality one can experience, namely, freedom *(nirvāṇa),* as well as to conception. Even a text like the *Parivāra,* the conclusion of the *Vinaya Piṭaka,* looked upon both freedom *(nibbāna)* and conception *(paññatti)* as undeniably non-substantial *(anatta;* see Chapter IX).

However, there is one Buddhist school to which the philosophical teachings of the *Lotus* can be related. There is strong evidence that as far as its philosophical standpoint and its reputation are concerned, it has a kinship to the Sautrāntikas, though the two schools are not identical. That relationship may be explained as follows.

We have pointed out that the Sautrāntikas, who were opposed to the substantialist Sarvāstivādins, adopted an essentialist perspective and eventually propounded a theory of nominalism *(prajñaptivāda).* The difference between the Sautrāntika position and that of the mainline Buddhist tradition regarding the evaluation of a concept (variously termed *saṅkhā* and *paññatti* or *prajñapti*) is that the former does not provide it with experiential content, while the latter does. However, the Sautrāntika nominalism moved in a different direction to offer a foundation for the metaphysical conception of a person *(pudgalavāda),* while the nominalism of the *Lotus* moved in the direction of asserting the conception of the ultimate person (i.e., the Buddha).

In terms of reputation, too, the two schools are related. For example, the *Lotus* is the first major text that claimed to be part of the Vaipulya tradition. *Vaipulya* (derived from *vipula,* meaning "great" or "comprehensive") represents the culmination of the transcendentalism *(lokuttaravāda)* known to the *Kathāvatthu.* Thus, by the time the *Lotus* came to be finalized, even some of the texts like the *Mahāvastu* and the *Lalitavistara,* belonging to the Sarvāstivādins but emphasizing the transcendence of the Buddha, were included under the category of the *vaipulya-sūtras.*[10] Not only did the *Lotus* exalt these *sūtras,* it also condemned the discourses belonging to the earlier period[11] and derided the early disciples as people "delighting in the lowly" *(hīnābhiratā)* and as not wise *(aviddasu).*[12] It is understandable that those branded as such by the *Lotus* would respond by condemning the *Lotus* as well as the Vaipulya tradition. Thus we have the rather derogatory term *vaitulyavāda* ("heretical teachings") used by the later commentators of Abhidhamma texts like the *Kathāvatthu,* who identified the transcendentalist views criticized therein as the views of the *vaitulyavādins,* even though this term may not have been in use at the time of the compilation of the *Kathāvatthu* itself.[13] Thus, in the eyes of the opponents of the *Lotus* and its philosophical standpoint, any school that leans toward the *Lotus* is a "heretical school" *(vaitulyavāda).* It is not insignificant that the *Abhidharmadīpa,* a work of the neo-Sarvāstivāda,[14] refers to the Sautrāntikas as "those who have reached the portals of *vaitulyaśāstra.*"[15] If these early commentators understood the philosophical standpoints of the different Buddhist schools, then this statement of the neo-Sarvāstivādins would be no more than an assertion that the essentialist Sautrāntika nominalism is what finally led to the absolute nominalism of the *Lotus,* and therefore of popular Mahāyāna.

Within this absolute nominalism of the *Lotus,* the concrete historical Buddha, the concrete teachings relating to man and morals as embodied in the early discourses, as well as the equally concrete individuals who devoted their lives to the perfection of morality, have no place. Their elimination, coupled with the recognition of an Absolute, compelled the *Lotus* to propound a moral philosophy that is very different from that of the mainline Buddhist tradition. The contextual pragmatism that encouraged adoption of a life conducive to the happiness of oneself as well as others had to be abandoned. The wayfarer has no opportunity to reflect on the consequences of his or her actions, as was encouraged in the Buddha's discourse to the Kālāmas. All he is left with is the "unproduced *dharma*" *(anutpattika-dharma),* the noumenon, of which he has no understanding until the attainment of buddhahood. Hence the *Lotus* encourages the acquiescence *(kṣānti)* of the noumenon,[16] and this is achieved primarily through faith.[17] Faith in the ultimate *dharma,* that is, the Buddha, can be so firm[18] that the wayfarer should be prepared to lay down his own life for it.[19] Sacrifice of one's own happiness, and even life, becomes the ideal way of life. The remaining portions of the *Lotus,* though of enormous religious appeal, are of little philosophical significance.

The religious appeal of the *Lotus* is different from that of the *Bhagavadgītā,* with which it is sometimes compared.[20] Even though the description of the Buddha in the *Lotus* may compare with the *Gītā*'s representation of Nārāyana as clad in all the glory and majesty of a sovereign, the illuminator and vivifier of the world, the two descriptions vary in intent. Whereas the *Gītā* may be interested in compelling the recalcitrant Arjuna to accept its conception of duty by making him realize that the universe, including himself, is the creation of the Almighty, the Buddha of the *Lotus* plays no such role. The glorification of the Buddha in the *Lotus* is done with an altogether different intention. Indeed, it creates a sense of the wondrous and the marvelous *(āścarya, adbhuta)* far beyond what one can find in the earlier Buddhist tradition. But when this is combined with the description of the suffering of ordinary human beings moving through the repeated cycle of births and deaths, it is intended to generate an excitement *(samuttejana)* eventually culminating in appeasement *(sampahaṃsana),* as a result of the realization that all beings are on their way to that ultimate buddhahood. It is in this sense that the *Lotus* is looked upon as a *dhāraṇī* not only to be recited daily but also to be copied and passed around for use by the multitude.

CHAPTER XVIII

The *Laṅkāvatāra-sūtra* and the Great Emptiness *(Mahā-śūnyatā)*

The *Laṅkāvatāra-sūtra* or *Discourse on the Descent into Laṅkā* (hereafter abbreviated as the *Laṅkā*) has a twofold historical significance. First, the title suggests that it is a discourse on the descent or entry into Lanka, and there cannot be much doubt that Lanka refers to the island of Sri Lanka, where Buddhism was established during the reign of the Emperor Aśoka in the third century B.C. The text itself was compiled in India during the fourth century A.D., almost eight centuries later. Yet it is never mentioned in any literature belonging to the Sri Lankan Buddhist tradition, despite the fact that the tradition possesses a carefully compiled set of chronicles such as the *Dīpavaṃsa* and *Mahāvaṃsa,* which include some of the legendary material utilized in the *Laṅkā* itself. Second, the *Laṅkā* is one of the most important texts of the so-called Mahāyāna, being included in the category called the Vaipulya-sūtras. In the East Asian Buddhist tradition, it became the most sacred text of the Tsao-tung Ch'an (Sōtō Zen) school, being introduced into China by Bodhidharma, the first patriarch of the Ch'an tradition. The competent authority on this text, D. T. Suzuki, has downplayed the importance of the first historical fact and emphasized the second. However, both are of tremendous value when assessing the contents of this discourse, especially in the context of the history of Buddhist philosophical thought. Therefore, we have provided an appendix in which an attempt is made to trace the historical background of the compilation of the *Laṅkā*.

Ideologically, the *Laṅkā* follows the doctrines of the *Lotus,* even though the philosophical method itself is derived from the *Vajracchedikā*. We have already seen that the method of the *Vajracchedikā* consisted of the deconstruction of substantialist concepts, Buddhist as well as non-Buddhist, and the reconstruction of empirically meaningful concepts without allowing for ontological *commitment* (see Chapter XV). In fact, the *Laṅkā* refers to the *Vajracchedikā* rather indirectly and quotes the famous passage, "even the dharmas are to be abandoned, and how much more adharmas."[1] However, the method is not applied in the same way as in the latter. The following analysis will clarify the difference.

The second chapter of the *Laṅkā* begins by raising a series of questions. Although the number of questions is mentioned as being 108, there are many more, pertaining to more than 122 topics, some of which are repeated.[2] The topics are mostly those that are discussed in the Abhidharma and previously treated in a more systematic form by an exponent of the Yogācāra idealism, namely, Asaṅga (see Appendix). The Buddha's responses, which come after all the questions have been listed, are equally unsystematic, in that some of the topics on which questions are raised are not even examined. Instead of explaining this as the characteristic Zen method, as perceived by some interpreters, of providing unrelated or meaningless answers to questions, it should be taken as representative of the unsystematic nature of the composition itself. Despite this lack of systematic treatment, it is possible to examine the significance of the Buddha's responses, all of which are presented in identical form. The first relates to "arising" *(utpāda)* being formulated as

utpādapadam anutpādapadaṃ,[3]

which may be translated in two ways:

1. A term for arising is no term for arising.
2. A term for arising is a term for non-arising.

Using *T* for the term and *S* for that which is signified, these may be symbolized as follows:

1. T is S
   $\sim T$ is S
2. T is S
   T is $\sim S$

If we are to adopt the former rendering for the *Laṅkā,* as Suzuki does, then what is rejected is the term or its ability to signify, leaving intact what is signified. This would be to assume that the signified is beyond description. The second possibility would leave the term or the concept intact, but without the signified content. This allows for pouring some new content into the term or concept, which is exactly what the *Vajracchedikā* tried to achieve. According to it,

T is S
T is $\sim S$
$\therefore$ "T is S"

This last statement can accommodate the modification or qualification of both the term and the content (see Chapter xx).

The *Laṅkā* does not adopt the three steps involved in the process of deconstruction and reconstruction. It retains only two steps, intended to achieve deconstruction of all concepts. This would mean adopting a philosophical standpoint in relation to words or concepts that is totally different from what appeared in the earlier Buddhist traditions. We have already seen that the Buddha, the Ābhidhammikas, the *Vajracchedikā,* and Nāgārjuna adopted the same standpoint in their evaluation of concepts. The *Lotus,* on the contrary, recognized the incorruptibility of concepts. Now the *Laṅkā* comes up with a theory that negates the value of concepts altogether.

In the *Laṅka,* Mahāmati comes up with the following argument:

> Fortunate One, is it not because of the reality of words that all things are? If not for words, Fortunate One, there would be no arising of things. Hence, Fortunate One, the existence of all things is by reason of the reality of words.[4]

The Buddha's response, as presented in the prose section, is twofold. First, there are words without objects, that is, empty words such as hare's horns, tortoise's hair, and barren woman's child. Second, words are not available in the real worlds, the buddha-lands *(buddha-kṣetra),* where ideas are expressed by looking steadily, by gestures, by a frown, movement of the eyes, laughing, yawning, by clearing the throat, by recollection, or by trembling.[5] It is interesting to note that this form of communication without words is highlighted by some of the Ch'an (Zen) schools.

This latter enables the *Laṅkā* to accommodate the unspeakable, including the "most excellent Samādhis." However, in the verses that follow, concepts, to which the mainline Buddhist tradition would be prepared to give validity, are taken up and rejected as the imaginations of the ignorant.

> As space, the hare's horns, and barren woman's child are non-entities except as expressed in words, so is *this existence* imagined.
> When causes and conditions are in combination, the ignorant imagine the birth [of this world]; as they fail to understand this reason, they wander about in the triple world which is their dwelling.[6]

The *Laṅkā,* like the *Lotus,* is thus committed to a hierarchy of three degrees of knowledge: (1) worldly *(laukika),* (2) supernormal *(lokottara),* and (3) transcendental *(lokottaratama).*[7] While the characterization of the last form of knowledge as *lokottaratama* ("transcendental" or "super-transcendental") occurs here for the first time, the description of the manner in which it is attained is slightly different from that of the

Lotus. It is described as knowledge generated by "a thorough examination of the imagelessness or appearance-less-ness of dharmas" *(nirābhāsa-dharmapravicaya),* "perceiving non-ceasing and non-arising" *(anirodhānutpādadarśana),* and "the realization of the non-substantiality at the stage of Tathāgata" *(tathāgatabhūminairātmyādhigama).*[8]

The introduction of the two concepts of "imagelessness" or "absence of appearance" *(nirābhāsa)* and the "stage of Tathāgata" *(tathāgatabhūmi)* seems to distinguish the *Laṅkā* from many of the Buddhist texts examined so far. The former leads the *Laṅkā* to an extreme or absolute form of idealism, thereby eliminating any and every form of discrimination as subject and object. The Buddha in the *Laṅkā* was concerned that this concept of the imagelessness would contribute to a negativist view:

> Mahāmati, there are philosophers who are addicted to negativism according to whose philosophical view the non-existence of the hare's horns is ascertained by means of the discriminating intellect which affirms that the self-nature of things ceases with the destruction of their causes, and they say that all things are non-existent like the hare's horns.[9]

This would mean that the theory of "imagelessness" *(nirābhāsa)* can cause the first two natures *(svabhāva)* recognized in the *Laṅkā,* namely, the imagined *(parikalpita)* and the relative *(paratantra),* to cancel each other out, leaving a completely negative feeling. In fact, the seven forms of emptiness include emptiness of relativity or mutuality as well *(itaretara-śūnyatā).*[10]

For the *Laṅkā,* the conception of the "stage of Tathāgata" *(tathāgatabhūmi)* is the only way out of this negativism. It has to be a state in which there exists a positive content, but which is, at the same time, completely free from any conceptualization, discrimination, or thought process. The only candidate for this is the state of cessation *(nirodhasamāpatti),* or the highest stage of the contemplation *(jhāna,* Skt. *dhyāna),* defined in the early Buddhist tradition as the "cessation of perception and what is felt" *(saññāvedayitanirodha).* Even though, according to early Buddhism, any blissful feeling can be experienced only after emerging from the state of cessation because, in the state of cessation, what is felt is eliminated, the *Laṅkā* describes it as "abiding in the triple bliss which characterizes self-realization attained by noble wisdom."[11] It is called the *tathāgata dhyāna,* and is further explained as follows:

> A yogin, while in his exercise, sees the form of the sun or the moon, or something looking like a lotus, or the underworld, or various forms like sky, fire, etc. All these appearances lead him to the way of the philosophers, they throw him down into the state of Śrāvakahood, into the realm of the Pratyekabuddhas. When all these are tossed aside and there is a state of image-

lessness, then a condition in conformity with the Tathatā presents itself; and the Buddhas will come from all their countries and with their shining hands will stroke the head of the benefactor.[12]

What early Buddhism looked upon as a non-cognitive state of rapture *(samādhi, jhāna)* now becomes the stage of Tathāgata *(tathāgatabhūmi)* or the womb of Tathāgata *(tathāgatagarbha)*. It is a state of ultimate experience totally free from discrimination *(nirvikalpa)* and imagelessness *(nirābhāsa)*,[13] and hence is referred to as *nirvikalpaka-samādhi*, the highest experience a practitioner of yoga *(yogācārin)* can hope to achieve.

Psychology in the Laṅkāvatāra

The denial of the validity of all concepts left the *Laṅkā* with the responsibility of accounting for how all such concepts are formed. This represents its psychological enterprise. It is appropriate to begin our examination of that undertaking with the *Laṅkā*'s reference to the four things to be achieved by a practitioner of yoga in order to become a great yogin *(mahāyogin)*.[14]

1. Cultivation of the idea that the visible *(dṛṣya)* is one's own mind *(svacitta)*.
2. Renunciation of the views relating to arising, enduring, and ceasing.
3. Perception of the non-existence of external entities.
4. Thoroughly understanding that the realization of the noble wisdom is within one's own self.

The first three are steps leading to the realization mentioned in the fourth. The first is the inevitable conclusion of the skepticism that usually plagues sensory experience. Doubts concerning what is experienced through the senses lead the yogin to compare it with dream experience, with eye-disease, with a hare's horns or barren woman's child. What is left over after such doubting is the experiencing mind.[15]

One of the reasons for the uncertainty regarding the perception of the object is its instability. Very often, even the most enlightened philosophers have been compelled to assume that if something is real or true, it must be real or true always. The yogin who has already come to the conclusion that the object of perception is simply the experiencing mind is therefore led to the conclusion that arising, duration, and ceasing are acts of mind and not produced by any external event. This constitutes his perception of the unreality of the objective world, which is the third level of achievement.

Here the yogin is at the threshold of the highest experience, often referred to in the *Laṅkā* as the realization of the noble wisdom within one's own self *(svapratyātmāryajñānādhigama).* This realization is achieved instantaneously.[16] Thus the *Laṅkā* can accommodate both the gradual *(krama)* and sudden *(yugapad)* ways to enlightenment.

The epistemological foundation is thus laid for outlining an idealistic psychology. The mainline Buddhist tradition had recognized mind *(mano)* as a faculty *(indriya),* along with six types of consciousness *(viññāṇa)*—five based on the five physical sense organs and objects, plus mental consciousness *(manoviññāṇa),* representing the contact between mind and concepts *(dhammā).* For the idealist of the *Laṅkā,* these seven, including the mind *(mano),* which earlier was viewed as a faculty *(indriya),* are forms of consciousness *(vijñāna).*[17] Since these were defined by the metaphysicians as being momentary, the idealist of the *Laṅkā* needed a form of consciousness that accounts for continuity. The Sautrāntika metaphysicans had already posited a receptacle *(āśraya)* in which the momentary impressions are contained. This was not adequate for the idealist, who needed to explain not only continuity but also value judgments such as good and bad, which cannot be part of momentary forms of consciousness.[18] The idealist thus takes refuge in an important conception that was originally used by the Buddha to refer to attachment,[19] but that also conveyed the sense of receptacle. This is the concept of *ālaya.*

The *ālaya-vijñāna* thus becomes the eighth form of consciousness.[20] It is often compared with the ocean whose surface water is disturbed by the winds of activity, appearing in the form of constantly changing waves.[21] However, the wind of activity is not something external. The dispositional tendencies accumulated from time immemorial, which lie dormant in the *ālaya*-consciousness in the form of seeds, continue to create agitation within the *ālaya.*

In the earlier psychological speculations, the faculty of mind *(mano)* plays an active role in the creation not only of the notion of a permanent ego but also of eternal objects, and mental consciousness *(manoviññāṇa)* is simply a product of mind and concepts;[22] hence what is to be restrained is the mind. However, in the psychology of the *Laṅkā,* the mind or *manas* is responsible *only* for the belief in the ego, and it is the mental consciousness *(mano-vijñāna)* which discerns the world of objects and becomes attached to it.[23] The reason may be that the idealist of the *Laṅkā* wants to subordinate the five forms of consciousness—visual, auditory, olfactory, gustatory, and tactile—to mental consciousness without allowing them any objectivity. Getting rid of the external world being the primary task of the idealist, the *Laṅkā* insists on the elimination of the discriminating *mano-vijñāna,* and this is equated with *nirvāṇa.*[24]

Mental consciousness, functioning together with the five forms of consciousness, is also responsible for the discriminations of good and bad.

Furthermore, these six forms of consciousness, which are continuously and closely bound together, move on without remaining still even for a moment. It is this rapid movement that is called momentariness *(kṣaṇika)*.[25] Since the six forms of consciousness, along with the mind *(manas)*, are founded upon the *ālaya*-consciousness, the latter, too, in spite of being the "womb of the Tathāgata," is momentary. Momentary thoughts, as mentioned earlier, could not be associated with discriminations of good and bad. Thus the *Laṅkā* is compelled to recognize two aspects of the *ālaya* itself—the momentary *(kṣaṇika)*, which is defiled *(sāśrava)*, and the non-momentary *(akṣaṇika)*, which is free from defilements *(anāśrava)*.[26]

In another context, the "womb of Tathāgata," which is a synonym for the non-defiled and non-momentary *ālaya*-consciousness, is described as being bright and pure by nature *(prakṛti-prabhāsvara-viśuddha)*.[27] This brings the conception of *ālaya*-consciousness dangerously close to the theory of self *(ātmavāda)* advocated by the heretics. The *Laṅkā* responds with the following statement:

> No, Mahāmati, my teaching relating to the *garbha* is not the same as the theory of self of the heretics. For the Tathāgatas, Mahāmati, having formulated the instruction on the *tathāgatagarbha* in terms of emptiness *(śūnyatā)*, limit of existence *(bhūtakoṭi)*, freedom *(nirvāṇa)*, non-arising *(anutpāda)*, absence of a mysterious cause *(animitta)* and the unestablished *(apraṇihita)*, etc., teach the doctrine pointing to the *tathāgatagarbha*, the sphere of non-discrimination and imagelessness, in order to eliminate the anxiety on the part of the ignorant toward a theory of non-substantiality *(nairātmya)*.[28]

This would mean that the discourse on the *tathāgata* is itself empty, and the discourse on emptiness *(śūnyatā)* is also empty, a negative position not acceptable to *Laṅkā*, as discussed earlier. For this reason, all that can be asserted is that for the idealist of the *Laṅkā*, everything, including the discourse on the *tathāgata*, is empty, the only reality being *tathāgata* itself. Compared with the philosophy of the mainline Buddhist tradition, including Nāgārjuna, this certainly represents an absolute form of emptiness, or what the *Laṅkā*'s opponents, i.e., the Theravādins of Sri Lanka, called "the theory of great emptiness" *(mahāsuññatavāda)*. This great emptiness is well expressed in the dilemma of Rāvaṇa:

> [After this] the teacher and the sons of the Buddha vanished away in the air, leaving Rāvaṇa the Yakṣa himself standing [above] in his mansion. Thought he, "How is this? What means this? And by whom was it heard? What was it that was seen? And by whom was it seen? Where is the city? And where is the Buddha?

"Where are those countries, those jewel-shining Buddhas, those Sugatas? Is it a dream then? Or a vision? Or is it a castle conjured up by the Gandharvas? Or is it dust in the eye, or a *fata morgana,* or a dream-child of a barren woman or the smoke of a fire-wheel, that which I saw here?"

Then [Rāvaṇa reflected], "This is the nature as it is *(dharmatā)* of all things, which belongs to the realm of Mind, and it is not comprehended by the ignorant as they are confused by every form of imagination."[29]

CHAPTER XIX

Vasubandhu and the *Vijñaptimātratāsiddhi*

It is true that many Buddhist scholars of the ancient past were participants in an ongoing conflict between Theravāda and Mahāyāna. Even now, there are leading traditional Buddhist scholars who confine themselves to their particular schools without paying any attention to the literature belonging to or preserved by their so-called adversaries. While this kind of scholarship has been perpetuated for centuries, there is sufficient evidence to show that some of the truly outstanding philosophers of both traditions, after being nurtured in their own particular schools and mastering whatever literature was available to them, outgrew such sectarianism and were inspired by an altogether different ideal—namely, to go in search of the very person who began the whole enterprise and who was gradually being forgotten or enshrouded in a veil of mystery. This was the search for the historical Buddha and his original message. We have already seen how Moggalīputta-tissa tried to achieve this; so did Nāgārjuna, after reading the Prajñāpāramitā literature, go after the "other teachings of the Buddha." The author of a large number of works, his most mature treatise, the *Kārikā,* represents a concerted attempt to rediscover the historical Buddha. Two centuries after Nāgārjuna, during another golden age of Buddhist literary activity, emerged Vasubandhu, a man who lived to be eighty years old and thus had the opportunity to run the entire gamut of Buddhist philosophical and religious thought, moving from one tradition to another until he was able to compile his magnum opus (which, incidentally, is the briefest yet most comprehensive treatise on Buddhism). Our contention that the greatest thinkers in the Buddhist tradition transcended sectarianism to go in search of the Buddha's original message cannot receive better confirmation than from the writings of Vasubandhu.

Vasubandhu began by studying the Abhidharma commentaries called the *Vibhāṣā,* and summarized their contents in his famous *Abhidharmakośa.* He was able to weigh the teachings of the Sarvāstivādins against those of the Sautrāntikas and, for interesting reasons, favored the latter. Even in his early days, he was smart enough to realize that Sarvāstivāda could not represent the momentous revolution the Buddha had brought about in the Indian philosophical scene. His preference for the Sautrāntika standpoint earned him the wrath of that famous exponent of the Sarvāstivāda, Saṅghabhadra. Hsüan-tsang has provided interesting information about the dual between Vasubandhu and Saṅghabhadra up until the latter's death.[1]

Stefan Anacker's recent publication, *Seven Works of Vasubandhu: The Buddhist Psychological Doctor* (1984), contributes much to the understanding of Vasubandhu, especially by way of presenting translations and commentaries on seven of his major works. Unfortunately, the claims made by subsequent traditions, especially the Tibetan, seem to heavily influence his perspective, so that the other aspect of Vasubandhu's writings, namely, his attempt to reach out for the ideas expressed by the Buddha himself, remains unexamined. As far as the relationship between Nāgārjuna and Vasubandhu is concerned, Anacker is right in maintaining that the disagreements between the two are really those of the sixth-century followers of the two teachers. Yet Anacker's mistaken assumption that Nāgārjuna was involved in a "wholesale denial of causality"[2] makes it difficult for him to perceive a close affinity between Nāgārjuna and Vasubandhu, and hence between Vasubandhu and early Buddhism.

Another obstacle that lies in the way of appreciating Vasubandhu's contribution to the history of Buddhist thought, especially in the matter of unraveling the original insights of the historical Buddha, is his alleged conversion to Yogācāra by his half-brother Asaṅga. That Vasubandhu renounced his Sautrāntika leanings under Asaṅga's influence may be true, but to insist that he remained faithful to an absolutist idealism, comparable to the one propounded by Asaṅga, is to do great injustice to Vasubandhu's ingenuity.

Such problems are further compounded by what may be considered the mutilation of Vasubandhu's philosophically most sophisticated work, the *Vijñaptimātratāsiddhi, Establishment of Mere Conception,* probably as a result of misunderstandings on the part of his own disciples of the sixth and seventh centuries. The available Sanskrit text, edited by Sylvain Lévi, throws a smokescreen around the Chinese and Tibetan versions, all of which were completed after the damage was done to the original text, probably by commentators like Sthiramati and Dharmapāla, who were responsible for depicting Vasubandhu as an absolute idealist. Two noteworthy features of the existing Sanskrit text are (1) the absence of the introductory paragraph in Vasubandhu's autocommentary on the *Viṃśatikā* ("Twenty Verses"), and (2) the total loss of the autocommentary on the *Triṃśikā* ("Thirty Verses") and its replacement with a commentary by Sthiramati.

A careful philosophical analysis of Vasubandhu's arguments in the two texts indicates that he was no metaphysical idealist, a view that even Anacker wishes to espouse.[3] Vasubandhu avoided such an idealism by a judicious use of terminology. In this connection, Vasubandhu seems to have been able to read the discourses of the Buddha more accurately than some of his idealist followers. For example, the Buddha never considered the terms *citta* (thought), *mano* (mind), and *viññāṇa* (consciousness) as *synonyms.*[4] Neither does Vasubandhu, either in the verses or in the portion of his autocommentary on the *Triṃśikā* available in Sanskrit. The Buddha utilized the terms *saṅkhā* and *paññatti* to refer to concepts; the latter was preferred by Nāgārjuna. Sometimes we find the Buddha as well as the Ābhidharmikas employing the term *viññatti* (Skt. *vijñapti*) in the sense of "intimation." Vasubandhu's ingenuity lay in the fact that he realized the significance of the term *vijñapti* as a means of expressing the proper function of a concept, namely, intimating what is available through a cognition *(vijñāna).* It is most unfortunate that in the first paragraph of his autocommentary, lost in the available Sanskrit version and reconstructed from the Chinese and Tibetan translations, all these four terms—*citta, manas, vijñāna,* and *vijñapti*—are lumped together and defined as synonyms *(paryāya).* Furthermore, the term *citta-mātra,* "mere thought," occurring repeatedly in the *Laṅkā,* is introduced in this paragraph but does not occur anywhere else in Vasubandhu's own composition that follows. There was no better way to make an idealist out of Vasubandhu.

The loss of Vasubandhu's autocommentary on the *Triṃśikā* adds to our perplexity. An author who deemed it necessary to compile his own commentary on the *Viṃśatikā,* which primarily refutes the metaphysical extremes, would certainly have written a commentary on the *Triṃśikā* in order to elaborate on his main thesis. All that we have is the commentary by Sthiramati, whose interpretation of Vasubandhu is most suspicious.[5] The following analysis is based on the ideas I have already expressed in *The Principles of Buddhist Psychology* (1987), and focuses on the philosophical and psychological content of Vasubandhu's *Vijñaptimātratāsiddhi,* a work that remains unparalleled in several respects—its profundity, clarity and, above all, precision. Utilizing only twenty-two verses, Vasubandhu was able to analyze the various implications of two metaphysical views—eternalism and nihilism—that have plagued philosophical thinking for centuries. With another thirty verses, he expounded the teachings of the Buddha as embodied in thousands of discourses.

Vasubandhu's Philosophical Inheritance

Anyone reading Nāgārjuna's *Kārikā* will get the feeling that he was almost obsessed with criticizing the theories of identity *(svabhāva)* and difference *(parabhāva).* His criticism of these two theories was so penetrating and severe that most interpreters, classical as well as modern, have assumed that he was abandoning causation altogether. After Nāgārjuna's criticism, the Buddhists—even those who propounded the theories of identity and difference—were reluctant to return to them. While criticizing these two metaphysical theories, Nāgārjuna was leaning toward the solution offered in the early discourses, the Abhidharma as well as the *Vajracchedikā,* by focusing on conception, which he referred to by the term *prajñapti.* This was a move toward philosophical psychology in the solution of the above metaphysical problems. No sooner did he do so than we find the metaphysician reemerging with an interpretation of conception that introduces a different set of problems. Instead of the questions of identity and difference, the Buddhist philosopher now comes up with the problems of the particular *(svalakṣaṇa)* and the universal *(sāmānyalakṣaṇa).* We have already seen how the *Lotus* advocated a conceptual absolutism. The idealist and transcendentalist *Laṅkā* often condemned the knowledge of the Śrāvakas and Pratyekabuddhas as being confined to particulars and universals,[6] explaining true knowledge as being non-conceptual.

It has been pointed out that Asaṅga's *Abhidharmasamuccaya* and the *Laṅkā* adopt the same philosophical standpoint. If Vasubandhu had recognized a non-conceptual truth or reality, we would have to assume that Asaṅga really was successful not only in turning his half-brother away from the Sautrāntika standpoint but in bringing him around to the idealistic mode of thinking. But if Vasubandhu actually renounced this idealistic stance as well, as more recent scholarship relating to his philosophy recognizes, then he was compelled to take the metaphysical bull by its two horns, i.e., the particular and the universal, and prevent a *conception* from deteriorating into a real particular or an empty universal. This deconstruction of absolutist metaphysics is the philosophical theme in the *Viṃśatikā.*

The existence of a real object *(sad artha)* is a presupposition of commonsense as well as metaphysical realism. The real object is not a simple object of perception but one that corresponds exactly to a concept, or one that exists whether or not it is perceived. Vasubandhu begins by refuting commonsense realism, which claims that the determinations of time and space, the possibility of shared experiences and fruitful activity, cannot be accounted for in the absence of a real object.[7] He cites the usual example of dream experience, along with that of experience in hell, to reject the claims of the realist, thereby giving the impression that *all* experiences are like dream experience, and so on. It is only after criticizing the theories of the metaphysical realist who reduces all objects to atomic particles, or their combination, that Vasubandhu returns to correct this wrong impression. The determination of mutually related concepts is based on mutual domination. In dream experience, thought is overwhelmed by torpor. Hence the difference in fruit.[8]

What is important here is that Vasubandhu recognizes a difference between dream and waking experiences. What he is not ready to accept is that waking experiences are absolutely incorruptible, as the commonsense and metaphysical realist would believe. Once belief in the incorruptibility of sense experience is abandoned, it is possible to appreciate the nature and function of concepts that are utilized in the expression of such experiences. Just as these experiences are not incorruptible and are conditioned by various factors, so are the concepts or conceptual schemes that are determined on the basis of their mutual relations. Thus, while a concept is a substitute for experience, the concepts *(vijñapti)* themselves are determined in terms of their mutual relations *(anyonyādhipatitva)*.

Vasubandhu's next move is to highlight the enormous influence of concepts, whether or not they are related to some experience. Thus, to take an example from modern Western philosophy, even an abstract concept like Gilbert Ryle's "regiment" may have causal efficacy, as does the more concrete "soldier." The only difference is that, epistemologically, the former is hazier than the individual soldiers, as dreams are in comparison with waking experience. To eliminate the absolute difference between the concept of the universal and the concept of the particular, Vasubandhu would argue that the death *(maraṇa)* of one person can be produced by a specific concept of another.[9] This may not be different from asserting that the conceptual framework of one person can cause the death of another, as in the case of Nero, whose conceptualization was undoubtedly the cause of the massacre of thousands of Christians.

In the *Viṃśatikā,* Vasubandhu is achieving several things. First, he is dissolving the absolute correspondence between a conception and an object of experience. Second, he is melting down the absolute lines of demarcation between concepts. Third, with the example of the dream experience, he is illustrating the possibility of there being empty concepts alongside concepts that have empirical content, so that the sharp dichotomy between the particular and the universal can be broken down.

Since all concepts are not empty of empirical content, and since most concepts, whether empty or with content, can produce consequences of some sort, Vasubandhu maintains that "all this is mere conception" *(vijñapti-mātram evaitad)*.[10] The philosophical significance of the term *mātra* ("mere" or "only") has already been examined in relation to the Buddha's explanation of the object of experience (Chapter VII) and his definition of conception (Chapter VIII). Vasubandhu, realizing the significance of the Buddha's insight, utilizes the same term in order to surmount the problems created by both realism and idealism. Thus it is not intended to deny the object, as assumed in the suspect introductory paragraph of the autocommentary,[11] but rather to accommodate the *fringes* of concepts, the elimination of which led to the sharp distinction between the particular and the universal *(sva-sāmānya-lakṣaṇa)*. This philosophical achievement—that is, the "establishment of mere conception" *(vijñapti-mātratā-siddhi)*—is gained not by simple speculation but by following the discipline of the Buddha *(buddha-gocara),* namely, analysis of the psychology of human experience. Thus the reconstruction of empirical concepts is the objective of the *Triṃśikā* or "Thirty Verses."

Philosophical Psychology

The *Triṃśikā* is best treated as a treatise on philosophical psychology because it is an attempt to deal with the perennial issues in philosophy through an analysis of human psychology. The analysis of human psychology should reveal how human beings formulate ideas, including those that are philosophically acceptable to the Buddhist and those that are not.

The very first statement that Vasubandhu makes becomes crucial, for he can tip the scale in the direction of either realism or idealism. The Buddha began his explanation of the process of experience with the sense organ and the sense object, and then the *arising* of consciousness, thereby emphasizing the fact that consciousness is dependently arisen, not representing any ultimate and permanent self. Since that statement had been made, speculation regarding the process of sense experience had reached such a sophisticated level that the slightest wrong move on Vasubandhu's part would have thrown him into one of various camps, such as materialism or behaviorism, essentialism, idealism, and so on. For example, if he maintained that all ideas arise depending on consciousness *(vijñāna),* he would immediately be characterized as an idealist. He carefully avoids this by speaking of evolution of consciousness *(vijñāna-pariṇāma).* The statement that all ideas that prevail *(pravartate)* occur in the transformation of consciousness does not entail the denial of a human body in which consciousness occurs, nor does it imply that there is no external object. If there is anything that is denied, and this is also only through implication, it is that there is either a mysterious agent behind the subject, that is, the evolution of consciousness, or a mysterious metaphysical object that exists without ever becoming part of that evolution of consciousness, that is, objects never perceived.

Evolution of consciousness *(vijñāna-pariṇāma)* is philosophically significant for other reasons as well. This will become evident when the description of that process of evolution is analyzed. The process is explained in terms of three functions, referred to as

> (1) resultant *(vipāka),* (2) mentation *(manana),* and (3) conception of the object *(viṣayasya vijñapti).*[12]

The resultant is then identified as the *ālaya-vijñāna,* further defined as conveyer of all its seeds *(sarva-bījaka).* The description of the evolving consciousness as a resultant is intended to avoid any essentialist perspective. This means looking at evolution at the point of its bearing fruit, rather than at its beginning. In addition, it means adopting the radical empiricist approach of the Buddha, who formulated the principle of dependent arising, by focusing on the dependently arisen *(pratītyasamutpanna),* which is also the fruit or the resultant.

The second characterization of *ālaya*-consciousness, as containing all of its seeds, highlights another important philosophical approach. Unfortunately, because of the loss of Vasubandhu's autocommentary and its replacement with a rather suspect explanation by Sthiramati, a metaphysical interpretation of *ālaya*-consciousness in terms of a theory of moments *(kṣaṇa-vāda)* has survived until the present day. The basis of the Sautrāntika theory of mind is the conception of moments, which Vasubandhu renounced early in his career. His theory of *ālaya*-consciousness therefore requires a different explanation. The evolution of *ālaya*-consciousness determined by dispositional tendencies *(vāsanā)* accumulated through one's behavioral responses *(karma)* to the world of experiences[13] does not require either a theory of discrete moments or a conception of substance, if Vasubandhu were to adopt the radical empiricist approach mentioned above. When Vasubandhu defines *ālaya*-consciousness as containing all its seeds *(sarva-bījaka),* he is trying to accommodate precisely these dispositional tendencies, which provide for its identity and character without making the *ālaya*-consciousness either a stream of disconnected, momentary flashings or a mental substance.

The above characterization of the *ālaya*-consciousness as resultant and as containing all the dispositional tendencies that determine its character and identity leaves Vasubandhu with a major descriptive problem. For him, it is certainly not originally bright and pure *(prakṛti-prabhāsvara-viśuddha),* as it was for the *Laṅkā,* for that would not make it a resultant *(vipāka)* but the original. However, while presenting the *ālaya*-consciousness the way he does, Vasubandhu also has to explain how the *false* notions of self *(ātman)* and the objects *(dharma)* arise. Thus, while maintaining that the *ālaya*-consciousness is possessed of activities such as contact, attention, feeling, perception, and *even* volition,[14] which characterize empirical consciousness, Vasubandhu insists that it is unidentified or unsolidified in terms of concepts of object *(upādi)* and location *(sthāna).*[15] This does not mean that the disposition *(vāsanā)* for such identification or solidification is totally absent in the *ālaya*-consciousness, for the seeds *(bīja)* are there.

However, the reason Vasubandhu does not want to describe *ālaya*-consciousness as consciousness that has already *solidified* in terms of concepts of object and location is that he wants to maintain the *possibility* of freedom *(nirvāṇa)* within the context of *ālaya*-consciousness. Unlike in the discourses of the Buddha, where the emphasis is on the negation of a subjective metaphysical self even though the negation of a substantial object is not unavailable (the reason being that the Buddha had to contend more with the Upaniṣadic notion of self than with any other conception), Vasubandhu, and Nāgārjuna before him, had to deal more with the scholastic solidification of the objective elements *(dharma)* than with the subject *(pudgala)*. We have already seen how Nāgārjuna emphasized the appeasement of the object *(draṣṭavyopaśama)* first, and devoted the first fifteen chapters of his treatise to this purpose, taking up the question of the individual self *(pudgala)* in the second part of his *Kārikā*. Similarly, Vasubandhu wants to begin his definition of consciousness by indicating that even though the conceptual solidification of the object has occurred in the *ālaya*-consciousness in the past—hence the tendency *(vāsanā)* to do so—each successive occurrence of consciousness is not invariably associated with such solidification. The future solidification of the concept of the object, as the stream of consciousness continues to flow like the current of a stream *(srotasaughavat)*, becomes a major concern for Vasubandhu.

Thus, when Vasubandhu proceeds to explain the consciousness of the person who has attained *arhatva* (*arhat* being the title for the Buddha, as well as for his disciples who have attained freedom), he refers to the dissipation *(vyāvṛtti)* of the particular form of consciousness that he described earlier as *ālaya (ālayākhyaṃ vijñānam)*,[16] that is, the consciousness that *tends* to get solidified into concepts of incorruptible and ultimately real objects every time it occurs. It is not the complete dissipation of every form of empirical consciousness, but only of the actual or potential solidification into concepts of real objects.

The next step is to describe how, on occasions of sense experience, consciousness leads to such solidified concepts. Vasubandhu now returns to the heart of the Buddha's doctrine. He realizes that, according to the Buddha, all ideas (*dhammā,* in its broadest application) have mind *(mano)* as a precondition.[17] Even though the Buddha looked upon the mind as a faculty *(indriya),* along with other sense faculties (eye, ear, nose, tongue, and body), he was careful not to make it a metaphysical substance sharply distinguishable from other faculties; hence his definition of mind as the function of mentation *(maññatīti mano)*. For Vasubandhu, who inherited a mass of metaphysical theories relating to the mind authored by the Buddhists themselves, mind is another form of consciousness *(mano nāma vijñāna),* with the function of mentation *(mananātmakaṃ)*.[18] This may seem very idealistic, but for Vasubandhu —who was keen on refuting the claims of the realist that the *concept* of the external object is totally independent of a perceiving mind, and that consciousness or cognitive awareness, together with its dispositional tendencies, have a role to play in the formation of such concepts—there was no such fear. Furthermore, the appeasement of the object *(draṣṭavyopa-*

śama) referred to by Nāgārjuna can be achieved not by changing the object itself but by appeasing the consciousness that plays a major role in the formation of the concept relating to the object. In other words, the concept of the object is undoubtedly the result of the interaction between the object and consciousness or, to put it in more Buddhistic terms, their interdependence. There is no denial that the objective world forces itself on the perceiving consciousness with irresistible force, producing what is sometimes referred to as the "objective pull."[19] But that does not mean that there is a way in which the human person can form an absolutely incorruptible conception of that object, unless he is omniscient. It may be noted that the problem for Vasubandhu is not the consciousness *(vijñāna)* of the object, but rather the conception *(vijñapti)* formed on the basis of cognitive awareness. There is nothing wrong with the concept as long as it is not believed to be incorruptible or to stand for an equally incorruptible object, the former being incompatible with the limited human capacity for *conceiving* and the latter being unavailable to a limited human capacity for *perceiving.*

It is because of the anxiety generated by these limitations that human beings often try to go beyond them and postulate conceptions of eternal selves or immutable substances. This becomes a craving *(tṛṣṇā)* and, hence, a defiling tendency *(kleśa)*. Thus, for Vasubandhu, the *ālaya*-consciousness, which is already susceptible to the generation of such defilements, gives rise to the four defilements on occasions of sense experience, namely, self-view, self-confusion, self-esteem, and self-love. These four defilements are not in the worthy one *(arhat)* because they have been eliminated. They are also not found in the state of cessation *(nirodha)* and the supramundane path *(lokottara-mārga)* because they are (temporarily) suspended.[20] Here again, the defilements consist of the wrong view *(dṛṣṭi)*, confusion *(moha)*, esteem *(māna)*, and love *(sneha)*. This means that the concept of the self *(ātma)*, without being elevated to the level of an incorruptible object, can remain at an empirical level, if and when the four defilements are eliminated.

The defilements that produce a subjective metaphysical self also force the individual to grasp the object *(viṣayasya upalabdhi)*, and this emotional attachment generates a sharp dichotomy between what is good *(kuśala)* and bad *(akuśala)*, which is then tagged onto the object itself, the person hardly realizing that in doing so he is all the time conceiving. The implication is that there are no *inherently* good or bad objects. This, indeed, is an affirmation of the Buddha's view that objects are neither true nor valuable in themselves, and that their truth or value depends on their function. Here, then, is the deconstruction of a metaphysical subject as well as an equally metaphysical object, by insisting that what is involved in both cases is "mere conception" *(vijñapti-mātra)*.

Conception *(vijñapti)*, thus, is the story of the evolution of consciousness *(vijñāna-pariṇāma)*. To conceive of the existence of something beyond that conception, whether it relates either to the subject or to the object, is simply false conception *(parikalpita)*. The interdependence between the subject and object is also reflected in the interdependence between conception *(vijñapti)* and consciousness *(vijñāna)*. Without the former, the latter is blind; without the latter, the former is empty. This interdependent nature *(para-tantra-svabhāva)* represents the basic teaching of the Buddha, namely, dependent arising *(pratītyasamutpāda)*. The realization of this fact represents the highest achievement *(pariniṣpanna)*. This latter describes the highest freedom, for it is simply the absence of false conception *(parikalpa)* in relation to the interdependent *(paratantra)*.[21] Here there is no *hierarcy* of three forms of knowing or three *independent* substances or natures, as in the case of the *Laṅkā* (see Chapter XVIII), but the achievement of freedom from obsessive conception, i.e., conceptions of ultimately real selves or ultimately real objects. This is not a renunciation of all conceptions but a way of dissolving the absolute dichotomy between the particular and the universal.

CHAPTER XX

Dignāga's Epistemology and Logic

According to our understanding, the last of the great Buddhist philosophers of India who attempted to remain faithful to the original Buddhist tradition was Dignāga. Like many other Buddhist luminaries who preceded him, Dignāga was born to a brahman family of Kāñci in South India; like many others, including his teacher, Vasubandhu, he began his career by being an advocate of a certain metaphysical school of Buddhism, only to move away from it and become a faithful disciple of the Buddha. Thus, according to the available records, he started as a Vātsīputriya, the school of Personalists, whose views probably attracted him because of his Brahmanical background. Dissatisfied with this doctrine and those who propounded its tenets in South India, he is said to have traveled north, where he became a pupil of Vasubandhu. The period in which Vasubandhu lived was marked by heated debates among the different Buddhist schools, as well as between the Buddhist and Brahmanical traditions. Dignāga, who lived during the latter part of the fifth and the early part of the sixth century (ca. 480–540 A.D.),[1] seems to have inherited this fervor for debating and wrote several works refuting the views of his adversaries. Thus, unlike his teacher—whose more mature treatise, the *Vijñaptimātratāsiddhi,* was an attempt to reexamine the psychological speculations of the Yogācāra tradition, especially its theory of three substances *(tri-svabhāva),* thereby making it an extremely significant work in philosophical psychology—Dignāga focused on the appropriate methods of reasoning, and this involved him in a project that underscored the importance of logic and epistemology.

Unfortunately, just as Vasubandhu's psychological speculations were given an idealistic turn by his commentator, Sthiramati, so Dignāga's epistemology received additions and revisions at the hands of his commentator, Dharmakīrti, and these have dominated the interpretation of his thought for centuries. Just as we know more of Candrakīrti than of Nāgārjuna, so we know more of Dharmakīrti than of Dignāga. To add to our difficulties in understanding Dignāga, his most important treatises are not available in their original versions. We at least have the mutilated version of Vasubandhu's primary treatise, but Dignāga's important works can be recovered only from quotations or later translations. The loss of Dignāga's important works in their original versions tells the sad story of Buddhist literature in India. As will be seen, Nāgārjuna, Vasubandhu, and Dignāga were philosophers who remained faithful to the mainline Buddhist tradition. Yet none of their important treatises would have survived if not for the commentaries written on them during the sixth and seventh centuries by Candrakīrti (ca. 650), Sthiramati (ca. 550), and Dharmakīrti (ca. 650), the first two rendering Nāgārjuna's and Vasubandhu's thoughts in an absolutist and idealist mold, respectively, and Dharmakīrti giving Dignāga's thought an essentialist twist.[2]

Pramāṇa or the source of knowledge is foremost in the mind of the epistemologist Dignāga. For him, the proper understanding of the object depends on the source of knowledge *(pramaṇādhīno hi prameyādhigamaḥ).*[3] Hattori seems to contrast Nāgārjuna and Dignāga by arguing that Nāgārjuna denied the possibility of apprehending *prameya* (the object) by means of *pramāṇa* (the source of knowledge) because these, being mutually conditioned, lack independent substantiality,[4] and that Dignāga assumed the source of knowledge to be substantial while the object is not. It will be seen that unless we adopt an essentialist perspective in explaining Dignāga's epistemology, there is no need to assume that for Dignāga all that matters is the source of knowledge *(pramāṇa),* the object of that knowledge being a mere conceptual construction. Such an interpretation emerges as a result of Dignāga being considered an idealist. On the contrary, Dignāga underscored the importance of the source of knowledge in order to achieve what Nāgārjuna called the "appeasement of the object" *(draṣṭavyopaśama).*[5] While trying to find ways and means to appease the conception of the object, Nāgārjuna also had to devote much time to the problem of the subject *(ātman).* Hence his emphasis on the non-substantiality of both subject and object. However, coming after Vasubandhu, who provided an extremely sophisticated psychological analysis of the philosophical problem of the subject, Dignāga was left to battle with his contemporaries regarding the nature of the object—especially with Buddhists like the Sautrāntikas, who reduced the object to a unique particular *(svalakṣaṇa),* and with Brahmanical thinkers like Bhartṛhari, who insisted on the real object being a universal *(sāmānyalakṣaṇa).*

For Dignāga, there are only two sources of knowledge, perception *(pratyakṣa)* and inference *(anumāna).* He then enumerates two aspects *(lakṣaṇa)* of the object that correspond to the two sources, the particular *(svalakṣaṇa)* being the object of perception and the universal *(sāmānyalakṣaṇa)* the object of inference.[6] Even though Dignāga begins his description with such correspondence between the source of knowledge *(pramāṇa)* and the object *(prameya),* as the discussion progresses one can see how he dissolves the sharp dichotomy between the particular and the universal.

Dignāga begins with the primary source of knowledge, namely, perception *(pratyakṣa)*. His is the most succinct description of perception available anywhere in Buddhist literature. It is so brief that its interpretation became quite varied. The definition runs thus:

pratyakṣaṃ kalpanā'poḍhaṃ.[7]

The term *kalpanā,* which is crucial here, is generally rendered as "conceptual construction," thereby leaving the impression that *pratyakṣa* is "perception" free from conceptual construction, and hence non-conceptual. A careful analysis of the conceptions discussed by Dignāga in light of the treatment of concepts or conceptions in the mainline Buddhist tradition discussed earlier may enable us to understand what Dignāga is negating in the present context. The concepts are:

1. Arbitrary words *(yadṛcchā-śabda),* i.e., proper names such as Diṭṭha, etc.
2. Genus-words *(jāti-śabda),* i.e., common nouns such as "cow," etc.
3. Quality-words *(guṇa-śabda),* i.e., adjectives such as "white," etc.
4. Action-words *(kriyā-śabda),* i.e., terms expressive of agency such as "cook," etc.
5. Substance-words *(dravya-śabda),* i.e., terms expressive of ownership such as "staff-bearer," "horn-bearer," etc.[8]

Dignāga distinguishes two interpretations of these concepts. The first recognizes a correspondence between the term and the thing expressed by the term. This, undoubtedly, is the interpretation of the Realist. Unfortunately, this identification of the standpoint of the Realist has escaped Masaaki Hattori's attention, because he assumes that the correspondence pertains only to the agent-words and substance-words,[9] whereas no such distinction is made in Dignāga's explanation. The second interpretation is that these concepts do not stand for anything, and hence are devoid of any meaning *(artha-śūnya-śabda).* This is the standpoint of the Nominalist, who would not want to say that a name designates something. For Dignāga, perception *(pratyakṣa)* is devoid of *such* discriminations *(eṣā kalpanā)* only, not of all or any and every form of conception. How a similar situation obtained among the transcendentalist interpreters of Nāgārjuna has already been pointed out.[10] A transcendentalist can ignore the meanings of words and sentences, even though he uses them all the time to affirm his standpoint, but an analytical philosopher cannot afford to ignore the nuances of language. Dignāga, like Nāgārjuna and

Vasubandhu before him, was an analytical philosopher. Hence, in the above context, he could not have used the term "such" *(eṣā)* to mean "all" *(sarvaṃ)*.

Furthermore, the history of Buddhism—beginning with the Buddha himself, through the Abhidhamma, especially the *Kathāvatthu,* and the non-idealistic Mahāyāna, represented by the *Vajracchedikā,* Nāgārjuna, and Vasubandhu—represents a gigantic effort to avoid the extreme standpoints of Realism and Nominalism in the interpretation of meaning and use of conceptions. The final defender of that Buddhist faith in the flexibility, limitations, and usefulness of conception is Dignāga, as has become clear from our analysis.

If the conceptions or discriminations *(kalpanā)* that are eliminated *(apoḍha)* are the two types mentioned above, and if there could be other forms of genuine conception, then perception *(pratyakṣa)* need not be looked upon as totally non-conceptual. Dignāga's theory of the non-conceptual *(nirvikalpa)* is therefore not absolute but relative to the metaphysical conceptions of the Realist and the Nominalist. It is a search for the "middle standpoint" adopted by the Buddha in the explanation of language.[11]

After defining the negative characteristic of perception, that is, the absence of *metaphysical* discriminations *(kalpanā'poḍha),* Dignāga proceeds to explain its positive characteristics. Here he follows the Buddha in designating perception in terms of the sense organ, because the latter is the specific cause of the former.[12] The phrase "specific cause" *(asādhāraṇa-hetu)* can be construed as implying a unique cause. However, Dignāga's intention is to explain the role of the sense organ in determining the nature of the perception of the object. The object as perceived is not an absolutely incorruptible one. Even before other subjective elements, such as dispositions, interfere with the determination of the nature of the object, there are physical conditions, such as the constitution of the physical organ,[13] that contribute to the conception of the object. In other words, Dignāga attempts to highlight the fact that the object "as it is" is never known, and that any conception of it should take into consideration the limiting factors, among which the sense organ is the first.

At this point, Dignāga reiterates his idea that perception is devoid of metaphysical conceptual construction.[14] This is clarified by making the distinction, for example, between cognizing "blue" *(nīlaṃ vijānāti)* and cognizing something "as blue" *(nīlaṃ iti vijānāti)*.[15] The former represents the awareness of a colored object *(arthe 'rtha-saṃjñī)* and the latter an object possessing the color *(arthe dharmasaṃjñī)*.[16] The former is perception *(pratyakṣa)* that involves the conception of color; the latter is metaphysical construction that assumes the color to be a characteristic or property *(lakṣaṇa)* of a really existing object. It is only recently that Western philosophers have begun to realize that it is discriminations like these that contribute to problems relating to objectivism. In the words of Hilary Putnam,

> . . . the problem with the "Objectivist" picture of the world . . . lies deeper than the postulation of "sense data"; sense data are, so to speak, the visible symptoms of a systemic disease, like the pock marks in the case of smallpox. The deep systemic root of the disease . . . lies in the notion of an "intrinsic property," a property something has "in itself," apart from any contribution made by language or the mind.[17]

If by direct perception *(pratyakṣa)* is meant cognition, awareness, or consciousness *(vijñāna)*—for *vijñāna* is the nominal form of the verb *vijānāti*—that direct perception is not totally free from the activities of *manas,* which has its own objects, namely, concepts *(dharma).* Wherever *manas* is operative, concepts will also appear. *Manas* as a faculty *(indriya)* is distinguished from other faculties, such as the eye and ear, because of its involvement with concepts that the other faculties cannot deal with. In other words, when the faculty of eye *(cakṣu)* operates on an object *(rūpa),* that operation is not complete—i.e., it does not yield awareness *(vijñāna)*—unless *manas* makes its own contribution,[18] and this contribution pertains to recognition in terms of concepts *(dharma).* There cannot be cognition without recognition. The assumption of cognition without recognition is a fundamental thesis of the essentialist, not of a radical empiricist.

Thus, when Dignāga says that "perception caused by the five kinds of sense organs is devoid of conceptual construction,"[19] as a good Buddhist he cannot mean that no conceptions whatsoever are involved in perception. Instead, he is claiming that *certain* forms of conception, that is, those relating to absolute distinctions, are not involved in perception. It is the fixing of the concept (= *nilam iti vijānāti*) that does not take place in perception, a process comparable to what Vasubandhu referred to as the *viṣaya-vijñapti.*

This determination or fixing of the object represents the extended activity of *manas,* namely, the activity of cognizing itself. Dignāga even raises the question as to whether "the awareness of such conceptual construction" *(kalpanā-jñāna)* can be a cognition. Allowing it as an internal awareness, he refuses to recognize it as an objective perception, for it is the very act of discriminating the object.[20] In other words, Dignāga is not willing to make "conceptual construction" a transcendental activity, because that would leave the human person without any control over an activity which, according to the Buddha, leads either to bondage or to freedom.

Dignāga's next endeavor is to specify and account for the erroneous perceptions or what, in the light of the perception discussed earlier, is a non-perception. He lists illusion *(bhrānti)*, knowledge of conventional reality *(saṃvṛti-sat-jñāna)*, inference *(anumāna)*, the inferred *(anumānika)*, the recollected *(smārta)*, and the desired *(abhilāśika)*, all of which he describes as apparent perceptions *(pratyakṣābhaṃ)* that are accompanied by obscurity *(sataimiraṃ)*.[21] This is what his teacher Vasubandhu explained as the "thought destroyed by torpor" *(middhenopahataṃ cittaṃ)*, like the dream experience.[22] Furthermore, following Vasubandhu, Dignāga perceives the fruit *(phala)* as that which distinguishes valid knowledge *(pramāṇa)*, and he utilizes the same criterion to distinguish perception from non-perception or the apparent perceptions listed above.[23] The fruit is not merely the end product but the continuous working of the process *(savyāpāra-patīta)*. By providing such an explanation, Dignāga is not demonstrating his unfamiliarity with the concept of "causal efficiency" *(artha-kriyā)*, as Hattori seems to think,[24] but is actually avoiding its formulation in metaphysical terms popular with the Sautrāntikas and with Dharmakīrti.

Fruitfulness is also an aspect of self-cognition or the cognition cognizing itself *(svasaṃvitti)*. This means that even the concepts formed on the basis of cognition cognizing itself can produce consequences. This relationship is indeed significant, for it is what fuses fact and value. It was mentioned earlier that direct perception is like perception of blue *(nīlam vijānāti)*. A determination or fixing of that object *(artha-niścaya)* is the work of the cognition cognizing itself, which is equivalent to perceiving blue as blue *(nīlam iti vijānāti)*. According to Dignāga, decisions regarding value, that is, desirability and undesirability, occur at this stage.[25] Interestingly, fruitfulness occurs at two different levels: at the level of perception, which determines the validity or invalidity of an object of perception, and at the time of conceptual construction *(kalpanā)*, which accounts for its desirability or undesirability. It would be difficult to find a better explanation of the psychology of the pragmatic notions of truth and value.

Finally, for Dignāga, whatever the form in which a cognition appears —that is, whatever the object of cognition *(prameya)*—it again bears fruit *(phalate)* as the source of knowledge *(pramāṇa)*. The three factors that are involved, namely, the subject *(grāhaka)*, the form of the object *(ākāra)*, and the cognition cognizing itself *(svasaṃvitti)*, are not clearly distinguished.[26] Yet Dignāga distinguishes two forms of cognition: (1) knowledge of the object *(viṣaya-jñāna)*, and (2) knowledge of that [knowledge] *(tajjñāna)*.[27] The former represents the direct perception *(pratyakṣa)* and the latter, the cognition of that through the internal sense *(svasaṃvitti)*, which is the *extended* activity of *manas* (mind). It is this extended activity of *manas,* referred to as *manana* by Vasubandhu, which leads to the fixing of the boundaries of the object *(artha-niścaya)* and which Dignāga calls *kalpanā* (discrimination). In other words, absolute distinctions, such as white and non-white, cow and non-cow (to quote oft-used examples), are not part of direct experience *(pratyakṣa)* but are the results of the rational enterprise directed at determining the boundaries of conceptions. It is this form of discrimination that is also involved in the absolutist distinction between the particular *(svalakṣaṇa)* and the universal *(sāmānyalakṣaṇa).*

The above description of perception does not make it error-free in any way, nor does it give any suggestion that perception, in its most valid form, is pure and transcends the empirical. The idea that perception is transcendent emerges from the wrong interpretation of what Dignāga included under a non-perception, namely, *saṃvṛti-sat-jñāna.* Hattori renders this as the "cognition of empirical reality,"[28] which he then contrasts with a conception of the ultimate *(paramārtha)* taken to be the object of a valid cognition. However, for Dignāga, even a valid cognition does not yield error-free knowledge; hence its object cannot be an ultimate reality. Indeed, it was Dharmakīrti who added the further qualification that perception is "non-illusory" *(abhrānta).*[29] This, in itself, is the result of the rationalist enterprise explained earlier: if illusion *(bhrānti)* is a non-perception, then perception must be non-illusory. For Dignāga, this kind of discrimination is the result of "exclusion" *(apoha),* a discrimination that gets eliminated along with the exclusion of metaphysical conceptual construction *(kalpanā'poḍha).*[30]

As noted earlier, Dignāga began his *Pramāṇasamuccaya* saying that he would explain how the particular *(svalakṣaṇa)* is the object of perception *(pratyakṣa)* and the universal *(sāmānyalakṣaṇa)* the object of inference *(anumāna).* Contrary to what the subsequent interpreters of Dignāga expected, he left no room for the interpretation of the particular as a momentary or instantaneous flash of experience[31] undiluted by past experience and memory.[32] All that is absent in that experience is the activity of the cognition cognizing itself. It is not prereflective in the sense of involving no memory of the past, for, according to the Buddha, the most significant knowledge, namely, *yathā-bhūta-ñāṇa,* is one where memory or mindfulness *(sati)* is most prominent. It is the cognition cognizing itself *(svasaṃvitti)* that introduces the metaphysical discriminations. Cognition is prereflective only in this latter sense—unless, of course, the cognition is interpreted as being instantaneous, and therefore absolutely pure at every moment of its occurrence. Thus, for Dignāga, the individual or the particular *(svalakṣaṇa)* is not an indefinable and indescribable unique moment of experience, but rather a whole or a "thing possessing many properties," *all* of which are not captured by the senses.[33] While this description eliminates the clarity and precision with which the essentialist thinkers would view the particular, it also introduces elements of the universal *(sāmānyalakṣaṇa),* so that the object of cognition retains its "fringes" that can account for the empirical relations. In other words, all that is admitted is the fact that in cognition the empirical content *(svalakṣaṇa)* of the object is *dominant.*

This position is reversed with inference *(anumāna),* which, as seen by Dignāga, is a non-perception (see above). The universal *(sāmānyalakṣaṇa)* is *preeminent* here. Its preeminence does not mean that one can treat logic as a way of discovering ultimate structures in language. Such an enterprise could be espoused only if one were to adopt the perspective of a philosopher like Bhartṛhari, who would insist that a single utterance of a word embodies an object qualified by *all* its qualifiers simultaneously.[34] For Dignāga, as for the Buddha, inference is a way of knowing the object with some measure of certainty when direct cognition or experience is not available. It is to facilitate such knowledge that the knowledge of the universal becomes relevant. Thus the universal is an abstraction from particular experiences, not an innate idea that enables us to understand experiences and that is embodied in language from beginningless time. Giving up the sacredness and authority of language *(śabda),* which his Brahmanical opponents were trying to justify, Dignāga was compelled to discover a method of determining a universal, so that language would not be rendered totally meaningless or empty *(artha-śūnya),* and so that knowledge by way of inference would not be regarded as completely invalid, and hence useless. Thus the problem with the universal is the same as the problem with the concept of the particular or the individual: it can be neither real (= Realism) nor unreal (= Nominalism). It is here that Dignāga demonstrated his greatest ingenuity.

Looking back at his tradition, it was not difficult for a perceptive thinker like Dignāga to realize that whenever a statement, which takes the form of a universal, was made—either in the discourses of the Buddha or by the prominent philosophers of the tradition, including his teacher Vasubandhu—it was almost always concretized. The following statements can be quoted as examples:

The Buddha: All *this* is suffering *(sabbam idaṃ dukkhaṃ).*
Nāgārjuna: All *this* is empty *(śunyam idaṃ sarvaṃ).*
Vasubandhu: [All] *this* is mere conception *(vijñapti-mātram evedaṃ).*

Considering these three statements, it is easy to understand why Dignāga did not follow the system of deduction, comparable to what is found, for example, in Aristotle:

1. All men are mortal.
2. Socrates is a man.
3. Therefore, Socrates is mortal.

As a logician involved in debates with his absolutist and essentialist adversaries, Dignāga could see that this method of deduction cannot be operative in a non-absolutist system. Therefore he devised the following:

1. This is impermanent. (The statement of the object of proof)
2. This is a product. (The statement of reason)
3. Whatever is a product is impermanent. (A universal statement)

This takes the form of an induction rather than a deduction, and hence is deprived of the sort of theoretical certainty that one looks for in a deductive argument. Dignāga's solution to this problem is embodied in his famous theory of exclusion *(apoha):*

4. Whatever is not impermanent is not a product. (A contraposed universal statement)

Taking a = demonstrated "this," Ia = "a is impermanent," and Pa = "a is produced," the above argument can be symbolized as follows:

1. $\mathrm{I}a$
2. $\mathrm{P}a$
3. $(x)(\mathrm{P}x > \mathrm{I}x)$ (generalization)
4. $(x)(\sim \mathrm{I}x > \sim \mathrm{P}x)$

The fourth step, involving exclusion, is Dignāga's response to the realist treatment of universals. In the context in which he wrote, it was a reply to the Brahmanical thinker Bhartṛhari, who insisted on the reality and eternality of every word *(śabda)*. Following the Buddha's analysis of the nature of linguistic convention (see Chapter v), Dignāga was not willing to subscribe to Bhartṛhari's view. However, as a logician he would run into difficulties if he were to accept the flexibility or corruptibility of concepts. Let us consider an example, from a textbook on logic, of a logically invalid argument whose premises and conclusion are said to be true:

If I am President, then I am famous.
I am not President.
Therefore, I am not famous.
$(\mathrm{P} > \mathrm{Q}$
$\sim \mathrm{P}$
$\therefore \sim \mathrm{Q})$

The invalidity of this argument is said to be evident when we look at another one of similar form:

If Rockefeller is President, then he is famous.
Rockefeller is not President.
Therefore Rockefeller is not famous.[35]

In formal logic, this is considered to be an invalid argument with an obviously false conclusion. However, if we are to follow Dignāga's analysis, it seems that the reason the conclusion is false is not because it does not follow from the premises or because it is evident that Rockefeller is famous, but because the concept of "famous" in the major premise is not the same as the concept of "famous" in the conclusion. Linguistic convention does not provide us with an absolute meaning for the term "famous." A person can be famous because he is the President of the United States, because he is rich, because he can influence the President as a result of his wealth, and so on. Therefore, if we are to strengthen the argument above, we need to circumscribe the meaning of the term "famous," and this is precisely what Dignāga achieves with his method of exclusion *(apoha)*. Dignāga will argue:

If Rockefeller is President, then he is famous.
[If Rockefeller is not famous, then he is not President.]
Rockefeller is not President.
Therefore Rockefeller is not famous.

This shows that the major premise of a deductive argument and the conclusion of an inductive argument, both of which involve universals or generalizations, cannot be true unless they are qualified. In Western logic, such qualifications were attempted through counterfactuals, due to the inordinate urge to safeguard the unconditioned reality of the universals, that is, the Platonic legacy. Dignāga's solution undercuts this whole enterprise. While allowing the logician the satisfaction of providing a valid argument, Dignāga alerts him to the limitation of that validity. In other words, he is saying that the construction involved in an argument is much more than the construction that goes into sense experience. Thus white-ness is determined not on the basis of black-ness but in relation to non-white-ness. Theoretical certainty, which is all one can have in formal logic, is increased by the principle of exclusion *(apoha)*, while at the same time it helps to demarcate the boundaries of an abstract concept. We have already referred to the Buddha's warning against the dangers involved in truth-claims based on exclusion (see Chapter III). A precursor of Dignāga's elaborate theory of exclusion *(apoha)* is Nāgārjuna's statement in the *Kārikā:*

> The occurrence of self-nature through causes and conditions is not proper. Self-nature that has occurred as a result of causes and conditions would be something that is made.
> Again, how can there be a self-nature that is made? Indeed, an unmade self-nature is also non-contingent upon another.[36]

In other words, neither the Buddha nor Nāgārjuna nor Dignāga was willing to consider logic as the "royal road" to the discovery of truth. Furthermore, the inference becomes a source of knowledge *(pramāṇa)* in that it is not totally divorced from experience or perception *(pratyakṣa),* even though the end product is not a perception as such. Here, then, is why the universal *(sāmānyalakṣaṇa)* becomes the object of inference.

Just as the particular *(svalakṣaṇa)* is not an absolute particular, like that of the essentialist empiricist, so the universal *(sāmānyalakṣaṇa)* is not an absolute universal, as it is in the case of the absolutist rationalist. This eliminates the difficulties one encounters in negotiating the gap between the conceptual object and the perceptual one.[37] Thus the concepts of the particular and the universal in Dignāga are as non-substantialist *(anātman)* as any other idea based on experience or reason, and in this sense Dignāga remained faithful to the mainline Buddhist tradition.

Radhika Herzberger has mentioned the difficulties that some of the earlier writers on Dignāga, such as de La Vallée Poussin, Keith, and Randle, encountered in understanding how logic could have its beginnings in an idealistic system.[38] Herzberger herself tried to resolve this puzzle, even though her own interpretation recognizes the existence of a metaphysical scheme with which Dignāga's logic needs to be reconciled.[39]

If Dignāga had been perceived in the background of the mainline Buddhist tradition, these so-called puzzles would not have been generated in the first place. Dignāga, like his predecessors Nāgārjuna and Vasubandhu, was a preeminent epistemologist. As such, it is not appropriate to regard Dignāga's thought as a strictly logical system nor even as the "beginning" in Buddhist logic. For all intents and purposes, Dignāga's logic is already implicit in the writings of Nāgārjuna and Vasubandhu, if not in the discourses of the Buddha. Second, Dignāga was not an idealist. He may have started his career as an idealist, and Dharmakīrti subsequently made him an essentialist, but in between, Dignāga happened to be a radical empiricist. Third, Dignāga's is not a *system* of logic in any conventional sense. Indeed, his was an excellent demonstration of the futility of attempting to construct logical systems or linguistic structures in order to overcome human anxieties relating to the future. Finally, there was no mystical experience recognized by Dignāga that would come into conflict with his logical investigations.

The Buddha had realized that metaphysical systems, linguistic structures, absolute laws, and so on formulated on the basis of inference were the results of human anxiety. He argued:

> Beings dominated by prediction *(akkheyya),* established upon prediction, not understanding prediction, come under the yoke of death. However, having understood prediction, one does not assume oneself to be a fore-teller. When such a thought does not occur to him, that by which he could be spoken of, that does not exist for him.[40]

It is to Dignāga's credit that he was able to demonstrate to the traditional logician that the certainties that logical thinking generates through the formulation of absolute universals, which are then perceived to be inherent in language and which are supposed to determine experience itself, are no more than metaphysical conceptual constructions *(kalpanā).* For Dignāga, these metaphysical constructions are far removed from the flesh and blood of genuine experience, and are accompanied by obscurity *(sataimiraṃ).* In demonstrating this, he was simply clarifying the statement of his teacher, the Buddha, that there can be reasoning that is well done *(sutakkita)* and badly done *(duttakkita),* valid *(tathā pi hoti)* and sometimes invalid *(aññathā pi hoti).*[41]

CHAPTER XXI

Buddhaghosa, the Harmonizer

While many brilliant thinkers studded the history of Buddhist thought in India—some remaining faithful to the original teachings of the Buddha, others deviating from it, and still others being venerated as the founders of new schools—there is only one name that has remained prominent in the Theravāda countries of South Asia. That name is Buddhaghosa. Rhys Davids summed up in a few words most of what can be said about him: "Of his talent there can be no doubt; it was equalled only by his extraordinary industry. But of originality, of independent thought, there is at present no evidence."[1] More recent work by a scholar-monk who was part of the tradition dominated by Buddhaghosa contains the following defense: "Modern critics have reproached him with lack of originality: but if we are to judge by his declared aims, originality, or to use his own phrase, 'advertising his own standpoint,' seems likely to have been one of the things he would have wished to avoid."[2]

If the claim of the faithful followers of the Theriya tradition is that Buddhaghosa did not interpret or add anything to the Theravāda, or that he simply summarized the ideas expressed in the original Sinhalese commentaries and translated them into Pali, then these followers *cannot* claim to be the custodians of the original teachings of the Buddha as embodied in the discourses and in the Abhidhamma, which they themselves have preserved. The reason is that neither the *Visuddhimagga (Path of Purification),* Buddhaghosa's most significant work, nor the commentaries he compiled on most of the canonical texts preserves the philosophical standpoint we have attributed to the Buddha, to the compilers of the Abhidhamma literature, and even to Moggalīputta-tissa. This is so because it is not impossible to trace some metaphysical speculations, such as those of the Sarvāstivādins, the Sautrāntikas, and even the Yogācārins, in the works attributed to Buddhaghosa. What is most significant is that these ideas are introduced in an extremely subtle manner, and that it took a few centuries for them to blossom into full-fledged, openly stated metaphysical positions. Yet even if Buddhaghosa possessed no originality, or if his capacity for innovative thinking was suppressed by the context in which he had to work, a history of Buddhist thought would be incomplete without a chapter devoted to his writings, especially considering the tremendous influence he exerted on Buddhism in countries like Sri Lanka, Burma, Cambodia, Thailand, and Vietnam. For the traditional Buddhist scholars in this region, Buddhaghosa is literally the "voice" *(ghosa)* of the Buddha.

Buddhaghosa's life story is cloaked in mystery, as in the case of his predecessors. The Sri Lankan chronicle entitled the *Cūḷavaṃsa* (thirteenth century) and the biography of Buddhaghosa, the *Buddhaghosuppatti* (compiled by the Burmese monk Mahāmaṅgala during the early part of the fifteenth century), speak of Buddhaghosa as a native of Bodhgayā, where the Buddha attained enlightenment. This association with Bodhgayā is understandable, especially in view of his name, "the voice of the Buddha," given to him after he became a Buddhist monk. However, Buddhaghosa's own writings indicate that he was *living* in South India, close to Nāgārjunikoṇḍa, before his trip to Sri Lanka.[3] This means that he was closely associated with the centers of Buddhist learning in South India (see Appendix).

The nature of Buddhaghosa's writings is best understood in the context in which they were undertaken and completed. He arrived in Sri Lanka during the reign of King Mahānāma (409–431 A.D.), who was not favorably disposed toward the Mahāvihāra, the center of Theravāda.[4] Mahānāma is said to have erected several monasteries for the benefit of the monks of Abhayagiri,[5] the fraternity with which Sanghamitra was associated, while his queen favored the Mahāvihāra. Under these circumstances, and against the background of the traumatic experiences of the reign of King Mahāsena (see Appendix), the monks of the Mahāvihāra had to be more cautious in dealing with a scholar-monk from South India who wanted to translate the Sinhalese commentaries into Pali for the use of Indian Buddhists. Buddhaghosa was not given access to the Mahāvihāra library until he demonstrated his abilities. This, according to the tradition, is the reason for the compilation of the *Visuddhimagga*. Furthermore, in the colophons to each of his commentaries, Buddhaghosa makes reference to a monk from the Mahāvihāra whom he says invited him to compile that particular work. Given the initial wariness of the Theravāda monks, we cannot be certain whether the monk in question was inviting him to compile the commentary or scrutinizing how Buddhaghosa was performing the task of summarizing and translating the Sinhalese commentaries.

Just as the Theravāda monks were cautious in welcoming Buddhaghosa, so Buddhaghosa was careful in introducing any new ideas into the Mahāvihāra tradition in a way that was too obvious. There seems to be no doubt that the *Visuddhimagga* and the commentaries are a testimony to the abilities of a great harmonizer who blended old and new ideas without arousing suspicion in the minds of those who were scrutinizing his work. One prominent example shows how Buddhaghosa achieved his goal. In the commentary on the *Dhammasaṅganī,* Buddhaghosa makes a very important remark regarding the theory of moments *(khaṇa-vāda).* He says, "herein, the flowing present *(santati-pacuppanna)* finds mention in the commentaries *(aṭṭhakathā),* the enduring present *(addhā-paccuppanna)* in the discourses *(sutta).* Some say *(keci vadanti)* that the thought existing in the momentary present *(khaṇa-paccuppanna)* becomes the object of telepathic insight."[6] This account leaves the upholders of the theory of moments unidentified. The identification was made only by Ānanda, who compiled subcommentaries on Buddhaghosa's commentaries a few centuries later. The theory, even according to Buddhaghosa, was found neither in the discourses nor in the commentaries preserved at the Mahāvihāra, which Buddhaghosa was using for his own commentaries in Pali. Yet this momentary telepathic insight *(khaṇika-samādhi)* appears as an extremely important theory in his *Visuddhimagga.*[7] Furthermore, Buddhaghosa utilized the theory of moments rather profusely in this and other works, especially in his explanation of the functioning of the mind and of the experience of material phenomena.[8] It is important to note that the application of the theory of moments in explaining insight or intuition was popular in the Mahāyāna schools before and after Buddhaghosa, while its use in the explanation of empirical phenomena was common among the Sarvāstivādins and Sautrāntikas. It is not possible to say whether the monks of the Mahāvihāra were aware of the far-reaching consequences of Buddhaghosa's adoption of the theory of moments. There is no question that it did change the character of the original teachings introduced by Mahinda immediately after Moggalīputta-tissa's refutation of the heretical views during the third century B.C.

The *Visuddhimagga*

It is almost impossible to summarize the doctrines discussed in the *Visuddhimagga.* Unlike the treatises compiled by previous Buddhist scholars like Nāgārjuna and Vasubandhu, in which attempts were made to resurrect the original teachings of the Buddha by adopting various approaches prompted by the nature of the prevalent metaphysical ideas, Buddhaghosa's treatise is no more than an encyclopedic treatment of the path of purification, with a profuse use of the early discourses, and whatever was available in the Sinhalese commentaries, along with a variety of doctrines with which he was familiar before he arrived in Sri Lanka. These latter include ideas emphasized by the Sarvāstivādins, Sautrāntikas, Mādhyamikas, and Yogācārins. It is a gigantic synthesis. If there is any ingenuity in Buddhaghosa, it lies, as noted by Rhys Davids, not in any originality or independent thought on his part but in how he was able to analyze and synthesize the contents of the enormous body of literature with which he worked and about which he possessed an awesome knowledge.

It is possible that the *Vimuttimagga (Path of Freedom)* served as a model for Buddhaghosa's *Visuddhimagga.* The authorship of that work is attributed to Upatissa. It was available only in a Chinese translation of the sixth century A.D. until it was claimed to have been discovered in Sri Lanka in its Pali version, published in 1963.[9] Even though Buddhaghosa makes no mention of it, his successor in the commentarial tradition, Dhammapāla, refers to it.[10]

The *Visuddhimagga* treats its subject matter under three headings: morality or virtue *(sīla),* concentration *(samādhi),* and insight *(paññā).* In fact, Buddhaghosa begins the treatise with a verse in which the Buddha himself explains how to disentangle this tangle or puzzle of life:

> A wise man, a monk [who] is ardent and sagacious, having established [himself] in morality, and developing his thought and insight, will disentangle this entangle.[11]

The entire treatise is supposed to be a commentary on this verse. However, Buddhaghosa begins by analyzing the title of his work, "path of purification," into two elements, namely, the purification and the path leading to it. He equates purification with *nirvāṇa.* Being free from all defiling tendencies, it is utterly pure; it is the one goal. However, there can be many paths *(magga)* leading to that one goal *(ekāyana).* Quoting statements from the discourses, he lists at least six different ways of attaining the goal:

1. Insight *(paññā)*
2. Contemplation and insight *(jhāna* and *paññā)*
3. Action *(kamma)*
4. Morality or virtue *(sīla)*
5. Mindfulness *(sati)*
6. Right effort *(sammā vāyāma),* etc.[12]

However, Buddhaghosa is interested in presenting the path as a gradual one, so he opts for the explanation in terms of the threefold division of morality, concentration, and insight.

Morality or virtue *(sīla)* is examined in a variety of ways. Questions such as What is morality? In what sense is it morality? What are its characteristics, etc.? What are the benefits of morality? How many kinds of morality are there? and finally, How is it defiled? and How is it cleansed? are raised. Most of the answers are extremely authoritative, for they are substantiated by a profusion of quotations from the early discourses of the Buddha. However, one question for which Buddhaghosa fails to provide substantiation from the early discourses is that relating to characteristics and the like.[13] Yet for Buddhaghosa this is an extremely important question. Not finding appropriate quotations from the early discourses of the Buddha, he attributes the answer to the wise ones *(viññū),* and he continues to apply this definition in clarifying almost every concept he has to deal with. The definition is made in terms of four conditions: characteristic *(lakkhaṇa),* quality *(rasa),* manifestation *(paccupaṭṭhāna),* and foundation *(padaṭṭhāna).* The explanation of morality in terms of these four conditions is as follows:

1. Morality, in spite of its diverse elements, has the characteristic of composing *(sīlana),* like visibility in the case of different forms of visible data *(rūpa).*
2. Its quality is twofold: functional and consummative. Its functional quality or act-character is the destruction of bad moral habits *(dussīlya)* and its consummative quality is the attainment of blamelessness *(anavajja).*
3. It manifests in the form of purity *(soceyya).*
4. Its foundation consists of sensitivity *(ottappa)* and modesty *(hirī),* for without these there would be no moral life.

In the first place, Buddhaghosa's inability to quote any authoritative text from the early discourses in support of this definition weakens its authority, especially in the context of the hermeneutical principles laid down by the Buddha under the *mahāpadesas* (see Chapter V). Second, Buddhaghosa does not even refer to the definition or interpretation of concepts in the more authoritative non-canonical hermeneutical treatise, preserved at the Mahāvihāra, called the *Netti (Guide),* which contained a sophisticated method of conveying *(hāra)* the meanings of concepts.[14] Even though that treatise was pre-Buddhaghosan, he seems to have ignored it. Dhammapāla, who followed Buddhaghosa, is said to have compiled the existing commentary on it. One reason Buddhaghosa may have disregarded this work is that its sixteen modes of conveying or determining the meanings of concepts were too cumbersome compared to the fourfold definition. But more important is the fact that the fourfold definition enabled Buddhaghosa to introduce, rather surreptitiously, the substantialist as well as essentialist standpoints of the Sarvāstivādins and Sautrāntikas. Dhammapāla did so more openly, and in the end the Mahāvihāra tradition seems to have been overwhelmed by such interpretations.

The fourfold definition demonstrates Buddhaghosa's capacity to harmonize several strands of thought that had by then emerged in the Buddhist tradition. The categories that created much controversy among Buddhists—namely, the particular or the unique *(sabhāva = svabhāva)* and the universal or the abstract *(sāmañña = sāmānya)*—are here introduced under the guise of characteristics *(lakkhaṇa = lakṣaṇa),* and came to be identified as such in later manuals.[15] The recognition of such categories would not have been problematic if not for the fact that they were thus distinguished by later Theravādin philosophers, thereby allowing for the emergence of metaphysical theories of identity and difference comparable to those criticized by Nāgārjuna. Thus the particular *(sabhāva, salakkhaṇa)* came to be looked upon as the absolutely unique character not shared by anything else *(anaññasādhāraṇa),* the universal *(sāmañña)* being identified with the common or the shared *(sādhāraṇa).*[16] This was more or less the standpoint of the essentialist. With the pursuit of such an essentialist conceptual enterprise, the explanation of events or entities in terms of their dependence *(paṭiccasamuppāda)* was relegated to the background.

The second definition, in terms of quality *(rasa),* enabled Buddhaghosa to accommodate the description of an event, entity, or thing in terms of its function. He was keenly aware of the significance of such a definition in the discourses of the Buddha.

The third condition, manifestation (*paccupaṭṭhāna,* lit., "serving toward"), is more teleological in implication. The problems created by the previous essentialist interpretation probably called for such a definition, which eventually strengthened the essentialist enterprise by assigning specific goals for each of the processes assumed in the second condition.

The fourth condition, foundation *(padaṭṭhāna),* tightens the entire typological process by indicating definite conditions under which an event takes place. It is in some sense a counterfactual required by the first of the conditions. It is the foundation that specifies the conditions necessary for an event to occur.

The above definition may appear to be harmless so long as Buddhaghosa's endeavor was to explain the empirical constituents and conditions of morality *(sīla).* These, according to the Buddha, are non-substantial *(anatta);* hence neither the category of characteristics (*lakkhaṇa,* involving the particular/universal dichotomy) nor the category of foundation *(padaṭṭhāna)* should be understood in a rather strict sense as defining the *ultimate meaning* of the nature and constituents of morality. Yet for Buddhaghosa, the fourfold definition is intended to determine the precise meaning of morality, that is, to answer the question, In what sense is morality? *(Ken' aṭṭhena sīlaṃ).* It is therefore not a simple empirical description but one intended to bring out the essential and real meaning. Thus the fourfold definition is not a hermeneutical device but a language of precision intended to replace the empirical description *(sammuti, vohāra)* with more precise and technical vocabulary *(paramattha-vacana)*.

A philosophically correct language is not in itself an unreasonable ideal for a philosopher, but it need not be pursued at the expense of veridical knowledge. Unfortunately, Buddhaghosa's philosophical language eliminated not only metaphysical conceptions, such as permanent and eternal subjects and objects, but also empirical distinctions like woman *(itthi)* and man *(purisa)*, retaining only the aggregates *(khandha)*.[17] The fact that this is an essentialist enterprise is made clear by his analysis of human life into discrete momentary events, which he justifies by quoting a passage that is supposed to be from the Buddha but that has not yet been traced in any of the early discourses.[18]

It seems that, because of the manner in which Buddhaghosa introduced this essentialist definition, which he used extensively in the *Visuddhimagga* and the entire set of commentaries he compiled on the three collections *(tipiṭaka)*, the Mahāvihāra monks did not realize its far-reaching implications. Even if they were aware of them, they were probably fearful of being as aggressive as they had been on previous occasions. The consequences of this essentialist definition became apparent only in the writings of Theravāda teachers like Anuruddha and Sāriputta a few centuries later.

Buddhaghosa's use of the abovementioned essentialist perspective is most evident in his explanation of the restraint of the senses *(indriya-saṃvara)*, which is an aspect of the moral life *(sīla)*. His explanation of the sensory process and how it can be restrained is stated as follows:

> Herein, there is neither restraint nor non-restraint in the actual eye-faculty, since neither mindfulness nor forgetfulness arises in dependence on the eye-sensitivity. On the contrary, when a visible datum as object comes into the eye's focus, then, after the life-continuum has arisen twice and ceased, the functional mind-element accomplishing the function of adverting arises and ceases. After that, eye-consciousness with the function of seeing; after that, resultant mind-element with the function of receiving; after that, resultant inoperative mind-element-consciousness with the function of investigating; after that, the inoperative mind-consciousness-element accomplishing the function of determining arises and ceases. Next to that, impulsion impels. Herein, there is neither restraint nor non-restraint on the occasion of the life-continuum, or on any of the occasions beginning with adverting. But there is non-restraint if immorality or forgetfulness or unknowing or impatience or idleness arises at the moment of impulsion. When this happens, it is called "non-restraint of the eye-faculty."[19]

This explanation may appear to bring out the essential features of the process of perception, and these essential features are couched in precise and technical vocabulary. Yet, obviously, the very creative process of perception is thereby rendered sterile or lifeless. While very speculative, it also introduces concepts that are extremely metaphysical from the mainline Buddhist standpoint. We have here the recognition of an "unconscious" consciousness, referred to as "life-continuum" *(bhavaṅga),* to account for the continuity in the otherwise dissected and unrelated series of momentary mental events. Philosophically, this is not much different from the metaphysical conception of *ālaya*-consciousness presented in the *Laṅkā,* except that it is not looked upon as originally pure.

The essentialist perspective thus introduced in the analysis of morality *(sīla)* is then applied in the explanation of concentration *(samādhi)* and insight *(paññā).* Part II (Chapters III–XI) of the *Visuddhimagga* provides a detailed description of the process of concentration *(samādhi).* This is the fourfold definition of concentration:

1. Characteristic = non-distraction *(avikkhepa)*
2. Quality = elimination of distraction *(vikkhepa-viddhaṃsana)*
3. Manifestation = non-wavering *(avikampana)*
4. Foundation = happiness *(sukha)*[20]

Keeping this definition in view, Buddhaghosa elaborates on forty different meditative techniques leading up to concentration. As Ñāṇamoli has noted, the account of each single meditation subject given here is incomplete unless taken in conjunction with the whole of Part III, namely, the section on insight *(paññā),*[21] because the concentration discussed here relates to the eight attainments *(aṭṭha-samāpatti),* which provide a feeling of ease and comfort rather than knowledge and understanding. Interestingly, Buddhaghosa adds two more chapters in the section on concentration in order to explain the various forms of psychic powers (Chapter XII) and the five forms of higher knowledge (Chapter XIII), which he describes as mundane higher knowledge *(lokiyābhiññā).*

Part II (Chapters XIV–XXIII) of the *Visuddhimagga* also provides an exhaustive analysis of insight *(paññā).* Buddhaghosa's way of distinguishing insight from perception *(saññā)* and consciousness *(viññāṇa)* may appear to be rather simple and uncontroversial until we get to the actual definition, when it becomes rather complicated. Utilizing a simile that became rather popular in the Theravāda after him, Buddhaghosa illustrates the distinctions thus:

> Perception is like the child without discretion seeing the coin, because it apprehends the mode of appearance of the object as blue and so on. Consciousness is like the villager seeing the coin, because it apprehends the mode of the object as blue, etc., and because it extends further, reaching the penetration of its characteristics. Insight is like the money-changer seeing

> the coin, because, after apprehending the mode of the object as blue, etc., and extending to the characteristics, it extends still further, reaching the manifestation of the path.[22]

Thus perception *(saññā)* is direct sensory awareness, such as the perception of blue, etc. Consciousness *(viññāṇa)* provides understanding of characteristics such as impermanence, unsatisfactoriness, and non-substantiality. Having stated that it is not easy to distinguish perception and consciousness from insight,[23] and recognizing the moral content of insight by indicating that it has the capacity to manifest the path to freedom, Buddhaghosa proceeds to define it in terms of the four conditions mentioned earlier:

1. Characteristic = penetration into the essential nature of phenomena *(dhamma-sabhāva-paṭivedha)*
2. Quality = abolishing the darkness of confusion that conceals the essential nature of phenomena *(sabhāvapaṭicchādaka-mohāndhakāraviddhaṃsana)*
3. Manifestation = non-delusion *(asammoha)*
4. Foundation = concentration *(samādhi)*[24]

What Buddhaghosa means by essential nature *(sabhāva)* is not clear. His commentator takes this to mean both the particular or the unique *(sakabhāva)* and the general or the universal *(samānabhāva)*.[25] If this were the case, it would justify the view expressed in the *Laṅkā* that the insight of the *śrāvakas* and *pratyekabuddhas* is confined to the particular and the universal (*svasāmānyalakṣaṇa;* see Chapter XVIII). But if the essential nature of phenomena is to be understood in the sense of *dhammatā* (i.e., the dependent nature of phenomena),[26] then the object of insight would not be much different from the object of consciousness as described by Buddhaghosa above. The only difference would be that the former will be positive and the latter negative. However, this would contradict the three levels or tiers of understanding illustrated by the simile of the coin, with the knowledge of the money-changer bordering on absolute knowledge regarding the nature and value of the coin. In that explanation, the pragmatic as well as the moral content of knowledge is lost, and what we are left with is an extremely sophisticated, detailed, and value-free knowledge comparable to that of a typical scientist who is expected to be interested in the knowledge of phenomena for its own sake.[27]

One cannot help thinking of such theoretical knowledge when reading Chapters XIV to XVII of the *Visuddhimagga.* Here we find experience being dissected and the separated components described and grouped in several alternate patterns. In most cases Buddhaghosa adopts the fourfold essentialist definition mentioned above, which involves an exhaustive analysis of the aggregates and the various modes of the principle of dependence *(paṭiccasamuppāda).*

In contrast, Chapters XVIII to XXI are practical. They provide instructions on how the theoretical knowledge of the earlier part can be internalized, that is, analyzed in terms of the meditator's individual experience in order to attain the five kinds of purification *(visuddhi):*

1. Purification of view *(diṭṭhi-visuddhi)*
2. Purification by overcoming doubt *(kaṅkhā-vitaraṇa-visuddhi)*
3. Purification by knowledge and vision of the path and the non-path *(maggāmagga-ñāṇa-dassana-visuddhi)*
4. Purification by knowledge and vision of practice *(paṭipadā-ñāṇa-dassana-visuddhi)*
5. Purification of knowledge and vision *(ñāṇa-dassana-visuddhi)*

Thus the five forms of purification are achieved by thoroughly examining the object of knowledge *(ñāta)* as well as knowledge itself *(ñāṇa).*[28] Progress occurs in relation to the eight forms of knowledge[29] aimed at the clarification of objective experience and the consequent modification of the subjective attitudes, until the meditator reaches the three gateways to freedom. These are reflections *(anupassanāni)* relating to (1) the absence of a mysterious cause *(animitta),* (2) the non-established (that is, the absence of a foundation, *appaṇihita*), and (3) the empty *(suñña).*[30] These reflections are then utilized to generate the four types of activity in relation to the four noble truths, namely,

1. Thorough understanding *(pariññā)* of the truth of suffering *(dukkha)*
2. The relinquishing *(pahāna)* of the arising *(samudaya)* of suffering
3. The cultivation *(bhāvanā)* of the path *(magga)* leading to the cessation of suffering
4. The realization *(saccikiriya)* of the cessation *(nirodha)* of suffering

Quoting a passage from the *Saṃyutta-nikāya,*[31] where the Buddha maintains that a person who perceives suffering also perceives its arising, its cessation, and the path leading to its cessation, Buddhaghosa insists that all these four different activities take place simultaneously "during one moment" *(ekakkhaṇe):*

> For this is said by the Ancients *(porāṇā):* Just as a lamp performs four functions simultaneously in a single moment—it burns the wick, dispels darkness, makes light appear, and uses up the oil—so, too, path-knowledge penetrates to the four truths simultaneously in a single moment—it penetrates

> to suffering by penetrating to it with full understanding *(pariññā)*, penetrates to arising by penetrating to it with relinquishing *(pahāna)*, penetrates to the path by penetrating to it with cultivating *(bhāvanā)*, and penetrates to ceasing by penetrating to it with realizing *(saccikiriyā)*.[32]

This is an ingenious way of harmonizing two different paths—the gradual path, with which he began the treatise, and sudden realization based on momentary concentration *(khaṇika-samādhi)*. It is also an interesting way to reconcile two philosophical standpoints—the foundationalism or essentialism with which he began the work, and the anti-foundationalism or anti-essentialism embodied in the three gateways to freedom *(animitta, appaṇihita,* and *suñña)*. It is indeed a work of highest erudition on the part of a great harmonizer.

CHAPTER XXII

Tantras and *Parittas:* The Voiceful Tradition

Tantras

The Vajrayāna, represented by the *Tantras,* is generally regarded as the final phase of Buddhism in India. Since the conquest of Tibet by the People's Republic of China and the exodus of the Dalai Lama, together with several hundred thousand of his followers, the Vajrayāna, which remained almost isolated in the Himalayan kingdom, has gained extreme popularity in the West, especially in America, where it is gradually replacing the study of Ch'an (Zen), which has been pursued with enthusiasm for several decades. Western studies of Buddhism have undergone paradigm shifts comparable to those in the scientific world. Early studies of Mahāyāna in Europe were challenged by the discovery and dissemination of Theravāda by British orientalists. "Pearl Harbor" seems to have precipitated the study of Japanese Zen (and its Chinese version, Ch'an), and the "Fall of Tibet" has brought forth an avalanche of Tibetan and Tāntric studies. Such enthusiasm, while promoting valuable academic pursuits, can also deteriorate into dogmatic, uncritical adoration as well as misunderstandings and misinterpretations.

A large number of books on Tibetan Buddhism has appeared during the last two decades. These include editions and translations of Tāntric texts, the commentaries on them by scholars and teachers of the classical Tibetan tradition, poetic compositions, traditional Tibetan tales, and popular indigenous literature. Critical studies of the Tibetan Buddhist tradition and publications on Tibetan paintings, arts, and crafts fill library shelves. There cannot be any doubt that these publications have enriched world literature and provide valuable information about a culture that was almost closed to the outside world for centuries.

A controversy has already arisen regarding the meaning of the *Tantras,* the sacred books of the Vajrayāna. Indian scholars, some of whom were nurtured in the Hindu Tāntric tradition, view the Buddhist *Tantras* as no more than Buddhist adaptations of their own religious literature. In any case, rarely do we come across a modern Hindu scholar who would look upon Buddhism and Hinduism as two totally different philosophical and religious traditions. Western scholars, once again nurtured in different philosophical and religious traditions, have joined the controversy. There are at least three different interpretations of the *Tantras* by Western scholars. First, there are those who, like Alex Wayman, believe that the *Tantras* represent a mixture of old Vedic and Upaniṣadic ideas with those of Buddhism.[1] This is based on wrong translations of important philosophical and psychological terms occurring in the *Tantras*. Second, there are others, like H. V. Guenther, who insist on the purity of the Buddhist Tāntric ideas, emphasizing that these represent the culmination and quintessence of the Buddha's teachings.[2] Even though these scholars make a concerted attempt to distinguish the Buddhist from the Hindu *Tantras,* they continue to recognize a linear evolution of Buddhist thought from humble beginnings to elaborate systems, as advocated by some of the medieval Buddhist historians like Bu-ston. Hence this position is most popular among the Tibetan *lamas* and laity alike. Third is an interpretation of the *Tantras* that is critical of the second view but insists on the genuine Buddhist component in Tāntricism while simultaneously recognizing its "magical," "mystical," and "erotic" content. This last view appears in the most recent work by David Snellgrove, a recognized authority on the Tibetan language but a scholar whose interpretation of the Buddhist tradition can hardly be considered authoritative; it seems to be a diatribe against the more sympathetic scholars of the Western tradition who have attempted to make sense out of the seemingly incomprehensible Tāntric texts. Translating the important Sanskrit term *mantra* as "spell," Snellgrove remarks:

> I am aware that the present day Western Buddhists, specifically those who are followers of the Tibetan tradition, dislike this English word used for mantra and the rest because of its association with vulgar magic. One need only reply that whether one like it or not, the greater part of the tantras are concerned precisely with vulgar magic, because this is what most people were interested in then, just as they are interested chiefly nowadays in scientific achievements and technological inventions. . . . A spell is an enunciation of certain syllables, which should have a spontaneous (viz., magical) effect, when correctly pronounced by someone who is initiated into its use. In translating all these many tantric texts, the Tibetans did not normally translate the actual spells, because the change of enunciation might threaten their efficacy. They merely transliterated them into Tibetan script, as I have done into English script with the more tractable ones. The early Tibetan commentators usually understood the Sanskrit terminology, but except for a minority of serious practitioners who have studied under competent teachers, the recitation of these spells has all too often become a form of gibberish, a term that has been applied rather more unfairly to the use of spells by whomever they are recited under whatever circumstances.[3]

The so-called magical formulae appear mostly at the end of the Tāntric texts, and they are generally brief compared with the actual text. However, the impression one gets from Snellgrove is that the entire Tāntric literature consists of magical formulae. If the Tibetan teachers viewed the texts as described above, which is the way the Brahmanical priests perceived the *Vedas,* the Tibetans would certainly have developed ancillary sciences comparable to the *vedāṅgas,* consisting of treatises on etymology, grammar, semantics, and so on, in order to preserve every syllable of the text unchanged. However, one hears of no such ancillary literature in the Tibetan tradition.

Leaving aside for the moment the concluding *dhāraṇīs* or so-called magical formulae, Snellgrove also has difficulty distinguishing the primary contents of the Buddhist *Tantras* from those of the Hindu *Tantras.* His inability to understand the significance of the use of symbolism compels him to a literal interpretation of the texts, hence his perception of "eroticism" as an important ingredient of the Buddhist *Tantras,* a perception that would not be shared by the more educated and enlightened *lamas.* Finally, his analysis of the most important conception in the *Tantras,* namely, *vajra,* from which the Vajrayāna tradition derives its name, appears so superficial that the entire tradition becomes alienated from the previous forms of Buddhism, including Mahāyāna.

The analysis that follows avoids both perspectives mentioned above, namely, that the *Tantras* represent *either* a corruption *or* a culmination of Buddhism in India. Instead, it places the Tāntric texts in the context of the history of Buddhist thought, outlined in the present work, and evaluates the significance of the *mantras* (that is, the *Tantras* as recited) in the light of Buddhist religious practices.

The *Tantras,* as mentioned earlier, are the sacred texts of the Vajrayāna. Therefore, it seems appropriate to begin our explanation of the Tāntric texts with an analysis of the conception of *vajra.* In tracing the history of a conception in any philosophical or religious tradition, it is not sound scholarship to begin from a mid-way point, especially when the conception in question occurs in the literature of an earlier period. For example, the term *vajira,* symbolizing analytical knowledge *(ñāṇa-vajira)* that disintegrates the grasping of consciousness *(viññāṇānaṃ pariggaha),* occurs in the statement of a disciple of the Buddha named Migajāla, who was presenting a description of the noble eightfold path.[4] The grasping of consciousness, when it relates to conception, is ontological commitment. It is this same grasping or ontological commitment that prevented the followers of Brahmanism and Jainism from understanding —or led them to refuse to understand—the Buddha's analysis of theories such as caste *(vaṇṇa),* even when this analysis was accompanied by empirical arguments. The dogmatism with which they upheld their beliefs could be eliminated only under threat, which a buddha could not resort to. Hence the appearance of a threatening or fear-generating personality, often symbolized as a *yakkha,* in whose hand is placed the *vajira,* and who is hence called *Vajirapāṇi.*[5] The compilers of the *Tantras* were not unaware of the incident relating to the conversion of Ambaṭṭha, the hard-nosed brahman who insisted on the superiority of the Brahmana class, and who was threatened by Vajrapāṇi. Explaining the role of Vajrapāṇi, a Tāntric texts says:

> Placing his vajra on his heart, he said to all the Buddhas: "O all you Blessed Tathāgatas, I do not comply." They said: "O why?", and he replied: "O Blessed Ones, there are evil beings, Maheśvara and others, who have not been converted by all of you Tathāgatas. How am I to deal with them?" In response the Resplendent One [Vairocana] relapsed into the state of composure known as Wrathful Pledge-Vajra, the great compassionate means of all the Tathāgatas, and enunciated the syllable HŪṂ. At once there emerged from the vajra at the heart of Vajrapāṇi the Lord Vajradhara who manifested a variety of fearful Vajrapāṇi-forms, reciting this verse:
>
> Oho! I am the means of conversion, possessed of
> all great means.
> Spotless, they assume a wrathful appearance so
> that beings may be converted by these means.[6]

The passage goes on to describe the confrontation between Vajrapāṇi and Maheśvara, the creator god of the Hindu pantheon, until the latter was reduced to a dead body, along with his retinue of gods. This, undoubtedly, is an echo of the incident related in the *Ambaṭṭha-sutta* referred to above.

Considering this latter function of generating fear in the individual to loosen up his dogmatism, the interpretation of *vajirapāṇi* as a "demon with a thunderbolt in hand" may not be totally inappropriate. However, to restrict it to that interpretation alone is to lose the subtler and more important allusion to analytical knowledge that engenders fear in the minds of those who are prone to ontological commitment.

It is no doubt this more significant meaning of *vajra* (interpreted simply as an "instrument," without indicating what it is)[7] that is expressed by the famous Tāntric writer, Advayavajra:

> The vajra is twelve finger-spans in length because it eliminates the twelvefold causal nexus. The syllable HŪṂ on the rounded middle-part indicates the unsurpassable essential truth *(dharmatā):* H representing freedom from causality *(hetu),* Ū representing freedom from argumentation *(ūha),* and the Ṃ the groundlessness of all dharmas. The five points that emerge [at each end of the vajra] from the lotus-flower source of existence [its middle part] represent the Sages *(muni)* as fivefold since by emerging in bodily form they

eliminate the five aggregates of personality. Four of them face toward the center one indicating that body and the rest (viz., feelings, perceptions and impulses) depend upon consciousness. Furthermore, they all have four sides in order to indicate their universality. Then men of wisdom who understand the Vajradharma, having attained to the fivefold form of salvation, spread out in the form that causes the syllable HŪṂ to resound. On all sides there are trifoliate patterns indicating Voidness, Signlessness and Effortlessness. That such is the nature of the Five Wisdoms, namely, Mirrorlike Wisdom, the Wisdom of Sameness, Discriminating Wisdom, Active Wisdom and the Wisdom of the Pure Absolute, all this must be learned from one's preceptor. Indicating the indivisibility of wisdom we have this concise statement:

> Firm, substantial and solid, of uncuttable and
> unbreakable character,
> Unburnable, indestructible, the Void is said to
> be the vajra.[8]

This is the elaboration of the "diamond-like knowledge" *(ñāṇa-vajira)* which is referred to in the early discourses *sans* the metaphysics and which served as the inspiration for the *Vajracchedikā,* where the elimination of ontological commitment is practiced with great fervor, especially through utilization of the concepts of the empty *(śūnya,* Pali *suñña),* the absence of a mysterious cause *(animitta),* and the groundless or the unestablished *(apratiṣṭhita,* Pali *appatiṭṭhita* or *appaṇihita).*

In light of the above references in the early discourses, where the concepts of *vajra* as well as *vajrapāṇi* occur, it would be rather dogmatic to begin an analysis of these concepts only in relation to texts such as the *Perfection of Wisdom in Eighty Thousand Verses (Aṣṭasāhaśrikāprajñāpāramitā)* or the *Sutra of Golden Light (Suvarṇaprabhāsottama-sūtra).*[9] Thus the conclusion is irresistible that the more exalted meaning of the concept of *vajra* in the early discourses is what appears in the *Vajracchedikā,* with no references to Vajrapāṇi. The two Mahāyāna sources cited above retain only the further popularization of that symbolism in the form of Vajrapāṇi as it occurs in the early discourses of the Buddha. Utilizing the conception of the "diamond" *(vajra)* and the more popular symbolism of the "demon with diamond in hand" *(vajrapāṇi-yakṣa),* it is thus possible to explain the so-called incomprehensible Tāntric texts as well as their religious significance when they are utilized as *mantras,* that is, texts for recitation.

In terms of literary style, the Tāntric texts seem to differ from the previous canonical literature, primarily the discourses *(sūtra)* of early Buddhism and Mahāyāna, in three respects, even though one or the other of these features may be noticeable in some of the later Mahāyāna sūtras. The three main characteristics of the literary style of the *Tantras* are: (1) the paradoxical nature of the description of the doctrine; (2) the profuse

use of symbolism, especially in expressing the various positive categories in the Buddhist doctrine, and (3) concluding statements that often express, either in brief or in detail, a feeling or experience of peace and happiness, and that are generally considered to be magical formulae.

The seemingly paradoxical statements in the Buddhist *Tantras* must relate themselves to those of the earlier Buddhist sūtras like the *Vajracchedikā* if they are to be characterized as the primary sources of Vajrayāna in Buddhism. We have already explained how the apparently paradoxical statements of the *Vajracchedikā* are not intended to assert an ultimate reality, as in Hinduism, but rather to avoid ontological commitment in relation to concepts. The assertion-negation-assertion process was utilized to deconstruct fossilized concepts and reconstruct them in order to accommodate flexibility and relativity. Thus the two processes of deconstruction and reconstruction are beautifully combined in the two systems of Nāgārjuna and Vasubandhu. Nāgārjuna's *Kārikā* emphasizes the process of deconstruction, utilizing the conception of "emptiness" *(śūnyatā)* without abandoning reconstruction altogether, such reconstruction being the function of Chapter XXVI of that work. Vasubandhu's *Triṃśikā,* in contrast, emphasizes reconstruction in terms of "mere concept" *(vijñaptimātra)* without renouncing deconstruction altogether, such deconstruction being the purpose of the *Viṃśatikā.* These two philosophers together have provided an excellent exposition of the *Vajraccedikā,* and both these processes should be embodied in the *Tantras* in order for them to be considered genuine Buddhist texts.

However, the *Tantras* were not meant to be simple philosophical or psychological treatises. They had a specific role to play as texts to be recited at rituals and ceremonial occasions, without, however, losing their doctrinal content. This is achieved through the introduction of symbolism, of which the *Tantras* make such extensive use that they become almost unintelligible, just as a classical Sanskrit text like the *Kādambarī* is not intelligible to anyone unfamiliar with the mythological allusions of the Hindus. There seems to be little doubt that the introduction of symbolism was intended to popularize the Buddhist teachings at a time when the Hindu *Tantras* were gradually becoming the vogue and posing a challenge to the Buddhists. The fact that the Buddhist *Tantras* were intended to be recited as *mantras* at religious ceremonies does not mean that either the doctrinal contents of the *Tantras* or the benefits anticipated from such recitations had to be identical with those of the Hindu *Tantras.* Their contents need not be mystical, and their consequences need not be magical.

Thus the substitution of demons, gods, and *bodhisattvas* for philosophical concepts proved a more effective way of retaining the attention of the ordinary listener when these texts were being recited: the demons appear as personifications of enormous power and, sometimes, of evil;

the gods are embodiments of pleasurable existences or experiences; and the buddhas and *bodhisattvas* are invariably representations of the ultimate goal of the moral life. To take an example of the last form of symbolism, we have the five aggregates of the human personality replaced by five buddhas, explained in terms of their functions as follows:

1. Body *(rūpa)*—Vairocana—ethics
2. Feeling *(vedanā)*—Ratnasambhava—concentration
3. Perception *(saṃjñā)*—Amitābha—appreciation
4. Disposition *(saṃskāra)*—Amoghasiddhi—freedom
5. Consciousness *(vijñāna)*—Akṣobhya—vision in freedom[10]

An ordinary, uninitiated disciple would get excited when he heard that the human personality consists of the buddhas Vairocana, Ratnasambhava, Amitābha, Amoghasiddhi, and Akṣobhya. Even if he did not know what these buddhas stand for, the mere mention of their names, with which he would be familiar, would keep his mind focused on a higher ideal. Yet doctrinally the symbolism is not meaningless, for it represents a non-substantialist interpretation of the relationship between *saṃsāra* and *nirvāṇa,* an interpretation embodied, for example, in Nāgārjuna's statement that

> The life-process has no thing that distinguishes it from freedom. Freedom has no thing that distinguishes it from the life-process.[11]

Presenting the five buddhas in relation to the five aggregates of the human personality, the *Tantras* were simply denying the mysterious "something" *(kiṃcit)* that the substantialist thinkers were looking for in order to explain freedom. Although this symbolism may have been inspired by Nāgārjuna's exposition of the Buddha's doctrine, since Nāgārjuna was closer in time to the compilers of the Tāntric texts than was the historical Buddha, it is not far removed from the meaning of the Buddha's statement that the world *(loka),* its arising, its cessation (= freedom), and the path leading to its cessation are all "within this fathom-long body associated with consciousness and mind" *(byāmatte kaḷebare saviññāṇake samanake).*[12]

The introduction of symbolism, as noted earlier, contributed much toward retaining the attention of ordinary laypeople. In the South Asian Buddhist countries, the mere mention of the Buddha's name during the course of a monk's sermon elicits praises like "Fortunate, indeed!" *(sādhu)* from the audience. However, such symbolism, though psychologically appealing to the *listener* when the *Tantra* is being recited, can cause enormous problems for the *learner* or student of the *Tantras,* who can be baffled by some of the equations—for example, the identification of the body *(rūpa)* with Buddha Vairocana, feeling *(vedanā)* with Buddha Ratnasambhava, and so on. The Tāntric texts that present such identifications are almost non-discursive in explaining the relationships. A whole mass of important doctrinal points can sometimes be incorporated in one symbol, as in the case of *vajra* referred to earlier. The explanation of such symbolism requires a comprehensive knowledge of the Buddhist tradition on the part of a teacher *(guru)*. He needs to be conversant with the fundamental teachings, at least the two major themes in the Buddha's doctrine symbolized by the *vajra*—namely, the process of deconstruction, implied by the doctrine of non-substantiality *(anātman)*, and reconstruction, signified by the theory of dependent arising *(pratītyasamutpāda)*.

However, even if the ordinary, uninitiated listener were initially to believe in the mysterious efficacy of Tantra recitation, the adept, like the physician who administers medicine, cannot succumb to such a view if he is to know his profession. Thus where a Hindu Tāntric text, in keeping with its doctrine of a transcendent self *(ātman)* and its creativity, emphasizes the notion of a mysterious power *(śakti)*, the person conversant with the Buddhist *Tantras* understands that the heart of the Buddhist doctrine embodied in these texts is the principle of dependence. In fact, the substantialist terminology of the Hindu *Tantras* is conspicuously absent in the Buddhist texts, even though some modern Western interpreters continue to use terms like "power" and "empowerment" in explaining both these texts and the rituals.[13] Equipped with such knowledge and understanding, the teacher can carefully guide the student into the intricacies of Tāntric symbolism. What is *not* required of him is any mystical experience, which, assuming that it is beyond linguistic expression, is not easily communicated from teacher to pupil except through an equally mysterious method of instruction, as in the Hindu Tāntric tradition.

Now, the uninitiated listener may view the *Tantras*, recited as *mantras*, as possessing magical power, for he does not have the opportunity of learning them or making sense out of their doctrinal content. Indeed, the danger that the statements in the *Tantras* will lead to ontological commitment, the belief in substances, may be less in the case of the listener than in that of the learner. It is true that the ordinary, uneducated person is prone to thinking in a substantialist way. However, it is the intellectual who is more likely to provide further support for such beliefs. Substantialist thinking is more deep-rooted in the intellectual than in the uneducated person, who is also more susceptible to correction than is his more learned counterpart. Thus the processes of deconstruction and reconstruction taking effect in the uneducated listener are less complicated than are those in the disciple who is being initiated into the meaning and significance of the *Tantras*. The psychological impact of the *man-*

tra is therefore far greater in the case of the former than in the case of the latter. The uneducated person is simply listening to a string of statements, most of them incomprehensible to him; hence there is no danger of any ontological commitment on his part. His attention is absorbed by the names of demons whom he fears, gods whom he respects, and buddhas and *bodhisattvas* whom he venerates. These can generate fear and trepidation in his mind, but not the same kind of fear and trepidation that is generated in the intellectual looking for the mysterious substance and not finding it.[14] The listener's fear and trepidation is caused by his realization of the existence of evil represented by the demons or *yaksas*, by the physical greatness or authority symbolized by the gods, and above all by the enormous moral undertakings and achievements signified by the *bodisattvas* and buddhas, respectively. Such fear and trembling is appeased as the recitation comes to a close.

The concluding statements of the *Tantras* are therefore intended to appease the agitated mind. Even though the listener is unable to understand the doctrinal significance of the entire *Tantra,* these last few statements are intelligible to him because they pertain to peace and happiness of mind. The psychological significance of that appeasement of mind cannot be overestimated. Those who interpret this psychological impact of the *mantra* or the recitation of the *Tantras* as magical are as mistaken as were those of the Buddha's contemporaries who assumed that he possessed the magical power of conversion *(āvaṭṭanī-māyā).*

Explaining the Buddha's method of language and communication, we have already mentioned (see Chapter V) that it consists of four stages, namely, pointing out *(sandasseti),* creating an agitation *(samuttejeti),* appeasing the mind *(sampahaṃseti),* and converting *(samādapeti).* Placing the Buddhist *Tantras* against the background of that method of discourse, we can understand both the significance of their contents and the psychological relevance of their recitation, without having to view them either as gibberish or as vulgar magic.[15]

Parittas

The Vajrayāna, with its emphasis on the recitation of the *Tantras,* is not without its counterparts in some of the other Buddhist countries. The *Tantras* themselves are popular in the East Asian countries. There are schools that do not utilize the *Tantras* but that have their own texts for chanting. The chanting of the *Lotus,* and even of the *Laṅkā,* is not unusual. Chanting is also an extremely popular ritual in the Theravāda tradition of Sri Lanka. In the latter context, the ritual is called *paritta* (lit., "protection")[16] and is intended to banish evil and bring good luck. It is generally traced back to the Buddha himself, especially to the events related in the *Khandha-sutta* of the *Aṅguttara-nikāya*[17] and the *Aṅgu-*

limāla-sutta of the *Majjhima-nikāya.*[18] According to the first discourse, when a monk died of snakebite, the Buddha advised his disciples to practice "friendliness" *(mettā)* toward all snakes as a protection from such danger. If the cultivation of friendliness can effectively eliminate the danger of conflict among human beings, there need be no absolute disbelief that friendliness and compassion would both work in the case of the relationship between humans and animals—unless, of course, we are to believe that a human is totally different from all other animals. The second discourse refers to the incident where the Buddha advised his disciple Aṅgulimāla to make an asseveration of truth in the presence of a woman who had been in labor for seven days. This is said to have enabled the woman to ease her suffering and give birth to her child. Whether or not the woman understood the meaning of the asseveration, the appearance of a Buddhist monk, himself an object of veneration, and his assertion that he had never *willfully* destroyed any life (in this case by a person who, before he became a disciple of the Buddha, had committed a large number of murders as a result of a wrong conception of a religious ritual) seem to have shifted her attention from her physical pain to something totally different. The therapeutic effect of such a psychological transformation is what is generally understood as the "magical" effect of meditation.

These two incidents provided an incentive for later Buddhists to develop the more elaborate ritual called *paritta.* In fact, the *Milinda-pañha,* an extremely popular non-canonical text of the first century B.C., mentions six discourses included under the category of *parittas.*[19] The anthology, as it is available today, consists of twenty-nine discourses. This final version is the text used for the elaborate ritual of all-night chanting. In the less elaborate ritual, three of the discourses are normally chanted. The text itself and the manner in which chanting is done are of considerable psychological significance.

It is interesting to note that some features of the *mantra* discussed earlier can be seen in the *paritta.* The texts themselves are, of course, different. The *parittas* are discourses *(sutta)* taken from the earliest collection *(nikāya).* As such, they do not contain any paradoxical statements. They are discourses that deal with the moral life, like the *Ratana-sutta,*[20] concerning the invocation of blessings that can be enjoyed following truthful words *(sacca-vajja)* relating to the Three Gems (*ratana;* see Chapter XI); the *Metta-sutta,*[21] inculcating the virtues of a life of friendliness *(mettā,* Skt. *maitrī);* and the *Mahāmaṅgala-sutta,*[22] describing the life of social harmony culminating in the attainment of ultimate freedom *(nibbāna).* The only symbolism is contained in the discourse called the *Āṭānāṭiya,*[23] where the so-called *yakkhas* approach the Buddha during the night and inform him that some of the them are pleased with his teachings and some are not, thus rendering the Buddha's disciples in need of protection from those who are not pleased and who could bring about harm. The king of the *yakkhas,* Vessavana, presents the Buddha with what he considers to be a protective charm *(rakkha)* containing statements praising the Buddha and a brief *dhāraṇī.*[24] In the morning, the Buddha tells his disciples what happened during the night and recommends that they study and preserve the protective charm. Thus symbolism is not a major component of the text that is chanted, although it does play a significant role in the designing of the setting for the ritual itself.

The close relationship between *mantra* and *paritta* becomes evident when we consider the manner of chanting and the nature of actual benefits gained. As in the case of the *Tantras,* while the monk who is chanting the discourse may understand the meaning and significance of the discourse recited, it may be incomprehensible to the ordinary layperson, since it is the Pali version of the text that is chanted. After the preliminary ceremonials are performed, the chanting begins in the evening, in a rather steady tone, with the more popular discourses being recited during the initial stages, reaching a climax after midnight, when the *Āṭānāṭiya-sutta* is recited. This recitation is done at the highest pitch or maximum loudness a monk can generate. It is intended to create agitation in the mind of the listener, who dares not leave the premises until the recitation is complete for fear that he will not be protected from the *yakkhas* who are supposed to be displeased. Thereafter, the chanting continues in a smooth and soothing tone until the ritual is concluded around 5:00 A.M. with the distribution of *paritta* water and thread.

As in the case of the *mantra,* the agitation produced in the mind of the listener is appeased in the end. The sense of relief, the calm and satisfaction one feels at the conclusion of the ceremony can produce a psychological transformation that serves as an antidote to many a physical ailment or case of psychological distress. The *mantras* and the *parittas,* if they can claim to be part of the genuine Buddhist tradition, need to be evaluated in light of their psychological significance, not in terms of any mysterious or magical effect. Indeed, neither tradition can claim superiority over the other, for similar or identical benefits are claimed on the basis of chanting totally different texts.

CHAPTER XXIII

Silent Meditation and Ch'an (Zen): The Voiceless Tradition

In my previous analysis of the Ch'an (Zen) tradition, I tried to relate its two major schools, Ts'ao-tung (Sōtō) and Lin-chi (Rinzai), with the Yogācāra and Mādhyamika schools, respectively. Although I have radically revised my explanation of what is meant by Mādhyamika and Yogācāra, and which philosophers and texts belong to these two traditions, it is still possible for me to maintain that relationship by identifying Ts'ao-tung with the metaphysical teachings of the *Laṅkā* (see Chapter XVIII) and Lin-chi with the analytical tradition of the *Vajracchedikā* (see Chapter XV). Unfortunately, this has been made more difficult by the writings of some classical as well as modern interpreters, whose explanations tend to obliterate some of the significant doctrinal differences between these two schools, even though their ultimate spiritual goals may not be at odds with each other. This is not much different from the scenario in India during the seventh century and afterward, when Buddhist philosophers like Candrakīrti, Sthiramati, and Dharmakīrti synthesized the metaphysical and analytical traditions in Buddhism. For example, reading the interpretation of the Ch'an tradition by Chang Chung-yuan, who pays very little attention to the teachings of the first six patriarchs from Bodhidharma to Hui-neng, and who deals at length with the ideas expressed by the subsequent Ch'an masters, one can see hardly any difference in the philosophical standpoints of the two schools.[1] The same is true of the writings of the most influential interpreter of the Japanese Zen tradition in the modern world, D. T. Suzuki.[2] Whether the statements of the founders of these two schools, Tung-shan Liang-chieh of the Ts'ao-tung school and the Lin-chi I-hsuan of the Lin-chi, can be interpreted in the way Chang and Suzuki do, especially adopting transcendentalist perspectives, is open to question. Suzuki goes one further step toward providing what may be called an ahistorical interpretation of Zen:

> But when we come to Zen after a survey of the general field of Buddhism, we are compelled to acknowledge that its simplicity, its directness, its prag-

> matic tendency and its close connection with everyday life stand in remarkable contrast to the other Buddhist sects. Undoubtedly, the main ideas of Zen are derived from Buddhism, and we cannot but consider it a legitimate development of the latter; but this development has been achieved in order to meet the requirements peculiarly characteristic of the psychology of the Far-Eastern people. The spirit of Buddhism has left its highly metaphysical superstructure in order to become a practical discipline of life. The result is Zen. Therefore, I make bold to say that in Zen are found systematized or rather crystallized, all the philosophy, religion and life itself of the Far-Eastern people, especially of the Japanese.[3]

There may be certain characteristics of East Asian peoples reflected in the Zen Buddhist tradition. However, Suzuki seems to go far beyond these in asserting the independence of Zen from Buddhism:

> Zen claims to be Buddhism, but all the Buddhist *teachings* propounded in the sūtras and śāstras are treated by Zen as mere waste of paper whose utility consists in wiping off the dirt of intellect and nothing more.[4]

Suzuki, unfortunately, was misled by some of his contemporaries—both South Asian exponents of the Pali tradition and his own Japanese colleagues involved in the study of the (Chinese) Āgamas—who reduced the Buddhist philosophical tradition to the "Four Noble Truths, the Twelvefold Chain of Causation, the Eightfold Path of Righteous Living, the doctrine of the Non-ego *(Anātman)* and Nirvana."[5] One scholar's mistakes do not justify another's. The history of Buddhist philosophy, as analyzed in the previous chapters, would seem to indicate that, while the themes mentioned by Suzuki may constitute its most prominent doctrines, more important is the philosophical standpoint that serves as the basis for these doctrines. If Suzuki had investigated the literature that the two schools of Ch'an Buddhism utilized as their source material, he would have obtained a better understanding of the relationship between the two Ch'an traditions and Buddhism.

Since it is not possible, in the course of a short chapter like this, to examine the statements of each one of the later Ch'an masters and see whether the interpretations provided by such competent scholars as Chang and Suzuki are in keeping with the two different philosophical standpoints represented by the Ts'ao-tung and the Lin-chi, I will confine my investigation to the early history of Ch'an, from the time of Bodhidharma until the major revolution initiated by Hung-jen and Hui-neng. Without assuming that philosophy has no place in Ch'an Buddhism, but taking the controversy initiated by the Fifth Patriarch, Hung-jen, and continued by Hui-neng to be representative of a major shift in philosophical standpoint, I will try to show that the conflict between the

Ts'ao-tung and Lin-chi schools is a replay of the philosophical controversy among Buddhists on the Indian subcontinent.

Let us start with what came to be known subsequently as the Ts'ao-tung tradition. If Bodhidharma was the founder of the Ch'an tradition in China, and if the *Laṅkā* was the sacred Buddhist text he brought with him for propagation, then it is obvious that Ts'ao-tung is the classic version of Ch'an, as represented by the famous statement attributed to Bodhidharma, but which is said actually to have been formulated much later, when Ch'an had reached a high point of development and maturity. The statement runs thus:

> A special transmission outside the scriptures;
> No dependence upon words and letters:
> Direct pointing at the mind of the man;
> Seeing into one's own nature and the attainment
> of Buddhahood.[6]

There is little doubt that among the different philosophical standpoints adopted by the Buddhists, as explained in the previous chapters, the one that comes closest to the ideas expressed in this statement is that of the *Laṅkā*. We have pointed out the force of the method of negation in that work. It is an outright denial of all forms of conceptual thinking, with no attempt whatsoever to redefine the nature and function of concepts. The consequences of adopting such a standpoint are twofold. First, any literary tradition, which invariably involves conceptualizations, has to be rejected, even though the *Laṅkā* itself does not openly advocate such a project. The first part of the statement attributed to Bodhidharma specifically insists on such a rejection. Second, the rejection of the literary tradition, and, along with it, all forms of conceptualization, involves nihilism, which the *Laṅkā* avoided by recognizing a transcendent subjective reality. The second part of Bodhidharma's statement asserts exactly this subjective reality.

The Ch'an tradition thus began with the most extreme form of Mahāyāna, emphasizing the voiceless practice of silent meditation symbolized by Bodhidharma's "wall-gazing" for the duration of nine years. The Ts'ao-tung, giving priority to this silent meditation, was thus responsible for the popularization of *tso-ch'an (zazen)* in the Chinese Buddhist tradition. The purpose of such silent meditation is well expressed in the statement of Shen-hsiu:

> The body is the Bodhi-tree,
> The mind is like a clear mirror.
> At all times we must strive to polish it,
> And must not let dust collect.[7]

Even though this is a voiceless practice, it is not possible for a beginner to proceed with it unless he has some clue as to what he should be doing. He should have an idea as to what the dust represents that settles on the clear mirror or the originally bright and pure mind (*prakṛti-prabhāsvara-citta;* see Chapter XVIII). The *Laṅkā* identified that dirt as conception (*vikalpa*) of every sort. But to quote the *Laṅkā* as an authority is to go back to the scriptures. Such scriptural authority was condemned in the statement attributed to Bodhidharma, even though he himself handed it down to his students. In the developed Ch'an tradition, this lacuna was filled by the *kung-an (kōan)* or so-called public record.[8] These are no more than the responses of the patriarchs and masters to the queries made by their disciples. A careful analysis of these statements reveals that they do not differ doctrinally from the expositions of Buddhist doctrine found in the thousands of texts translated into Chinese from Indian originals. As will be explained below, they differ only in the *form* in which ideas are expressed, not in the ideas themselves. In fact, their form reminds us of the cryptic dialogues between Confucius and his students or interlocutors, as recorded in the *Analects.* Therefore the more significant contribution of these *kung-an*s was the naturalization of Buddhism in China, for by presenting them as the words of indigenous Buddhist masters dependence on foreign sources was eliminated. That there were no doctrinal differences between Buddhism and Ch'an, only differences relating to the literary form in which the doctrines were presented and also to the authorship of these statements, will become clear from the following analysis.

Yet, in the Ts'ao-tung tradition, the *kung-an* played a secondary role.[9] This is because it emphasized "the direct pointing at the soul of man; seeing into one's own nature and the attainment of Buddhahood," which was to be achieved by abandoning all forms of conceptualization, as in the *Laṅkā.* It is rather unfortunate that no attempt has been made to distinguish the *kung-an*s or *kōan*s utilized by the Ts'ao-tung from those employed by the Lin-chi, despite almost universal acceptance of the differences in their philosophical standpoints. If the silent meditation (*tso-ch'an,* or *zazen*) in both schools is the same, for it is said to be indescribable, and the goal to be achieved (namely, buddhahood) is also identical, the only difference between the two schools is the *form* in which the inexpressible is expressed, and this pertains to the *kung-an.* Since the Ts'ao-tung, following the methodology of the *Laṅkā,* denied every form of conception, the *kung-ans* employed by those belonging to this school should reflect a similar absolute negation of conceptual thinking. Otherwise they would be contradicting themselves, whereas by adopting such an absolute negation, they would be leaving room for the recognition of an ultimate or absolute reality beyond conceptual thinking (if that is possible). The following *kung-an*s seem to reflect such a philosophical standpoint:

> A monk asked Chao-chou (Joshu), "I read in the Sutra that all things return to One. But where does this One return to?" Answered the master, "When I was in the province of Tsing I had a robe made which weighed seven *chin.*"[10]

Again,

> A monk asked Chao-chou, "When the body crumbles all to pieces and returns to the dust, there eternally abides one thing. Of this I have been told, but where does this one thing abide?" The master replied, "It is windy again this morning."[11]

Thus, from the time of Bodhidharma (520 A.D.) until the time of Hung-jen (602–675), the voiceless or silent meditative tradition seems to have been nurtured by the *Laṅkā,* which served as a sourcebook for Bodhidharma. However, with Hung-jen it was to take a different turn. Hui-neng specifically states that after he composed the verse (see below) contradicting the ideas expressed in Shen-hsui's verse, Hung-jen explained the *Vajracchedikā* to him.[12] Yet Suzuki does not agree with this view.[13] Given the two different philosophical standpoints presented in the *Vajracchedikā* and the *Laṅkā,* the revolution that took place in Ch'an Buddhism at this time seems to be of tremendous significance. We have already pointed out that the *Vajracchedikā* represents an attempt to return to the Buddha's teachings, which were gradually becoming infested with absolutist and transcendentalist metaphysics. Philosophers like Nāgārjuna, Vasubandhu, and Dignāga later elaborated on the same theme. *The Platform Sūtra* of the Sixth Patriarch and the legend incorporated therein are best understood in light of that Indian context.

Shen-hsui's verse, quoted above, and the Fifth Patriarch's response to it are interesting. The Ch'an tradition had already been fossilized by the metaphysics of the *Laṅkā.* The search for one's own nature and for buddhahood, two mysteries not revealed by any form of conceptual thinking, had become obsessions *(prapañca).* As far as ordinary disciples were concerned, Hung-jen was willing to admit the verse's usefulness,[14] even though it does not reflect the understanding of an enlightened person but only of one who has reached the portals.[15]

The Sixth Patriarch, Hui-neng, is represented as an uneducated person, unable to read and write. But after getting someone to read Shen-hsui's verse to him, his response was the following verse:

> Bodhi originally has no tree,
> The mirror also has no stand.
> Buddha nature is always clean and pure;
> Where is there room for dust?[16]

Against the background of Shen-hsui's verse, this verse represents abandoning the search for a metaphysical entity (that is, one's own nature, identified with an ultimate reality in the highest state of meditation) and recognizing an ultimate goal of morality (namely, buddhahood, or what was referred to in the *Vajracchedikā* as the *dharmakāya*). Thus it depicts the deconstruction of metaphysical concepts without having to abandon concepts altogether. Indeed, the statement that "Buddha nature is always clean and pure" need not be confused with assertions involving metaphysical concepts about "Buddha nature," which for many thinkers means an eternal reality or entity that is inherent in all human beings. The legend depicting Hui-neng as an illiterate person is a symbolic representation of an innocence not permitting ontological commitment.

It is not without interest that on the day Hui-neng composed his verse, the Fifth Patriarch, Hung-jen, invited him into the hall at midnight and explained to him the *Vajracchedikā*.[17] This was sufficient for Hui-neng to realize the nature of the Buddha's teaching, as in the case of Nāgārjuna before him. Fearing that Hui-neng would have to face the dogmatism of the prevalent Ch'an tradition, Hung-jen blessed him with the robe that entitled him to the position of sixth patriarch and sent him away with the words: "From ancient times the transmission of the Dharma has been as tenuous as a dangling thread. If you stay here there are people who will harm you. You must leave at once."[18] Hung-jen's statement seems to reflect his awareness of the recurrent dangers the Buddhist doctrine had encountered from its very outset. These dangers, as explained in Chapter XII, were posed by the people who were prone to absolutist thinking of one form or another.

At the end of this lengthy discourse, where Hui-neng makes a deliberate and persistent attempt to reconcile the old and the new in Chinese Ch'an—the older form of silent meditation popularized by Bodhidharma and the new one introduced by Hung-jen, based on the *Vajracchedikā*—we come across a rather significant statement by Hui-neng. This statement represents the method of the *Vajracchedikā,* of Nāgārjuna, and of many other philosophers who struggled to eliminate absolutistic and transcendentalist metaphysics without abandoning experience and conception altogether:

> Deluded, a Buddha is a sentient being;
> Awakened, a sentient being is a Buddha.
> Ignorant, a Buddha is a sentient being;
> With wisdom, a sentient being is a Buddha.
> If the mind is warped, a Buddha is a sentient being;
> If the mind is impartial, a sentient being is a
> Buddha.

When once a warped mind is produced,
Buddha is concealed within the sentient being.
If for one instant of thought we become impartial,
The sentient beings are themselves Buddha.
In our mind itself a Buddha exists,
Our own Buddha is the true Buddha.
If we do not have in ourselves the Buddha mind,
Then where are we to seek the Buddha?[19]

The first part of this is reminiscent of Nāgārjuna's famous statement regarding *saṃsāra* and *nirvāṇa.*[20] The second part reflects the way an enlightened Buddhist would advise lay followers to perceive the Buddha (see Chapter XI), without having to commit themselves to metaphysical propositions but simply accepting the fact that moral perfection is to be sought within "this fathom-long conscious body."

Thus the *kung-an*s that can be related to the above philosophical standpoint must be different from those mentioned earlier. They should reflect not only the deconstruction of metaphysical concepts but also the reconstruction that allows for meaningful concepts. *Kung-an*s involving repetition have the same force as the statements of the *Vajracchedikā,* without the negation. Thus we have the *kung-ans* attributed to T'ou-tzu Tai-t'ung of the T'ang dynasty, such as the following:

Who is the Buddha?
The Buddha.

What is the way?
The way.

What is the *dharma?*
The *dharma.*[21]

Such responses would certainly have the same effect as the *kung-an* from the *Vajracchedikā:*

Dharma.
[No-*dharma.*]
Therefore *"dharma."*

It is possible that a more careful study of *kung-an*s will reveal the two different philosophical approaches to conceptual thinking in the two Ch'an traditions, and also distinguish the Ch'an masters who adopted these two different philosophical standpoints.

It is silent meditation *(tso-ch'an, zazen),* coupled with the *kung-an*s based on the philosophical method of the *Vajracchedikā,* that can be considered creative, for all creativity in knowledge is said to take place in terms of conception, not without it. The *kung-ans* that serve as a means of denying the validity of all conceptual thinking can be as stultifying as any anesthesia, allowing the person to be manipulated while he himself reverts to inaction.

Silent meditation is not an innovation of the Ch'an tradition. The rigorous practice of such meditation, sometimes more strenuous than that ascribed to Bodhidharma, is known from the Theriya tradition in Sri Lanka. Walpola Rahula reports, on the basis of the commentaries of Buddhaghosa, many instances of monks practicing extreme forms of meditation.[22] One of them was a *thera* called Mahānāga who, according to Buddhaghosa, is said to have spent twenty-three years in meditation (fourteen more than Bodhidharma) without talking to anyone except to answer an unavoidable question. He is also said to have spent seven years walking and standing without ever sitting or lying down.[23] Rahula informs us that the fame of this *thera* as a holy man had spread as far as India.[24]

Another interesting story is related in the *Visuddhimagga.* It refers to a *thera* named Cittagutta (lit., "concealed mind" or "protected mind") who lived in a cave called Kuraṇḍaka, near Mahāgāma in the southern part of Sri Lanka. In this cave there were some beautiful paintings of the renunciation scenes of the Seven Buddhas. Some monks who visited these caves saw these paintings and remarked on their beauty to Cittagutta. The latter's response was, "Friends, I have lived here for over sixty years. But I did not know that there were these paintings."[25] A more interesting story about the same *thera* takes the form of a *kung-an* of the Ts'ao-tung tradition. The king, who had heard about the great virtues of the *thera,* was anxious to see him and pay homage to him. Thrice the *thera* refused the king's invitation to visit the capital. The king adopted a perverse and unusual device to make the holy man come. He ordered the breasts of all suckling mothers to be tied and sealed, and declared that the children would not get milk until the *thera* came. Through compassion for the children, the monk finally visited the capital and the king had the opportunity to entertain him. Whether it was the king who worshiped him or whether it was the queen, Cittagutta always bestowed blessings saying, "Be happy, O Mahārāja [Great King]!" The other monks remarked, "Sir, regardless of whether it is the king who worships you or the queen, you say, 'Be happy, O Mahārāja!' " "I do not discriminate between the king and the queen," was the *thera*'s unconcerned reply.[26] After sixty years of such meditation, he probably did not have any meaningful use for concepts, and Rahula rightly remarks that this certainly is not the kind of restraint that the Buddha advocated.

The Buddhist monks of South and Southeast Asia have increasingly come to accept this form of silent meditation, which they also export to Western countries as well as to Australia and New Zealand. Unfortunately, a replay of the conflict between the extremes of textual study *(gantha-dhura)* and silent meditation *(vipassanā-dhura)* characterized the life of monks during the medieval period,[27] a conflict introduced into China by Bodhidharma during the same time, as is evident from the statement attributed to him.

The philosophical speculations of Moggalīputta-tissa, Nāgārjuna, Vasubandhu, and Dignāga represented attempts to be in tune with the teachings of the Buddha. Although comparable speculations may not have been Hui-neng's forte, he was probably trying to get the religious life back on a track that avoided the extremes of textual study and silent meditation by reworking the *kung-an*s, which had previously been of little use in the Ch'an tradition.

EPILOGUE
PHILOSOPHY AND HISTORY

The peaceful spread of Buddhism throughout the Asian continent has baffled many historians. However, although actual bloodshed in the propagation of the doctrine was nil, and in the preservation of the tradition rare and apart, Buddhism cannot boast of ideological harmony. In addition to the many disputes among the minor sects, a major conflict, sometimes rather bitter, has plagued the Buddhist tradition for centuries. This is the rivalry between Theravāda and Mahāyāna. Whatever the actual historical circumstances that occasioned this rift, it was widened and deepened for posterity during the second century A.D., as a result of a change in the philosophical paradigm on the basis of which peace and harmony had been achieved in the first instance.

The Buddha's own proposal for achieving peace *(araṇa)* and avoiding conflict *(raṇa)* was the middle path, theoretical as well as practical. On the theoretical side, it was a middle path between extremist viewpoints. Thus, in epistemology, it was a middle path between absolutism and skepticism; in ontology, between eternalism and nihilism; in ethics, between deontology and emotivism; and in linguistic philosophy, between what may be called realism and nominalism. With the renunciation of such extremes, the Buddha was compelled to adopt some form of relativism. For him relativism was not an evil as long as a person does not commit some other error that makes relativism unpalatable. What makes relativism unpalatable to many is the commonly held but mistaken view that one theory has to be superior to another, one belief superior to another, one perspective superior to another, independent of the conditions under which the theory is formulated, the belief held, or the perspective adopted. If there were absolute certainty regarding the validity of the theory or belief or perspective, then holding it to be superior would be justified. But our analysis of the Buddha's epistemology and logic provided no evidence that he claimed such certainty; on the contrary, he was extremely critical of those who made such claims.

If our presentation of the Buddha's doctrine in the first part of this work is accurate, then it is evident that, according to the Buddha, human knowledge, the conception of reality, moral principles, and means of communication are to be recognized as valid so long as they are useful and contribute to happiness and peace among living beings. This does not mean that there can be no sophistication and advancement in these areas, but these are not the only criteria for determining what is relevant or irrelevant in a given situation. Whether some theory is sophisticated or unsophisticated, advanced or primitive, in the final analysis its value lies in how it contributes to the weal and woe of living beings in that particular context. *When the criterion is pragmatic in this sense, it would be most inappropriate to adopt a hierarchical model of evaluation, where one theory is judged to be absolutely the best and all others are placed in descending order, the last being characterized as the worst.* This form of relativism lurks in the background of an absolutist perspective, where one theory *is* recognized as the best under all circumstances and at any time.

Most of the discourses included in the *Aṭṭhakavagga (Section on Meaning)* of the *Sutta-nipāta* are intended to drive home the idea that the above method of evaluating a view or a conception leads not only to dogmatism (which is avoided in the Buddha's epistemology; see Chapter III) but also to strife *(kalaha)* and conflict *(viggaha)*. To claim that one's own view is superior *(seṭṭha)* and to condemn another's as low and vile *(hīna)* is the easiest way to generate unnecessary animosity in the mind of that other person. Regretfully, it is this method of evaluation of the different schools of Buddhism in the *Saddharmapuṇḍarīka-sūtra* (see Chapter XVII) and the *Laṅkāvatāra-sūtra* (see Chapter XVIII) that enlarged the rift between Theravāda and Mahāyāna, the latter calling the former the "low vehicle" *(hīnayāna),* to which the former responded by branding the latter a "heresy" *(vaitulyavāda).* Indeed, the *Saddharmapuṇḍarīka* went to the extent of maligning the Buddha himself, who is made to characterize his immediate disciples who had attained enlightenment as people of "low dispositions" *(hīnādhimukti).* Furthermore, the Buddha is represented as enjoying the rift among his disciples when he is made to say that, as a result of the departure, in protest, of those whom he had characterized as low, the assembly has been cleared of trash.

The original schism that took place during the Second Council (about a century after the death of the Buddha) is said to have resulted in the formation of two major schools: Theravāda, representing the conservatives, and Mahāsaṅghika, constituting the liberals. It is assumed that the Mahāsaṅghikas were the precursors of Mahāyana. However, from the information available about the doctrines of the Mahāsaṅghikas, there is nothing to suggest that they upheld or even provided incentive for any doctrines comparable to those advocated by the Mahāyāna of the *Saddharmapuṇḍarīka* and *Laṅkāvatāra.* Curiously, it was the Sarvāstivāda school that authored most of the theories in question, such as those of the absolute omniscience and transcendence of the Buddha, and these doctrines were the inevitable consequences of asserting the idea of an unchanging substance *(svabhāva)* in phenomena. It may be remembered that the Sarvāstivāda doctrines were refuted by the author of the *Kathāvatthu* (see Chapter XIII). Yet there is no condemnation of any of those doctrines as low or vulgar *(hīna)*. The impression one gets from the *Kathāvatthu* is that they were considered to be mistaken in relation to what was reported as the teachings of the Buddha in the early discourses, which were quoted by both Moggalīputta-tissa and his opponents. Comparable debates took place among the Buddhist schools, as between Saṅghabhadra, a proponent of Sarvāstivāda, and Vasubandhu, who has been identified as an idealist but who is more appropriately characterized as an early Buddhist. Such controversies and debates may signify a healthy and vibrant philosophical atmosphere. However, the tone of the two Mahāyāna sūtras does not indicate such an atmosphere.

It was mentioned that the *Saddharmapuṇḍarīka* was the first text to abuse the Theravāda, as well as early Buddhism, as low *(hīna)*. While it was guilty of initiating a conflict that was to create animosities, the response from the Theravāda itself, when it called Mahāyāna a heresy *(vaitulyavāda)*, did not help diffuse the situation. Instead of hurling abuse on each other, the two sides should have examined the pragmatic value of each theory in the context in which it was presented. If such an analysis had been undertaken, the ideological rift would have gradually disappeared.

Interestingly, in spite of Theravāda dependence on Buddhaghosa and Mahāyāna reliance on the *Saddharmapuṇḍarīka,* there is a lot of common ground between the two traditions, which some of their adherents are reluctant to admit, tending to overemphasize the differences and downplay the similarities. This common ground resulted from the endeavors of those enlightened teachers—Moggalīputta-tissa, who was highly respected in the Theravāda, as well as Nāgārjuna, Vasubandhu, and Dignāga, venerated in the Mahāyāna—who showed unmistakable signs of being non-sectarian in their advanced years. All were determined to resurrect the teachings of the historical Buddha. Their writings have influenced both traditions and served as a thread of continuity between them, despite the unfortunate ideological disagreement that has survived for centuries.

APPENDIX
HISTORY OF THE *LAṄKĀVATĀRA*

The title of the *Laṅkāvatāra* discourse *(Descent into Laṅkā;* abbreviated *Laṅkā)* and the period of its compilation suggested by historians (i.e., the fourth century A.D.) provide interesting clues to understanding a text that is highly venerated by one of the major schools of Zen Buddhism, albeit considered to be an extremely unsystematic work by its followers. Unfortunately, the significance of the title and the period of compilation were ignored by the most competent authority on the text, D. T. Suzuki. The fact that the *Laṅkā* was adopted as a basic text of the Sōtō Zen tradition does not necessarily mean that the intention of its compilers was to propagate the doctrines of this particular school. Regarding the title, Suzuki has the following to say:

> *Laṅkāvatāra* literally is "entering into Laṅkā," while Lanka is one of the islands in the south of India. It is popularly identified with Ceylon, but scholars are not certain about it. "Entering" probably refers to the Buddha's coming over to the island. The sūtra is supposed to have been delivered by the Buddha while staying there. The dialogue takes place between him and Mahāmati who is the chief one of Bodhisattvas assembled there. *It is unusual for a Buddhist sūtra to be delivered in such an out-of-the-way place as Lanka, a solitary island in the middle of the Indian ocean* [emphasis added].[1]

In the first place, to ignore the very title of the work, which has never been controverted, is not serious scholarship. Second, Suzuki is almost silent regarding the philosophical and religious atmosphere in which the text was compiled. Considering the enormous impact of this work on East Asian Buddhism and the controversies surrounding its history and compilation, it would seem appropriate to piece together whatever scanty information can be collected in order to determine the significance of the title and the historical context in which the text came to be compiled. In fact, the text was compiled during a rather complicated era in the history of Buddhism, so critical evaluation of the history of the text is all the more important. However, the following information is presented not without sensitivity to the feelings of those who view this work as the primary source of their philosophical views and spiritual exercises. This is simply evidence that stares at you when you are involved in historical scholarship.

Suzuki and many others who commented on the *Laṅkā* believe that two chapters—the first and the eighth—are later additions. There is no doubt that, without these two chapters, the rest of the work appears to be a self-contained unit. Yet, examining this self-contained unit in the context of one of the major treatises of the idealistic Yogācāra Buddhism, namely, Asaṅga's *Abhidharmasamuccaya,* one can raise questions regarding its relevance. Asaṅga's *Abhidharmasamuccaya* is an extremely well-organized and comprehensive text that attempts to provide an idealistic interpretation of the categories or phenomena *(dharma)* that were the subject matter of the Abhidharma. The idealistic interpretation emerges when the *dharmas* are analyzed in terms of the three truths—the false *(parikalpita),* the relative *(paratantra),* and the ultimate *(pariniṣpanna)*—considered in a hierarchical order. Presented in the form of questions and answers, Asaṅga's treatise deals with almost every category and subcategory of phenomena examined in the Abhidharma tradition. If the historians are correct, the *Abhidharmasamuccaya* is older than the *Laṅkā.* (Asaṅga's major works were composed between 333–353 A.D., while the *Laṅkā* is believed to have been compiled between 350–400.)[2] Even if they were contemporary, one cannot help asking why it was necessary to compile an obviously unsystematic *sūtra* like the *Laṅkā* when there was a more systematic, coherent, and detailed treatment of the same subject in the *Abhidharmasamuccaya.*

The second chapter of the *Laṅkā* (i.e., the beginning of the so-called self-contained original text) starts with a series of questions, 108 in number.[3] The questions deal with a variety of topics and are presented, unlike in Asaṅga's treatise, in an extremely unsystematic way, indicating that the work was put together in haste.

However, there are two important differences between Asaṅga's work and the *Laṅkā.* First, Asaṅga's treatise contains questions and answers presented in an impersonal way, as in the Abhidharma. The *Laṅkā,* on the contrary, introduces a little-known *bodhisattva,* Mahāmati, as the questioner and the Buddha as the respondant. This is probably to give the appearance of a "discourse" *(sūtra),* which would carry more authority than a philosophical treatise compiled by an individual. Second, the topics on which Mahāmati questions the Buddha are immediately negated. This is reminiscent of one aspect of the methodology adopted in the *Vajracchedikā,* a theme discussed in Chapter XVIII.

In spite of this difference, the question raised earlier calls for an answer. Why was it necessary for the idealistic Yogācāra tradition to put together a *sūtra* in such haste, especially when there was already a more comprehensive and systematic treatment of idealism in the work of Asaṅga? The answer is contained in the title of the work and in the first and eighth chapters, all of which baffled Suzuki. The title *Descent into Laṅkā* implies the introduction of Mahāyāna transcendentalism into a country that had remained faithful to the earlier, pragmatic form of Buddhism introduced during the third century B.C.

Chapter 1 is interesting because the interlocutor here is not the Bodhisattva Mahāmati but the mythical King of Laṅkā, Rāvaṇa, the Lord of the Yakṣas, who is said to have ruled Laṅkā before the advent of the Sinhala race. At Rāvaṇa's invitation, the Buddha is supposed to have appeared on the island and preached the *Laṅkā,* embodying "the innermost state of consciousness realized by them [the Tathāgatas,] which is not found in any system of doctrine."[4] Rāvaṇa is here depicted as an extremely intelligent, pious person who had no difficulty understanding the doctrine taught by the Buddha. In fact, Rāvaṇa was able to realize the empty nature of all phenomena *(dharmatā)* without a great deal of effort.[5] Criticism of him is rare; he is more often praised as a great person.

In contrast, Chapter 8 is, by allusion, a most severe condemnation of the Sinhala race, which is believed to have colonized the island during the sixth century B.C., and which by this time had come to preserve the Buddhist tradition introduced to the island during the time of Emperor Aśoka. One wonders why a chapter entitled "Meat Eating" *(Maṃsabhakṣana)* should be a conclusion to such an important philosophical treatise. An allusion to the Sinhala race is found in the following paragraph:

> Mahāmati, there was another king who was carried away by his horse into the forest. After wandering about in it, he committed evil deeds with a lioness out of fear for his life, and children were born to her. Because of their descending from the union with a lioness, the royal children were called the Spotted-Feet, etc. On account of their evil habit-energy *(vāsanā)* in the past when their food had been flesh, they ate meat even [after becoming] king [*sic*]. . . . Falling into such, it will be with difficulty that they can ever obtain a human womb; how much more [difficult] attaining Nirvana![6]

The allusion is clear. The Sinhala race traced its origin to Siṃhabāhu and Siṃhasīvalī, who were believed to have been the children born to an Indian princess, Suppādevi, who ran away into the jungle and lived with a "lion" *(siṃha).*[7] Prince Vijaya, who colonized the island around the sixth century B.C. (long after Rāvaṇa), is said to have been the progeny of Siṃhabāhu and Siṃhasīvalī, and is supposed to have been banished from India because he was the product of incest. Thus the custodians of the

Buddhist tradition at the Mahāvihāra belonged to the so-called Lion-race *(siṃhala)*. The chapter on "Meat Eating" thus appears to be no more than a condemnation of the Mahāvihāra tradition, for a philosophical treatise like the *Laṅkā* could have dealt with more important moral issues than meat-eating. In fact, the compilers of the *Laṅkā* were quite aware that the Mahāvihāra followed the rather liberal views of the Buddha, and even go to the extent of denying a statement in the early discourses attributed to the Buddha regarding meat-eating.[8]

This is the internal evidence that the *Laṅkā* was meant as a textbook for the conversion of Laṅkā to Mahāyāna Buddhism. The external evidence for this view is even more compelling. Laṅkā does not appear to be a simple, out-of-the-way, solitary island, as Suzuki thought, if we keep in mind the extended ideological battles between the Theravādins and the Mahāyānists staged in this part of the world during the third and fourth centuries A.D. While the Mahāvihāra in Sri Lanka remained the center of Theravāda Buddhism, more cosmopolitan Buddhist centers were coming into prominence in South India, especially in places like Nāgārjunikoṇḍa. These centers attracted scholars from various parts of the world, including Sri Lanka. It may be remembered that South India produced a number of leading Buddhist scholars like Nāgārjuna, Dignāga, Buddhaghosa, and Dhammapāla.

We have already seen how transcendentalism *(lokuttaravāda)*, which came into prominence during the time of Moggalīputta-tissa, reached its culmination in the *Lotus*. The condemnation of the *arhats* in the *Lotus* could not have gone unnoticed by the Theravādins of Sri Lanka, who even had a Sinhalese monastery in Nāgārjunikoṇḍa.[9] It is during the third century A.D. that we hear of the first major invasion of Sri Lanka by the Mahāyānists. It may have been during this time that the Theravādins, who were angered by the Mahāyāna characterization of their teachings as *hīnayāna* (the lowly vehicle), began referring to their opponents as Vaitulyavādins. According to historical records, the *vaitulyavāda* (Pali, *vetullavāda*) made its first appearance in Sri Lanka during the reign of Vohārika-tissa (269–291 A.D.).[10] Urged on by the monks at the Mahāvihāra, the king suppressed the teachings and expelled their adherents from the island. Its second appearance was during the reign of Goṭhābhaya (309–322), and was associated with the monastery called Abhayagiri, whose monks had broken away from the Mahāvihāra. It was probably received with favor by the monks at Abhayagiri, since they had been influenced by the doctrines of the Sautrāntikas,[11] who (as mentioned in Chapter XVII), were referred to as those who had "arrived at the portals of *Vaipulyaśāstra*."

Goṭhābhaya is said to have held an inquiry, suppressed the Vaitulyavādins, burnt their books, and exiled sixty of their leaders from the island. Some of the exiled monks took up residence in Kāvīrapaṭṭana, in the

Chola country in South India. Walpola Rahula observes that this period coincided with the activities of the Yogācāra school in India.[12] Furthermore, the Sri Lankan monks who lived in exile in Kāveri became friendly with a dynamic young monk named Saṅghamitra. It was Saṅghamitra who came to Sri Lanka, befriended King Mahāsena (334–362), and wreaked havoc in the Theravāda tradition, compelling the monks of the Mahāvihāra to flee to the south of the island. For almost a decade, the Mahāvihāra was deserted. It is reported that Saṅghamitra got the king to demolish the buildings at the Mahāvihāra, including the seven-story Lohapāsāda ("the brazen palace"), and used some of that material to erect new buildings at Abhayagiri.[13] Saṅghamitra's activities sent a shock wave through the length and breadth of the country.

King Mahāsena himself was unaware of the enormous influence of the Mahāvihāra until one of his close friends, Meghavaṇṇa-Abhaya, who had fled to the South, raised an army and challenged him. Mahāsena is said to have awoken from his slumber, met with his friend, regretted the damage done to the Mahāvihāra, and promised to restore it.

It is not insignificant that Saṅghamitra's activities in Sri Lanka coincided with the compilation of the *Laṅkā.* Even a cursory glance at the *Laṅkā* can convince the reader that its basic teachings are not far removed from what the Theravāda perceived to be the theory of the "Great Emptiness" *(mahāsuññatavāda)* or the tradition of the Vaitulyakas (see Chapter XVIII).

If the internal evidence that the *Laṅkā* was a Mahāyāna handbook to be used in converting Sri Lanka is valid, then Saṅghamitra and his followers could have propagated no better discourse during their fateful sojourn on that island. Indeed, it would be surprising had Saṅghamitra, who was committed to converting the island, arrived there empty-handed. He needed to replace the scriptures of the Mahāvihāra with his own. Given the seriousness with which he undertook his mission, one cannot easily reject the view that a work entitled *Descent into Laṅkā* or *The Invasion of Laṅkā (Laṅkāvatāra),* which was subsequently included among the Vaipulya-sūtras, was a handbook for Saṅghamitra. The reason none of this literature survived in the Sri Lankan Buddhist tradition is that Saṅghamitra and his followers were dealt with so severely after the revolt by Meghavañña-Abhaya. Sinhalese historical records say that after the reconciliation between Mahāsena and Meghavaṇṇa-Abhaya, the angry crowd went on a rampage. One of the king's favorite wives, who was bitter about the suffering of the Mahāvihāra monks, got a carpenter to kill Saṅghamitra. Nothing associated with Saṅghamitra survived. Even one of his closest friends, a Sinhalese minister named Soṇa, was slain. It would have been a miracle had any Mahāyāna literature from this period remained on the island. These events left an extremely bitter feeling among the Theravāda monks, so much so that, when Buddhaghosa arrived from the same part of India two centuries later, he was treated with great suspicion (see Chapter XXI).

If these historical events have any validity, and if our surmise about the original intention of the compilers of this work is not too farfetched, there is no reason to be baffled by the *Laṅkā*'s extremely unsystematic treatment of subject matter or crude presentation of important philosophical questions. Suzuki himself puts this rather mildly: "For thoughts of deep signification are presented in a most unsystematic manner. As I said in my *Studies,* the *Laṅkā* is a memorandum kept by a Mahāyāna master, in which he puts down perhaps all the teachings of importance accepted by the Mahāyāna followers of his day."[14] Unfortunately, despite the *Laṅkā*'s popularity in East Asia, it failed to attract the attention of Buddhists in Sri Lanka, who were too deeply rooted in the tradition representing the less mystical, more empirical and pragmatic teachings of the historical Buddha.

NOTES

Chapter I

1. See Benimadhab Barua, *A History of Pre-Buddhistic Indian Philosophy* (Delhi: Motilal Banarsidass, 1970), for a detailed treatment of the early Indian philosophers and their reflections.
2. *Ṛgveda* x.81.4.
3. Ibid. x.129; tr. Walter H. Maurer, *Pinnacles of India's Past: Selections from the Ṛgveda,* University of Pennsylvania Studies in South Asia, vol. 2 (Amsterdam and Philadelphia: John Benjamins, 1986), pp. 283–284.
4. K. N. Jayatilleke, *Early Buddhist Theory of Knowledge* (London: George Allen & Unwin, 1963), p. 27.
5. *Ṛgveda* I.164.46.
6. See Thomas Nagel, *The View from Nowhere* (Oxford: Oxford University Press, 1986).
7. *Ṛgveda* VII.86.
8. Ibid. x.90.
9. *Bṛhadāraṇyaka Upaniṣad* I.4.1–16; tr. R. E. Hume, *The Thirteen Principal Upaniṣads* (London: Oxford University Press, 1934).
10. *Ṛgveda* x.90.
11. *Tattvopaplavasiṃha of Jayarāśi Bhaṭṭa,* ed. S. Sanghavi and R. C. Parikh, Gaekwad Oriental Series 87 (Baroda: Oriental Series, 1940), p. 1.
12. *Ṣaḍdarśanasamuccaya* of Haribhadra, Bibliotheca Indica (Calcutta: Asiatic Society of Bengal, 1905), p. 306.
13. *D* 1.53. This Buddhist discourse is considered to be one of the earliest sources for the study of Ājīvikism, of which no literary tradition has survived. See A. L. Basham, *History and Doctrines of the Ājīvikas* (London: Luzac, 1951).
14. *M* 1.81–82.
15. Barua, *Pre-Buddhistic Indian Philosophy,* p. 395.
16. See *Immanuel Kant's Critique of Pure Reason,* tr. Norman Kemp Smith (London: Macmillan, 1963), p. 34.
17. Quoted in Barua, *Pre-Buddhistic Indian Philosophy,* p. 397.
18. *Sūtrakṛtāṅga* I.1.2.4 (see tr. H. Jacobi, *The Jaina Sūtras,* Sacred Books of the East, vol. 45 [Oxford: Clarendon Press, 1895]).

19. For details, see S. Radhakrishnan, *Indian Philosophy* (New York: Macmillan; London: George Allen & Unwin, 1962), vol. 1, pp. 302–304.
20. Ibid., vol. 1, pp. 299–301.
21. P. S. Jaini inappropriately argues for similarity regarding the conceptions of "omniscience" *(sarvajñatva)* in the Jaina and Buddhist literature; see his article "On the Sarvajñatva (Omniscience) of Mahāvīra and the Buddha," in *Buddhist Studies in Honour of I. B. Horner,* ed. L. Cousins et al. (Dordrecht: D. Reidel, 1974), pp. 71–90.
22. *M* 1.373.
23. Barua, *Pre-Buddhistic Indian Philosophy,* p. 399.
24. *M* 2.222.
25. *Vin* 1.40.
26. *M* 1.497–501.

Chapter II

1. See M. Winternitz, *A History of Indian Literature,* second ed. (Delhi: Munshiram Manoharlal, 1972), vol. 1., pp. 268–289.
2. M 1.163.289.
3. *S* 5.421–423.
4. Ibid. 2.17–18.
5. *Vin* 1.43.
6. See tr. Mrs. C. A. F. Rhys Davids, *Psalms of the Early Buddhists,* 2 vols. (London: PTS, 1948).
7. *Thag* 866–891.
8. Ibid. 341–349.
9. G. De, *Democracy in Early Buddhist Sangha* (Calcutta: Calcutta University Press, 1955), p. xv.
10. *D* 2.154.
11. G. C. Pande, *Studies in the Origins of Buddhism* (Allahabad: University of Allahabad, 1957), p. 330.
12. *D* 2.149–150.
13. Ibid. 2.128, 134, 137; *Ud* 83–84.

Chapter III

1. *D* 1.12ff.
2. Ibid. 1.13.
3. Ibid. 1.16.
4. Ibid. 1.13.
5. *M* 2.170.
6. Ibid. 2.170–171.
7. Ibid. 1.108ff.
8. Ibid. 1.111–112.
9. *D* 1.41ff.
10. *M* 1.112.
11. William James, *Some Problems of Philosophy,* ed. F. Burkhardt (Cambridge, Mass.: Harvard University Press, 1979), pp. 31–60.

12. *M* 1.163–166.
13. *D* 1.73.
14. Ibid. 2.156.
15. Ibid. 3.230.
16. *S* 4.295.
17. *M* 1.296.
18. *D* 1.76.
19. Ibid. 1.77.
20. *Vin* 2.110–112.
21. *M* 1.502.
22. Ibid. 2.169.
23. Ibid. 1.375, 381; *A* 2.190, 193.
24. *D* 2.190.
25. Ibid. 3.134.
26. See Hajime Nakamura, *Indian Buddhism* (Osaka: KUFS Publication, 1980), p. 306.
27. *M* 1.403.
28. Ibid. 1.292–293.
29. *D* 1.84, 177, 203; *M* 2.39.
30. *J* 1.75 *(sabbaññū)*; *Sn* 177, 211; *Dhp* 353 *(sabbavidū)*; *M* 1.92 *(sabbadassāvī)*.
31. *M* 1.481ff.
32. *S* 4.15.
33. *Sn* 1122.
34. *PTSD,* p. 320, s.v. *diṭṭhi.*
35. *Dhp* 421.
36. *S* 1.11.
37. Ibid. 2.58.
38. W. V. O. Quine, *Elementary Logic* (New York: Harper, 1965), p. 6. This is what logic is all about, even though Quine's later ideas are somewhat less rigid.
39. Ibid.
40. *Sn* 884.
41. *M* 1.169.
42. William James, *The Will to Believe,* ed. F. Burkhardt, (Cambridge, Mass.: Harvard University Press, 1976), p. 89.
43. Jayatilleke, *Early Buddhist Theory of Knowledge,* pp. 345–346.
44. *A* 2.25.
45. Jayatilleke takes proposition iii to be a contradiction by introducing the phrase "both." To be consistent, he should insert the same word in proposition iv, as "both neither p nor not-p", which would mean that it is not an excluded middle (see his *Early Buddhist Theory of Knowledge,* p. 345). It seems that the Buddha would have characterized the excluded middle as *musā,* not *kali.* As such, Jayatilleke's attempt to give truth-value to proposition iv seems inappropriate.
46. David J. Kalupahana, *Causality. The Central Philosophy of Buddhism,* (Honolulu: University of Hawaii Press, 1975), pp. 187ff.
47. *D* 1.3.

48. *Sn* 1076.
49. *S* 2.19.
50. The reason Jayatilleke wanted to give truth-values to the propositions that were negated, when the Buddha would not even think of doing so, becomes evident when one reads the conclusion of his work, wherein he maintains that the person who has attained *nibbāna* survives death even though he cannot be spoken of. This would explain the questions laid aside by the Buddha (i.e., *ṭhapanīya,* or *avyākata*) as those that pertained to an ineffable reality, which would be the position of the Jainas.
51. Irving M. Copi, *Introduction to Logic* (New York: Macmillan, 1978), p. 264; also repeated in idem, *Symbolic Logic* (New York: Macmillan, 1973), pp. 6–7.
52. See notes 5 and 6 above.
53. *M* 1.394. Jayatilleke, struggling under the yoke of the essentialist conceptions of truth and falsity, perceives no direct inquiry into the nature of truth, in an epistemological sense, in the Buddhist texts. His evaluation of the contents of the Buddha's discourse to Prince Abhaya therefore remains unenthusiastic.
54. See Introduction to William James' *Pragmatism and the Meaning of Truth,* ed. A. J. Ayer (Cambridge, Mass.: Harvard University Press, 1978), pp. xxviff.
55. *S* 2.17.

Chapter IV

1. *S* 2.36. Referring to the Buddha's explanation of *paṭiccasamuppāda,* his disciple Ānanda says, *Acchariyaṃ bhante abbhutaṃ bhante yatra hi nāma ekena padena sabbo attho vutto bhavissati.* ("It is wondrous, O Venerable Sir, it is marvelous, O Venerable Sir, that with one word the entirety of meaning comes to be expressed.")
2. Ibid. 2.25–26.
3. Ibid. 2.26; *ahosiṃ nu kho atītaṃ addhānaṃ,* etc.
4. Ibid. 2.77.
5. Ibid.
6. The term *khaṇa* occurs in two important instances: (1) *Sn* 333 = *Dhp* 315, where it means "opportunity"; and (2) *A* 4.137, where the impermanence of human life is explained, emphasizing the shortness of one's life span. The simile of the river *(nadi)* is used to deny any stability in that life span.
7. See David J. Kalupahana, *A Path of Righteousness (Dhammapada),* (Lanham, Md: University Press of America, 1986), p. 18.
8. See Kalupahana, *Causality.*
9. *S* 2.58.
10. *D* 2.12–15; *M* 1.324.
11. *Sphuṭārthābhidarmakośa-vyākhyā,* ed. U. Wogihara (Tokyo: Publishing Association of the Abhidharmakośavyākhyā, 1932–1936), p. 174.
12. *S* 2.25.
13. Ibid. 2.26.
14. *M* 1.167.

15. Ibid. 1.262ff.; *S* 2.28.
16. *S* 2.16–17.
17. *M* 1.167.
18. Ibid.
19. *Dhp* 421.
20. *M* 1.167.

Chapter V

1. See two lists, one at *DA* 1.199 and *DhpA* 1.22, and the other at *DhsA* 38.
2. Wilhelm and Magdelene Geiger, *Pali Dhamma, vernehmlich in der kanonischen Literatur* (München: Bayerischen Akademie der Wissenschaften, 1921).
3. *D* 3.85–86.
4. George Zipf, *Psychobiology of Language,* quoted in W. V. O. Quine, *Quiddities: An Intermittently Philosophical Dictionary* (Cambridge, Mass.: Belknap Press of Harvard University Press, 1987), p. 111.
5. Quine, *Quiddities,* p. 111–112.
6. *D* 3.85–86.
7. *M* 3.234ff.
8. Quine, *Quiddities,* pp. 111–117.
9. Ibid.
10. See Winternitz, *A History of Indian Literature,* vol. 1, pp. 268–289.
11. *Vin* 2.139.
12. *AA* 1.92–93.
13. *A* 2.102ff. This is also evident from the priority given to the rehearsal of the *Vinaya Piṭaka* at the First Council.
14. See Walpola Rahula, *History of Buddhism in Ceylon* (Colombo: M. D. Gunasena, 1966), pp. 158–159.
15. *M* 1.294.
16. *D* 1.3.
17. *D* 2.123–126; *A* 2.167–170.
18. *M* 1.167.
19. *D* 3.229; *A* 1.197.
20. *M* 1.190–191.
21. *A* 147; *S* 4.216, etc.
22. *S* 1.140.
23. *DA* 1.99.
24. *M* 2.55.
25. Ibid. 1.375.
26. *Chung A-han Ching* 31.1 (*TD* 1.623b).

Chapter VI

1. *M* 1.485ff.
2. Ibid.
3. Ibid. 1.140.
4. Ibid. 1.136.

5. *S* 2.3ff.
6. Ibid. 3.19.
7. *M* 1.389.
8. Karl R. Popper and John C. Eccles, *The Self and Its Brain* (New York: Springer International, 1985, corrected second printing), pp. 38ff.
9. *D* 2.199.
10. James, *Some Problems of Philosophy,* p. 32.
11. *M* 1.292.
12. Ibid. 3.239.
13. Ibid. 1.421–423; see also Y. Karunadasa, *Buddhist Analysis of Matter* (Colombo: Department of Cultural Affairs, 1967), pp. 16ff.
14. See Karunadasa, *Buddhist Analysis of Matter,* p. 93.
15. *S* 2.150.
16. *D* 2.62.
17. *M* 1.260.
18. Ibid. 1.261.
19. *D* 2.118.
20. Ibid. 3.134.
21. *M* 1.261ff.
22. *S* 3.87.
23. Ibid. 1.135.
24. James, *Some Problems of Philosophy,* p. 32.
25. *D* 3.105.
26. Ibid. 2.62–63.
27. *A* 2.79.
28. *D* 2.157.
29. *Kant: Foundations of the Metaphysics of Morals,* ed. Robert Paul Wolff (New York: Macmillan, 1985), p. 85.
30. Donald Davidson, "Mental Events," in *Readings in Philosophy of Psychology,* ed. Ned Block (Cambridge, Mass.: Harvard University Press, 1980), vol. 1, pp. 107–119.
31. *M* 1.85.
32. Ibid. 1.85–87.
33. Ibid. 1.341.
34. *S* 1.122.

Chapter VII

1. List of three, *Sn* 793, 798, 901, 914; list of four, ibid. 1122; *S* 4.73.
2. *M* 1.135.; *S* 3.203.
3. *D* 2.93; *M* 1.37; *S* 2.69; *A* 1.149.
4. See *Cpd,* p. 6.
5. *D* 1.202.
6. *Bṛhadāraṇyaka Upaniṣad* 3.7.3ff.; see Bhikkhu Ñāṇananda, *Concept and Reality in Early Buddhist Thought* (Kandy: Buddhist Publication Society, 1971), p. 50, note 1.
7. *M* 1.1ff.
8. *Sn* 1122.

9. *S* 4.73.
10. *D* 2.302; *S* 2.72.
11. See Karunadasa, *Buddhist Analysis of Matter,* p. 1.
12. *D* 1.70.
13. Ibid. 1.245; *M* 1.85.
14. *M* 1.266–267.

Chapter VIII

1. *D* 1.83–84; see *M* 1.175, where *āsavakkhaya-ñāṇa* = *paññā.*
2. *S* 5.421.
3. Ibid.
4. James, *Will to Believe,* p. 153.
5. *D* 1.12ff.
6. *M* 1.265.
7. *S* 2.274.
8. *Dhp* 278.
9. *S* 3.96.
10. *A* 1.189; *S* 5.421.
11. *Dhp* 277.
12. Ibid. 288.
13. *D* 2.199.
14. *S* 2.17; 5.423.

Chapter IX

1. *M* 1.193.
2. Ibid. 1.167; *S* 1.136.
3. *Sn* 796.
4. Ibid. 841.
5. Ibid. 886.
6. *Dhp* 5.
7. *Sn* 840.
8. *S* 2.58.
9. Ibid. 3.143; *Sn* 1086.
10. *A* 2.24.; *It* 122.
11. *Thag* 419.
12. *D* 1.95; *M* 1.231.
13. *M* 1.117, 347, 377, etc.
14. *S* 4.175; *Sn* 454.
15. *Thig* 350.
16. *S* 1.174.
17. *Ud* 80–81.
18. *A* 2.37–39.
19. *D* 3.260.
20. *Sn* 268.
21. *Thag* 1002–1003.
22. *S* 4.62.

23. *J* 3.51–56.
24. *Sdmp*, p. 164.
25. *A* 2.52.
26. *S* 4.235.
27. Ibid.
28. See Lily de Silva, "Sense Experience of the Liberated Being," in *Buddhist Philosophy and Culture*, ed. David J. Kalupahana and W. G. Weeraratne (Colombo: N. A. Jayawickrema Felicitation Volume Committee, 1987), pp. 13–21.
29. *It* 38.
30. *M* 1.12–13.
31. *Vin* 5.86, *nibbanañ c' eva paññatti anattā iti nicchayā.*
32. *Ud* 80.
33. *D* 3.246.
34. *Ud* 66–69.
35. *M* 1.426.
36. *S* 3.109–115.
37. *M* 1.483–489.
38. Ibid. 1.426–432.
39. *It* 38.
40. Ibid.
41. *M* 1.396–400.

Chapter X

1. Nagel, *The View From Nowhere*, pp. 193ff.
2. *M* 1.135.
3. James, *The Will to Believe*, p. 153.
4. *M* 2.27.
5. Ibid., 1.145ff.
6. C. A. F. Rhys Davids, *Buddhism: Its History and Literature*, American Lectures on the History of Religions, 1894–1895 (New York and London: P. G. Putnam's Sons, 1896), p. 139.
7. *Sn* 824.
8. *S* 2.22.
9. *M* 2.27.
10. Ibid. 2.73.
11. Ibid. 1.270.
12. *D* 2.93; *S* 1.9; *A* 3.258, etc.
13. *A* 3.254.
14. *S* 1.189.
15. *M* 1.373.
16. Ibid. 1.415.
17. Ibid. 1.55–56.
18. *Vin* 3.171–173.
19. *A* 2.69–70.
20. *D* 3.225–226.
21. *M* 1.56.

22. *D* 3.275.
23. Ibid. 1.13; *M* 2.233; *S* 3.45.
24. *M* 1.395.
25. *Vin* 1.56, 238.

Chapter XI

1. The most recent of such studies is *Great Tradition and Little Tradition in Theravāda Buddhist Studies,* ed. Terrence P. Day (Queenston, Ontario: Edwin Mellon Press, 1987). See also *Village India: Studies in the Little Community,* ed. Marriot McKim (Chicago: University of Chicago Press, 1955).
2. *D* 3.5, 227.
3. Ibid. 2.100.
4. Ibid. 1.193.
5. *Confucius. The Analects,* 8.7 (tr. D. C. Lau [Middlesex: Penguin Books, 1979], p. 93).
6. *D* 2.100.
7. *Dhp* 276.
8. *S* 2.228.
9. *D* 3.5, 227.
10. *A* 2.25.
11. *S* 4.15.
12. *A* 1.188ff.
13. *M* 2.170.
14. Ibid. 1.228.
15. *Ud* 80.
16. *M* 1.136.
17. *D* 3.5, 227.
18. *M* 1.55–56.
19. Ibid. 1.148.
20. *S* 2.17.
21. *M* 1.55–63.
22. *Thag* 303.
23. *Dhp* 160.

Chapter XII

1. *Vin* 1.8.
2. William James, *Pragmatism,* ed. F. Burkhardt (Cambridge, Mass.: Harvard University Press, 1975), p. 95.
3. *M* 1.482.
4. Ibid. 3.8.
5. *A* 3.38–39.
6. *D* 1.18, 84; *A* 1.63; 2.82, 159, 203, etc.
7. *M* 1.256ff.
8. *S* 3.1ff.
9. *M* 2.170.
10. *KvuA* 7.

11. *Kvu* I.1.
12. See *Sarvadarśanasaṃgraha,* ed. V. S. Abhyankar (Poona: Bhardarkar Oriental Research Institute, 1951), p. 36.
13. *Akb* 461.
14. *Kvu* I.6.
15. See *Adv,* pp. 259ff.
16. *Akb,* p. 329.
17. Ibid., p. 330.
18. Ibid., p. 331.
19. *AK* 2.50; see *Akb,* p. 82.
20. Quine, *Quiddities,* pp. 145–146.
21. Winternitz, *A History of Indian Literature,* vol. 2, p. 248.
22. *KvuA* 167, *mahāsuññatavādasaṅkhātānañ ca vetullakānaṃ,* which Jayawickrema, in his new edition (*KvuA,* London: PTS, 1979 p. 168), corrects to *mahāpuññavādisaṅkhātānaṃ.*

Chapter XIII

1. *KvuA* 10.
2. For example, the Siamese version reads *paramaṭṭha;* see *Kathāvastuprakaraṇa,* Buddha Jayanti Tripitaka Series, vol. xliv (Colombo: Government of Ceylon, 1967), vol. 1, p. 2, n.
3. *Kvu* 1.
4. See Jayatilleke, *Early Buddhist Theory of Knowledge,* pp. 412–415.
5. *KvuA* xx–xxi.
6. *Kvu* 1–2.
7. Ibid. 65.
8. Ibid.
9. Ibid. 68.
10. Ibid. 69.
11. Ibid. 115.
12. Ibid. 140.
13. Ibid. 140–141 (cf. *S* 3.70–73).
14. Ibid. 142 (cf. *S* 4.52–53).
15. Ibid.
16. Ibid. 142–143 (cf. *S* 2.100).
17. Ibid. 143.
18. Ibid. 559.
19. Ibid.
20. Ibid. 559–560.
21. Ibid. 560.
22. Ibid.
23. Ibid. 549–557.
24. Ibid. 556.

Chapter XIV

1. Indeed, they have identified the doctrines of the Abhidhamma with those of the commentaries. Thus, in a modern critical treatment of the Buddhist doc-

trine such as E. R. Saratchandra's *Buddhist Psychology of Perception* (Colombo: Ceylon University Press, 1958), one finds a chapter on "Perception in the Abhidhamma" that is entirely based on the commentaries of Buddhaghosa, without a single reference to any of the canonical Abhidhamma texts.

2. For example, almost every commentarial tradition, and almost every modern treatise on the Abhidhamma, makes profuse uses of the dichotomies of conventional *(sammuti)* and ultimate *(paramattha, paramartha)* or substance *(svabhāva)* and qualities *(lakkhaṇa, lakṣaṇa)* in characterizing its contents. Thus Nyanatiloka Mahāthera, following the commentarial tradition, explains the difference between Sutta and Abhidhamma as follows (*Guide Through the Abhidhamma-Piṭaka* [Kandy: Buddhist Publication Society, 1971], p. 2):

> Regarding the difference between Sutta and Abhidhamma, the "Higher Doctrine," it does not really so much concern the subject, but rather its arrangement and treatment. The subject matter in both is practically the same. Its main difference in treatment, briefly stated, may be said to consist in the fact that in the Suttas the doctrines are more or less explained in the words of the philosophically incorrect "conventional" every-day language *(vohāra-vacana)* understood by anyone, whilst the Abhidhamma, on the other hand, makes use of purely philosophical terms true in the absolute sense *(paramattha-vacana)*.

3. Ibid., p. 12.
4. *A Buddhist Manual of Psychological Ethics,* tr. of *Dhammasaṅganī,* with Introductory Essay and Notes, by C. A. F. Rhys Davids (London: PTS, 1974).
5. See Nyanatiloka, *Guide,* pp. 25–26.
6. Ibid., p. 88.
7. Ibid.
8. Ibid., p. 91.
9. Kalupahana, *Causality,* pp. 163–166.
10. Ibid., pp. 166–176.
11. Nyanatiloka, *Guide,* p. 57.
12. *Pug* 1.
13. Nyanatiloka, *Guide,* pp. 57–58.
14. *Pug* 2–3.
15. Ibid. 38.

Chapter XV

1. Nakamura, *Indian Buddhism,* p. 159.
2. *Dhp* 204.
3. *Vajra,* pp. 34–35.
4. *S* 5.422.
5. *M* 3.230ff.; see Kalupahana, *Buddhist Psychology,* pp. 156–157.
6. Ibid., p. 33.
7. Unfortunately, as in the interpretation of the contents of the Abhidhamma,

where modern scholars depended heavily on a commentarial tradition from a period far removed from the canonical texts themselves, the contents of the *Vajracchedikā* have also been analyzed in relation to ideas that emerged much later in the Buddhist tradition. Thus we find Edward Conze, who did yeoman's service for the study of the Prajñāpāramitā literature by editing and translating it, setting the tone for the interpretation of the text as follows (*Vajracchedikā-prajñāpāramitā,* ed. and tr. Edward Conze, Serie Orientale Roma, no. 13 [Rome: Instituto italiano per il medio ed Estremo Oriente, 1957], pp. 12–13):

> The phrase [*tenocyate*] is a common ingredient of Buddhist definitions and argumentations, in the texts of all schools, and it indicates a logical relation which is plausible and can be assented to. In this Sūtra, however, it is used to indicate a paradoxical, inconclusive and illogical relation between what precedes and what follows. *It frequently brings out the opposition which exists between esoteric truth and mere speaking, between the true state of affairs as it is, and the words in which it is expressed* [emphasis added].

If this is true of the *Vajracchedikā,* then those who take it to be the correct philosophical standpoint of the so-called Mahāyāna cannot legitimately claim superiority over the Sarvāstivāda, Sautrāntika, or even the post-Buddhaghosan Theravāda. It is as metaphysical a point of view as any other, including that of traditional Brahmanism. For this reason, the methodology of the *Vajracchedikā* needs to be freshly evaluated, and this is best accomplished by keeping in mind the Buddha's own assessment of language, truth, and logic as well as the threefold methodology of enumeration, classification, and synthesis adopted in the Abhidharma to preserve the temper of the Buddha-word.

Conze's interpretation of the formula does not seem to be consistent with the teachings either of the Buddha or of the Abhidharma as explained in the present text. He has the following to say about the formula (pp. 11–12):

> *Logically,* the Sūtra teaches, that each one of the chief Buddhist concepts is equivalent to its contradictory opposite. A special formula is here employed to express this thought, i.e., "A mass of merit, a mass of merit," as no-mass that has been taught by the Tathāgata. In that sense He has spoken of it as a "mass of merit."

To say that every Buddhist concept is equivalent to its contradictory would mean that every Buddhist concept can be formulated as $p = \sim p$. This would immediately render the Buddhist concept meaningless, leaving room for the recognition of an ineffable and mystical truth or reality. Hence the final statement, "In this sense He has spoken of it as a 'mass of merit,' " would simply mean that "merit" *(puṇya)* is a mere name, an empty term.

8. I am indebted to my student, Dr. John F. Gregory, who brought this to my attention.
9. See *Vajra,* pp. 11–12, where Conze (see note 7 above) lists the variety of concepts to which the formula is applied.

10. *M* 1.1ff.; see Kalupahana, *Buddhist Psychology,* pp. 57–58.
11. *Vajra,* p. 32.
12. *S* 3.142.
13. *Vajra,* p. 62.
14. Ibid., pp. 56–57; cf. *Thag* 469.
15. *S* 3.120.
16. *D* 3.219; *S* 4.296.
17. *S* 1.122.

Chapter XVI

1. K. R. Subramanian, *Buddhist Remains in Andhra* (Madras: Diocesan Press, 1932), pp. 53–63.
2. Nakamura, *Indian Buddhism,* p. 235.
3. K. V. Ramanan, *Nāgārjuna's Philosophy* (Varanasi: Bharatiya Vidya Prakashan, 1971), p. 25.
4. Ibid., p. 26.
5. Ibid.
6. Nakamura, *Indian Buddhism,* p. 187.
7. *Kārikā* XVIII.12.
8. Ibid. XV.7.
9. Critics of my work on Nāgārjuna have continued to insist that dependence on the *Kārikā* alone in order to understand Nāgārjuna's philosophy is a methodological error. They propose that Nāgārjuna's philosophy must be examined in light of all the works attributed to him, rightly or wrongly, whether they represent his early writings or his later ones. This is understandable, especially in a context where scholars sometimes continue to devote their valuable time to examining theories which the author of that theory has himself rejected. For example, it is not unusual to find someone specializing in early Wittgenstein when Wittgenstein himself rejected his earlier theories as mistaken. The *Kārikā* is the last major work of Nāgārjuna and also contains the most complete treatment of the major doctrines of Buddhism. As such, it supercedes any other work he may have compiled during his early years. To expound Nāgārjuna's philosophy on the basis of such a comprehensive work should not be considered a methodological error. Indeed, my critics have not come up with any superior methodology that can stand the test of critical inquiry.
10. *Kārikā* I.3.
11. Ibid.
12. Ibid. II.24–25.
13. Nagel, *The View From Nowhere,* pp. 11, 78.
14. *Kārikā* V.8.
15. Ibid. XV.3.
16. Ibid. XV.7.
17. *Akb,* pp. 461ff.
18. *S* 3.138.
19. Ibid. 2.17.
20. *Kārikā* XXV.24.
21. Ibid. XXIV.18.

Chapter XVII

1. Nakamura, *Indian Buddhism,* pp. 186–187.
2. *Scripture of the Lotus Blossom of the Fine Dharma (The Lotus Sūtra),* tr. from the Chinese of Kumārajīva by Leon Hurvitz (New York: Columbia University Press, 1976), p. xvi.
3. Ibid., p. xxiii.
4. Ibid., p. 110; also *Sdmp,* p. 91.
5. Ibid., p. 111.
6. Ibid., pp. 113–114; *Sdmp,* p. 93.
7. Ibid., p. 30f.
8. *Sdmp,* p. 93.
9. Ibid., p. 89, v. 34.
10. Ibid., p. 30, v. 5.
11. Ibid., vv. 44–45.
12. Ibid., v. 46.
13. The identification of some of the controversies regarding transcendence, etc. is made in Buddhaghosa's commentary; see *KvuA,* pp. 168, 174f., 213.
14. Nakamura, *Indian Buddhism,* p. 112.
15. *Adv,* p. 101.
16. *Sdmp,* p. 92.
17. *Scripture of the Lotus,* tr. Hurvitz, p. 114.
18. *Sdmp,* p. 22.
19. Ibid., p. 164.
20. See *The Saddharmapuṇḍarīka or the Lotus of the True Law,* tr. H. Kern, Sacred Books of the East, vol. 21 (Oxford: The Clarendon Press, 1884), p. xxvii.

Chapter XVIII

1. *Laṅkā,* p. 17; *The Laṅkāvatāra Sūtra,* tr. D. T. Suzuki (London: Routledge & Kegan Paul, 1966), pp. 16–17.
2. Ibid., pp. 24–34; tr. Suzuki, pp. 23–31.
3. Ibid., pp. 34–37.
4. Ibid., p. 104; tr. Suzuki, p. 91.
5. Ibid., pp. 104–105; tr. Suzuki, p. 91.
6. Ibid., pp. 105–106; v. 166–167; tr. Suzuki, p. 92.
7. Ibid., p. 156.
8. Ibid.
9. Ibid., p. 51; tr. Suzuki, p. 46.
10. Ibid., p. 74.
11. Ibid., p. 98.
12. Ibid.; tr. Suzuki, p. 86.
13. Ibid., p. 78.
14. Ibid., pp. 79–80.
15. Compare the Cartesian *cogito.*
16. *Laṅkā,* p. 26.
17. Ibid., p. 235.
18. Ibid.

19. *M* 1.167.
20. *Laṅkā*, p. 235.
21. Ibid., pp. 2, 127.
22. See Kalupahana, *A Path of Righteousness*, pp. 18–19.
23. *Laṅkā*, p. 126.
24. Ibid.
25. Ibid., p. 235.
26. Ibid.
27. Ibid., p. 77.
28. Ibid., p. 78.
29. Ibid., pp. 8–9; v. 40–42; tr. Suzuki, pp. 8–9.

Chapter XIX

1. See Stefan Anacker, *Seven Works of Vasubandhu. The Buddhist Psychological Doctor* (Delhi: Motilal Banarsidass, 1984), pp. 7–24.
2. Ibid., p. 3.
3. Ibid., p. 2.
4. *S* 2.94–97, which is often quoted as an instance where the three terms are used synonymously. However, the statement need not necessarily imply the synonymity of the three terms. Instead, it can be a listing of three different items, as: "Whatever is called 'citta' and is called 'mano' and is called 'viññāṇa'; therein an ordinary uneducated person is incapable of being disenchanted, of being detached, of being freed." While these refer to different parts of the psychophysical personality, the uses of these three terms in other contexts certainly indicate that they are not synonyms.
5. See Kalupahana, *Buddhist Psychology*, pp. 193, 195, 209.
6. *Laṅkā*, pp. 59, 63, 67, etc.
7. *Vims* 2.
8. Ibid. 18.
9. Ibid. 19.
10. Ibid. 1.
11. *Vijñaptimātratāsiddhi*, p. 1.
12. *Triṃś* 2.
13. *Viṃś* 6–7; *Triṃś* 18–19.
14. *Triṃś* 3.
15. Ibid.
16. Ibid. 2.
17. *Dhp* 1–2.
18. *Triṃś* 5.
19. W. V. Quine, *Word and Object* (Cambridge, Mass.: M.I.T. Press, 1960), pp. 5ff.
20. *Triṃś* 7.
21. Ibid. 21.

Chapter XX

1. Masaaki Hattori, *Dignāga, On Perception* (Cambridge, Mass.: Harvard University Press, 1968), p. 4.

2. In my article on "Dignāga's theory of immaterialism" (*Philosophy East and West,* 20 [1970]: 121–128), I attempted to indicate that his *Ālambana-parīkṣā* was devoted to a criticism of the belief in a material object existing totally independent of human experience, not at eliminating the world of objective experience altogether. Keeping that analysis in mind, I shall try to explain the most important ideas expressed by Dignāga on the problem of perception, as expressed in the first section of Chapter 1 of his *Pramāṇasa-muccaya,* available in Hattori's *Dignāga* (pp. 239–244). In doing so I shall try to steer clear of two ways Dignāga has been often perceived, namely, those of Sautrāntika essentialism and Yogācāra idealism. Just as it is senseless to utilize Sautrāntika doctrines like momentariness to explain Vasubandhu's most mature work, the *Vijñaptimātratāsiddhi,* because he had already renounced these ideas, so it is meaningless to employ the essentialist concepts of the Sautrāntikas to interpret Dignāga, even though during the early part of his career he prepared a summary of his teacher's earlier work, the *Abhidharma-kośa,* which is known as *Abhidharmakośa-marmadīpa.* In fact, it would not be surprising if Dignāga's *Pramāṇasamuccaya* is no more than an epistemological film laid over the psychological painting in Vasubandhu's *Vijñaptimātratāsiddhi.* Similarly, I shall avoid using Dignāga's earlier treatise, the *Yogāvatāra,* in analyzing his epistemological theories, thereby not committing myself to the assumption that he was an idealist.
3. Hattori, *Dignāga,* p. 239.
4. Ibid., p. 76.
5. *Kārikā* v.8; Hattori, *Dignāga,* p. 76.
6. Hattori, *Dignāga,* p. 24.
7. *PS* I.3.
8. Hattori, *Dignāga,* p. 25.
9. Ibid.; note addition by Hattori in parentheses.
10. See Kalupahana, *Nāgārjuna,* p. 248.
11. *S* 3.70–73.
12. *PS* I.4.
13. *M* 1.190.
14. Hattori, *Dignāga,* p. 26.
15. Ibid.
16. Ibid.
17. Hilary Putnam, *The Many Faces of Realism* (LaSalle, Ill.: Open Court, 1987), p. 8.
18. *M* 1.295.
19. Hattori, *Dignāga,* p. 27.
20. *PS* I.7.
21. *PS* I.7–8.
22. *Vims* 18.
23. Hattori, *Dignāga,* p. 28.
24. Ibid., p. 80.
25. *PS* I.9; Hattori, *Dignāga,* p. 29.
26. Here my explanation differs from Hattori's.
27. *PS* I.11; Hattori, *Dignāga,* pp. 29, 108.
28. Hattori, *Dignāga,* p. 28.

29. *Nyāyabindu-prakaraṇa,* with Dharmottara's *Nyāyabindu-ṭīkā,* ed. F. E. Stcherbatsky (Osnabruck: Biblio Verlag, 1970), p. 6.
30. A detailed analysis of Dignāga's philosophy of language and logic in more recent times is by Radhika Herzberger (*Bhartṛhari and the Buddhists* [Dordrecht: D. Reidel, 1986]). Her description of Dignāga's theory of experience and language is not very different from that outlined above. The one significant difference is that she arrives at her conclusions on the basis of an examination of the philosophies of Kātyāyana and Bhartṛhari. She perceives Dignāga's contribution as emerging from an attempt to embody in his theory the seemingly irreconcilable ideals presented in Kātyāyana's aphorisms and Bhartṛhari's speculations (p. 112). Such an evaluation of Dignāga's contribution becomes necessary because she perceives him to be violating his Buddhist commitments. These commitments are listed as follows (p. 113):

    1. *Nirvāṇa* is beyond name and form *(nāma-rūpa).*
    2. Words always fall short of reality, on the one hand, and distort reality, on the other.
    3. Language, for Dignāga, as it is for all good Buddhists, is the product of a "beginningless *vāsanā*" (the phrase is Dharmakīrti's).

    The preceding nineteen chapters of the present work should provide interesting evidence as to whether the above commitments can be attributed to "all good Buddhists." In light of the evidence provided, we cannot assume that the *mainline* Buddhist tradition, beginning with the Buddha himself, made any of the commitments that Herzberger attributes to it. Indeed, she herself suspects the so-called refinements introduced by Dignāga's commentator, Dharmakīrti (pp. xxii, 212ff.).

    The fact that Dignāga lived almost immediately after Kātyāyana and Bhratṛhari does not necessarily mean that he was compelled to reconcile their irreconcilable ideals. Even a cursory glance at the history of Buddhist philosophy will justify Dignāga's main thesis that, as stated by Herzberger herself, "The phenomenal world directly contributes to the meaning of some names" (p. 113). If she had seen the Buddhist tradition prior to Dignāga without attributing to it the commitments mentioned earlier, she would not have been forced to see Dignāga's *Upādāyaprajñapti-prakaraṇa* as anti-Buddhist. A more positive description is in fact appropriate, for this work represents the continuation of the Buddha's analysis of *paññatti,* the Ābhidhammika definition of *upādāya-paññatti,* Nāgārjuna's own analysis of *upādāya prajñapti* in the *Kārikā,* and Vasubandhu's definition of *vijñapti* associated with the *paratantra-svabhāva.* In all these instances, a genuine concept is understood as one that is dependent without being absolutely unique. This eliminates the essentialist standpoint that emerges from Hattori's translation of Dignāga, which Herzberger rightly rejects (p. 115).

    Despite an extremely detailed and critical analysis of Dignāga's ideas, Herzberger is left with the problem of negotiating a "gap between the conceptual object and the perceptual one" (p. 138, n. 3; Herzberger herself raises the question as to how we can achieve this). The reason is that even after such a careful analysis, she is reluctant to renounce the idea that

Dignāga was an idealist. After quoting a passage from one of his earliest texts, the *Yogāvatāra,* she says (pp. 165–166):

> The above is from one of the very early works of Dignāga. Here Dignāga viewed reality as an unstructured realm of pure experience. It is a vision that Dignāga was to carry over into his last work, the PS [*Pramāṇasamuccaya*]. That purely perceptual realm in which no element is conceptual, is the only reality posited by the PS. There perception is defined as that which is without construction *(kalpanā'poḍham)*. . . . The realm of pure perception includes presentation of the senses and also the mystical experience of enlightenment.

This, of course, takes her back to Hattori's interpretation (p. 189, n. 4). In fact, putting together the *Yogāvatāra* and the *Pramāṇasamuccaya* would be like combining Wittgenstein's *Tractatus* and his *Philosophical Investigations.*

31. Hattori, *Dignāga,* p. 29.
32. Herzberger, *Bhartṛhari,* p. 106.
33. *PS* I.5.
34. Herzberger, *Bhartṛhari,* p. 111.
35. Copi, *Symbolic Logic,* p. 5.
36. xv.1–2; see also Kalupahana, *Nāgārjuna,* pp. 228–229.
37. Herzberger, *Bhartṛhari,* p. 138.
38. Ibid., p. 165.
39. Ibid., pp. 187–189.
40. *S* 1.11.
41. *M* 2.170–171.

Chapter XXI

1. *Hasting's Encyclopaedia of Religion and Ethics,* vol. 2, p. 887, quoted in E. W. Adikaram, *Early History of Buddhism in Ceylon* (Colombo: M. D. Gunasena, 1953), p. 4.
2. Bhikkhu Ñyāṇamoli, *Buddhaghosa: The Path of Purification* (tr. of *Visuddhimagga*), (Colombo: Semage, 1964), p. xix.
3. Ibid., p. xvi, esp. n. 8.
4. Adikaram, *Buddhism in Ceylon,* p. 93.
5. Ibid.
6. *DhsA* 421.
7. *Vism* 144, 290, 291, etc.
8. Ibid. 140–141, 475, 509, 560, 600, 613, 631–632, 691ff.
9. *Vimuttimagga,* ed. G. Siri Ratnajoti and K. Siri Ratnapala (Colombo: Government Press of Ceylon, 1963).
10. See Ñyāṇamoli, *Buddhaghosa,* p. 104.
11. *S* 1.13.
12. *Vism* 2.
13. Ibid. 8–9.
14. See *Nettippakaraṇa,* ed. E. Hardy (London: PTS, 1961); also George Bond,

"The Netti-pakaraṇa: A Theravāda Method of Interpretation," in *Buddhist Studies in Honour of Walpola Rahula,* ed. Somaratne Balasuriya, et. al. (London: Gordon Fraser, 1980), pp. 16–28.
15. See *Abhidhammatthavikāsinī,* ed. A. P. Buddhadatta (Colombo: Anula Press, 1961), p. 11.
16. *Visuddhimagga-ṭīkā (Paramatthamañjusā),* ed. M. Dhammananda (Colombo: Mahabodhi Press, 1928), p. 211.
17. *Vism* 526.
18. Ibid. 328.
19. Ibid. 21.
20. Ibid. 85.
21. Ñyāṇamoli, *Buddhaghosa,* p. xxxi.
22. *Vism* 437.
23. Ibid. 437–438.
24. Ibid. 438.
25. Ñyāṇamoli (*Buddhaghosa,* p. 481, n. 3) takes the latter to mean "existing essence" (*samāna* = present participle from *as,* "to exist"). However, in the present context it is more appropriate to understand it in the sense of "like," "similar" *(samāna),* as opposed to "unlike," "dissimilar" *(asamāna). Samāna* would then be a synonym for *sādhāraṇa* or "common."
26. *A* 5.3, 313; see also *Kārikā* xxii.16.
27. Note the interesting comments by C. S. Peirce, *Collected Works of Charles Sanders Peirce,* ed. Charles Hartshorne and Paul Weiss (Cambridge, Mass.: Belknap Press of Harvard University Press, 1960), 1.76.
28. *Vism* 642.
29. Ibid. 639.
30. Ibid. 658.
31. *S* 5.437.
32. *Vism* 690.

Chapter XXII

1. Alex Wayman, *Yoga of the Guḥyasamājatantra: The Arcane Lore of Forty Verses* (Delhi: Motilal Banarsidass, 1975).
2. Herbert V. Guenther, *The Tantric View of Life* (Boulder and London: Shambhala, 1976).
3. David Snellgrove, *Indo-Tibetan Buddhism* (Boston: Shambhala, 1987), vol. 1, p. 143.
4. *Thag* 419.
5. *M* 1.231; *D* 1.95.
6. Snellgrove, *Indo-Tibetan Buddhism,* vol. 1, p. 136.
7. Ibid., p. 133.
8. Ibid., pp. 133–134. I leave the translation of some of the Buddhist terms into English as they are, even though these can be replaced by less metaphysical terms more appropriate in the Buddhist context.
9. Ibid., pp. 134–135.
10. See Guenther, *Tantric View,* p. 105.
11. *Kārikā* xxv.19.

12. *S* 2.62.
13. Snellgrove, *Indo-Tibetan Buddhism,* vol. 1, pp. 135, 146, etc.
14. *M* 1.136.
15. Snellgrove, *Indo-Tibetan Buddhism,* vol. 1, p. 134.
16. A detailed study of the symbolism of this ritual is found in Lily de Silva's "The Paritta Ceremony of Sri Lanka: Its Antiquity and Symbolism," in *Buddhist Thought and Ritual,* ed. David J. Kalupahana (New York: Paragon House, 1991), pp. 139–150.
17. *A* 2.72.
18. *M* 2.72.
19. *Miln* 150.
20. *Sn* 222–238.
21. Ibid. 143–152.
22. Ibid. 258–269 (ed. and tr. R. Chalmers, *Buddha's Teachings,* Harvard Oriental Series, vol. 37 [Cambridge, Mass.: Harvard University Press, 1932], pp. 46–47).
23. *D* 3.1094–206.
24. Ibid. 3.201.

Chapter XXIII

1. Chang Chung-yuan, *Original Teachings of Ch'an Buddhism* (New York: Random House, 1969).
2. *Zen Buddhism: Selected Writings of D. T. Suzuki,* ed. William Barrett (New York: Doubleday, 1956); *The Essentials of Zen Buddhism,* selected from the writings of Daisetz T. Suzuki, ed. with introduction by Bernard Phillips (New York: E. P. Dutton, 1962).
3. Suzuki, *The Essentials of Zen Buddhism,* p. 8.
4. Ibid., p. 9.
5. Suzuki, *Zen Buddhism,* p. 34.
6. Idem, *The Essentials of Zen Buddhism,* p. 106.
7. *The Platform Sūtra of the Sixth Patriarch,* tr. from the Chinese Philip B. Yampolsky (New York and London: Columbia University Press, 1967), p. 130.
8. Isshu Miura and Ruth Fuller Sasaki, *The Kōan* (New York: Harcourt, Brace and World, 1965), p. 4.
9. Ibid., p. xi.
10. Suzuki, *Zen Buddhism,* p. 122.
11. Ibid., pp. 122–123.
12. *The Platform Sūtra,* tr. Yampolsky, p. 133.
13. Suzuki, *The Essentials of Zen Buddhism,* p. 129.
14. *The Platform Sūtra,* tr. Yampolsky, p. 130.
15. Ibid., p. 131.
16. Ibid., p. 132.
17. Ibid., p. 133.
18. Ibid.
19. Ibid., p. 180.
20. *Kārikā,* xxv.19; see my translation, in Kalupahana, *Nāgārjuna,* p. 366.

21. Suzuki, *Zen Buddhism,* p. 125.
22. Rahula, *History of Buddhism in Ceylon,* pp. 199ff.
23. *DA* 1.190.
24. Rahula, *History of Buddhism in Ceylon,* p. 208.
25. *Vism* 38.
26. Ibid. 38–39.
27. Rahula, *History of Buddhism in Ceylon,* pp. 159ff.

Appendix

1. D. T. Suzuki, *Studies in the Laṅkāvatāra* (London: Routledge, 1930), p. 3.
2. Nakamura, *Indian Buddhism,* pp. 231, 264, n. 1.
3. *Laṅkā,* p. 23, v. 9. The number 108 puzzled Suzuki. See tr. Suzuki, p. 31, n. 2, continued on p. 32. One explanation is that the title of the chapter "Collection of All Thirty-six Thousand Dharmas" *(Ṣaṭtriṃśat-sāhasra-sarva-dharma-samuccaya),* which Suzuki mistranslates following the Chinese versions (p. 117), possibly refers to 36 *dharmas,* namely, 5 aggregates *(skandha),* 12 faculties *(āyatana, indriya),* and 18 elements *(dhātu),* to which the Yogācārins were compelled to add *ālaya-vijñāna,* not previously included among the 18 elements. When these 36 items are analyzed in relation to the 3 degrees of truth accepted by Yogācāra, one can have 108 propositions; hence the number of questions. Yet some of the questions raised here have no relevance to the above *dharmas,* nor can one be sure of the number of questions—some are single, others contain several queries within one question.
4. *Laṅkā,* p. 5, v. 10.
5. Ibid., pp. 8–9, v. 38–44; tr. Suzuki, pp. 8–9.
6. *Laṅkā,* tr. Suzuki, pp. 216–217.
7. See *The Mahāvaṃsa,* tr. Wilhelm Geiger (Colombo: Government of Ceylon, Information Department, 1960), pp. 51ff.
8. *Laṅkā,* tr. Suzuki, pp. 217–218.
9. *2500 Years of Buddhism,* ed. P. V. Bapat (New Delhi: Ministry of Education and Broadcasting, Government of India, 1959), p. 295.
10. See Rahula, *History of Buddhism in Ceylon,* pp. 87ff.
11. David J. Kalupahana, "Schools of Buddhism in Early Ceylon," *Ceylon Journal of the Humanities,* Peradeniya: I (1970):159–190.
12. Rahula, *History of Buddhism in Ceylon,* p. 93.
13. Ibid., p. 94.
14. *Laṅkā,* tr. Suzuki, p. xi.

SELECT BIBLIOGRAPHY

Part One: Early Buddhism

Primary Sources

NON-BUDDHIST SOURCES

ṚgVeda, tr. Walter H. Maurer, *Pinnacles of India's Past: Selections from the ṚgVeda,* University of Pennsylvania Studies in South Asia, vol. 2 (Amsterdam and Philadelphia: John Benjamins, 1986). A clear and precise translation of a good selection of Vedic hymns.

Sūtrakṛtāṅga, tr. H. Jacobi, *The Jaina Sutras,* Sacred Books of the East, vol. 45 (Oxford: The Clarendon Press, 1895). This represents the more philosophical work of the Jaina canon.

Upaniṣads, tr. R. E. Hume, *The Thirteen Principal Upaniṣads* (London: Oxford University Press, 1934). An excellent, widely used translation of the earlier Upaniṣads.

BUDDHIST SOURCES

Discourses from the First Four Collections

Aggañña-suttanta (*D* 3.80ff.); *Discourse on the Beginning of Things* (*SBB* 4.77ff.); *TD* 1.36ff. The Buddha adopts a theory of evolution based on the principle of dependence *(paṭiccasamuppāda)* to refute the Brahmanical caste system. The continued process of evolution and dissolution is recognized in the explanation of the physical world; social, economic, and political institutions; and the means of communication, especially language.

Aggivacchagotta-sutta (M 1.483ff.); *Discourse to Vacchagotta on Fire* (*MLS* 2.162ff.); *TD* 2.245ff. A detailed analysis of the epistemological reasons for the Buddha's reluctance to provide answers to the so-called undeclared *(abyākata, avyākrta)* metaphysical questions.

Alagaddūpama-sutta (M 1130ff.); *Discourse on the Parable of the Water-snake* (*MLS* 1.167ff.); *TD* 1.763ff. An extremely complex discourse, yet one that sets out the fundamental Buddhist attitude toward theories or views *(diṭṭhi)* that pervaded the tradition from the *Aṭṭhakavagga* of the *Sutta-nipāta* to the writings of some of the Ch'an (Zen) masters in China and Japan. It is the attitude of "non-grasping" of views or the ideal of "letting go," well illustrated by the simile of the raft *(kulla, kola)*, an oft-quoted simile in later Buddhist literature.

The discourse begins with the Buddha rebuking a monk named Ariṭṭha for his insistence that what the Buddha considered to be tendencies inimical to human progress are actually not so. After stating that the wrong pursuit of the *dhamma* (i.e., the study of the doctrine as recorded in the discourses, etc.) is comparable to taking a snake by its tail, the Buddha proceeds to examine six types of views regarding the nature of self and the world, all of which are based on the belief in permanence. Human anxiety *(paritassanā)* is looked upon as the reason for grasping such views about the self and the world. The Buddha reiterates the significance of the realization of the three characteristics of existence.

Ambalaṭṭhikā-Rāhulovāda-sutta (*M* 1.414ff.) *Discourse on Exhortation to Rāhula at Ambalaṭṭhikā* (*MLS* 2.87ff.); *TD* 1.436ff. A discourse to Rāhula (the Buddha's son) on the value of reflection *(paccavekkhana)* in deciding what constitutes good or bad behavior.

Apaṇṇaka-sutta (*M* 1.400ff.). *Discourse on the Sure* (*MLS* 2.69ff.). This is Buddha's formulation of what has come to be popular in Western philosophy as "Pascal's Wager." The Buddha is here utilizing the belief in the survival of the human personality or the possibility of rebirth as a wager or a rational or prudent (lit., "unquestionable" = *apaṇṇaka*) means of encouraging the pursuit of a moral life. The discourse also represents a criticism of the Materialist philosophy that denied survival and, therefore, morality.

Araṇavibhaṅga-sutta (*M* 3.230ff.); *Discourse on the Analysis of the Undefiled* (*MLS* 3.277ff.); *TD* 1.701ff. A discourse devoted to the analysis of non-conflict or peace *(araṇa)*. Non-conflict is here traced to the adoption of the middle path in moral philosophy (first enunciated in the *Tathāgatena vutta* or the *Dhammacappavattana-sutta*), which is then related to how one communicates with others and finally to the attitude one adopts with regard to the means of communication, especially language. The ideal of non-conflict and its relationship to linguistic philosophy were emphasized subsequently in the *Vajracchedikā*.

Ariyapariyesana-sutta (*M* 1.160ff.); *Discourse on the Aryan Quest* (*MLS* 1.203ff.); *TD* 1.775ff. As a historical document this remains unsurpassed, for here we have, in the Buddha's own words, a description of his quest for a solution to the riddles of human existence. It took him to Āḷāra Kālāma and Uddaka Rāmaputta, two contemplatives who probably belonged to the Upaniṣadic tradition. Dissatisfied with the mental training he received under their tutorship, he left them and, striving on his own, realized the nature of existence and a solution to the problem of human suffering.

Brahmajāla-suttanta (*D* 1.1ff); *The Perfect Net* (*SBB* 2.1ff.); *TD* 1.88ff. The Buddha explains how his disciples should respond either to criticism or to praise of the Buddha, the doctrine, and the community. In the process of outlining his own intellectual and moral achievements, the Buddha refers to his understanding and criticism of sixty-two philosophical theories known to him regarding the nature of the self and the world. This discourse is a valuable source of information about pre-Buddhist Indian philosophy.

Cakkavattisīhanāda-suttanta (*D* 3.58ff.); *The Lion's Roar of a Universal Monarch* (*SBB* 4.53ff.); *TD* 1.39ff., also 1.520f. A comprehensive treatment of the Buddhist conception of a "universal monarch," including a statement of the basic features of the Buddha's views on political and economic affairs.

Caṅkī-sutta (*M* 2.164ff.); *Discourse with Caṅkī* (*MLS* 2.354ff.). In a discussion with a brahman named Caṅkī, the Buddha explains how to achieve the safeguarding of truth *(saccānurakkhaṇa)*, the realization of truth *(saccānubodha)*, and the attainment of truth *(saccānupatti)*.

Cūḷa-Malūṅkya-sutta (*M* 1.426ff.); *Lesser Discourse to Māluṅkya(putta)* (*MLS* 2.97ff.); *TD* 1.804ff. A statement of the pragmatic reasons for not answering metaphysical questions.

Dhammacakkappavattana-sutta (see *Tathāgatena-vutta*)

Gaṇaka-Moggallāna-sutta (*M* 3.1ff.); *Discourse to Gaṇaka-Moggallāna* (*MLS* 3.52ff.); *TD* 1.652f. A discourse emphasizing the gradualness of the path to enlightenment and freedom.

Kaccāyana-gotta-sutta (*S* 2.17f.); *Discourse to Kaccāyana* (*KS* 2.12ff.); *TD* 2.85. Quoted in full in Chapter IV, this is the Buddha's discourse on the philosophical middle path, which became a paradigm discourse for many of the leading philosophers and schools of later Buddhism.

Kālāma-sutta (*A* 1.188ff.); *Those of Kesaputta* (*GS* 1.170ff.); *TD* 1.438f. Questioned by the Kālāmas of Kesaputta as to how to act when a plurality of views have been expressed by different religious teachers and philosophers, the Buddha refers to the variety of epistemological standpoints adopted by them and argues that one should make up one's own mind about these matters based on important moral considerations, which are in turn based on one's own experience of what conduces to happiness and to suffering.

Kammavibhaṅga (*Cūḷa-* and *Mahā-*)-*suttas* (3.202ff.); *Discourses on (the Lesser- and Greater-) Analysis of Deeds* (*MLS* 3.248ff.); *TD* 1.703ff. The smaller version explains how a person becomes an inheritor of his own actions or karma, while the larger version attempts to avoid the deterministic interpretation of karma that could emerge from such a statement. This is done by placing karma in the larger context of dependent arising.

Khandha-saṃyutta (*S* 3.1–188); *Kindred Sayings on Elements* (*KS* 3.1–154); roughly corresponding to *TD* 2.1–22. Contains 158 short discourses devoted to an analysis of the five aggregates *(khandha)*, explaining the concept of a human person with emphasis on the three characteristics of existence: impermanence *(anicca)*, unsatisfactoriness *(dukkha)*, and non-substantiality *(anatta)*. This is done from a wide variety of perspectives.

Loṇaphala (*A* 1.249ff.); *A Grain of Salt* (*GS* 1.177ff.). An attempt to distinguish between a deterministic theory of karma and one based on conditionality.

Madhupiṇḍika-sutta (*M* 1.108ff.); *Discourse on the Honeyball* (*MLS* 1.141ff.); *TD* 1.603ff. A Śākyan named Daṇḍapāṇī questions the nature of the Buddha's teachings. The Buddha responds that he teaches a way to remain in the world without coming into conflict with it. This is achieved by not letting perceptions overwhelm a person through not being attached to sense pleasures, overcoming doubt by avoiding excessive demands on understanding (i.e., by renouncing Cartesian doubt), and abandoning craving for existence and non-existence. Daṇḍapāṇī leaves without being able to comprehend the

Buddha's statement. Questioned further by one of his disciples, the Buddha adds that when obsessed perceptions and conceptions assail a person, he should neither take delight in nor be engrossed by them. This also was too brief a statement, and the monks resorted to Venerable Mahākaccāyana for further clarification. Mahākaccāyana's detailed analysis of the process of sense experience (which received the Buddha's approval and designation as the "method of the honeyball," *madhupiṇḍika-pariyāya*) has served as a *locus classicus* for all future discussions of the psychology of perception, especially in the mainline Buddhist tradition.

Mahā-assapura-sutta (*M* 1.271ff.); *Greater Discourse at Assapura* (*MLS* 1.325ff.); *TD* 1.724ff. Explains in detail the moral life that renders meaningful the designation of the Buddha and his disciples as ascetics *(samaṇa).*

Mahā-maṅgala-sutta (*Sn* 258ff.); *The Boon of Boons* (*Buddha's Teachings,* tr. R. Chalmers, Harvard Oriental Series, vol. 37 [1932], p. 65ff.). A succinct statement of moral virtues starting from the simplest, such as taking care of one's parents and family, up to the ultimate moral perfection involving the attainment of freedom and overcoming of suffering.

Mahā-nidāna-suttanta (*D* 2.55ff.); *The Greater Discourse on Causation* (*SBB* 3.50ff.); *TD* 1.60ff. This lengthy discourse contains a detailed treatment of the principle of dependent arising, followed by a criticism of the Brahmanical theory of self *(atta).*

Mahā-parinibbāna-suttanta (*D* 2.72ff.); *The Book of Great Decease* (*SBB* 3.78ff.); *TD* 1.11ff. This famous discourse is believed to be originally part of a chronicle (the other part being Chapters 11 and 12 of the *Cullavagga* of the *Vinaya Piṭaka*) compiled by the Buddha's immediate disciples after his death. The longest discourse in the collection, it contains valuable historical information about the last days of the Buddha's life as well as a philosophically important account of his final passing away.

Mahā-taṇhāsaṅkhaya-sutta (*M* 1.256ff.); *Greater Discourse on the Destruction of Craving* (*MLS* 1.311ff.); *TD* 1.766ff. This discourse contains the famous "Sāti's heresy," namely, the assumption that, to explain the possible continuity of human life after death, there ought to be a mysterious psychic agent that remains unchanged. The Buddha's application of the principle of dependent arising *(paṭiccasamuppāda)* to account for any form of continuity is highlighted. It represents the best explanation of the relation between the negative conception of non-substantiality *(anatta)* and the positive doctrine of dependent arising *(paṭiccasamuppāda).*

Mahā-vedalla-sutta (*M* 1.292ff.); *Greater Discourse on the Miscellany* (*MLS* 1.350ff.); *TD* 1.790ff. The two *Vedalla-suttas (Mahā-* and *Cūḷa-)* are generally viewed as forerunners of the Abhidhamma method of analysis and are therefore held in high esteem. Both deal with straightforward definitions of concepts. What is significant in the system of definitions is that it focuses on the functional rather than the essentialist meaning. The reluctance to make absolute distinctions between concepts expressive of cognitive and psychological content, e.g., between feeling or sensation *(vedanā)* and perception *(saññā)*, is a notable feature; hence its relationship to the methodology of the Abhidhamma.

Nidāna-saṃyutta (*S 2.1–133); Kindred Sayings on Cause* (*KS* 2.1–94); roughly corresponding to *TD* 2.79–86. Ninety-three short discourses deal with almost every aspect of the Buddha's conception of causality or dependent arising.

Poṭṭhapāda-suttanta (*D* 1.178ff.); *Discourse to Poṭṭhapāda* (*SBB* 2.159ff); *TD* 1.109f. A detailed explanation of the causality of perception *(saññā)*, placed against the background of theories that advocated either non-causation, an internal agent *(atta)*, the interference of a powerful ascetic or brahman, or even the activity of a powerful divinity. After stating that perception is due to causes and conditions, the Buddha argues that training *(sikkhā)* is a way of determining how perceptions occur. The restraint of the sense faculties and their resulting perceptions is then described, indicating how a state of total cessation *(nirodha)* of perceptions can be induced. Even after all this discussion, Poṭṭhapāda, the interlocutor, continues to introduce the conception of *atman*, whereupon the Buddha undertakes a detailed refutation of this conception, comparing the soul-theorist to a man who has fallen in love with a beauty queen *(janapada-kalyāni)* whom he has never seen. The Buddha concludes that self *(atta)* is a worldly linguistic convention that he himself utilizes without ontological commitment *(aparāmasaṃ)*. The discourse represents the most detailed treatment of metaphysical questions.

Sāmaññaphala-suttanta (*D* 1.47ff.); *The Fruits of a Life of a Recluse* (*SBB* 2.65ff.); *TD* 1.107ff. A discussion between the Buddha and King Ajātasattu of Magadha on the fruits of recluseship. Ajātasattu reports to the Buddha his encounters with the six ascetics, Pūraṇa Kassapa, Makkhali Gosāla, Ajita Kesakambali, Pakudha Kaccāyana, Nigaṇṭha Nātaputta, and Sañjaya Bellaṭṭhiputta. His account of their views represents the earliest and most authentic version available, except that of Nigaṇṭha Nātaputta, whose doctrines are preserved in the Jaina canon. Against the background of these theories, the Buddha presents his conceptions of morality, concentration, and wisdom. The explanation of the higher forms of knowledge in this discourse is rather unique.

Sandaka-sutta (*M* 1.513ff.); *Discourse to Sandaka* (*MLS* 2.192ff.). Ānanda, the Buddha's constant companion, meets with a wanderer named Sandaka. The conversation that ensues relates to the so-called higher life *(brahmacariya)* recommended by the ascetics on the basis of their views regarding the nature of human life. This is then contrasted with the higher life advocated by the Buddha.

Satipaṭṭhāna-sutta (*M* 1.55ff.); *Applications of Mindfulness* (*MLS* 1.70ff.); *TD* 1.582ff. Deals with the enormous significance of establishing mindfulness as a means of attaining enlightenment and freedom. It is the Buddha's justification of what may be called radical empiricism.

Sundarīka-Bhāradvāja-sutta (*S* 1.167ff.); *The Sundarikāyan* (*KS* 1.209ff.); *TD* 2.320f. Highlights the importance of subjective moral purification over the performance of purely external rituals.

Suññata (Cūḷa- and Mahā-)-suttas (*M* 3.104ff); *Lesser* and *Greater Discourse on Emptiness* (*MLS* 3.104ff.); *TD* 1.736ff. These two discourses explain the Buddha's notions of the empty *(suñña)* and the not empty *(asuñña)*, which should serve as a corrective to the total negation of conceptual thinking advocated by some of his later disciples as well as modern interpreters. The second discourse specifically deals with how the conception of emptiness can be made part of experience.

Tathāgatena-vutta (popularly known as the *Dhammacakkappavattana-sutta,*) (*S* 5.421ff.); *Said by the Tathāgata* (*KS* 5.356ff.); *TD* 2.103. The first discourse of the Buddha, delivered at Sarnath, to his five erstwhile friends who attended him during the years he undertook extreme self-mortification. It lays out a middle path in moral behavior between the extremes of self-indulgence and self-mortification, and contains a detailed explanation of the four noble truths examined from a variety of perspectives. The middle path is defined as the noble eightfold path.

Tevijja-suttanta (*D* 1.235ff.); *On Knowledge of the Vedas* (*SBB* 2.300ff.); *TD* 1.104ff. The Buddha examines the claims of the Brahmanical teachers such as Caṅkī, Tārukkha, Pokkharasāti, Todeyya, and Jānussoṇi, who were his contemporaries, about "union with Brahma" *(brahmasahavyatā)*. A discussion of the three *Vedas* as handed down by the seers of old (mentioned by name) and the invoking of gods to achieve the unachievable are followed by the Buddha's own version of "union with Brahma," namely, the restraining of the senses and overcoming of defiling tendencies.

Tevijja-Vacchagotta (*M* 1.481ff.); *Discourse to Vacchagotta on the Threefold Knowledge* (*MLS* 2.159ff.) A discussion with Vacchagotta in which the Buddha disclaims omniscience comparable to that claimed by the Jaina leader Mahāvīra. Such knowledge is said to be constantly available whether one is moving around or stationary, sleeping or awake. In contrast, the Buddha claims a threefold knowledge consisting of clairvoyance and retrocognition, both of which can be developed whenever he wishes, and the knowledge of the waning of influxes, which is constant.

Works of Importance from the Fifth Collection

Dhammapada, text and tr., David J. Kalupahana, *A Path of Righteousness* (Lanham, Md.: University Press of America, 1987). An extremely popular text used by Buddhists in the South and Southeast Asian countries as a handbook summarizing the teachings of the Buddha. The original version consists of 423 verses, most of which are taken from the early discourses and arranged into 24 chapters. Even though tradition holds that each of the verses was used by the Buddha as a theme of a discourse, there are strong reasons to believe that it was compiled by later Buddhists as a response to the *Bhagavadgītā*.

Itivuttaka, ed. E. Windish (London: PTS, 1948); *As it was said, Minor Anthologies,* vol. 2, tr. F. L. Woodward (London: PTS, 1935). A collection of 112 brief discourses, each of which discusses a theme in prose and then summarizes the ideas in verse. Some of the discourses contain discussions on important problems, like freedom *(nibbāna),* not found elsewhere in the canon.

Sutta-nipāta, ed. H. Smith (London: PTS, 1913); ed. and tr. R. Chalmers, *Buddha's Teachings,* Harvard Oriental Series, vol 37 (Cambridge, Mass.: Harvard University Press, 1932). Philosophically one of the most important—and linguistically one of the very archaic—parts of the Buddhist canon. The work consists of 71 discourses divided into 5 sections. The discourses are mostly in verse (a total of 1,149). Section 4, on "meaning" (*aṭṭhaka-vagga,* the traditional interpretation being "section on octads"), is philosophically the most significant part.

Thera- and *Therīgāthā,* ed. H. Oldenber and R. Pischel (London: PTS, 1966); tr. *Elders' Verses,* 2 vols., by K. R. Norman (London: PTS, 1969, 1971). Statements of more than 300 early disciples who had attained enlightenment and freedom. Some of these include poignant stories about their lives before and after enlightnment.

Udāna, ed. P. Steinthal (London: PTS, 1948); *Verses of Uplift, Minor Anthologies,* vol. 2, tr. F. L. Woodward (London: PTS, 1931). This consists of 80 short discourses divided into 8 sections, the eighth being the philosophically most important.

Secondary Sources

PRE-BUDDHIST INDIAN PHILOSOPHY

Barua, Benimadhab, *A History of Pre-Buddhistic Indian Philosophy* (Delhi: Motilal Banarsidass, 1970). One of the best and most detailed treatment of pre-Buddhist Indian philosophical systems.

Basham, A. L., *History and Doctrines of the Ājīvikas* (London: Luzac, 1951). The only comprehensive treatment of the doctrines of the Ājīvikas available.

Radhakrishnan, S., *Indian Philosophy* (New York: Macmillan; London: George Allen & Unwin, 1962), vol. 1. A free-flowing account of early Indian philosophy. However, the author's interpretation of Buddhism, especially its Vedantic slant, has been a subject of much controversy.

Gopalan, S., *Outlines of Jainism* (New Delhi: Wiley Eastern Private, 1973). A clear and concise account of Jaina philosophical thought.

EARLY BUDDHIST PHILOSOPHY

Conze, Edward, *Buddhist Thought in India: Three Phases of Buddhist Philosophy* (London: George Allen & Unwin, 1962). The three phases are archaic Buddhism, Sthaviravāda, and Mahāyāna, a classification that was popular for a long time and that is questioned in the present work.

Horner, I. B., *The Early Buddhist Theory of Man Perfected* (London: Williams & Norgate, 1936). A very comprehensive account of the concept of a freed person *(arahat)* in early Buddhism.

Jayatilleke, K. N., *Early Buddhist Theory of Knowledge* (London: George Allen & Unwin, 1963). Hailed as a "masterpiece by any standard" when it was first published, this is the most comprehensive treatment of the early Buddhist theory of knowledge. In addition to a detailed analysis of the background to early Buddhism, it contains exhaustive discussions of the problems of authority, reason, analysis and meaning, logic and truth, means and limits of knowledge, based on the Pali canon.

———. "The Principles of International Law in Buddhist Doctrine," *Recueil des cours* 2 (1967):445–566. Contains five lectures dealing with the problem of ethics and law from the early Buddhist perspective.

———. *Survival and Karma in Buddhist Perspective* (Kandy: Buddhist Publication Society, 1969). An essay devoted to explaining the early Buddhist theories of karma and rebirth in light of recent research in parapsychology.

Johansson, Rune E. A., *The Psychology of Nirvāṇa* (London: George Allen & Unwin, 1969). A comprehensive work on the conception of freedom *(nibbāna),* based on the source material in the Pali Nikāyas and an interpretation in terms of Western psychology.

Kalupahana, David J., *Causality: The Central Philosophy of Buddhism* (Honolulu: University Press of Hawaii, 1975). A detailed analysis of the problem of causality or dependent arising *(paṭiccasamuppāda),* based on the source material in the Pāli Nikāyas and the Chinese Āgamas, together with an examination of the developments in the later Buddhist schools.

———. *The Principles of Buddhist Psychology* (Albany: State University of New York Press, 1987). A more recent work dealing with Buddhist psychology. The first part is devoted to an analysis of the psychological speculations in early Buddhism; the second deals with later Buddhism. Also included are translations and annotations of Maitreya's *Madhyāntavibhāga* (Chapter 1) and Vasubandhu's *Vijñaptimātratāsiddhi.*

Kalupahana, David J., and Indrani Kalupahana, *The Way of Siddhartha: A Life of Buddha* (Lanham, Md.: University Press of America, 1987).

Karunadasa, Y., *Buddhist Analysis of Matter* (Colombo: Department of Cultural Affairs, 1970). A comprehensive treatment of the Buddhist conception of matter based on the early discourses and the Abhidharma literature.

Malalasekera, G. P. and Jayatilleke, K. N., *Buddhism and the Race Question* (Paris: UNESCO, 1958). A very authoritative monograph on the early Buddhist conception of a person and his place in nature. An in-depth criticism of the theories of caste and race in the Indian context and the Buddha's detailed criticism of these views, as well as a comparison of the Buddha's views with more recent theories.

Nakamura, Hajime, *Indian Buddhism* (Osaka: KUFS Publication, 1980). In this work of rare scholarship, Nakamura, the doyen of Buddhist studies in the modern world, has provided information about the doctrines, literature, personalities, and history of Buddhism to which the even the advanced Buddhist scholar has little access. This will serve as a handbook for the researcher for years to come.

Ñyāṇamoli, Bhikkhu, *The Life of the Buddha* (Kandy: Buddhist Publication Society, 1972). It consists of translations of selections from the entire Pali canon. These selections have been carefully sorted out and identified, especially with regard to their authors, as for example, reports by Ānanda or Upāli, who were Buddha's immediate disciples, or explanations provided by traditional commentators, like Buddhaghosa.

Ñāṇananda, Bhikkhu, *Concept and Reality in Early Buddhist Thought* (Kandy: Buddhist Publication Society, 1971). A valuable research monograph on the psychology of perception, especially the concept of *papanca* (which the author translates as "conceptual proliferation"), based on material in the early discourses.

Pande, G. C., *Studies in the Origins of Buddhism* (Allahabad: University of Allahabad, 1957). An extremely valuable analysis of the origin and development of some of the major concepts in early Buddhism.

Piyadassi Thera, *The Buddha's Ancient Path* (London: Rider, 1964). An authoritative account of the four noble truths by a highly respected scholar-monk attempting to build a bridge between tradition and modernity.

Rahula, Walpola, *What the Buddha Taught* (New York: Grove Press, 1959). Undoubtedly one of the best introductions to Buddhist doctrines, especially the four noble truths, the doctrine of non-substantiality, and theory of mental concentration, presented by a leading scholar-monk from Sri Lanka who spent a good part of his life in the Western world confronting the Western intellectual tradition.

Rhys Davids, C. A. F., *Buddhist Psychology* (London: Luzac, 1914). One of the earlier and more reliable works by Rhys Davids, first published in 1914 before the death of her son during the first World War. In her subsequent writings she tended to attribute to the Buddha a stronger version of self *(atta)* almost identical with that of the *Upaniṣads,* arguing that the theory of no-self *(anatta)* was the fabrication of later Buddhist monks.

Saddhatissa, H., *Buddhist Ethics* (New York: George Braziller, 1971). A traditional analysis of morality by a highly respected Buddhist monk.

Saratchandra, E. R., *Buddhist Psychology of Perception* (Colombo: Ceylon University Press, 1958). A research monograph on the problem of perception in early Buddhism, in the Abhidharma commentarial tradition, and in Yogācāra. The author, excessively influenced by the Western positivist tradition, considers the early Buddhist theory of mind as a form of epiphenomenalism.

Smart, Ninian, *Doctrine and Argument in Indian Philosophy* (London: George Allen & Unwin, 1964). An innovative work presenting the concepts in Indian philosophy without using Indian terms but translating every concept and every name into English. A generous treatment of Buddhist epistemology and metaphysics is included.

Thomas, E. J., *The History of Buddhist Thought* (London: Kegan Paul, Trench, Trubner, 1933). One of the pioneering works on Buddhist thought, which has remained generally accurate in spite of its age.

———. *The Life of Buddha as Legend and History* (London: Routledge & Kegan Paul, 1960). Another work of great erudition, critically evaluating the scanty historical material and the vast collection of legends relating to the life of Buddha.

Vajirañāṇa, Paravahera, *Buddhist Meditation in Theory and Practice* (Colombo: M. D. Gunasena, 1962). An exhaustive analysis of the theory and practice of meditation, based on the Pali canon and its interpretation by Buddhaghosa.

Warder, A. K., *Indian Buddhism* (Delhi: Motilal Banarsidass, 1970). An extremely detailed analysis of the Buddhist tradition in India, starting from early Buddhism through Mādhyamika philosophy.

Wijesekera, O. H. de A., *Buddhism and Society* (Colombo: Bauddha Sahitya Sabha, 1951). A brief but extremely valuable essay on the Buddha's conception of society.

Part Two: Continuities and Discontinuities

Primary Sources

TEXTS OF THE *ABHIDHAMMA PIṬAKA*

Dhammasaṅganī, ed. E. Muller (London: PTS, 1978); tr. C. A. F. Rhys Davids, *A Buddhist Manual of Psychological Ethics* (London: PTS, 1974). Traditionally considered to be the first book of the *Abhidhamma Piṭaka,* it contains definitions of 1,599 concepts relating to the psychophysical elements *(dhamma),* examined from the standpoints of experience as well as moral relevance.

Vibhaṅga, ed. C. A. F. Rhys Davids (London: PTS, 1978); tr. U. Thittila, *The Book of Analysis* (London: PTS, 1969). A further analysis of the concepts enumerated and defined in the previous work, but this time by placing each concept in the context of other related concepts to bring out the similarities as well as the differences in meaning. Thus we have the concept of form *(rūpa)* examined as one variety, two, three, and up to ten varieties. The flexibility in the use of the concept of form is thus established.

Dhātukathā, ed. E. R. Gooneratne (London: PTS, 1963); tr. U. Narada, *Discourse on Elements* (London: PTS, 1962). A shorter text dealing with the various categories, such as the five aggregates, the twelve gateways, the eighteen elements, and the four noble truths, analyzing them in terms of how they are associated or dissociated, related or distinguished.

Puggalapaññatti, ed. R. Morris (London: PTS, 1972); tr. B. C. Law, *Designation of Human Types* (London: PTS, 1922). Another brief treatise dealing specifically with the variety of concepts of personhood, the genuine and the empty.

Kathāvatthu, ed. A. C. Taylor (London: PTS, 1979, 2 vols. published as one); tr. S. Z. Aung and C. A. F. Rhys Davids, *Points of Controversy or Subjects of Discourse* (London: PTS, 1960). The only canonical text attributed to someone other than the Buddha, this work by Moggalīputta-tissa is of tremendous historical importance. It deals with some of the major philosophical controversies that emerged in the Buddhist tradition during its first 250 years (see Chapter XIII).

Yamaka, ed. C. A. F. Rhys Davids, 2 vols. (London: PTS, 1987); *(Book of Pairs),* untranslated. Another attempt to clarify concepts by considering them in pairs to see how two related concepts are mutually exclusive or inclusive.

Paṭṭhāna, ed. C. A. F. Rhys Davids, 2 vols. (London: PTS, 1988); tr. U. Narada, *Conditional Relations* (London: PTS, 1969). A book enumerating 24 causal relations, hence providing a synthetic view of the material subjected to analysis in some of the previous books.

NON-CANONICAL ABHIDHARMA TEXTS

Abhidhammatthasaṅgaha of Anuruddha, ed. T. W. Rhys Davids, in *Journal of the Pali Text Society,* 1884; tr. *Compendium of Philosophy,* by S. Z. Aung and C. A. F. Rhys Davids (London: PTS, 1910). A handbook summarizing the contents of the Pali Abhidhamma Piṭaka by a Sri Lankan monk who lived sometime between the ninth and eleventh centuries. The work is very popular in the Theravāda countries.

Abhidharmadīpa, with *Vibhāṣāprabhāvṛtti,* ed. P. S. Jaini (Patna: K. P. Jayaswal Research Institute, 1959); untranslated. This is a response to Vasubandhu's *Abhidharmakośa,* which presents the Sautrāntika standpoint in the interpretation of the Abhidharma and an attempt to establish the Vaibhāṣika (Sarvāstivāda) point of view.

Abhidharmakośa and *-bhāṣya* of Vasubandhu, ed. P. Pradhan (Patna: K. P. Jayaswal Research Institute, 1967); untranslated. The Chinese version by Hsuan Tsang (including his own annotation) has been translated into French by Louis de La Vallée Poussin, *L'Abhidharmakośa de Vasubandhu,* 6 vols., including the index volume (Bruxelles: Institute Belge des Hautes Études Chinois, 1971). This latter has served as the primary source for the study of Sarvāstivāda and Sautrāntika ideas in the West for a considerable period of time.

MISCELLANEOUS SOURCES IN PALI AND BUDDHIST SANSKRIT

Laṅkāvatāra-sūtra, ed. B. Nanjio (Kyoto: Otani University Press, 1956); tr. D. T. Suzuki, *The Laṅkāvatāra Sūtra* (London: Routledge & Kegan Paul, 1966). For an analysis of the text, see Chapter XVIII and Appendix.

Mūlamadhyamakakārikā, text and tr., *Nāgārjuna: The Philosophy of the Middle Way,* by David J. Kalupahana (Albany: State University of New York Press, 1986), and *Nāgārjuna: A Translation of His Mūlamadhyamakakārikā,* by Kenneth Inada (Tokyo: Hokuseido Press, 1970). For an analysis of the text, see Chapter XVI.

Nāgārjuna's Letter to King Gautamīputra (*Sahṛdlekhā* or "Friendly Epistle"), tr. from Tibetan by Lozang Jamspal, Ngawang Samten Chophel, and Peter Della Santina (Delhi: Motilal Banarsidass, 1978). An extremely interesting compilation (123 verses) by Nāgārjuna, wherein he provides moral guidance to his royal friend, the Sātavāhana king, Gautamīputra Śātakarṇi. Some of the verses are identical with those of the *Dhammapada.*

Nyāyabindu-prakaraṇa of Dharmakīrti, with Dharmottara's *Nyāyabindu-ṭīkā,* ed. F. Stcherbatsky (Osnabruck: Biblio Verlag, 1970); tr. F. Stcherbatsky, *Buddhist Logic,* vol. 2 (New York: Dover, 1962).

The Platform Sūtra of the Sixth Patriarch, tr. from the Chinese by Philip B. Yampolsky (New York and London: Columbia University Press, 1967). One of the foundational texts of Ch'an Buddhism. The translator's lengthy introduction is one of the best accounts of Chinese Ch'an. For a discussion of some of the contents, see Chapter XXIII.

Pramāṇasamuccaya, Dignāga's most mature work, is available in several Tibetan versions. Text and translation of Chapter 1, with annotations, is found in Masaaki Hattori's *Dignāga, On Perception* (Cambridge, Mass.: Harvard University Press, 1968).

Saddharmapuṇḍarīka-sūtra, ed. P. L. Vaidya (Dharbhanga: Mithila Institute, 1960); tr. H. Kern, *The Saddharmapuṇḍarīka or the Lotus of the True Law,* Sacred Books of the East, vol. 21 (Oxford: Clarendon Press, 1884); tr. from the Chinese of Kumārajīva by Leon Hurvitz, *Scripture of the Lotus Blossom of the Fine Dharma (The Lotus Sūtra),* (New York: Columbia University Press, 1976). For a discussion of the text, see Chapter XVII.

Vajracchedikā-prajñāpāramitā, ed. and tr. Edward Conze, Serie Orientale Roma, no. 13 (Rome: Instituto italiano per il medio ed Estremo Oriente, 1957). The contents of the text are analyzed in Chapter XV.

Vijñaptimātratāsiddhi, Viṃśatikā and *Triṃśikā,* text and tr., *The Principles of Buddhist Psychology,* by David J. Kalupahana (Albany: State University of New York Press, 1987). See Chapter XIX for a discussion of the subject matter.

Visuddhimagga, ed. C. A. F. Rhys Davids, 2 vols. (London: PTS, 1920–1921); tr. Bhikkhu Ñyāṇamoli, *Buddhaghosa: The Path of Purification* (Colombo: Semage, 1964); P. Maung Tin, *Buddhaghosa: The Path of Purity,* 3 vols. (London: PTS, 1922–1931). Discussion of the contents in Chapter XXI.

Secondary Sources

Anacker, Stefan, *Seven Works of Vasubandhu. The Buddhist Psychological Doctor* (Delhi: Motilal Banarsidass, 1984). Seven important works by Vasubandhu are translated and presented with introductions. Presents valuable information regarding the interpretation of Yogācāra.

Chi, Richard S. Y., *Buddhist Formal Logic* (London: Royal Asiatic Society, 1969). A highly technical work covering the development of Buddhist logic in India and China.

Dayal, Har, *Bodhisattva Doctrine in Buddhist Sanskrit Literature* (London: Kegan, Paul, Trench, and Trubner, 1932). By far the best treatise on the concept of *bodhisattva* in Buddhism.

Guenther, Herbert V., *Philosophy and Psychology in the Abhidharma* (Lucknow: Buddha Vihara, 1959). One of the early works of Guenther, which contains an extremely stimulating analysis of the Abhidharma material.

———. *The Tantric View of Life* (Boulder and London: Shambhala, 1976). An excellent work that explains the philosophical and psychological underpinnings of the *Tantras.*

Herman, Arthur, *A History of Buddhist Thought* (Lanham, Md.: University Press of America, 1984). An excellent analysis of the early and later Buddhist schools by a philosopher trained in the Western analytical tradition.

Herzberger, Radhika, *Bhartṛhari and the Buddhists* (Dordrecht: D. Reidel, 1986). A detailed study of Dignāga in relation to Bhartṛhari, the famous philosopher of language in India. An advancement in the interpretation of Dignāga compared to those of Stcherbatsky and Hattori.

Inada, Kenneth, *Nāgārjuna: A Translation of his Mūlamadhyamakakārikā* (Tokyo: Hokuseido Press, 1970). Contains an extremely valuable general introduction as well as short introductions to each of the 27 chapters. Here Nāgārjuna's philosophy is perceived as a beautiful blend of early Buddhism and the metaphysics of Mahāyāna.

Kalupahana, David J., *Nāgārjuna. The Philosophy of the Middle Way* (Albany: State University of New York Press, 1986). An attempt to see Nāgārjuna as resurrecting the teachings of the Buddha, as recorded in the Nikāyas and the Āgamas, avoiding the more metaphysical schools of Mahāyāna Buddhism.

———. *The Principles of Buddhist Psychology* (Albany: State University of New

York Press, 1987). The second part of this work tries to delineate the empirical and metaphysical trends in Buddhist psychology as they developed in the later Buddhist schools.

Kochumuttom, Thomas A., *A Buddhist Doctrine of Experience* (Delhi: Motilal Banarsidass, 1982). Another translation and interpretation of some of Vasubandhu's important works.

Mookerjee, Satkari, *The Buddhist Philosophy of Universal Flux: An Exposition of the Philosophy of Critical Realism as Expounded by the School of Dignāga* (Delhi: Motilal Banarsidass, 1975). A detailed study of the Sautrāntika school of thought, based primarily on Śāntarakṣita's *Tattvasaṃgraha,* mistakenly identified with the thought of Dignāga.

Murti, T. R. V., *The Central Philosophy of Buddhism: A Study of the Mādhyamika System* (London: George Allen & Unwin, 1955). A work that became highly respected as the most authoritative interpretation of Nāgārjuna. The analysis of Nāgārjuna is done mainly on the basis of Candrakīrti's commentary. Recent research has raised questions about the appropriateness of adopting Candrakīrti's exegesis on Nāgārjuna's philosophy because of the former's Vedāntic leanings.

Nakamura, Hajime, *Indian Buddhism;* see under Early Buddhism, Secondary Sources.

———. *A Critical Survey of Tibetology and Esoteric Buddhism Chiefly Based on Japanese Studies* (Tokyo: Tokyo University Press, 1965). Another scholarly treatment that betrays the incredible versatility of this academic stalwart.

Rahula, Walpola, *History of Buddhism in Ceylon: The Anurādhapura Period, 3rd* B.C.*–10th* A.D. (Colombo: M. D. Gunasena, 1966). The most scholarly work on the history of Buddhism in South Asia, especially Sri Lanka, which was a hub of activity during this period. Of invaluable assistance in understanding the controversies and conflicts between the so-called Theravāda and Mahāyāna.

Robinson, Richard, *Early Mādhyamika in India and China* (Madison: University of Wisconsin Press, 1967). A scholarly treatment of the school of Mādhyamika in India and China by one who was competent in philosophy as well as Asian languages.

Stcherbatsky, F., *Buddhist Logic,* vol. 1 (New York: Dover, 1962). For a long time the only comprehensive treatise on Buddhist epistemology and logic available in English, and hence a work that set the standard for modern discussions. Unfortunately, it is based on Dharmakīrti's essentialist epistemology. What Stcherbatsky failed to realize is that Dharmakīrti's epistemology is not the same as Dignāga's. Recent scholarship has challenged Stcherbatsky's view in this regard.

Suzuki, D. T., *Essays in Zen Buddhism* (London: Rider, 1949). The essays deal with the history of Ch'an (Zen) Buddhism from its inception until the time of Hui-neng.

———. *Zen Buddhism: Selected Writings of D. T. Suzuki,* ed. William Barrett (New York: Doubleday, 1956).

———. *Essentials of Zen Buddhism,* selected from the writings of Daisetz T. Suzuki, ed. with introduction by Bernard Phillips (New York: E. P. Dutton, 1962). Two collections of essays from a prolific writer.

INDEX